SCRIBAL HABITS AND SINGULAR READINGS
IN CODEX SINAITICUS, VATICANUS, EPHRAEMI, BEZAE,
AND WASHINGTONIANUS IN THE GOSPEL OF MATTHEW

SCRIBAL HABITS AND SINGULAR READINGS
IN CODEX SINAITICUS, VATICANUS, EPHRAEMI, BEZAE,
AND WASHINGTONIANUS IN THE GOSPEL OF MATTHEW

GREGORY S. PAULSON

GlossaHouse
Wilmore, KY
GlossaHouse.com

SCRIBAL HABITS AND SINGULAR READINGS IN CODEX SINAITICUS, VATICANUS, EPHRAEMI, BEZAE, AND WASHINGTONIANUS IN THE GOSPEL OF MATTHEW

Copyright © 2018 by GlossaHouse, LLC

All rights reserved. No part of this work may be reproduced or transmitted in any form or by any means, electronic or mechanical, including photocopying and recording, or by means of any information storage or retrieval system, except as may be expressly permitted by the 1976 Copyright Act or in writing from the publisher. Requests for permission should be addressed in writing to the following:

GlossaHouse, LLC
110 Callis Circle
Wilmore, KY 40390

Scribal Habits and Singular Readings in Codex Sinaiticus, Vaticanus, Ephraemi, Bezae, and Washingtonianus in the Gospel of Matthew by Gregory S. Paulson

xxiv, 345 p.   22.86 cm. — (GlossaHouse Dissertation Series; volume 5)

A revision of the author's ETD dissertation, University of Edinburgh, 2013.

Includes bibliographical references and indexes.

ISBN 9781942697459 (paperback)
ISBN 9781942697565 (hardback)

1. Bible. Matthew—Criticism, Textual. 2. Codex Sinaiticus (biblical manuscript) 3. Codex Vaticanus (biblical manuscript) 4. Codex Ephraemi Rescriptus (biblical manuscript) 5. Codex Bezae (biblical manuscript) 5. Codex Washingtonianus (biblical manuscript) I. Title. II. Series.

BS2575.52.P38 2018   226.2
Library of Congress Control Number: 2018938148

Cover Design by T. Michael W. Halcomb
Typesetting by Fredrick J. Long
The fonts used to create this work are available from
www.linguistsoftware.com/lgku.htm

To Steve and Sally Paulson

GlossaHouse
Dissertations Series

Series Editors

Fredrick J. Long
T. Michael W. Halcomb

GLOSSAHOUSE DISSERTATION SERIES

The goal of the GlossaHouse Dissertation Series to facilitate the creation and publication of innovative, affordable, and accessible scholarly resources, whether print or digital, that advance research in the areas of both ancient and modern texts and languages.

TABLE OF CONTENTS

Abbreviations, Critical Signs, and Collation Key xvi
Acknowledgments xxiv

Chapter 1: Introduction 1
1.1. The Selection of Manuscripts and the Gospel of Matthew 3
1.2. Methodology 4
1.3 The Ensuing Study 10

Chapter 2: Codex Sinaiticus 13
2.1. The Scribes and Extent of Matthew in Sinaiticus 13
2.2. The Singular Readings of Scribe A in Sinaiticus in Matthew 13
2.2.1. Orthography 14
2.2.1.1. Itacisms 14
2.2.1.2. Other Vocalic Changes 14
2.2.1.3. Consonantal Changes 15
2.2.1.4. Omissions and Additions of Letters 15
2.2.2. Other Spellings 15
2.2.3. Nonsense in Context 15
2.2.4. Parablepsis 16
2.2.4.1. Haplography 16
2.2.4.2. Dittography 19
2.2.4.3. Corrected Leaps 20
2.2.5. Transpositions 21
2.2.6. Influence from Context 22
2.2.7. The Use of Conjunctions 27
2.2.8. Definite Articles 28
2.2.9. Other Substitutions 29
2.2.10. Other Omissions 31
2.2.11. Inexplicable Changes 34
2.2.12. Koine Grammar 34
2.2.13. Other Construed Singular Readings 35
2.2.14. Possible Theological Readings and Interpretation of the Text 36
2.3. The Singular Readings of Scribe D in Sinaiticus in Matthew 38

2.4. Conclusion..41
2.4.1. Scribal Habits in General 41
2.4.2. Longer and Shorter Readings 42

Chapter 3: Codex Vaticanus 45
3.1. The Scribe and Extent of Matthew in Vaticanus....................45
3.2. The Singular Readings in Vaticanus in Matthew 45
3.2.1. Orthography and Spelling 46
3.2.1.1. Itacisms 46
3.2.1.2. Other Vocalic Changes 46
3.2.1.3. Consonantal Orthography 46
3.2.1.4. Misconstrued Spellings 47
3.2.2. Not Construed in Context...48
3.2.3. Parablepsis...48
3.2.3.1. Haplography 48
3.2.3.2. Dittography..50
3.2.4. Transpositions..50
3.2.5. Influence from Context 51
3.2.6. Inexplicable Readings..52
3.2.7. Attic and Koine Greek 53
3.2.8. Aorist Constructions 54
3.2.9. Synonym Substitutions 55
3.3. Conclusion..56
3.3.1. Scribal Habits in General 56
3.3.2. Longer and Shorter Readings 58

Chapter 4: Codex Ephraemi..59
4.1. The Scribe and Extent of Matthew in Ephraemi 59
4.2. The Singular Readings in Ephraemi in Matthew 59
4.2.1. Orthography and Spelling 60
4.2.1.1. Itacisms 60
4.2.1.2. Vocalic Orthography..61
4.2.1.3. Consonantal Orthography 61
4.2.2. Letter Omissions..61
4.2.3. Letter Additions...61

4.2.4. Omission and Addition of Syllables 62
4.2.5. Other Spellings 62
4.2.6. Not Construed In Context 63
4.2.7. Parablepsis 63
4.2.7.1. Within Words 64
4.2.7.2. Whole Words 65
4.2.8. Influence of Context 66
4.2.9. Inexplicable Readings 67
4.2.10. Textual Improvement 68
4.2.11. Harmonization to Mark 68
4.3. Conclusion 69
4.3.1. Scribal Habits in General 69
4.3.2. Longer and Shorter Readings 70

Chapter 5: Codex Bezae 73
5.1. The Scribes and Extent of Matthew in Bezae 73
5.2. The Singular Readings in Codex D in Matthew 73
5.2.1. Orthography 74
5.2.1.1. Itacisms 74
5.2.1.2. Vocalic Changes 75
5.2.1.3. Consonantal Orthography and Other Spellings 75
5.2.1.4. Consonant Changes 76
5.2.2. Letter Additions 77
5.2.3. Letter Omissions 77
5.2.4. Syllable Omissions 77
5.2.5. Not Construed in Context 77
5.2.6. Inexplicable Readings 77
5.2.7. Parablepsis 78
5.2.7.1. Haplography 79
5.2.7.2. Dittography 80
5.2.8. Transpositions 81
5.2.9. Synonym Substitutions 81
5.2.10. Definite Articles 83
5.2.10.1. Proper Nouns 84
5.2.10.2. Common Nouns 84

5.2.10.3. Verbs 85
5.2.10.4. Genitive Absolute Construction 85
5.2.11. Attic, Koine, Hebraic, and Latin Constructions 85
5.2.12. Influence from Context 88
5.2.13. Agreement Between the Greek and Latin Columns 92
5.2.14. Noun and Adjective Changes 94
5.2.15. Use of Pronouns 94
5.2.16. Textual Improvement 95
5.2.17. Use of Verbs 97
5.2.18. Other Omissions 100
5.3. Conclusion 101
5.3.1. Scribal Habits in General 101
5.3.2. Longer and Shorter Readings 103

Chapter 6: Codex Washingtonianus 105
6.1. The Scribe and Extent of Matthew in Washingtonianus 105
6.2. The Singular Readings in Washingtonianus in Matthew 105
6.2.1. Orthography 106
6.2.1.1. Itacisms 106
6.2.1.2. Other Vocalic Changes 106
6.2.1.3. Consonant Orthography 107
6.2.2. Other Spellings 108
6.2.3. Not Construed in Context 108
6.2.4. Parablepsis 109
6.2.4.1. Haplography 109
6.2.5. Transpositions 110
6.2.6. Influence from Context 112
6.2.7. Attic and Hebraic Influence 114
6.2.8. Synonym Substitutions 116
6.2.9. Doublets/Triplet 117
6.2.10. Textual Emphasis 117
6.2.11. Various Editing 118
6.2.12. Concerning Pharisees 120
6.2.13. Conflations 121
6.3. Conclusion 122

6.3.1. Scribal Habits in General 122
6.3.2. Longer and Shorter Readings 123

Chapter 7: Conclusion 125
7.1. Comparisons of Scribal Habits via Singular Readings 125
7.1.1. Orthography 125
7.1.2. Attic and Koine Dialects 126
7.1.3. Influence from Context 127
7.1.4. Remote Gospel Harmonizations 127
7.1.5. Conflations 128
7.1.6. Theological Readings 128
7.2. Longer and Shorter Singular Readings 128
7.3. Summary and Areas for Further Research 131

Appendix 1: Select Details of II–V/VI Century Greek Manuscripts
Containing the Gospel of Matthew 135

Appendix 2: Singular Readings in Sinaiticus in Matthew 139
1. Scribe A 139
2. Scribe D 152

Appendix 3: Singular Readings in Vaticanus in Matthew 155

Appendix 4: Singular Readings in Ephraemi in Matthew 163

Appendix 5: Singular Readings in Codex D in Matthew 170

Appendix 6: Singular Readings in Washingtonianus in Matthew 191

Appendix 7: Non-Singular Readings in Sinaiticus in Matthew 201

Appendix 8: Non-Singular Readings in Vaticanus in Matthew 212

Appendix 9: Non-Singular Readings in Ephraemi in Matthew 220

Appendix 10: Non-Singular Readings in Codex D in Matthew 224

Appendix 11: Non-Singular Readings in Washingtonianus in Matthew 261

Appendix 12: Itacisms in Sinaiticus in Matthew 268
1. αι > ε 268
2. ε > αι 277
3. ει > ι 277
4. ι > ει 288
5. Singular Readings with Non-Singular Orthographic Exchanges. 289

Appendix 13: Itacisms in Vaticanus in Matthew 291
1. ι > ει 291
2. Singular Readings with Non-Singular Orthographic Exchanges. 293

Appendix 14: Itacisms in Ephraemi in Matthew 294
1. αι > ε 294
2. ε > αι 294
3. ει > ι 294
4. ι > ει 294
5. Singular Readings with Non-Singular Orthographic Exchanges. 295

Appendix 15: Itacisms in Codex D in Matthew 296
1. αι > ε 296
2. ε > αι 296
3. ει > ι 298
4. ι > ει 298
5. Singular Readings with Non-Singular Orthographic Exchanges. 308

Appendix 16: Itacisms in Washingtonianus in Matthew 310
1. αι > ε 310
2. ε > αι 311
3. ει > ι 313
4. ι > ει 314

5. οι > υ 316
6. Singular Readings with Non-singular Orthographic Exchanges .. 317

Appendix 17: Singular Omissions (-) and Additions (+) of Words .. 319

Bibliography 323

Index of Modern Authors 331

Index of Subjects 335

Scripture Index 336

Abbreviations, Critical Signs, and Collation Key

This book generally follows the conventions prescribed by *The SBL Handbook of Style for Biblical Studies and Related Disciplines*, 2nd ed. (Atlanta: SBL Press, 2014). Common abbreviations and others are as follows.

General Conventions and Abbreviations

1s, 1pl, 2s, etc. First person singular, first person plural, second person singular, etc.

INTF   Institut für Neutestamentliche Textforschung

MS(S)   Manuscript(s)

decl.   Declension.

>   This symbol is not used in collations but in prose when describing variants. The sign represents a change from one variant to another. For example, when a verb in the present tense is substituted for a verb in the aorist tense, it can be described as "present > aorist". The sign can also show the order of words that have been transposed. The word order in B in 18:31 (αυτου οι συνδουλοι) is transposed as genitive pronoun > article > subject.

|| Parallel lines indicate a Gospel parallel. For example, Matt 27:17 has a parallel in both Mark 15:9 and John 18:39, displayed in prose as: Matt 27:17 || Mark 15:9; John 18:39.

___   Underlining in words in prose points to possible causes of parablepsis. For example, when describing a leap from θελ<u>ω</u> to οδ<u>ω</u>, the omegas are underlined as a possible cause of the leap.

Critical Editions

BHS *Biblia Hebraica Stuttgartensia.* Edited by K. Elliger and W. Rudolph. Stuttgart: Deutsche Bibelgesellschaft, 1997.

LXX Unless otherwise noted: *Septuaginta: Id est Vetus Testamentum graece iuxta LXX interpretes.* Edited by Alfred Rahlfs. Stuttgart: Deutsche Bibelgesellschaft, 1979.

NA[27] *Nestle-Aland Novum Testamentum Graece.* 27th ed. Edited by Barbara and Kurt Aland, Johannes Karavidopoulos, Carlo M. Martini, Bruce M. Metzger. Stuttgart: Deutsche Bibelgesellschaft, 2001.

NA[28] *Nestle-Aland Novum Testamentum Graece.* 28th ed. Edited by Barbara and Kurt Aland, Johannes Karavidopoulos, Carlo M. Martini, Bruce M. Metzger, revised by Luc Herren, Marie-Luise Lakmann, Beate von Tschischwitz, and Klaus Wachtel, under the direction of Holger Strutwolf. Stuttgart: Deutsche Bibelgesellschaft, 2012.

Reference Works

BDAG Danker, Frederick William, Walter Bauer, William F. Arndt, and F. Wilbur Gingrich. *Greek-English Lexicon of the New Testament and Other Early Christian Literature.* 3rd ed. Chicago: University of Chicago Press, 2000.

BDF Blass, Friedrich, Albert Debrunner, and Robert W. Funk. *A Greek Grammar of the New Testament and Other Early Christian Literature.* Chicago: The University of Chicago Press, 1961.

Liddell-Scott Liddell, Henry George, and Robert Scott. *A Greek-English Lexicon.* New ed. Henry Stuart Jones and Roderick McKenzie. Oxford: Clarendon Press, 1966.

Liste   Kurzgefasste Liste des Griechischen Handschriften des Neuen Testaments. Rev. and enl. ed. Edited by Kurt Aland. ANTF 1. Berlin: Walter de Gruyter, 1994.

Moulton-Milligan   Moulton, James Hope and George Milligan. *The Vocabulary of the Greek Testament: Illustrated from the Papyri and Other Non-Literary Sources.* Grand Rapids: Eerdmans, 1930.

TDNT   *Theological Dictionary of the New Testament.* Edited by Gehard Kittel and Gerhard Friedrich. Translated by Geoffrey W. Bromiley. 10 vols. Grand Rapids: Eerdmans, 1964–1976.

TLG   *Thesaurus Linguae Graecae.* Edited by Maria C. Pantelia. Irvine, University of California. http://www.tlg.uci.edu.

Abbreviations of Textual Witnesses

Abbreviations of textual witnesses have been reproduced from printed editions (see pages 8–10), without attempting to adhere to a single standard or create consistency. The most important, and commonest, abbreviations relevant to this study are as follows:

א   Codex Sinaiticus. Gregory-Aland 01. Folio numbers are from the British Library digital manuscript. The siglum for the scribes and correctors have been adopted from the British Library (see "Production of the Manuscript" and "Revisions", http://www.codexsinaiticus.org/en/project/transcription_detailed.aspx).
On-line http://www.codexsinaiticus.org/en/manuscript.aspx.

B   Codex Vaticanus. Gregory-Aland 03. The siglum for scribes and correctors have been adopted from the INTF's New Testament Transcripts Prototype http://nttranscripts.uni-muenster.de/.

C   Codex Ephraemi. Gregory-Aland 04. Lyon's corrections of Tischendorf's transcription have been included. Folio numbers reflect

Abbreviations, Critical Signs, and Collation Key

the Bibliothèque nationale de France digitization of the MS. On-line http://gallica.bnf.fr/ark:/12148/btv1b8470433r.

D   The Greek text of Codex Bezae. Gregory-Aland 05. Folio numbers are from the University of Cambridge Digital Library edition of Codex Bezae. On-line http://cudl.lib.cam.ac.uk/view/MS-NN-00002-00041/1.

W   Codex Washingtonianus. Gregory-Aland 032. Folio numbers are from Henry A. Sanders, *Facsimile of the Washington Manuscript of the Four Gospels in the Freer Collection* (Ann Arbor: University of Michigan, 1912).

d   The Latin text of Codex Bezae. Folio numbers are from the University of Cambridge Digital Library edition of Codex Bezae.

Critical Signs and Conventions Used in Collations

The critical signs used in the study here basically agree with the conventions in the NA²⁸ (see pages 879–90), but some have been elaborated or modified slightly.

°   The word following in the text is omitted by the witnesses cited.

▫ ... ˋ   The words, clauses, or sentences following ▫ in the text are omitted by the witnesses cited. The sign ˋ marks the end of the omitted text.

⌜   The word following in the text is replaced with one or more words by the witnesses cited. When there is more than one word replaced in the text, then ⌜¹ marks the first word, ⌜² marks the second word, etc. The sign ⌜om. notes that the following witnesses cited omit the word.

ABBREVIATIONS, CRITICAL SIGNS, AND COLLATION KEY

⊤ The sign marks the location where one or more words, sometimes a whole verse, is inserted. When there is more than one instance of a textual insertion, then ⊤¹ marks the first insertion, ⊤² marks the second insertion, etc.

ˢ ... ᶻ The words following in the text are replaced with other words by the witnesses cited. The second sign s marks the end of the replaced text.

| A solid vertical line separates the various alternative readings from each other within a single instance of variation.

2314 Variants of word order are represented by italic numerals which correspond to the order of the words in the text (*1* = the first word in the text, etc.).

( ) Witnesses which show only minor differences are noted in parentheses ( ) along with the witnesses for the main variant. MSS in parentheses contain a very similar reading to the one they are cited for and usually differ only by an itacism or transposition (unless the point of citing the variant is to show an itacism or transposition, then the MSS in parentheses differ in another insignificant, minor way). The witnesses in parentheses differ in a way that does not affect the discussion of the variant.

[NA²⁸] When the NA²⁸ is enclosed within brackets, that means the text found in the NA²⁸ is enclosed within brackets, indicating that the editors are not certain of the best reading.

α̣ Letters with a dot below them are difficult to see in the MS.

[...] An ellipsis within brackets signifies non-extant text. Letters within brackets are reconstructed, non-extant text.

om. The variant is omitted in the witnesses cited.

\-   Minus sign. Normally, when a MS is cited with a minus sign, it indicates either the MS is lacunose or the MS omits the text. Rarely, it indicates that a MS's reading has been deemed not significant to cite since it would not affect the discussion of the variant.

*   Identifies the original reading of a MS when a correction has been made.

^{c} Identifies a correction made by a later unidentified hand, but sometimes also by the first hand. Such corrections are retained in *rell* unless otherwise noted.

^{A}, ^{B} A correction made by an identified hand known as scribe A, or scribe B, etc. These identifiable corrections of our MSS (Codex Sinaiticus, Vaticanus, Ephraemi, Bezae, and Washingtonianus) are never subsumed in the abbreviation *rell*, but rather explicitly noted.

$^{Corr.C}$ When an identified hand is referred to as "scribe C", it is cited as "corrector C" or $^{Corr.C}$ so as not to be confused with an unidentified correction marked as ^{c}.

^{mg} (*in margine*) Indicates a reading in the margin of a manuscript without being identified as either a correction or an alternative reading.

^{vid} (*ut videtur*) Indicates that the reading attested by a witness cannot be determined with absolute certainty.

et al. (*et alii*)   And some

pc (*pauci*)   A few

pler (*plerique*) Many

plu (*plures*)   Most

rell (*reliqui*) Remaining. Unless otherwise noted, the NA^{28} is retained in *rell* for all collations.

ABBREVIATIONS, CRITICAL SIGNS, AND COLLATION KEY

Explanation of Textual Collations in Appendices 2–16

The MSS supplied for each variant are typically cited in the Gregory-Aland order (papyri, majuscules, minuscules, versions, and Patristic sources) when they occur within the same unit. In order to give the reader bearing for locating the text within its fuller context, the first reading displayed is normally the text of the NA²⁸. If the text of a MS contains an abbreviation (e.g. numeric or *nomen sacrum*), the word is usually written in full (if it occurs in one of our primary MSS, it is discussed in one of the main chapters). The text of the early versions is expressed in Greek or Latin for ease of reading, rather than the original language in the case of Syriac, Coptic, etc.

In appendices two through eleven, the text supplied for a variant does not always comprise a complete sentence, clause, or phrase. The words surrounding a variant are included as merely reference points for locating the text in printed editions. Sometimes two or more lines are needed to express all known variation within one variation unit. An example of a collation is as follows:

12:4b ουκ εξον ην   *rell* |132 D
       ουκ ⌜εξον   Chr^com et^mo6 |⌜εξην Or |⌜εξεστιν C 16 33 118 726 1010 1375 1579 1675 |⌜εξεστι 28

Above, the reading of Codex D in Matt 12:4b is ουκ ην εξον. The reading known by Chrysostom is ουκ εξον. Origen attests the reading ουκ εξην. Codex C, along with several minuscules reads ουκ εξεστιν. Similarly, 28 reads ουκ εξεστι (which I have not regularized as ουκ εξεστιν). The remaining MSS and the NA²⁸, which are subsumed *rell*, read ουκ εξον ην.

In the orthography appendices, twelve through sixteen, there are usually no additional words supplied along with the variant; and if the same word is found in two or more instances in the same verse, the first occurrence of the word is cited with the superscript numeral one and the second occurrence is cited with the superscript two, etc. Some orthographic spellings in a MS reoccur throughout Matthew. In these instances, they are recorded as,

1:24; 18:25*; 19:3, 9*; 22:24, 25*   ⌜γυναικα *rell* |⌜γυνεκα ℵ

This indicates that the spelling of γυναικα in ℵ is γυνεκα in 1:24; 19:3; and 22:24, as well as in 18:25; 19:9; 22:25 in ℵ*.

There are also instances where citing "*rell*" is inaccurate, and therefore other spellings are placed in parentheses. For example,

6:11, 12; 13:36 (ημην L); 15:33; 20:12; 21:25; 22:25 (εμιν Θ); 24:2, 3; 25:8 (υμιν 157), 11 (υμιν 1346); 26:63, 68   ⌜ημιν *rell* |⌜ημειν D

In all instances above, Codex D reads ημειν, but in 13:36 Codex L reads ημην, in 22:25 Codex Θ reads εμιν, in 25:8 157 reads υμιν, and in 25:11 1346 reads υμιν. The purpose of the collation is to show that the reading of Codex D in these instances is an orthographic spelling, not a word substitution or other type of textual change.

Acknowledgements

The present work is a revised version of my Ph.D. dissertation accepted by the University of Edinburgh for graduation in 2013. I offer my heartfelt thanks to many individuals who helped get the manuscript through its various phases from inception to publication. Foremost, I owe Dr. Juan Hernández, Jr. a debt of gratitude since he has selflessly looked over numerous iterations of my dissertation and provided helpful feedback at every stage.

My supervisors at the University of Edinburgh, Prof. Paul Foster and Prof. Larry Hurtado, provided academic support during my stint in Scotland and offered valuable input for the dissertation. My examiners, Dr. David Mealand and Dr. Peter M. Head, helped correct many errors in detail and illogical statements. Post-graduation, Dr. Michael Holmes and Dr. James R. Royse looked over revised drafts, correcting many errors of composition, logic, and my understanding of scribal habits. I am grateful that Dr. Fredrick J. Long and Dr. T. Michael W. Halcomb at GlossaHouse accepted this work into their dissertation series, and for the proofreading by Dr. Shawn I. Craigmiles and the proofing and typesetting by Dr. Fredrick J. Long.

My parents, Dr. Steven and Sally Paulson, have supported me in my intellectual and spiritual journey every step of the way. Their example has taught me far more than is possible to state here, and it is to them that I dedicate this work. Their tireless patience, authenticity, strong work ethic, and love of learning have all deeply shaped the way I conduct my life. I am grateful for their feedback on this work.

And my dear wife, Dr. Katie Leggett, who has been supportive, patient, and helpful, has provided many encouraging and challenging conversations. Her feedback and ideas have not only helped shape this study, but have given me a new lens to look through at life. Her sacrifices have made it possible to have this work in print.

CHAPTER 1
INTRODUCTION

Although studies on the text of the New Testament may be plentiful, studies on the scribes who transmitted the text are not. Considering this lacuna, and that many biblical MSS still have much to offer, this study intends to offer portraits of scribal habits in several important biblical MSS through the lens of singular readings.

The study of singular readings (i.e. variants that do not occur anywhere else in the MS tradition, generally assumed to be created by the scribe—cf. §1.2) in New Testament MSS is a relatively recent area of interest and development within New Testament textual criticism. The 1960s saw an important work published, Ernest C. Colwell's "Scribal Habits in Early Papyri: A Study in the Corruption of the Text,"[1] and then essentially unchanged and republished as "Method in Evaluating Scribal Habits: A Study of $\mathfrak{P}^{45}$, $\mathfrak{P}^{66}$, $\mathfrak{P}^{75}$."[2] In this work, Colwell was one of the first to use singular readings systematically as a tool to study copying practices of scribes. Other similar studies since his have been carried out. The most comprehensive of them is James R. Royse's *Scribal Habits in Early Greek New Testament Papyri*, where the author assesses the singular readings of six NT papyri, giving each scribe a unique profile.[3] Another study, by Juan Hernández Jr., also uses singular readings, which demonstrates that a method using singular readings to portray scribal habits could be applied to a

---

[1] Ernest C. Colwell, "Scribal Habits in Early Papyri: A Study in the Corruption of the Text," in *The Bible in Modern Scholarship*, ed. J. Philip Hyatt (Nashville: Abingdon, 1965), 370–89.

[2] Ernest C. Colwell, "Method in Evaluating Scribal Habits: A Study of $\mathfrak{P}^{45}$, $\mathfrak{P}^{66}$, $\mathfrak{P}^{75}$," in *Studies in Methodology in Textual Criticism of the New Testament*, NTTS IX (Leiden: Brill, 1969), 106–24.

[3] James R. Royse, *Scribal Habits in Early Greek New Testament Papyri*, NTTSD 36 (Leiden: Brill, 2008).

single book within a MS and can produce enough evidence to argue for theological motives behind scribal activity.[4] Of course not all studies of singular readings are so theologically sensational, as Peter M. Head[5] and Kyoung Shik Min[6] demonstrate with their conclusions that no theological tendencies exist in the data they analyze; but indeed, this is also valuable information about scribal practices and the MSS they studied.

The present study, similar to the ones above, is an analysis of the singular readings of several NT MSS—Codex Sinaiticus, Vaticanus, Ephraemi, Bezae, and Washingtonianus—in one book of the NT, the Gospel of Matthew. Looking at the singular readings *in situ*, the study offers possible reasons behind scribal activity in these MSS and suggests conditions under which the scribes would make certain changes during the transcription of their text. In addition, the work will give special attention to the quantity and frequency of omissions and additions in the scribes' work. The study offers, to date, the only survey of singular readings in these MSS in the Gospel of Matthew.[7]

---

[4] Juan Hernández, *Scribal Habits and Theological Influences in the Apocalypse: The Singular Readings of Sinaiticus, Alexandrinus, and Ephraemi*, WUNT 2, 218 (Tübingen: Mohr Siebeck, 2006).

[5] Peter M. Head, "The Habits of New Testament Copyists: Singular Readings in the Early Fragmentary Papyri of John," *Bib* 85 (2004): 399–408; and Observations on Early Papyri of the Synoptic Gospels, Especially on the 'Scribal Habits'," *Bib* 71 (1990): 240–47.

[6] Kyoung Shik Min, *Die früheste Überlieferung des Matthäusevangeliums (bis zum 3./4. Jh.)*, ANTF 34 (Berlin: de Gruyter, 2005).

[7] By analyzing more MSS than Hernández's study and including a lengthier survey text than Hernández's book of Revelation and most of Royse's papyri, I also aim to conduct a wider scale analysis than has previously been undertaken in a single study. There are approximately 404 verses in Revelation; and with at least one letter extant per verse, Royse's papyri contain 803 verses in $\mathfrak{P}^{45}$, 1,620 verses in $\mathfrak{P}^{46}$, 127 verses in $\mathfrak{P}^{47}$, 831 verses in $\mathfrak{P}^{66}$, 191 verses in $\mathfrak{P}^{72}$, and 1,385 verses in $\mathfrak{P}^{75}$. A potential advantage of Royse's study is the range of text incorporated—his papyri cover at least a portion of 18 of the 27 canonical NT books (2 Thess, 1 and 2 Tim, Titus, Phlm, Jas, and 1, 2, and 3 John are not extant in his papyri).

1.1. The Selection of Manuscripts and Gospel of Matthew

This study uses a common backdrop, a single book of the NT, to execute a study of singular readings. The Gospel of Matthew is chosen because it sits at a place of primacy in the NT as the most frequently cited gospel of the early church and has enjoyed positive canonical reception early on.[8] Practically speaking, the Gospel of Matthew provides an ample amount of text for this study, approximately 1,067–1,071 verses.[9]

The MSS chosen for the study here are Codex Sinaiticus (fourth century),[10] Codex Vaticanus (fourth century), Codex Ephraemi (fifth century), Codex Bezae (fifth century), and Codex Washingtonianus (fourth-fifth century).[11] These are selected because they are consistently cited MSS in the NA^{28} for Matthew[12] and because they have enough extant text (unlike the early papyri that contain the text of Matthew) with which to garner sufficient data for an analysis of scribal habits.[13] Codex Alexandrinus (fifth century) is an obvious candidate for analysis, but because a large portion of Mathew is missing in the codex, it lacks sufficient textual data for the study here (it has 18.7%

---

[8] Cf. *BiPa* (see Head, "Observations," 240–41, 240 n. 7).

[9] Several verses of Matthew are not universally included in the MS tradition: 16:3; 17:21; 18:11; 21:44; and 23:14. Of these five verses, the NA^{28} includes only 17:21; 18:11; and 23:14 as the established text.

[10] Scribe A of Sinaiticus is responsible for 88.51% of the transcription of Matthew, and riding A's coattails into the study is scribe D who is responsible for 11.49% of the transcription of Matthew.

[11] The dates reflect the INTF *Liste*, http://ntvmr.uni-muenster.de/liste.

[12] NA^{28}, 62*.

[13] For a quantitative description of all extant NT MSS up to and including the fifth/sixth centuries, see APPENDIX 1. This list does not include MSS dated to the sixth century, but includes MSS that the *Liste* dates to the fifth/sixth centuries. The quantitative description of each MS has been generous to designate a single letter of a verse as an extant verse, which is also the method of the NA^{28} (i.e., "It should be noted that for purposes of description here a verse is counted present if a single letter of it is preserved" [NA^{28}, 86*]). Therefore, the quantity of verses has been maximally estimated, not to provide greater authority to the MSS, but in order to clarify what portions, if any, a particular MS contains. Each papyrus listed in APPENDIX 1 contains less than 6% of Matthew—most contain less than 1% of Matthew.

of the text of Matthew extant, from 25:7–end). The codices Sinaiticus, Vaticanus, and Washingtonianus have no lacunae in Matthew. Ephraemi has 75.2% of the text remaining, while Bezae (D) has 93.1% of the text remaining.[14]

1.2. Methodology

The data used in the study are singular readings from these five MSS in their text of the Gospel of Matthew. In general, there is not much debate about what a "singular reading" is. In the simplest of terms, Colwell states a singular reading is a reading "without other manuscript support."[15] He uses only evidence from Tischendorf for this endeavor and acknowledges that MSS not used by Tischendorf may witness the same singular reading. He states that it is also "highly probably that many readings with minor support in Tischendorf are scribal creations."[16] Nevertheless, if Colwell discovers that a singular reading has "support of recent finds" or other sources, he eliminates it from his study.[17]

Unlike Colwell, though, Royse goes "beyond the evidence of Tischendorf's apparatus" to define a singular reading.[18] In addition to Tischendorf, Royse uses textual evidence from the editions of von Soden, Clark (*Eight American Praxapostoloi*), the NA^{25}, NA^{26}, NA^{27}, the United Bible Societies *Greek New Testament* 3rd and 4th editions, Aland's *Synopsis* 14th ed., Legg (which includes only Matthew and

---

[14] Concerning the five verses that are not universally included in copies of Matthew, Sinaiticus and Vaticanus include only 21:44 (NB: 17:21 is added in Sinaiticus by ℵ^{cb2}, and is not included in the total of verses of the *prima manus*). Ephraemi and Washingtonianus include all five of these verses (NB: 18:11 and 23:14 would occur in lacunae in C, but the MS would presumably follow the majority of MSS in including these verses). Codex Bezae (D) includes 16:3; 17:21; and 18:11. Therefore, the total number of verses likely copied by the *prima manus* in Sinaiticus and Vaticanus are 1,067; in Ephraemi and Washingtonianus are 1,071, and Bezae (D) are 1,069.

[15] Colwell, "Method," 108.
[16] Ibid., 108–9.
[17] Ibid., 109.
[18] Ibid.

Mark), *New Testament in Greek* (Luke and John), *Das Neue Testament auf Papyrus* (Catholic Letters, Paul's Letters), and Swanson (Matthew, Mark, Luke, John, Acts, Galatians, and Romans).[19] Hoskier and other editions are used by Royse when relevant. Except in certain cases, readings with versional and Patristic support are still counted as singular for Royse as long as there is no continuous-text Greek MS support.[20] Royse also includes corrected readings as long as the scribe of the MS, and not a later corrector, corrected them. In his study, Royse does not include established patterns of vocalic interchange, i.e. itacisms, nor several types of orthographic differences, as singular readings.[21]

In Hernández's extensive study of singular readings in Revelation, he uses Tischendorf, von Soden, Hoskier, Andrew of Caesarea, and NA[27] to determine MS attestation, and does not include those readings with versional support.[22] Hernández "also entertain[s] the possibility that some of our singulars may be 'original' (and therefore not 'created' readings), due to the Apocalypse's poor preservation and peculiar textual history."[23] Unlike Revelation for Hernández, the Gospel of Matthew for this study is not wrapped in such dilemmas since it is well attested in the early MS tradition. Nevertheless, it remains open that some singular readings under consideration could have been copied instead of created by the scribe.

However, not all who encounter singular readings are, at first, entirely positive that they were created by the scribe at hand. Holger

---

[19] Royse, *Scribal Habits*, 65. In his pre-publication dissertation, Royse used Tischendorf, von Soden, NA[25], NA[26], UBS[3], and Hoskier for Revelation (James R. Royse, "Scribal Habits in Early Greek New Testament Papyri" [Th.D. diss., Graduate Theological Union, 1981], 4).

[20] Royse states that "quite a few of our readings that are considered singular in fact have such support [of versions and Fathers]." He continues, "a certain amount of such 'support' from versions is likely to be illusory, resting only on an editor's mistake, nescience of the language or of the translational idiosyncrasies of the version ... " (Royse, *Scribal Habits*, 68–69).

[21] On itacisms see ibid., 79–81; on orthography see ibid., 81–83.

[22] Hernández, *Scribal Habits*, 47.

[23] Ibid.

Strutwolf, for example, is pessimistic about the ability to attribute a singular reading to a scribe, yet he uses them as primary data to portray copying practices. He believes that there are serious doubts about the thesis of "Royse and his followers," stating,

> One of these objections is that it is far from sure that the singular readings a manuscript contains really are the individual readings of the scribe who produced the manuscripts. Since we only possess a small portion of the vast number of manuscripts that ever existed, in most cases we do not know the real ancestors of the manuscript in question. So the singular readings of a certain manuscript might have been invented by its scribe, but could also already have existed in the ancestor or even have been passed down through three or more generations of ancestors now lost.[24]

Strutwolf states that since the publication of the *ECM* of the Catholic Epistles,[25] twelve readings that Royse identified as singular in $\mathfrak{P}^{72}$ are now *not* singular. Royse does in fact note that these twelve readings are no longer singular according to the available resources, though were counted as singular in his dissertation—*pre-publication*, and in some cases Royse now shows more support from witnesses than what Strutwolf notes. About these former singular readings, Royse says,

> An examination of the wealth of material contained [in the *ECM*] has led to substantial changes to the list of singular readings [from the 1981 dissertation to the 2008 publication] and to

---

[24] Holger Strutwolf, "Scribal Practices and the Transmission of Biblical Texts: New Insights from the Coherence-Based Genealogical Method," in *Editing the Bible: Assessing the Task Past and Present*, ed. John S. Kloppenborg and Judith H. Newman, RBS 69 (Atlanta: Society of Biblical Literature, 2012), 142.

[25] *Novum Testamentum Graecum Editio Critica Maior*, ed. The Institute for New Testament Textual Research, IV Catholic Letters, ed. Barbara Aland *et al.*, Installment 1: James, Installment 2: The Letters of Peter, Installment 3: The First Letter of John, Installment 4: The Second and Third Letter of John and the Letter of Jude (Stuttgart: Deutsche Bibelgesellschaft, 1997, 2000, 2003, 2005). The second edition of the *ECM* of the Catholic Letters was published in 2013, after Royse's *Scribal Habits*.

the textual changes throughout.... Most of these newly asterisked readings involve common errors (such as orthographic variation), and in none of them would I be inclined to see a genetic relationship.[26]

After noting the problems of identifying the true singularity of a variant, Strutwolf identifies the singular readings of 2186, a late Byzantine MS.[27] He makes the case that these readings are similar to the types Royse found in his study, and states that these are the scribal habits of the copyist of 2186.[28] Strutwolf concludes that the singular readings of 2186 witness more omissions than additions, a common phenomenon discovered in studies of singular readings and scribal habits, which is congruent with Royse's study.[29] In sum, while Strutwolf is reticent to use singular readings, he agrees that singular readings can display scribal habits.

Considering these dilemmas, a singular reading in the present study is a reading (such as a transposition, a word replacement, a word omission or addition, as well as an orthographic spelling, but not an itacism) that occurs in only one Greek NT MS. If a non-continuous Greek MS, version, or Patristic citation supports the reading, the reading is not included in the study. Thus, the selection of singular readings is intentionally restrictive so as to diminish as much as possible the probability that the scribe copied the reading.

This study also pays special attention to the longer and shorter readings created by the scribes, but not in the sense normally taken with the probability of *lectio brevior potior*. For one, a study of *lectio brevior potior* should include only intentionally created readings,

---

[26] Royse, *Scribal Habits*, 556.
[27] See Strutwolf, "Scribal Practices," 145–46 for his analysis of 2186.
[28] Ibid., 146.
[29] Strutwolf states, "If we apply the method of Royse to some Byzantine manuscripts which still have many singular readings, we come to the astonishing conclusion that even here the majority of the singular readings are omissions. A concrete example is Manuscript 2186: Nearly all of its singular readings consist of omission" (ibid., 145).

which is the method of Royse; and two, this probability is normally used to account for how the text of the MS tradition grew over time. Neither does the present study provide an account of the MS tradition, especially since singular readings were not copied over the course of generations, nor does the study adjudicate whether the scribe *meant* to create the reading or not (except in the case of obvious errors), only that the scribe *did* create the reading. When considering how long or short a reading is, its length is calculated from the longest or shortest similar variant at the given location.

This study further departs from the methods of Royse and Hernández, where it follows Colwell, by not including readings corrected by the scribe. This study restricts itself to the parameters of uncorrected singular readings, conceding that a more precise study of scribal habits would not be confined only to the uncorrected *or* to the corrected readings made by the initial scribe, but an analysis and synthesis of the two. This study could be, in that sense, the first step of discerning scribal habits in our MSS. The desideratum of this research is to analyze the *prima manus* hand of each MS, excluding corrections by the *prima manus*.

In order to identify if a variant is singular, it is compared to the evidence in several printed critical editions to discover if it agrees with any other textual witnesses. The editions employed for this in the study here are either the same sources that similar studies have employed or are the latest editions available.[30] In praxis, to identify a singular reading, the reading will have no support in Tischendorf's 8th edition,[31]

---

[30] To determine singular readings, Larry Hurtado used Tischendorf and Legg (*Text-Critical Methodology and the Pre-Caesarean Text: Codex W in the Gospel of Mark* [Grand Rapids: Eerdmans, 1981], 68); Head used NA[27], Tischendorf, von Soden, and Swanson ("John," 400); and Dirk Jongkind, in the text of Paul, used NA[27], von Soden, and Tischendorf, as well as the International Greek New Testament Project's edition of the Gospel of Luke for Lukan text (*Scribal Habits of Codex Sinaiticus* [Piscataway, NJ: Gorgias, 2007], 202, 221).

[31] Constantine Tischendorf, ed., *Novum Testamentum Graece*, 8th ed. (Lipsiae: Giesecke & Devrient, 1869). Unless otherwise stated, all references to Tischendorf are to this edition.

von Soden,[32] Legg,[33] NA[27], NA[28] *NTG/ECM Parallel Pericopes*,[34] *Text und Textwert*,[35] Swanson,[36] and occasionally other sources.[37] After the initial collation of Sinaiticus and Vaticanus using the INTF's New Testament Transcripts Prototype[38] (these transcripts are now also

---

[32] Hermann Freiherr von Soden, *Die Schriften des Neuen Testaments in Ihrer Ältesten Erreichbaren Textgestalt Hergestellt auf Grund Ihrer Textgeschichte*, II. Teil: Text mit Apparat (Göttingen: Vandenhoeck und Ruprecht, 1913).

[33] S. C. E. Legg, ed., *Nouum Testamentum Greace: Secundum Textum Westcotto-Hortianum, Euangelium Secundum Matthaeum* (Oxford: Clarendon, 1940).

[34] *Novum Testamentum Graecum/Editio Critica Maior: Parallel Pericopes*, ed. Holger Strutwolf and Klaus Wachtel (Stuttgart: Deutsche Bibelgesellschaft, 2011).

[35] Kurt Aland *et al.*, ed., *Text und Textwert der Griechischen Handschriften des Neuen Testaments IV: Die Synoptischen Evangelien, 2: Das Matthäus-evangelium, Bd. 2.2: Resultate der Kollation und Hauptliste sowie Ergänzungen* (Berlin: de Gruyter: 1999). This volume lists 64 test passages in Matthew. Of these, only five of them are singular readings concerning our MSS: ℵ4:23; B6:33; B19:17 (albeit for a different reading that what is given in *Text und Textwert*); D12:36; and D13:1. See the following five chapters for more information about what *Text und Textwert* notes as "singular" for each MS.

[36] Ruben Swanson, ed., *Matthew*, vol. 1 of *New Testament Greek Manuscripts: Variant Readings Arranged in Horizontal Lines Against Codex Vaticanus* (Sheffield, England: Sheffield Academic, 1995).

[37] In some instances, Henry A. Sanders has found agreement between Codex W and a Church Father that is not indicated in these critical editions, and here Sanders is followed. For example, Sanders found agreement between W, Origen, and Chrysostom for the transposition in Matt 19:24 (*The New Testament Manuscripts in the Freer Collection, Part 1: The Washington Manuscript of the Four Gospels* [New York: Macmillan, 1912], 140), and the word order in 25:32 in W is similar to the Ethiopic (p. 63). In addition, Jacob Geerlings, *Family 13—The Ferrar Group: The Text According to Matthew* (Salt Lake City: University of Utah Press, 1961), Amy S. Anderson, *The Textual Tradition of the Gospels: Family 1 in Matthew* (Leiden: Brill, 2004), which includes corrections of Kirsopp Lake's study, *Codex 1 of the Gospels and its Allies*, TS: Contributions to Biblical and Patristic Literature, ed J. Armitage Robinson, vol. 7 no. 3 (Cambridge: Cambridge University Press, 1902), and Min's study of Matthean papyri (*Die Früheste Überlieferung des Matthäusevangeliums*), are also utilized on occasion to check readings. Adolf Jülicher, ed., *Itala das Neue Testament in Altlateinischer Überlieferung: 1, Matthäus-Evangelium* (Berlin: de Gruyter, 1938), is consistently used to check agreement between Codex Bezae and the Old Latin.

[38] Institut für Neutestamentliche Textforschung, "New Testament Transcripts Prototype," http://nttranscripts.uni-muenster.de/.

housed in the INTF's Virtual Manuscript Room),[39] and a collation of Ephraemi, Bezae, and Washingtonianus using Swanson, the readings have been checked against facsimiles, microfilm, digital images, and/or other transcriptions of the MSS to confirm the initial collations and to ensure accountability and accurateness. Unless otherwise stated, the NA^{27} and Rahlfs LXX modules for Logos Bible Software have been used to calculate the occurrences of words or phrases in the biblical text.

1.3. The Ensuing Study

The following five chapters each concentrate on a single MS and offer explanations as to why its singular readings were created. In each of these chapters, first, an overview of the contents of the MS and scribe are given, including the number of singular readings found in that MS in Matthew. Then, the singular readings are grouped together according their commonalities and discussed. These discussions are the bulk of the contribution of this work, where I attempt to offer explanations, when possible, as to why these unique readings were created and if they can be considered habitual on the part of the scribe. At the end of each chapter, a summary is provided, followed by an analysis of the readings that are either longer or shorter than the other known readings that those locations. The conclusion chapter offers a summary of the results of the study and a comparison of the five MSS under analysis to each other.

As already mentioned, APPENDIX 1 is a descriptive list of all extant NT MSS up to and including the fifth/sixth centuries. APPENDICES 2 through 6 record the singular readings of each MS, which is the primary data the study is based on. APPENDICES 7 through 11 contain the readings that are either nearly singular or were singular according to one source but not others—these are not considered as part of the

---

[39] Institut für Neutestamentliche Textforschung, "Virtual Manuscript Room," http://ntvmr.uni-muenster.de/home.

core singular reading data.[40] APPENDICES 12 through 16 record the orthography for each of our MSS.[41] Finally, the tables in APPENDIX 17 organize the singular readings by number of words omitted and added.

---

[40] Few of the readings as presented in these appendices are ostensibly singular but effectively witness no new reading. For example, Codex D in 22:38 does not contain an article, which agrees with many MSS, and has a transposition, which agrees with other MSS. Therefore, the reading of D for 22:38 is not included as a singular reading.

[41] The orthographic appendices each contain a subsection titled "Singular Readings with Non-Singular Orthographic Changes". Herein, a spelling will have at least two itacisms, but the MS will be the only MS that witnesses both. The result is a word-spelling that exists nowhere else but in that MS, yet each of its itacisms are not unique. The readings in these subsections are not counted among the singular readings in the study.

CHAPTER 2
CODEX SINAITICUS

2.1. The Scribes and Extent of Matthew in Sinaiticus

Three scribes, A, B, and D, provide the original transcription of Codex Sinaiticus. Although there is an argument for four scribes, A, B^1, B^2, and D, the difference, however, does not directly affect the text of Matthew.[1] There is no dispute that scribe A transcribed most of the NT, including most of Matthew. Other portions of Matthew are copied by scribe D: Matt 16:9 (starting with τη πετρα) through 18:12 (ending with ανθρωπω) and 24:36 (beginning with περι) through 26:6 (ending with λεπρου).[2] Scribe A copied 942 verses and scribe D copied 125 verses, which amount to 1,067 verses in Matthew. There are no lacunae in this MS in Matthew.

2.2. The Singular Readings of Scribe A in Sinaiticus in Matthew

In the Gospel of Matthew, scribe A creates 158 singular readings (that is one singular for every 6.75 of his verses).[3] The most fre-

---

[1] The scribes A, B, and D, were proposed by H. J. M. Milne and T. C. Skeat after determining that Tischendorf's scribe C was actually the work of the scribes A and D (*Scribes and Correctors of the Codex Sinaiticus* [Oxford: Oxford University Press], 22–29). See Amy Myshrall, "The Presence of a Fourth Scribe?" in *Codex Sinaiticus: New Perspectives on the Ancient Biblical Manuscript*, ed. Scot McKendrick *et al.* (London: The British Library), 139–48, for an argument for four scribes.

[2] Scribe D in the NT is also responsible for Mark 14:54 (beginning with θησεν of ηκολουθησεν) though the end of Mark; Luke 1:1 though 1:56 (ending with τον); 1 Thes 2:14 (beginning with συμφυλετων) through the end of 1 Thess; Heb 4:16 (beginning with προσερχωμεθα) through 8:1 (ending with του); and Rev 1:1 through 1:5 (up to and including νεκρων). See Milne and Skeat, *Scribes and Correctors*, 29, for a comprehensive list of the scribal work of A, B, and D in the LXX and the NT.

[3] See APPENDIX 2 for the list of singular readings. Coincidentally, Hernández also counts 158 significant singular readings of scribe A in the Apocalypse (Hernández, *Scribal Habits*, 60), which is noteworthy considering that Matthew is a longer book. Of the 64 test passages in Aland *et al.*, *Text und Textwert*, ℵ is reportedly

quent type of singular reading arises from parablepsis, and the second most frequent arises from the influence of textual context. Some readings may intend to improve the text, as perceived inconsistencies are amended or a theological statement is reworked, but these are the exceptions to otherwise patterns of readings that do not significantly change the meaning of the text.

2.2.1. Orthography

Apart from common itacisms, mostly of two types of changes, the orthography in the work of scribe A elicits a few irregular changes, such as consonantal changes and the addition and omission of single letters.[4]

2.2.1.1. Itacisms

In Matthew in Sinaiticus, some itacistic changes occur often in the transcription by scribe A, ει > ι (338)[5] and αι > ε (192), and their counterparts are considerably less frequent ι > ει (7) and ε > αι (3).[6]

2.2.1.2. Other Vocalic Changes

Apart from itacistic changes, other vocalic changes include α > ε (5:41), ο > α (9:20), ου > ω (26:15b),[7] and ω > ου (27:64).

---

singular in 4:23 (which is accurate, denoted as 4:23a here) and 23:3 (but I have found versional support).

[4] Hernández documents several non-itacistic vocalic changes in the work of scribe A in Revelation: α > ει (1), αι > α (1), ε > α (2), ε > η (1), η > ει (1), ο > α (1), and ο > ου (1). Hernández, *Scribal Habits*, 61. His count of singulars tallied 9.45% to be orthographic, which includes "confusion of nasal sounds (1), confusion of consonants (2), replacement of vowels (8), dropping of consonants (5), adding of consonants (1), and occurrence of un-contracted forms (2)" (ibid., 60). Apart from itacisms, scribe A in Matthew creates more than three time as many orthographic spellings as is found in his work in Revelation.

[5] In the text of Revelation in Sinaiticus, there are over one hundred non-singular readings that witness the change ει > ι. Cf. Juan Hernández, "A Scribal Solution to a Problematic Measurement in the Apocalypse," *JSNT* 56.2 (2010): 275.

[6] See APPENDIX 12. Callan also reports that ι > ει and ε > αι occur less frequently than their counterparts in Sinaiticus in 2 Peter (Terrance Callan, "Reading the Earliest Copies of 2 Peter," *Bib* 93.3 [2012]: 450).

[7] See APPENDIX 12 where this is also recorded as an αι > ε change.

2.2.1.3. CONSONANTAL CHANGES

Besides vocalic changes, there are palatal mute changes $\varkappa > \chi$ (1:14¹, 14²; 20:13), a labial change $\pi > \varphi$ (5:33), and another consonant change γ or $\delta > \zeta$ (8:28).[8]

2.2.1.4. OMISSIONS AND ADDITIONS OF LETTERS

Other than changes/substitutions, there is a vowel addition between a consonant and a vowel (26:65).[9] There are final vowel omissions (18:18; 22:16) and consonant omissions (12:33; 27:23). Omission of final nu in verbs is not relegated to occur only before vowels or consonants, but is omitted before either (21:25; 22:21; 22:30; 28:7).[10] In one instance, there is a nu added at the end of a word (12:49).[11]

2.2.2. OTHER SPELLINGS

There is a syllable omission (4:18) and a non-contracted preposition (14:7)[12] in the singular readings. Some singular readings in Sinaiticus in Matthew are not real words (13:25; 26:15a).

2.2.3. NONSENSE IN CONTEXT

"Nonsense" comes in two forms: "strictly nonsense" and "nonsense in context."[13] The following singular readings in Sinaiticus do not make grammatical or logical sense in context, but are real words.

A verb is changed to a noun by the addition of one letter

---

[8] Most of these (1:14¹, 14²; 8:28) occur in proper names.

[9] Cf. Francis Thomas Gignac, *Grammar of the Greek Papyri of the Roman and Byzantine Periods*, vol. 1 Phonology, Testi e Documenti per lo Studio Dell'antichità 55 (Milan: Instituto Editoriale Cisalpino-La Goliardica, 1976), 1:310.

[10] Of these, only the reading in 28:7 ends a line of text. See A.T. Robertson, *Grammar of the Greek New Testament in the Light of Historical Research* (Nashville: Broadmanm, 1934), 220.

[11] Perhaps the nu ending of the preceding την influenced an addition of nu to χιρα (an orthographic spelling of χειρα), although, in that case, χιρην might be expected. Cf. την χειραν in Jos. Asen. 4:7 (Eckart Reinmuth, ed., *Joseph und Aseneth*, SAPERE XV [Tübingen: Mohr Siebeck, 2009]).

[12] Cf. Gignac, *Grammar*, 1:315.

[13] Cf. Royse, *Scribal Habits*, 91; Hernández, *Scribal Habits*, 62, 63.

(6:6).¹⁴ Concerning pronouns, one case change creates nonsense (20:14b),¹⁵ as well as one number change (20:34).¹⁶ There is a nonsensical substitution of *Daniel* for (a contracted form of) *Israel* (24:15).¹⁷

2.2.4. PARABLEPSIS

2.2.4.1. HAPLOGRAPHY

There are many possible instances of haplography (25). These account for 15.82% of the singular readings in Sinaiticus (scribe A) in Matthew. Omissions of three words or more almost always seem to be due to haplography in the singular readings in Sinaiticus (of 14 instances where three or more words are omitted, 11 have evidence of parablepsis).

Some are omissions of an entire clause (7:27b;¹⁸ 13:39)¹⁹ or two

---

¹⁴ The text of ℵ* reads a genitive instead of a dative as *rell*.

¹⁵ There are no vocalic changes οι > υ in the singular readings of scribe A in Matthew, and thus the change from dative to nominative here creates a reading that is nonsense in context.

¹⁶ The text of ℵ* reads a singular pronoun, but should be plural to match the subject, δυο τυφλοι, from 20:30.

¹⁷ The text of ℵ* reads a *nomen sacrum* for Israel, which is not construed in context because no prophet called Israel, or Jacob who is called Israel (Gen 35:10), spoke such words of desecration as Matthew declares. The three letters of the abbreviation, ιηλ, are the same as the final three letters of the word it replaces, Δανιηλ. If there was confusion with the preceding preposition, δια, with δαν (the beginning of δανιηλ) then scribe must have skipped the δαν of δανιηλ, leaving διαιηλ. When the scribe encountered the word ιηλ, perhaps there was a natural inclination to place a bar over it since it resembles the *nomen sacrum* for Israel. This would assume the scribe was paying enough attention to the word he was copying to think it read *Israel*, but not enough attention, or knowledge, to realize that a prophet called Israel never said these things. Perhaps there is mention of (the man) Israel in the targumim or pseudepigrapha where he is associated with this, but if this reading were intentionally created by the scribe and means this, then the scribe would have had to have some familiarity of Jewish extra-canonical sources—though there is no evidence of such familiarity elsewhere by the scribe in Matthew.

¹⁸ In 7:27b, the text of ℵ* lacks a clause (probably due to the parablepsis of –μοι και).

¹⁹ In 13:39, an entire clause is lacking, probably due to the parablepsis of ο(ι) δε θερισ–.

clauses (9:15),[20] or are omissions of phrases (28:2–3).[21] Sometimes the omission may also be due to beginning a new line of text, involving entire phrases (10:9)[22] or one clause (5:45;[23] 10:39),[24] two clauses (19:18),[25] one word (21:19;[26] 27:53a),[27] or adjuncts consisting of one word (8:3;[28] 12:44).[29]

---

[20] Two full clauses are lacking here in ℵ*, probably by haplography (due to parablepsis of –ν ο νυμφιος).

[21] In 28:3, the words ην δε η ειδεα αυτου are lacking in ℵ*. It is likely due to the parablepsis of αυτου.

[22] In 10:9, the parablepsis of –ον μηδε could have caused an omission of the phrase (which is part of the complement), μηδε αργυρον, by the scribe. The μη of the first μηδε ends the final line of a column and the scribe could have lost his place as he began a new column.

[23] In 5:45, the text of ℵ* lacks an entire clause. The final word, αγαθους, is split between columns, ending with αγα on one column and beginning with θους on a new column (folio 202, line 1, column 4). Scribe A could have skipped text due to the –ους endings of the following words (δικαιους and αδικους), which would be an instance of homoeoteleuton. Apparently, the scribe noticed the mistake later and finished line 1 of column 4 with και βρεχει επι, and then added δικαιους και αδικους himself in the margin (the color of the ink used in the emendation here by ℵ^A is lighter than usual).

[24] In 10:39, the scribe leaps from one substantival participle to another substantival participle, perhaps due to the small parablepsis of the article, ο, or because of the grammatical parablepsis of substantival participles, resulting in an omission of entire clause in ℵ*.

[25] The text of ℵ* is lacking ου μοιχευσεις ου κλεψεις, which is probably a leap due to the parablepsis –εις ου. In the Markan parallel, 10:19, the text of ℵ* (and f^1) reads an omission of μη μοιχευσης, which could also have been due to a leap (from –ευσης μη to –ευσης μη).

[26] The predicator ευρεν is omitted, probably by homoeoteleuton due to the parablepsis of –εν in three consecutive words (ουδ<u>εν</u> ευρ<u>εν</u> <u>εν</u>).

[27] The text of Sinaiticus is lacking εισηλθον. The omission could result from a leap from εισ to εις and would be an instance of homoeoarchton. The preposition εις begins a new line of text.

[28] In 8:3, homoeoarchton may be found (due to parablepsis of initial epsilons), which omits the adjunct ευθεως. After the initial epsilon of εκαθαρισθη, the word continues onto the next line.

[29] The combination και ελθον "can be, in Semitic idiom, the protasis of a conditional sentence: 'and if he come and find it, etc.,' the apodosis being introduced

There are omissions of adjuncts with parablepsis of one letter (13:44;[30] 14:23),[31] and omissions of adjuncts with parablepsis of three letters (19:26).[32] Some are omissions of a single letter, occurring when the same letters are found back-to-back (6:14)[33] or a similar phenomenon (18:20;[34] 20:14a).[35]

There is one omission of the preposition εν (22:1),[36] as well as omissions of conjunctions (19:10;[37] 20:19)[38] and two omissions of a verb/participle (22:15;[39] 27:33).[40] Of these leaps, two involve parablepsis

---

by το/τε (v. 45)" (Alan Hugh McNeile, *The Gospel According to St. Matthew: The Greek Text with Introduction, Notes, and Indices* [Grand Rapids: Baker, 1980], 183). In ℵ*, the verb ελθον is omitted, perhaps by homoeoarchton in ℵ*, and creates a difficult reading.

[30] In 13:44, the adjunct εν τω αγρω is omitted in ℵ*, perhaps by parablepsis of a single letter, omega, prompting homoeoteleuton.

[31] In 14:23, the adjunct απολυσας τους οχλους is lacking, which may be because of the parablepsis of a single letter, alpha in απολυσας and ανεβη, prompting homoeoarchton.

[32] In 19:26, the text of ℵ* is lacking the adjunct, παρα ανθρωποις. Perhaps the parablepsis of –οις (also found in αυτοις) caused homoeoteleuton. The adjunct is added in the margin with the noun written as a *nomen sacrum*, α̅ν̅ο̅ι̅ς. Parablepsis is found either with the abbreviation or written in full as ανθρωποις.

[33] The previous word, παραπτωματα, ends with an alpha, which may account for the omission of the alpha in αυτων.

[34] The conjunction is omitted before the numeric abbreviation for three, Γ̅. Perhaps the vertical strokes of the eta and gamma were confused, creating a sort of modified homoeoteleuton; thus the word, η, could have been leaped over due to oversight.

[35] The text of ℵ* reads a dative relative pronoun (ω) instead of a dative article (τω). Merely omitting the tau, leaving the omega, creates the relative pronoun—perhaps it was an oversight as τουτω contains parablepsis with the article τω.

[36] The text of ℵ* does not read the preposition εν, perhaps due to parablepsis of the previous word, ειπ<u>εν</u>.

[37] The scribe of ℵ* could have leaped from iota to iota, thus omitting ει.

[38] The omission of και may be due to homoeoteleuton (parablepsis with the preceding –αι). It is the seventh and final occurrence και in the sentence (20:18–19).

[39] The omission of ελαβον, perhaps by homoeoteleuton, is part of a phrase meaning *take counsel* (cf. 28:12 below). The omission of the verb creates nonsense in context.

[40] In 27:33, the attributive participle, λεγομενον, may have been omitted due to the parablepsis of the –ον endings with τοπον preceding it. The reading of ℵ*

of εν (21:19; 22:1) and two involve the parablepsis of ον (22:15; 27:33).

Two pronoun omissions have one letter of parablepsis as well as preceding text that may have somehow aided in their omission (9:30;[41] 20:7).[42]

2.2.4.2. Dittography

There are several instances of dittography (9), which comprise 5.69% of the singular readings. In one instance (7:26),[43] the scribe repeats one or two words. In another instance, the scribe repeats two words (19:1).[44] There are instances where one letter in one word is repeated where the word is split between lines in the MS itself (1:18;[45] 8:26),[46] and where two letters are repeated when the word is split between lines (13:28).[47] There are instances where the final word of one line is repeated as the first word of the following line (11:19;[48] 21:43).[49] There is one instance where a letter below where the scribe

---

is still grammatically construed, but it is a difficult reading.

[41] The omission of the pronoun in א* could be an oversight, due to the parablepsis of nu endings with the previous word (ανεωχθησαν). A similar phrase, οφθαλμων αυτων, occurs prior in 9:29, and could have aided in the omission of the pronoun in v. 30, if αυτων was fresh in the scribe's mind.

[42] The pronoun ημας is omitted, perhaps by homoeoteleuton (final sigmas of ουδεις and ημας). The verb, εμισθωσατο, now does not have a direct object, unlike prior in 20:1: μισθωσασθαι εργατας.

[43] The text of א* repeats either και πας or just πας. The text of א* is difficult to see where a second και would be located. This is probably an instance of dittography.

[44] The scribe produces an obvious dittograph of και ηλθεν.

[45] The word μνηστευθισης in א* ends one line with μνησ and begins the next line with στευθισης.

[46] The word here begins θαλ on one line and continues λασση on the following line. This is probably not an intentional spelling with a double lambda, but dittography caused by the separation of the word onto two lines.

[47] The scribe repeats the final syllable of αυτα, writing the additional τα on a new line.

[48] Scribe A transcribed two consecutive καις, the first ends a line and the second begins a line.

[49] In א*, the letters καρ occur at the bottom of a column, and καρπους begins the following column. The scribe began the new column by transcribing the word anew.

was copying was reproduced above it (24:24).[50] One dittograph is a word substitution for a previous word (24:22).[51]

2.2.4.3. CORRECTED LEAPS

There are instances where it seems that the scribe leaped over text due to parablepsis, then returned to the omitted text and copied it, thus not *omitting* text in his copy, but rather copying text *out of order*. Several of these transpositions could have stemmed from correcting a leap (4:24b;[52] 9:28b;[53] 14:17;[54] 18:19;[55] 21:34–35;[56] 27:56ab).[57]

---

[50] The text of ℵ* reads an iota before ψευδοχριστοι. Almost directly below this in the MS, the iota of και is found, which is followed by ψευδοπροφηται. The aberrant iota before ψευδοχριστοι may be accounted for considering (1) the parablepsis of ψευδοχριστοι and ψευδοπροφηται, and that (2) the location of the words are almost directly on top of each other in the MS; and if the words were arranged similarly in the exemplar, the scribe could have created a dittograph of a letter below where he was copying.

[51] Instead of κολοβωθησονται, the text of ℵ* reads εκολοβωθησαν. The substitution could be influenced from the same word earlier in the verse, which are both followed by αι ημεραι εκειναι. In addition, εκολοβωθησαν and the word it replaces are similar in spelling, which could have aided in the change κολοβωθησονται > εκολοβωθησαν. The substitution is, however, nonsense in context.

[52] The reading is difficult to see in Sinaiticus here, but if it is as the British Library posits for ℵ*, σεληνιαζομενους (*lunatics*), then the scribe probably leaped from συνεχ<u>ομενους και</u> to δεμονιαζ<u>ομενους και</u> (thus omitting δεμονιαζομενους και) and copied the following και σεληνιαζομενους. The singular reading occurs in a location where several words have similar endings and/or beginnings that provide several occurrences of parablepsis; and thus several MSS contain omissions here, as easily seen in Swanson, e.g. M Δ 1346 1424 (Swanson, *Matthew*, 31).

[53] The text of ℵ* and some Latin MSS read a pronoun (found in a different location in ℵ*) that refers to Jesus' actions being done *to you*, i.e. the blind men. Assuming that Sinaiticus was copied from a Greek exemplar that had the pronoun in the location that the Latin MSS have (i.e. at the end of the sentence), there is evidence of parablepsis in the Greek (the αι endings of the surrounding verbs) that could have influenced a leap in ℵ* that, when noticed during the transcription process, could have been corrected so that τουτο ποιησαι was not deleted.

[54] There is a transposition in 14:17 between two clauses: ουκ εχομεν ωδε and ει μη πεντε αρτους και δυο ιχθυας. In the latter clause, one word (αρτους) from the complement (πεντε αρτους και δυο ιχθυας) has been placed in the former clause. The ωδε ends a line of text and αρτους begins the next line.

2.2.5. Transpositions

Other transpositions have no evidence of parablepsis. With one possible exception of an improvement (28:13),[58] these readings could be considered difficult or nonsense readings (4:12;[59] 7:28;[60] 14:1;[61]

---

[55] The complement (γενησεται) has been placed prior to the predicator (αιητησωνται). It is possible that the parablepsis (ται endings) could have initiated the transposition.

[56] Due to erasure, the writing of the *prima manus* is difficult to read in ℵ here. Tischendorf, Legg, and the NA[28] cite no variants for ℵ here. Swanson reads ινα λαβον, which would indicate a purpose clause in 21:34 here. The British Library *et al.*, "Electronic Version of Codex Sinaiticus," http://www.codexsinaiticus.org/en/manuscript.aspx, suggest και λαβον (with some uncertainty), which would be more grammatically congruent with the indicative λαβον rather than the infinitive λαβειν in *rell*. If the text of ℵ* did in fact read as the British Library suggests, then the alteration from και λαβον to λαβειν may result from a leap to και λαβοντες in v. 35, which was then corrected before the scribe completed λαβοντες. In addition, there are several instances of parablepsis involving ου that could have provided more opportunities to leap from the same to the same.

[57] In ℵ* in 27:56a, Μαρια η Μαγδαληνη και is omitted, and in 27:56b, η Μαρια is added in two instances. To create the singular reading in ℵ* in 27:56ab, the scribe could have leaped from the first Μαρια to the second Μαρια (v. 56a) and supplied Μαρια out of place twice (v. 56b). Legg states the omission in ℵ* is due to homoeoteleuton. The verse in full for ℵ* is, εν αις ην Μαρια η του Ιακωβου και η Μαρια η Ιωσηφ και η Μαρια η των υιων Ζεβεδεου. The verse in full in most MSS is, εν αις ην Μαρια η Μαγδαληνη και Μαρια η του Ιακωβου και (η ℵ[ca]) Ιωσηφ μητηρ και η μητηρ των υιων Ζεβαδαιου. In comparison to *rell*, then, the reading of ℵ* (1) has not specified that the first Μαρια was *Mary Magdalene*, (2) contains another possible Mary, who is *the mother of Joseph* and may not be the same Mary, *mother of James*, since the name is mentioned twice, and (3) has specifically stated that the mother of Zebedee's sons is named Mary (which is contrary to Mark's third woman, Salome, in Mark 15:40).

[58] The reading of Sinaiticus here contains an occurrence of two consecutive verbs of speech. (In the NT, two consecutive forms of λεγω are found in Matt 22:4; 24:3; 28:13; Luke 7:9; 13:27; 19:40; 20:2; 22:34; John 21:19.) The scribe transposed οτι to what is a more common syntactical location.

[59] The singular transposition in ℵ* creates a difficult reading because οτι follows Ιωαννης. As a result of the word placement, there could be potential confusion of the verbal (ακουσας) subject as *John* rather than the intended *Jesus*.

[60] The subject has been moved away from the verb in ℵ*.

[61] The result of the transposition in 14:1 separates Herod's title, ο τετρα-

23:34;[62] 26:44).[63]

2.2.6. INFLUENCE FROM CONTEXT

Many singular readings (25) have similar or verbatim text nearby that could have influenced a change, producing assimilation. These readings account for 15.82% of the singular readings.

Most of these readings seem to be influenced from the preceding text (4:23b;[64] 5:39;[65] 6:16b;[66] 9:12;[67] 10:21;[68] 11:23;[69] 12:22;[70]

αρχης, from his name.

[62] With the και transposed in ℵ*, the reading is nonsense.

[63] The transposition in ℵ* here places the adjunct (εκ τριτου) in the complement (τον αυτον λογον).

[64] The addition of αυτους in ℵ* is found in the context of Jesus teaching in Galilee and produces the translation, *teaching them*. Luz states that the following phrase in 4:23, *in their synagogues* (εν ταις συναγωγαις αυτων), "makes clear that the evangelist and his community have their own place outside these synagogues." He continues, noting that *teaching* and *preaching* are used together throughout the gospel (Ulrich Luz, *Matthew*, vol. 1 trans. Wilhelm C. Linss, CC [Minneapolis: Fortress, 1992]; vol. 2–3, trans. James E. Crouch, ed. Helmut Koester, Hermeneia [Minneapolis, Fortress, 2001–2005], 1:205). If the use of the pronoun after *synagogues* "reflects a feeling against the Jews as a hostile body" (cf. 7:29; 9:35; 10:17; 11:1; 13:54; McNeile, *Mathew*, 99), then the additional pronoun after *teaching* in ℵ* could reiterate such division. If, as Paul Foster states, in *Community, Law and Mission in Matthew's Gospel*, WUNT 2, 177 (Tübingen: Mohr Siebeck, 2004), 5, that "the references [in Matthew] either to 'their' or 'your synagogues' (Matt 4:23; 9:35; 10:17; 12:9; 13:54; 23:34) should not be underestimated as showing the boundary division between one community as opposed to the more dominant emergent Judaism," then the additional pronoun in ℵ* in 4:23b could stress the point more than without it. The singular reading, however, is not necessarily Anti-Judaic if "preaching" and "teaching" are perceived to be similar. Cf. Luz, *Matthew*, 1:205; John Nolland, *The Gospel of Matthew*, NIGTC (Grand Rapids: Eerdmans, 2005), 182. Therefore, the addition in ℵ* could be purely for grammatical repetition. The singular reading could have been unintentionally influenced by the previous pronouns in vv. 21 (αυτου, αυτων, αυτους) and 22 (αυτων, αυτω); thus αυτους in v. 23 was a natural grammatical fit because the participle διδασκων can take a direct object.

[65] The verb in ℵ here is aorist passive infinitive (as opposed to active in *rell*). In this context in the gospel, Matthew sets up the thesis-antithesis structure with αντι in v. 38 and αντιστηναι in v. 39 (Luz, *Matthew*, 1:324). Because of the connection between the two verses, the scribe could have recalled the passive of ερρεθη (v. 38)

12:34;⁷¹ 19:21;⁷² 20:18;⁷³ 21:7b;⁷⁴ 24:10a and 10b).⁷⁵ Some readings

and changed ανθιστημι in the following verse to passive, which fits well in context. Also in the context, Matthew may be quoting from LXX Isa 50:8. The Göttingen edition of Isiah only notes a change αντιστ. to ανθιστ in the Greek tradition (Joseph Ziegler, ed., *Isaias*, Septuaginta Vetus Testamentum Graecum Auctoritate Societatis Litterarum Gottingensis, vol. 14 [Göttingen: Dandenhoed & Ruprecht, 1939], 534). Cf. Robert H. Gundry, *Matthew: A Commentary on His Literary and Theological Art* (Grand Rapids: Eerdmans, 1982), 94. R. T. France, *The Gospel of Matthew*, NICNT (Grand Rapids: Eerdmans, 2007), 219, states that similar language is found in Lev 19:18; Deut 32:35; Prov 20:22; 24:29; 25:21–22; Sir 28:1–7, however, the infinitive verb in ℵ and *rell* does not exactly mirror the aorist active imperative verb, αντιστητω, in Isaiah.

⁶⁶ Connected with αμην, the addition of γαρ in ℵ* fits well in context. Cf. BDF, §452(3). The conjunction γαρ is used earlier in the same verse, which may have influenced a repetition later in the verse.

⁶⁷ The plural word in ℵ here, rather than singular in *rell*, matches the number of οι ισχυοντες immediately before.

⁶⁸ The scribe may have been influenced by the preceding nominative, thus changing αδελφον to nominative, but it should be accusative to be grammatical.

⁶⁹ The text of ℵ* reads a plural pronoun instead of a singular. The pronoun does not match συ, used earlier, but could perhaps refer to the inhabitants of Capernaum. There are several plural words preceding (i.e. αι δυναμεις αι γενομεναι), which could have influence the scribe to write a plural pronoun.

⁷⁰ The scribe may have interpreted the preceding δαιμονιζομενος τυφλος και κωφος as more than one person rather than two characteristics of the same person, hence the change from a singular to plural pronoun.

⁷¹ The phrase γεννηματα εχιδνων appears in three instances in Matthew (3:7; 12:34; 23:33), none of which are changed from plural to singular except here in ℵ*. Concerning 12:34, the preceding words, which are grammatically singular, του καρπου το δενδρον γινωσκεται (v. 33), could have influenced the scribe to continue with the singular number.

⁷² The scribe of ℵ* transcribes a 2pl verb rather than 2s as in *rell*. The 2pl is incongruent in context. The previous noun is plural (πτωχοις), which could have influenced a change in the verb.

⁷³ Instead of the instrumental dative in *rell*, θανατω, the classical use of the accusative is found in ℵ 700, θανατον. Cf. BDF, §195.2. The singular reading in Sinaiticus here is the addition of the preposition εις. The prepositional phrase earlier in the sentence, εις Ιεροσολυμα, may have influenced the addition of εις before θανατον later in the sentence in ℵ. The result is a doublet: it highlights the connection between Jerusalem and death, which emphasizes Jesus' prediction of his death

are influenced from following text (7:22;⁷⁶ 7:25;⁷⁷ 8:7;⁷⁸ 15:11;⁷⁹

---

in Jerusalem and puts the spotlight on him even more, as opposed to Jesus *and the disciples*, cf. Mark 10:32–34 (Luz, *Matthew*, 2:539).

⁷⁴ The scribe adds the preposition επι, which may have been influenced by the επι after επεθηκαν earlier in the verse, or perhaps influenced from the previous word, επανω, which is a synonym. (After επεθηκαν in v. 7, επ is read by ℵ B D L Z Θ Φ 33 69 174 788 892* 983 1295 1606 1689 *l*2211 sy^p NA²⁸; επανω is read by *rell* [except om. *f*¹³].) Reading επι after επανω is not construed in context because of its redundancy following the synonymic preposition. Never in the NT does a preposition occur with επανω (Matt 2:9; 5:14; 21:7; 23:18, 20, 22; 27:37; 28:2; Mark 14:5; Luke 4:39; 10:19; 11:44; 19:17, 19; John 3:31; 1 Cor 15:6; Rev 6:8; 20:3).

⁷⁵ The addition in ℵ in 24:10a was probably influenced by (or perhaps was a leap back to) παραδωσουσιν υμας εις θλιψιν in v. 9 (so Nolland, *Matthew*, 964; Donald A. Hagner, *Matthew*, 2 vols., WBC 33a–33b [Dallas: Word, 1995], 2:693 n. b). Gundry states that, "as a whole, v. 10 says that persecution will influence many church members to betray one another. Mutual hatred will result" (*Matthew*, 479). The reading of v. 10a emphasizes the *persecution* element with the addition of εις θλιψιν, but the omission (24:10b) of και μισησουσιν αλληλους overlooks the result of the very persecution that is emphasized, and thus the doublet of vv. 10–11, where each verse contains a cause and a result, is deemphasized.

⁷⁶ Most MSS read ονοματι δαιμονια εξεβαλομεν και τω σω ονοματι δυναμεις πολλας in 7:22. The text of ℵ* includes πολλα following δαιμονια and includes πολλας following δυναμεις: no other MS reads πολλα(ς) twice here as Sinaiticus does. The addition could be due to a similar, but not exact, parablepsis of δαιμονια and δυναμεις. Though the repetition is also not exact (πολλα and πολλας), the scribe could have nevertheless been influenced from the following text of δυναμεις πολλας.

⁷⁷ The verb must be plural to be construed with the subject, οι ανεμοι, not singular as it is in ℵ*. In context, there are singular nouns following the verb (τη οικια εκεινη), which may have contributed a to a nonsensical verbal number change.

⁷⁸ The addition of ακολουθι μοι in ℵ* anticipates τοις ακολουθουσιν in 8:10. Nolland states that the addition of ακολουθι μοι in ℵ* "forces the following clause [εγω ελθων θεραπευσω αυτον] to be construed as an indication of Jesus' intention" (*Matthew*, 352 n. d).

⁷⁹ The addition of τουτο after το στομα in 15:11 could be the result of assimilation to the phrase του στοματος τουτο later in the verse. The addition could modify στομα (*this* mouth) or it could act as τουτο does in later in the verse (*this* defiles man). The result of the addition in v. 11 is a doublet with του στοματος τουτο later in the verse.

21:39;⁸⁰ 23:4;⁸¹ 23:37;⁸² 24:17;⁸³ 26:21).⁸⁴
Some readings could be influenced from surrounding text, i.e., both preceding and following text (2:9;⁸⁵ 4:24a;⁸⁶ 6:28;⁸⁷ 27:16).⁸⁸

---

⁸⁰ The verb change from compound to simple avoids repetition of the following εξω.

⁸¹ The singular reading in ℵ in 23:4, adding μεγαλα between φορτια and βαρεα, "enhance[s] the solemnity of Jesus' words" by exaggerating the opponents' burden, which is in contrast to Jesus' light burden (το φορτιον μου ελαφρον εστιν, Matt 11:30) (Bruce M. Metzger, *A Textual Commentary on the Greek New Testament*, 2nd ed. [Stuttgart: Deutsche Bibelgesellschaft, 2002], 49). The complement later in the verse, *and hard to carry* (και δυσβαστακτα), is omitted in in ℵ L f^1 et al. According to the UBS committee, και δυσβαστακτα was omitted "due to stylistic refinement or accidental oversight [i.e. parablepsis]" (ibid.). The addition of μεγαλα in ℵ then, compensates for the absence of part of the complement later in the verse (though the complement may not have been known by the scribe, i.e. was not in his exemplar). On the other hand, the scribe could have anticipated the adjective βαρεα, and simply added a synonymous adjective, μεγαλα. In addition, the word μεγαλυνουσι, following in v. 5 (10 lines later in ℵ), could have somehow caught the attention of the scribe, influencing him to write μεγαλα in the previous verse (v. 4).

⁸² The *prima manus* of Sinaiticus could have committed haplography in the middle of a word: instead of αγαγ, the scribe wrote αγ. There are, however, no further instances where the scribe truncates a word due to parablepsis (except the misspelling in 6:14, but the parablepsis is composed in two words, not within one word). Perhaps, then, the subsequent present tense επισυναγει influenced a preemptive change in the aorist επισυναγαγειν to the present tense επισυναγειν here in ℵ*.

⁸³ In the *Sizt im Buch*, vv. 17–18, there are two "images of desperate urgency" (Nolland, *Matthew*, 972–973). The first image is the man on the roof: "to leave as quickly as possible would involve leaving everything in the house behind." The second image is a man working in the field, who has no time to retrieve his garment. The latter of the two images is grammatically singular, αραι το ιματιον αυτου, and may have caused a preemptive alteration in ℵ* in v. 17, from a plural article, τα, to a singular article, το.

⁸⁴ The scribe could have been influenced by the following λεγω to substitute ειπεν with λεγι. Hernández notes an instance in Revelation where scribe A replaces one verb for another, but the verb which influenced the change is located several sentences earlier: the replacement of ειδον with εδοθη in Rev 16:31a, and the earlier occurrence of εδοθη is in 16:8 (Hernández, *Scribal Habits*, 79; 79 n. 200; 206).

⁸⁵ The following word αυτους and/or the previous 3pl verbs may have caused the scribe change the verb in 2:9 προηγεν > προηγον. An orthographic change from ε > ο is not typically found in Sinaiticus in Matthew; therefore, the verb

Some of these readings produce nonsense in context (7:25; 10:21; 12:22; 19:21; 21:7b). These readings that seem to arise from influence of the textual context are some of the most common singular readings in Sinaiticus. This is similar to what Jongkind finds in the scribe's work elsewhere in the codex.[89] These singular readings never result in a loss of text.

---

takes τους μαγους (v. 7) as its subject, as opposed to ο αστηρ in *rell*, which creates a difficult reading in Sinaiticus.

[86] Instead of the dative form of βασανος (so *rell*), the text of ℵ* reads the accusative form. The change to accusative could have been influenced from the following accusatives, συνεχομενους, δαιμονιζομενους, σεληνιαζομενους, παραλυτικους. The words βασανοις and συνεχομενους stand almost directly on top of each other in the codex, especially the endings.

[87] The translation of ℵ* for the latter part of Matt 6:28 is, *Consider the lilies of the field, how they do not comb, nor spin, nor labor*. The singular portion of the reading in ℵ* is a verb substitution (αυξανουσιν > ξαινουσιν) and the addition of a negative particle ου. There are now three negatives in Sinaiticus and produces the structure " ... neither this, nor this, nor this ... " The change in ℵ* from αυξανουσιν (*they grow*) to ου ξαινουσιν (*they do not comb*) fits well in context, which is about clothing (ευδυματος) and lilies (κρινα). The verb in ℵ*, ξαινω, means to comb or clean (of wool), which corresponds well with νηθω in the same verse. There are several factors that could have prompted the change in ℵ* here: (1) the spelling of αυξανουσιν is similar to a word that fits well in context, though not a synonym, ξαινουσιν; (2) the addition of ου before ξαινουσιν is similar in spelling to the first two letters of <u>αυ</u>ξανουσιν and (3) ου could have been an assimilation of the following ου... ουδε construction.

[88] The text of ℵ* reads an accusative article (τον) and conjunction (τε) before δεσμιον (in place of τοτε). The alteration in ℵ* is simply the addition of a nu in the middle of τοτε (τον τε). The reading is grammatically construed, but in context is a difficult reading because the δε combined with τε produces the translation, *in addition*, or *also*, to which there is no addition. If this were an unintentional alteration, perhaps the accusative case of δεσμιον prompted an unintentional (and preemptive) inclusion of an accusative definite article, τον, and/or maybe the ending of ειχ<u>ον</u> influenced a nu to follow the omicron in τοτε—thus the result was τ<u>ον</u> τε.

[89] Jongkind states that "The scribe is likewise inclined to harmonise the text to its immediate environment" (*Scribal Habits*, 244).

2.2.7. THE USE OF CONJUNCTIONS

In several instances, καί is omitted (9:9;[90] 12:11;[91] 26:33;[92] 27:53b);[93] and sometimes it is omitted when it is repetitious (8:15b;[94] 9:35a).[95] Synonymic conjunctions are exchanged (10:40;[96] 18:30a;[97] 18:31).[98]

There are instances in which the addition of a conjunction eliminates asyndeton between sentences (27:24)[99] or eliminates conjunctive participle asyndeton (27:3).[100] A conjunction is added in another in-

---

[90] The second of three occurrences of καί in the sentence is omitted in ℵ*, but the narrative still progresses smoothly.

[91] The singular portion of the variant in ℵ here is the omission of καί, which still produced a grammatical construed sentence. The transposition in ℵ, similar in c ff[1.2] h vg[pler] sy[c.s.p] sah bo, may emphasize (illegal) action (εγερει) on the Sabbath.

[92] The conjunction ει introduces a real condition here in 26:33. Cf. Maximilian Zerwick, *A Grammatical Analysis of the Greek New Testament*, 5th ed. (Rome: Editrice Pontificio Instuto Biblico, 1996), 87; and *Biblical Greek: Illustrated Examples*, English ed. adapted from the fourth Latin ed. by Joseph Smith, 2nd reprint, Scripta Pontificii Instituti Biblici 114 (Rome: Editrice Pontificio Instituto Biblico, 1995), §306. The omission of ει in ℵ* creates an unnecessarily difficult reading.

[93] The sentence is wanting in narrative progression without the conjunction in 27:53b. The omission unnecessarily complicates sentence structure.

[94] The omitted καί in ℵ* is the second of two occurrences in the short sentence (it is the last of four occurrences of καί in the whole of v. 15). The sentence is still grammatically construed with its omission, but the progression of narrative seems hindered because the καί began a new clause.

[95] The scribe eliminates the third occurrence of καί in a sentence where καί is otherwise read in five instances.

[96] The use of δε here results in "additive relation" between the two clauses (BDAG, s.v. δέ) which are translated, *The one who receives you receives me and* (δε) *the one who receives me receives the one who sent me.*

[97] The αλλα refers to the δε at the beginning of the verse, see BDF, §447(1), but the substitution with καί in ℵ* is also grammatically construed.

[98] The text of Sinaiticus reads δε instead of καί here and adds an article for ελθοντες. The use of the nominative article with δε could mark "the continuation of a narrative," and is "common in all the historical books" (BDF, §251).

[99] Cf. BDF, §462(1).

[100] Scribe A wrote an indicative verb with a conjunction, μεταμεληθη καί, in place of μεταμεληθεις. The singular reading of ℵ* may have been intended to eliminate the repetitive, and perhaps awkward, asyndetic participles in the context.

stance, perhaps unintentionally (6:16a).[101] Most often when the singular readings involve conjunctions, a loss of text occurs in the MS.

2.2.8. DEFINITE ARTICLES

In Sinaiticus, definite articles are omitted, some substantival (6:9;[102] 27:11)[103] or in front of names (9:28a;[104] 22:32a;[105] 22:32b;[106] 22:42).[107] One article is added, creating an articular proper name (10:4).[108] Another is added, perhaps, due to influence of the context (23:16).[109] Omissions involving articles substantially outnumber addi-

---

Cf. BDF, §421. (The participles in Matt 27:3 have an unequal value: ιδων, ο παραδους, μεταμεληθεις.)

[101] The addition of και in ℵ* is grammatically unnecessary because of the δε that follows. Perhaps the addition of και fit naturally in its place if the scribe did not anticipate δε.

[102] The substantival article is omitted from a prepositional phrase in ℵ*.

[103] The article is omitted from a substantival participle by the *prima manus*.

[104] The article has been omitted in ℵ* here before the name *Jesus* ($\overline{ις}$, as it is contracted in the text of Sinaiticus). Perhaps repetition of the final two letters, iota and sigma, of the previous word with the contraction $\overline{ις}$ created confusion: αυτοισοισ.

[105] In 22:32a, the article is omitted before the second occurrence of θεος in the sentence. See the following note for 22:32b.

[106] The article is omitted before the third occurrence of θεος in the verse (22:32b), which is a quote of Exod 3:6. Along with the non-singular omission of the article before the fourth occurrence of θεος in this verse, Sinaiticus therefore reads the article only for the first occurrence of θεος here. Likewise, only the article for the initial θεος is found in LXX Exod 3:6 (most MSS), which may be an attempt at continuity in Sinaiticus in Matthew. Unfortunately, the book of Exodus is not extant in Sinaiticus, otherwise, the verse in Matthew could be compared to it to attest its textual harmony (as the scribe may attest in 21:42 with the quote of LXX Ps 117:22–23).

[107] The scribe creates an anarthrous name, Δαυιδ, which resembles the gospel parallels (Mark 12:35; Luke 20:41). This is, however, very unlikely an intentional harmonization due to the insignificance of change—such an alteration probably did not intend to elicit the parallel contexts, which are already similar.

[108] The additions of articles in ℵ*, ο Ιουδας ο Ισκαριωτης, create an articular proper name (only the article before Ιουδας constitutes a singular reading).

[109] The addition of οι before τυφλοι could be influenced from context as it precedes οι λεγοντες. In addition, the ending of the previous word, οδηγοι, could have also influenced an article with the same letters: οι.

tions of articles.

2.2.9. OTHER SUBSTITUTIONS

Some word substitutions work well in context (9:6;[110] 22:9;[111] 27:15;[112] 28:5b;[113] 28:12).[114] Some are similarly spelled to the words

---

[110] The text of ℵ* here reads πορευου instead of υπαγε in *rell*, which essentially mean the same in context. The imperative verb πορευου is used 16 times in the NT (most often in Luke-Acts) and serves a special purpose in every instance: it is used after Jesus heals someone, forgives sins, or when he gives a parabolic example to follow (Luke 5:24; 7:50; 8:48; 10:37; 17:19; John 4:50; [8:11]); it is spoken by God, the resurrected Jesus, the Spirit, and angels (Matt 2:20; John 20:17; Acts 8:26; 9:15; 10:20; 22:10; 22:21); and is used in pivotal contexts (it is used by Pharisees warning Jesus about Herod's murderous intentions, Luke 13:31, and is uttered by Felix to send Paul away, from which he never returns, Acts 24:25). Based on these uses, the text of Sinaiticus astutely employs a verb that fits well in the context of performing a miracle (i.e. healing the paralytic, Matt 9:2–8).

[111] The reading in ℵ* is difficult to see, but the British Library *et al.* "Electronic Version of Codex Sinaiticus," suggest υδατων for οδων. In Jesus' parable about the wedding banquet, in ℵ* the king's messengers sought people along *the waters*, rather than *the main roads*. The term υδωρ is generic enough to mean all types of water—in Homer it is rarely used to refer to seawater (Liddell-Scott, s.v. ὕδωρ).

[112] The word recorded by the *prima manus* of ℵ in Matthew here, παρητουντο, is the same in the Markan parallel (15:6) in ℵ* A B* Δ (also NA[28]) (most other MSS in Mark read ητουντο). In ℵ* in Matthew, then, the crowd *asked* for Barabbas to be released rather than *wished* him to be released; but in v. 17 and v. 21 (as well as the gospel parallels: Matt 27:17 ‖ Mark 15:9; John 18:39) (Matt 27:21 has no direct gospel parallel), Sinaiticus reads *wish* as do most other MSS, and not *ask* as in Matt 27:15. The notions of *asking* or *wishing* could be synonyms in context. Both verbs can emphasize "the coming free choice of Barabbas" (Gundry, *Matthew*, 560), but if a distinction could be made, perhaps *ask* involves more initiation—to *ask* for Barabbas could mean to actively speak—rather than perhaps passively *wishing* for him. The variant in ℵ* here resembles the Markan parallel, but it may not necessarily be an intentional harmonization because the text that is harmonized is small, just one word, and the texts are already similar to begin with. Harmonizations seem to be rare or even nonexistent in the singulars in Sinaiticus, but synonymic substitutions are more common which may be the case here (cf. 9:6, 9:27; 21:7a; 22:9; 24:28; 28:5b, 28:12).

[113] The verb in ℵ* here is aorist passive as opposed to present passive in other MSS. Concerning the verbal mood, if the ending of φοβηθηται is itacistic, ε > αι, then the verb is imperative (which would align the mood with *rell*). Such itacistic

they replace (9:27;[115] 21:7a;[116] 24:28).[117]

The singular substitution of *Antipatris* for *hometown* (13:54) is difficult to explain. Ropes argues that the reading is construed in con-

---

spellings are, however, rare in the work of scribe A in Matthew: two instances of ending changes, ε > αι, are found in the work of scribe A in Matthew (see APPENDIX 12). If the ending is not itacistic, which is probably the case here, then the verb seems to be subjunctive.

The particle μη with present imperatives forbids the continuation of an act, whereas μη with aorist subjunctives forbids a future act "with an absolute prohibition, as distinct from the prohibition 'in principle' conveyed by the present" (Zerwick, *Biblical Greek*, §246). The verbal emphasis with the μη + subjunctive in ℵ* here has compensated for Matthew's choice of a "weaker φοβεισθε ... to Mark's stronger εκθαμβεισθε" (Nolland, *Matthew*, 1249). Surely, the scribe did not intend to compensate for the evangelist Matthew's use of Mark, but the alteration does, however, result in a stronger grammatical negation than the present imperative found in *rell* in Matthew.

[114] The singular portion of the reading in ℵ* is the substitution of λαβοντες with εποιησαν. The use of συμβουλιον with λαμβανειν or ποιειν is a translation of the Latin phrase, *consilium capere* (BDF, §5.3). Cf. BDAG, s.v. συμβούλιον. It is used "in the sense 'counsel' (rather than 'council')" (C.E.B. Cranfield, *The Gospel According to Mark*, CGTC [Cambridge: Cambridge University Press, 2005], 122). In every instance in the NT where συμβουλιον is used with λαμβανειν or ποιειν (or διδωμι), there are variant readings in MSS witnessing one or the other verbs (in Matt 12:14 εποιησαν replaces ελαβον in L *l*184; in Matt 22:15 εποιησαν replaces ελαβον in 1527; in Matt 27:1 εποιησαν replaces ελαβον in D Latt Cop; in Mark 3:6 a form of ποιειν replaces εδιδουν in ℵ A C D W M *f*¹ *et al.*; and in Mark 15:1 λαβοντες replaces ποιησαντες in *l*13. The only other instance of συμβουλιον in the NT is in Acts 25:12 and is not used with one of the aforementioned verbs). The verbs λαμβανειν and ποιειν (and διδωμι) seem to be somewhat interchangeable when used in conjunction with συμβουλιον; and therefore, the substitution in 28:12 in ℵ* does not affect the meaning of the text, but is a construed substitution.

[115] The text of ℵ reads a form of κραυγαζω instead of κραζω as *rell*.

[116] The singular reading in ℵ* here is not significantly different than the other variants. It is comprised of a simple verb (also in D K N W Y Θ Π 700 1241) and is 3pl (as in ℵ^ca L 4 16 245 291 579 892). The same verb and form (εκαθισαν) is read in ℵ* in the Markan parallel (Mark 11:7).

[117] The text of ℵ* reads οπου > που. The reading can be construed in context because που does not need to be "strictly local" (Liddell-Scott, s.v. ποῦ, A.2). Cf. BDF, §103. If the change was unintentional in ℵ*, perhaps the previous genitive words, του υυ̅ του α̅ν̅ο̅υ̅ (v. 27), somehow affected the transcription of ορου (v. 28).

text, but Harris, Milne, and Skeat believe it could reveal provincial information of the codex.[118]

2.2.10. OTHER OMISSIONS

Some omissions may be mere oversights, but are still rendered sensical in context (18:12;[119] 23:11),[120] one of which is probably due,

---

[118] The text of ℵ* reads αντιπατριδα instead of πατριδα. The singular reading here has been pivotal for some scholars (e.g. Harris) in identifying a Caesarean provenance for Codex ℵ, noting that "as [the scribe] sat writing in the neighboring city of Caesarea," he unintentionally substituted a generic word (πατριδα) with the familiar proper noun (αντιπατριδα) (J. Rendel Harris, *Stichometry* [London: Clay, 1893], 75). The Judean city Antipatris was "founded by Herod the Great and named after his father ... on the road Lydda to Caesarea" (BDAG, s.v. Ἀντιπατρίς). Milne and Skeat agree, stating that Harris' argument "appears almost incontrovertible" and that "scribes as careless and ignorant as those of the Sinaiticus might easily have perverted πατριδα into a meaningless jumble, or substituted another word of approximately the same sound, but no one unconnected with Palestine would be likely to have produced Αντιπατριδα" (*Scribes and Correctors*, 67–68). It may not, however, be entirely reasonable to base the scribe's and/or the MS's provenance almost solely on the singular variant in 13:54 (as well as the reading *Caesarea* for *Samaria* in Acts 8:5). If there were more evidence of a Caesarean provenance, perhaps this variant would act as supplemental proof, but provenancial evidence may not so confidently and exclusively rest indirectly on a solitary variant or two. Not convinced of the explanation of Αντιπατριδα, Ropes conjectures that the scribe "coined a word (or else a very rare one) to mean 'foster-native-place'" (J. H. Ropes, *The Text of Acts*, vol. 3 of *The Beginning of Christianity*, ed. F. J. Foakes Jackson and Kirsopp Lake, part 1 [London: Macmillan, 1926], xlvii n. 1). Though Ropes intends to make sense of the reading, it could be simply that the reading is itself nonsense in context. See also Harry Y. Gamble, "Codex Sinaiticus in Its Fourth Century Setting," in *Codex Sinaiticus: New Perspectives on the Ancient Biblical Manuscript*, ed. Scot McKendrick *et al.* (London: The British Library), 6–13, for recent refutation of a Cesarean provenance.

[119] Fives lines after scribe A's transcription resumes after the transcription of scribe D (folio 210), an adjunct is omitted in 18:12 ([προβατα] επι τα ορη [και]). One way to account for the omission in ℵ* here is by homoeoarchton, which is possible only if the exemplar of Sinaiticus read προβατα ... πορευθεις, as do Β Θ *et al.* (the letters pi, rho, and omicron could possibly furnished a leap even though they are transposed: πορ/προ, and therefore could be metathesis). Sinaiticus is corrected with the addition επι τα ορη by ℵ^S1, but πορβατα and the following και are not included.

somehow, to the two scribes (A and D) ending and beginning their transcription within the MS (24:35).[121]

In two instances, the object of an object-complement construction is omitted (1:21;[122] 1:23).[123] Both of these involve naming Mary's child as Jesus/Emmanuel and witness the omission of the genitive pronoun, and unfortunately both of these readings are difficult to see (especially 1:21) due to deterioration of the folio or erasure.

Some omissions are seemingly inexplicable, but the word or phrase that is omitted can nevertheless be understood or implied in

---

Due to the correction not including προβατα, it may be more likely, then, that the exemplar of ℵ did not contain πορβατα, and thus the omission of επι τα ορη is not due to parablepsis, but rather is a scribal oversight.

[120] The pronoun υμων is not read in Sinaiticus here. In the longer form of the saying found earlier, Matt 20:26, the pronoun is read in Sinaiticus, εστε υμων διακονος; also, the genitive is found in Sinaiticus in the "similar saying" in Mark 9:35, και παντων διακονος (McNeile, *Matthew*, 332). The omission in 23:11 does not seem to have significant theological implications, but renders the translation, *The greatest among you will be a servant*, rather than *will be your servant*.

[121] The omission in ℵ* "is presumably a scribal oversight" (W. D. Davies and Dale C. Allison, *A Critical and Exegetical Commentary on the Gospel According to Saint Matthew*, ICC [Edinburgh: T&T Clark, 1988–1997], 3:368 n. 281); but what is the cause? Usually, large omissions in the singular readings of Sinaiticus have evidence of parablepsis, but that is not evident here. The omission occurs at the end of the last column of a page of codex ℵ (folio 213b). The omission is probably due to the changing of scribes in the MS because the work of scribe A ends here (and begins again with Matt 26:7) and scribe D picks up with 24:36.

[122] The original hand is difficult to see here. The *prima manus* may have written Ιησουν in full and omitted the pronoun αυτου.

[123] As in 1:21, the scribe in 1:23 omits the genitive pronoun after το ονομα. If ℵ* reads as the British Library tentatively suggests (with the omission of αυτου in 1:21, 23), then the combination of καλεω + ονομα + genitive pronoun + proper noun may have posed a problem for the scribe in these two instances. The genitive pronoun in the proximate εκαλεσεν το ονομα αυτου Ιησουν in 1:25, however, remains there. Perhaps the "known quantity" of ονομα, i.e. that a person has a name Daniel B. Wallace renders the possessive pronoun obsolete for the scribe. One difference between the two alterations (vv. 21, 23) and the phrase in v. 25 is that the future form of καλεω is found in vv. 21, 23 and the aorist is found in v. 25 (Daniel B. Wallace *Greek Grammar Beyond the Basics: An Exegetical Syntax of the New Testament* [Grand Rapids: Zondervan, 1996], 43 n. 21).

context. Perhaps there is a desire for concise expression or elimination of redundancy in these singular readings (4:23a;[124] 9:35b;[125] 12:37;[126] 21:30;[127] 27:48;[128] 28:10).[129]

---

[124] The singular reading in ℵ* here is the omission of ολη (in the Markan parallel, Mark 1:39, the reading in ℵ contains ολην). Specifically concerning the word ολη (*all*), Davies and Allison ask, "Is the universalism of the gospel (26:13; 28:19) foreshadowed in Jesus' preaching in '*all*' of Galilee, the land of the Gentiles (4:15)?" (*Matthew*, 1:413). Rudolph Schnackenburg states that "Galilee becomes the very region in which God's mercy is unveiled in Jesus' salvific activity" (Rudolph Schnackenburg, *The Gospel of Matthew*, trans. Robert R. Barr [Grand Rapids: Eerdmans, 2002], 39). If this detail is important, that *all* of Galilee is traversed by Jesus, then the scribe of ℵ* has done Jesus' ministry a disservice by stating he has not traversed the whole region; but nevertheless, the sense of the whole region, or *all*, can be implied in context even with the omission of ολη.

[125] The singular portion of the reading in ℵ* is the omission of πολλοι that is found in L Φ $f^{13(exc.124)}$ 7 *et al*. The reading of ℵ* then does not suggest how many people followed Jesus, as other MSS read "many", but the adjective "many" could easily be implied in ℵ*.

[126] There are several verbal person changes in the context of 12:37, which leads Nolland to believe that "the change from the second person plural of the opening of v. 36 and the third person plural of its body to the second person singular here suggests use of traditional material" (Nolland, *Matthew*, 507–508). Davies and Allison state the same notion (*Matthew*, 2:351). McNeile states that the material is "drawn from another context ... possibly a current proverb" (*Matthew*, 181). The pronoun σου in 12:37 in Matthew (which is omitted in Sinaiticus) could either aid in keeping track of the changes, from 2pl to 3s to 2s, or it could perhaps be seen as confusing. Nevertheless, the pronoun is understood in the verb καταδικασθηση, so its omission in Sinaiticus does not seem to affect the grammar or meaning of the text in any great way.

[127] The phrase, ο δε αποκριθεις ειπεν, is omitted in ℵ*. The same phrase occurs in the previous verse, and the parallelism between vv. 28, 29, and 30 is "nearly perfect" in *rell* (Davies and Allison, *Matthew*, 3:168). Plausibly, the omission in ℵ* may be for concise expression because ωσαυτως is not omitted, thereby noting the similarity between the verses.

[128] The partitive genitive (involving εκ + αυτων) is not omitted elsewhere in Matthew in ℵ (Matt 10:29; 18:12; 22:35; 25:2). The omission of part of the subject may be a scribal slip.

[129] The text of ℵ* does not read the genitive pronoun for τοις αδελφοις. (The previous occurrence when Jesus speaks of *my* brothers, 25:40, the pronoun is read in Sinaiticus.) It is still possible to infer μου from context, though the text flows

2.2.11. INEXPLICABLE CHANGES

One reading involves a verb change from an indicative verb to a participle (8:15a).[130] One noun is inexplicably changed from singular to plural (7:21).[131] Metaplasm is found in one instance (2:2).[132]

2.2.12. KOINE GRAMMAR

Some singular readings, grammatical in nature, situate the scribe in a Koine context, particularly using –ω verb endings in place of –μι verb endings (4:8;[133] 18:30b;[134] 26:46),[135] and using 1st aorist

---

better with its inclusion; and therefore, it is still possible to claim from the context that "the risen Lord continues to refer to his disciples as his brothers (and sisters) now even after they abandoned him" (Hagner, *Matthew*, 2:874).

[130] The verb in ℵ* here is a participle, εγερθις (with an itacism ει > ι), rather than indicative as in *rell*, ηγερθη. There was probably no influence from the surrounding verbs, as they are all indicative.

[131] The scribe changes the singular θελημα to plural. In the other instances of θελημα + του πατρος in Matthew (12:50; 18:14; 21:31), the singular readings do not witness alterations to θελημα. The text of ℵ* then states here that the person who does the *desires* of the Father will enter into heaven, rather than the one who does the *desire* of the Father.

[132] The masculine ending of αστερα is changed to feminine in both 2:2 and 2:10 (the latter occurrence is read by ℵ* C), which may be a kind of metaplasm (fluctuation of declension) (BDF, §49). In the singular readings, other occurrences of αστηρ are not likewise altered in Matthew. Another occurrence of the declined τον αστερα in Rev 2:28 is not altered in ℵ, but αστερας is found instead of αστερα in Rev 9:1 in ℵ*.

[133] The 3s primary verb ending for –ω verbs is used here in Sinaiticus in place of the 3s ending for –μι verbs. If verbs ending in –(νυ)μι in Koine were "give[n] place to synonyms or new formations in –ω" (Zerwick, *Biblical Greek*, §493), i.e., the new –ω formation of δεικνυμι is found in Matt 16:21; John 2:18; [Rev 22:8] in the majority of MSS, then perhaps the singular reading in Sinaiticus (δικνυει) was one of the new formations, or at least an acceptable formation. The "decline" of μι verbs is "strongly felt in Koine as compared with classical Greek" (BDF, §92). The BDAG states that δεικνυω goes back at least to Herodotus, fifth century B.C.E. (s.v. δείκνυμι). See also William W. Goodwin, *A Greek Grammar* (Surrey, UK: Thomas Nelson, 1992), §787.1, .2, where he states verbs in ημι and ωμι are inflected in εω and οω in Homer and Herodotus. The other occurrence of δεικνυσιν in the NT, John 5:20, reads δικνυσιν in ℵ (but δεικνυει in codex D).

[134] The aorist subjunctive 3s –μι verb is transcribed with an –ω verb ending.

verb endings in place of 2ⁿᵈ aorist endings (7:27a;[136] 15:12).[137]

2.2.13. OTHER CONSTRUED SINGULAR READINGS

Some case changes produce a good grammatical structure (3:15;[138] 19:15;[139] 20:31a;[140] 20:31b).[141]

---

[135] The verb παραδιδωμι is transcribed with an –ω verb ending (παραδιδω) in ℵ*, as opposed to a –μι verb ending.

[136] In Koine, the 1ˢᵗ aorist form is often substituted for an Attic 2ⁿᵈ aorist (BDF, §75), which may explain the 1ˢᵗ aorist active ending on ηλθαν in ℵ instead of the expected 2ⁿᵈ aorist ending. The word occurs at the end of a column line in the codex, so there is a bar over the alpha indicating moveable nu.

[137] The verb ειπον is transcribed with a 1ˢᵗ aorist active ending (ειπ<u>αν</u>), rather than the 2ⁿᵈ aorist (ειπ<u>ον</u>)—such a spelling is (normally) regularized in the apparatus of NA²⁸ (cf. ειπον as the reading of ℵ in the NA²⁸ here).

[138] The context of the variant is Jesus' response to John about how it is fitting for Jesus and John, i.e. *for us* (ημιν/ημας), to baptize Jesus *to fulfill all righteousness* (πληρωσαι πασαν δικαιοσυνην). Instead of the dative ημιν, ℵ* reads the accusative ημας as the subject of the infinitive πληρωσαι, which is construed because the subject (*us*) is different than the person (John) to whom Jesus is speaking. Cf. BDF, §409(3).

[139] The context of Matt 19:15 and the parallel Mark 10:16 is *the laying on of hands*, which is "a mark of blessing [that] appears in a variety of biblical contexts" (France, *Matthew*, 727). In the gospels and Acts, the blessing occasionally has the preposition επι with it (Matt 9:18; Mark 8:25; Acts 8:17; 9:17; 19:6), but it is most common not to have a preposition (Matt 8:3, 15; 9:29; 17:7; Mark 6:5; 7:32; 8:23; Luke 4:40; 13:13; Acts 6:6; 8:18, 19; 9:12; 13:3; 28:8. Cf. ibid., 727–728). Davies and Allison state that Matthew's change to αυτοις in 19:15 from Mark's επ αυτα (Mark 10:16) "enhance[s] the parallelism with 19:13" (*Matthew*, 3:34). Of all of the occurrences of the blessing throughout the NT, only in Matt 19:15 does the text of Sinaiticus include a preposition in the blessing (the MSS 483 484 also have the preposition in Matt 19:15). The inclusion of the preposition is probably more of an *aberration* here in Sinaiticus than it is a *harmonization* to the Markan parallel (Mark 10:16). The singular portion of the reading in Sinaiticus is the case change to accusative, which is construed as the object of the verb επιθεις.

[140] According to Nolland, Matthew's μειζον is a simplification of Mark's πολλω μαλλον (*Matthew*, 828). In Matt 20:31a, scribe A replaces μειζον with the "fairly rare" πολλω μαλλον (Wallace, *Greek Grammar*, 166), which aligns it with the Markan and Lukan parallels (Mark 10:48; Luke 18:39). The scribe does not alter the word μειζον in similar occurrences in Matthew: 12:6; 18:4; 23:11, 17 (23:19 is omitted in ℵ) (Davies and Allison, *Matthew*, 3:108). It seems that the variant in Sina-

2.2.14. POSSIBLE THEOLOGICAL READINGS AND INTERPRETATION OF THE TEXT

Several readings could be the result of forethought on the part of the scribe. Some omissions may intend to edit the text in some way, by clearing up an inconsistency (12:46;[142] 28:5a).[143] Sometimes the text

---

iticus may not be an *intentional* harmonization because the parallel texts are already very similar and the portion of text that is harmonized in Sinaiticus in Matthew is very small and does not elicit much difference in meaning. Cf. Michael W. Holmes, "Early Editorial Activity and the Text of Codex Bezae in Matthew" (Ph.D. diss., Princeton Theological Seminary, 1984), 138. Though the dative substantive + comparative adjective/adverb construction is rare, the scribe of Sinaiticus here provides a grammatically construed alteration.

[141] The text of ℵ* here reads a genitive υιος before Δαυιδ, rather than the nominative or vocative as in other MSS. (In the Lukan parallel, Luke 18:39, ℵ* also reads a genitive υιος, but in the Markan parallel, Mark 10:48, the vocative is found.) In Matthew, the relationship between the words *son* and *David* produce a genitive of relationship structure.

[142] Matthew places Jesus' mother and brothers at the scene while Jesus is speaking to the crowds, but it does not state in ℵ* that his mother and brothers were *seeking to speak to him* (ζητουντες αυτω λαλησαι). Several MSS (including ℵ*) omit the entirety of the following verse (v. 47), which is easy to account for due to parablepsis of ζητουντες and λαλησαι in v. 46 and v. 47 (Metzger, *Textual Commentary*, 26). McNeile states, v. 47 "is absent from the true text, Mt. having already summarized Mk.'s equivalent. It was added probably to supply an antecedent to τῷ λέγοντι αὐτῷ [of v. 48]" (*Matthew*, 184–85). The omission in ℵ* in v. 46, then, "is hard to account for" because the text of ℵ* lacks the parablepsis (ζητουντες and λαλησαι) of vv. 46 and 47 that could have produced haplography of the adjunct in v. 46, ζητουντες αυτω λαλησαι (Nolland, *Matthew*, 516 n. b-b). The portion of text that is omitted in ℵ* is not necessary for context to make sense, especially because Jesus' mother and brothers never *speak to him*, they are only *referenced by him*.

[143] Concerning the *Sitz im Buch* at Matt 28:5a, the women's fear has not been stated yet (but is stated in v. 8), only the guards' fear has been stated (found in the previous verse, v. 4). The omission of the adjunct, *the women*, in ℵ* resolves such perceived inconsistency: because they are not yet afraid, they cannot be told to be unafraid. Following, the emphatic υμεις (υμις in ℵ) no longer contrasts the two groups in ℵ*, the women and soldiers, by speaking only to the women (Davies and Allison, *Matthew*, 3:667), but combines them and now the angel speaks to both groups, not solely to the women.

is expanded upon, either by conflation of variants (14:29),[144] or other additions (15:5).[145]

One reading, though grammatically construed, may not produce a good interpretation of the text (21:42).[146] Another reading, perhaps one of the most interesting singulars in Matthew in Sinaiticus, concerns the confessional statement by the centurion (27:54a and

---

[144] The reading of ℵ* in 14:29 is a conflation of two variants (so Nolland, *Matthew*, 595 n. i-i.). It is comprised of the ελθειν from *rell* and the ηλθεν from B C* *et al.* An inferential ουν is added in ℵ* (or is a substitute for και from the reading in B C* *et al.*), which aids in separation of the two phrases (BDAG, s.v. οὖν). The reading in ℵ* may be an "exegetical expansion introduced by the scribe" as Metzger posits (*Textual Commentary*, 30) and is appealing as a theological reading since it occurs in a key soteriological passage in Matthew, as Andries G. van Aarde describes in "ΙΗΣΟΥΣ, the Davidic Messiah, as Political Saviour in Matthew's History," in *Salvations in the New Testament: Perspectives on Soteriology*, ed. Jan G. van der Watt, NovTSup 121 (Leiden: Brill, 2005), esp. 15–26; but since the scribe's contribution to the reading is merely a conjunction to combine two verbs, it is probably more likely an attempt to smooth what would have been an awkward reading without a conjunction.

[145] The text of ℵ* reads ουδεν εστιν after ωφεληθης in 15:5. The addition in ℵ* refers to the preceding δωρον as the subject. Nolland states that the scribe of ℵ* does not understand the custom (15:3, 6 παραδοσιν) of giving to the temple in lieu of supporting elderly parents; thus the meaning of ℵ* gives the sense, "The gift you would have gained from me is nothing" (Nolland, *Matthew*, 606 n. d). If the addition is read as a *commentary* on the custom, rather than the addition being a *misunderstanding* of the custom (so Nolland), then it resembles similar usage found in Matt 23:16 (ουδεν εστιν), meaning that the law is not binding and in this case that children should honor their parents (see BDAG, s.v. οὐδείς, 2.b.β). The addition in ℵ*, then, emphasizes the hypocrisy of the tradition along with the "very definite negation," ου μη immediately following in v. 6 (Luz, *Matthew*, 2:325 n. 1). This addition in 15:5 is perhaps an explanation of the text by the scribe.

[146] The singular reading in ℵ*, genitive > dative, is a portion of the LXX Ps 117:22–23 quote (which was also copied by scribe A in the OT portion of the codex, but contains the genitive *Lord*). (The Göttingen LXX edition gives no variants for παρα κυριου in Ps 117:23.) The preposition παρα with the genitive of person denotes source (*this was the Lord's doing*) as opposed to a rendering with υπο that would denote direct cause (*done by the Lord*) (Zerwick, *Grammatical Analysis*, 70). The scribe may have interpreted the variant in the very manner Zerwick cautions against by mistakenly supplying the dative of cause (*Biblical Greek*, §58).

54b).¹⁴⁷ These singular readings (21:42; 27:54a, and 54b), however, use minutiae that could either (1) produce drastic theological changes, which is unlikely intentional because such minutiae in the singulars is not used elsewhere to rework Matthew (cf. 6:6; 20:14b, 34 for nonsense in context; cf. 7:21; 8:15a for inexplicable changes), or (2) be a re-working of phrases that could have been perceived to be *grammatically* awkward rather than *theologically* awkward, or (3) be small errors that happen to make sense in context.

2.3. The Singular Readings of Scribe D in Sinaiticus in Matthew

There is comparatively little text transcribed by scribe D in Matthew, creating only 16 singular readings (that is one singular for every 7.81 verses he transcribes).¹⁴⁸ There are a few types of changes that are represented more than once, which are transpositions, pronoun changes to reflexive, haplography, and consonant changes, but none occur more than twice.

There is one itacistic change in the transcription of scribe D, αι

---

¹⁴⁷ There are two singular features in ℵ* in 27:54. The transposition (27:54a) within the complement (του θεου υιος) places the predicator (ην) between the genitive and nominative nouns. The inclusion of a definite article (27:54b) is also a singular reading in ℵ*; thus, the predicate is placed before the verb followed by an articular θεου could result in a slight emphasis of *the Son* of God. The grammatical construction in ℵ* resembles 27:40, ει υιος ει του θεου (but not 27:43, οτι θεου ειμι υιος; nor 14:33, θεου υιος ει), "to which the present confession is the positive counterpart" (Nolland, *Matthew*, 1221). In context, the centurion has "limited knowledge" of *the Son of God*, but he "recognises the presence of deity and has enough evidence to be profoundly convinced that Jesus is bona fide" (ibid., 1220). The change in ℵ* may intend to eliminate the possibility that the centurion meant *a son of God*, which would be allowed by the anarthrous υιος in its position in *rell* (so Gundry, *Matthew*, 578; France, *Matthew*, 1084 n. 50; Hagner, *Matthew*, 2:852). "In any case," states Zerwick, "the Christian reader is meant to recognize a confession of the whole truth" (*Grammatical Analysis*, 96), which is the result of the reading in ℵ*: *Jesus is the Son of God*. If this is *over translated*, however, there could be an emphasis on *the God* and not *the son*; but this may not be possible because υιος is transposed forward in the sentence.

¹⁴⁸ See APPENDIX 2.

> ε.[149] In the transcription of Matthew by scribe D, there is no elision in the particle αλλα (to αλλ) in one instance when it precedes a word beginning with a vowel (16:17).[150] There are two consonant omissions (18:3; 25:16) and one initial vowel omission (17:10). Milne and Skeat contend that "mannerisms of spelling can provide considerable assistance" in differentiating between the work of scribes A and D,[151] and Jongkind determined that the amount of itacistic spellings in the work of scribe D in the synoptics was significantly fewer per folio than scribe A.[152] When the established patterns of itacistic spellings of the two scribes gained from the study here are taken into account, there is an astonishing contrast in the singular readings in Sinaiticus in Matthew. In the transcription by scribe A, there are 539 singular itacistic changes, which amounts to one change for every 1.74 verses. In the transcription by scribe D, there is only one singular itacistic spelling, which, therefore, amounts to one change for every 125 verses. Compared to Jongkind's itacistic findings for Sinaiticus, the singular readings in Matthew display an exaggeration of the scribes' work. On the other hand, the *non-itacistic* spellings (that is, spellings outside of established patterns) amount to 5.69% of the text transcribed by scribe A, which is a relatively similar percentage to the orthographic changes in the transcription of scribe D, which amount to 3.2% of the text. Therefore, the purely itacistic spellings display a great contrast between the two scribes, but the amount of remaining vocalic and consonantal orthography is not helpful for differentiating the work of the two scribes in Matthew.

There are relatively few instances where scribe D omitted text where there is evidence of parablepsis (18:8;[153] 24:37).[154] There are

---

[149] Matt 24:40, παραλαμβανεται > παραλαμβανετε. See APPENDIX 12.

[150] Gignac, *Grammar*, 1:316.

[151] Milne and Skeat, *Scribes and Correctors*, 51. Milne and Skeat state three causes for scribe A's orthography: colloquialisms, phonetic errors, and indefensible blunders (i.e. carelessness) (ibid., 52). They conclude that D is "the most correct" of the scribes, "who alone reaches the standard of good literary papyri" (ibid., 53).

[152] Jongkind, *Scribal Habits*, 91.

[153] The scribe commits haplography due to parablepsis of σου σκανδαλιζει

only two singular transpositions in the text transcribed by scribe D (16:13;[155] 17:8),[156] none of which have evidence of parablepsis. Scribe D adds only one article, which may be a careless addition—perhaps caused by subsequent text (24:39).[157] There are instances where pronouns are substituted for reflexive (24:49;[158] 25:36),[159] or are substituted for articles (25:44a).[160] One noun has an inexplicable case change (16:19^1).[161] In one instance, an unnecessary second augment is found

---

σε ... καλον σοι εστιν in v. 8 and σου σκανδαλιζει σε ... καλον σοι εστιν in v. 9.

[154] There is an omission of part of the subject, perhaps by haplography, leaping from του to του.

[155] The verb λεγουσιν here is part of an interrogative predicate in the accusative case (Zerwick, *Grammatical Analysis*, 52). Scribe D places the verb closer to the following accusative predicate, τον υιον του ανθρωπου.

[156] The Aramaic proleptic pronoun construction is altered here (Zerwick, *Grammatical Analysis*, 55). The Aramaic proleptic pronoun construction is also found in Matt 3:4; Mark 2:21; 6:17, (18), 22; (12:36, 37); John 9:13. Cf. Nigel G. Turner, *Syntax*, vol. 3 of A Grammar of New Testament Greek, by James Hope Moulton (Edinburgh: T&T Clark, 1963), 41. The pronoun is no longer rendered proleptic (as in B* Θ 700) but as an antecedent pronoun, which is a common grammatical construction in the NT. Zerwick states, "The proleptic use of pronouns, i.e. their use to 'introduce' a noun which follows ... is a pure Aramaism, and has been almost entirely eliminated from the usual text" (*Biblical Greek*, §204; cf. §205). Cf. McNeile, *Matthew*, 251.

[157] The addition of an article in ℵ* before εως may be a scribal slip. The second word after εως is the same article, ο, which could have caused a preemptive addition before εως.

[158] When the word συνδουλους occurs in Matthew (the word does not occur in the other gospels: Matt 18:28, 29, 31, 33), a non-reflexive personal pronoun is used in all instances in Sinaiticus except here in 24:49, which is the only occurrence for which scribe D is responsible. (Not concerning συνδουλους, the previous occurrence of αυτου, 24:48, is changed to reflexive in ℵ 892.)

[159] The change here, με > εμε, occurs at the end of six instances of με in 25:35–36 and is the final word of a sentence. The location in the codex is the first and only word on the top line of a column (folio 214b). The alteration, similar to occurrences of αυτου > εαυτου, may be intended for emphasis.

[160] The singular element of the variant in ℵ* is the substitution of αυτοι for οι, which renders a similar translation with either variant, αυτοι or οι.

[161] The accusative is used here in ℵ* rather than the genitive in *rell*. In context, the difference between accusative and genitive when modified by επι is not

on an aorist verb (25:44b).[162] In one instance, the name *Jesus* is omitted, but is understood in context (17:17);[163] and in another instance the nonsacral name *lord* is omitted but is understood in context (25:22).[164]

2.4. Conclusion

2.4.1. SCRIBAL HABITS IN GENERAL

The singular readings in Sinaiticus in Matthew give distinct impressions of scribal behavior for scribe A, whereas for scribe D, the textual data via singular readings is scarce. For scribe D, there are only a few types of singular readings that occur more than once, such as haplography, transpositions, and pronoun changes to reflexive. Itacistic variation by scribe D is almost nonexistent (cf. §2.3), which is a great contrast to the work of scribe A (cf. §2.2.1.1). This disparity between the scribes is difficult to account for if both scribes copied the same exemplar by eye. Nevertheless, it is noticeable that different orthography is tolerated in a single MS even when scribes are working together. The itacistic differences between scribe A and D may be explained by the apparent lack of standardization of the time.

Concerning scribe A, who generates a wealth of singular readings, there is no apparent editorial attempt to re-present Matthew in a drastic way,[165] but there are a few noticeable habits and items worth

---

significant.

[162] The text of Sinaiticus here contains a second augment to the aorist διακονεω. A non-Attic spelling is found in *rell*, but an Attic rendering would be εδιακονησαμεν (BDF, §69.4).

[163] The text of ℵ* does not read Ιησους and places the article, ο, forward in the sentence. Although the Markan parallel is similar (Mark 9:19, omission of *Jesus*), it is not a harmonization because the name *Jesus* is still understood in context.

[164] The text of ℵ omits the nonsacral κυριε in 25:22. Its omission does not affect the meaning of the text because it is understood in context.

[165] Head arrives at a similar conclusion in his study of Sinaiticus in Mark. He states, "there is simply not a great deal of evidence for peculiar Sinaitican interpretive moves in the re-presentation of Mark" (Peter M. Head, "The Gospel of Mark in Codex Sinaiticus: Textual and Reception-Historical Considerations," *TC* 13 [2008]: §66).

mentioning. Perhaps the most noticeable theme among the singular readings is that the textual context seems to be an influence on the scribe. The scribe will skip or repeat text due to parablepsis (cf. §2.2.4); and if parablepsis is not involved, preceding and/or following text still influences changes (cf. §2.2.6). Although the nearby text seems to influence the scribe, the rare instances when singular readings seem to resemble a gospel parallel are probably a coincidence. Therefore, the scribe seems to be influenced most from the nearby context rather than remote parallels.

A preference for Koine grammar is also noticeable in some instances in the singular readings of scribe A (cf. §2.2.12). These Koineisms seem to stem from the scribe's own initiative, rather than mimicking nearby text or skipping text due to similar words as many other changes seem to be.

2.4.2. Longer and Shorter Readings

In Matthew in the work of scribe A, 31.64% of the singulars are omissions and 15.18% are additions (cf. APPENDIX 17). In Hernández's study of Sinaiticus in Revelation, he finds that 31.01% of the singulars created by the scribe are omissions,[166] which is a similar percentage compared to what is found in Matthew, and 25.32% are additions, mostly of one word.[167] Granted the criteria for what constitutes a singular reading is not identical between his study and the present study, it is nevertheless comparable and the results are congruent considering that more omissions are found in Sinaiticus in both Matthew and Revelation than additions.

Overall, there are 50 instances of omission and 24 instances of addition, practically a 2:1 ratio. There are 114 words omitted and 27 words added, which is greater than a four-to-one ratio. In Matthew, scribe A has a clear tendency to *omit* more often than add, and to *omit* more words than he adds.

---

[166] Hernández, *Scribal Habits*, 70.
[167] Ibid., 65.

Among the singular readings that affect the length of the text, it is evident that readings which have evidence of parablepsis most often result in a shorter text. When there is influence from context (with no evidence of parablepsis), however, *all* singular readings result in a longer text. Only in one instance is an article added, whereas all other singular readings that involve articles are omissions (cf. §2.2.8). Other changes often involve the omission of pronouns. The greatest *addition* is of two words, but Sinaiticus has *omissions* of one, two, three, four, five, six, eight, nine, and even thirteen words. Thus, overall, the scribe omits more often than adding, and omits greater units of words than what is displayed in the additions.

CHAPTER 3
CODEX VATICANUS

3.1. The Scribe and Extent of Matthew in Vaticanus

One scribe (scribe B) transcribed the entirety of the NT in Codex Vaticanus (who is responsible for portions of the OT as well).[1] In Vaticanus, Matthew contains 1,067 verses and no lacunae.

3.2. The Singular Readings in Vaticanus in Matthew

There are 95 singular readings in B in Matthew, which is among the lowest totals in our MSS in Matthew, and amounts to one singular reading for every 11.23 verses.[2] There are a relatively high number of transpositions and readings that are influenced from context, as well as several changes from Koine to Attic and *vice versa*, though rarely, if ever, do any of the readings change the meaning of the text. There are more instances of omissions in B than additions, but overall there are more words added to the text than subtracted. This, as far as I know, is the first documentation of such in a MS. The large number of word additions is due primarily to repetition of (nearby) text rather than, for example, an expansion of already existing content or harmonization to distant parallels.

---

[1] Scribe B copied 1 King 19:11–2 Esd and Hos–Dan. Scribe A copied Gen 46:28–1 King 19:11; Ps–Tob (Milne and Skeat, *Scribes and Correctors*, 87, 88).

[2] See APPENDIX 3 for a list of singular readings. Of the 64 test passages in Aland, *et al.*, *Text und Textwert*, Codex B is reportedly singular in 4:23 (but I found it has the support of versions); 6:33 (which is accurate); and 19:17 (for the omission of με, however 791 also omits it—but B* is indeed singular in its omission of εις in that variation unit which *Text und Textwert* does not document).

3.2.1. Orthography and Spelling

3.2.1.1. Itacisms[3]

In B in Matthew, there is only one type of itacistic change among the singular readings, ι > ει (73).[4]

3.2.1.2. Other Vocalic Changes

Vocalic (non-itacistic) changes are some of the most frequent types of changes in the singular readings in B in Matthew (13.68% of the singular readings). There are eight varieties of vocalic changes: α > ο (19:12; 26:53a), αι > α (13:48), ε > α (13:14), ε > η (25:10), ε > ι (26:53b), εα > ε (28:2–3), and ει > ε (10:22). In addition, several changes involve an iota omission in either και (6:19), οι (12:1b), or εαυτοις (21:38a). Iota is omitted before a back vowel (26:59),[5] and it is added in another instance which creates a hiatus (26:14).[6]

3.2.1.3. Consonantal Orthography

There are no orthographic consonantal *additions* in B in Matthew, but there are nine types of omissions and one substitution. Consonantal orthography is the most persistent type of singular reading in B in Matthew, found in 27.36% of the singular readings, due primarily to the spelling of *John*. In inflected forms of Ιωαννης, there is often a simplification of double nu (3:4; 4:21; 11:2; 11:4; 11:7;

---

[3] See APPENDIX 13.

[4] Stephen Pisano maintains that there are "consistent" ι > ει changes in B in Matthew ("The Text of the New Testament," in *Prolegomena: Exemplum Quam Simillime Phototypice Expressum Codicis Vaticani B (Vat. Gr. 1209) Praestantis Humanitatis Operis Rei Publicae Italicae Officina Typographica et Argentaria Sumptibus Suis Comparauit* [Vatican City: La Biblioteca Apostolica Vaticana e L'Instituto Poligrafico e Zecca Dello Stato, 1999], 34). In B in Mark, Voelz counts the change ι > ει in B "chief among its features" (James W. Voelz, "The Greek of Codex Vaticanus in the Second Gospel and Marcan Greek," *NovT* 48.3 [2005]: 211).

[5] A similar omission of iota is found in LXX Sus 1:60, ψευδομαρτυρας. Gignac states that "an accented ι is very frequently omitted before a back vowel," which may be the case in B* in 26:59 (Gignac, *Grammar*, 1:302).

[6] Cf. ibid., 1:109, 319.

11:11; 11:12; 11:13; 11:18; 14:3; 14:4; 14:8; 14:10; 21:26, 21:32).[7] Concerning other words, there is the simplification of a double mu (23:25),[8] omission of medial nu following mu (10:19),[9] omission of final nu (7:16; 21:17; 21:41), omission of a medial nasal before a dental stop (26:63),[10] omission of sibilant before a dental stop (3:12),[11] omission of initial sigma (12:33), omission of final sigma before a word beginning with a vowel (13:15),[12] and omission of final sigma before a word beginning with a consonant (15:32).[13] There is one singular dental change, κατ > καθ (20:17).[14]

3.2.1.4. MISCONSTRUED SPELLINGS

Some unusual spellings are found in B in Matthew (21:46;[15] 28:11).[16] There are some instances where a syllable has been omitted (17:23;[17] 18:9)[18] or where a word is simply misspelled (27:1).[19]

---

[7] The instances of νν > ν in Ιωαννης are simplification, though it is only found once in Gignac's study and not in a proper name (ibid., 1:158).

[8] Cf. Gignac, *Grammar*, 1:157.

[9] The text of B* reads μεριμνησητε > μεριμησητε. Gignac notes a similar occurrence in υπομνημα > υπομημα in *PMich.* 123 (ibid., 1:117).

[10] Such omissions are frequent in the Byzantine papyri. Cf. ibid., 1:116–7.

[11] Cf. ibid., 1:130.

[12] Cf. ibid., 1:125.

[13] Cf. ibid., 1:124–5.

[14] The dental change in 20:17, κατ > καθ, is also found in non-singular instances in B in Matthew, e.g. 17:1, 19; 24:3.

[15] The reading of B* is difficult to see here. If it is εκρατησαι (so NT Transcripts, similar to εκρατησα in Swanson), then the scribe has added an augment to the verb in the infinitive mood.

[16] The spelling σκουστωδιας in B* instead of κουστωδιας is flummoxing—it is not found in Gignac, Moulton-Milligan, Liddell-Scott, BDAG, nor TLG. The initial sigma could be a dittograph of the preceding της, but the same addition of sigma is found on κουστωδιαν in B* K in 27:65 (though not again in 27:66).

[17] The τη of τριτη is omitted in B*.

[18] The final syllable -ζει is missing from σκανδαλιζει in B.

[19] The word γενομενης is recorded as γομενης in B*.

3.2.2. Not Construed in Context

In some instances, the text of B contains a singular reading that is construed neither grammatically nor logically (13:30²;[20] 21:33).[21] One lengthy omission of ten letters does not have evidence of parablepsis (10:14).[22]

3.2.3. Parablepsis

The readings that involve an omission or addition of text due to similar or identical lettering nearby account for 8.42% of the singular readings. It is here that the longest amount of words are added, 6 words in one instance and 5 words in another, in all of the singular readings in Vaticanus, yet there are more *instances* of omission than addition.

3.2.3.1. Haplography

There are instances of omissions when there is evidence of one letter of parablepsis that could have resulted in homoeoteleuton (5:16;[23] 13:17).[24] There is an instance of homoeoarchton consisting of

---

[20] The text of B* reads a feminine pronoun where *rell* reads a neuter. The pronoun refers to the articular infinitive το κατακαυσαι, and is therefore not grammatically construed.

[21] The verb is 2pl in B*, but 3s would be the construed reading because of the 3s subject in 21:40, ο κυριος του αμπελωνος. The reading in B* could have been influenced by the 2pl verb that begins 21:33, ακουσατε, but the verbs surrounding εξεδετε are all 3s (εφυτευσεν, περιεθηκεν, ωρυξεν, ωκοδομησεν, and απεδημησεν). The word εξεδετε occurs in the middle of a line of text in B, so it is not the case of a moveable nu at the end of a line which would match the other –εν verbal endings.

[22] The omission of μη(ν) δεξηται υ renders the reading of B* nonsensical. A verb (i.e. δεξηται) should be present here for grammatical construal, but the greatest indicator of a scribal error present within the variation unit is the omission of the upsilon of υμας. The entire omission consists of ten letters if the exemplar of B* read as *rell* (if the exemplar read as B^c1, the omission is still of ten letters, consisting of the nu of μην and the contraction of αι to a single letter in δεξηται). This haplography does not consist of parablepsis, but it does align with other omissions of ten letters.

[23] The text of B does not read εργα following καλα. The word καλον "describes a work as it is seen by others," writes McNeile (*Matthew*, 57). He references

two letters of parablepsis (19:17).²⁵ There is an instance where a word is truncated, possibly due to parablepsis within the word itself (21:38b),²⁶ and a three-letter word reduced to one letter, perhaps due to parablepsis with the following word (27:45),²⁷ as well as a similar phenomenon (14:13).²⁸

---

two other instances in the gospels where καλον + εργον is used in a similar context, Matt 26:10 and John 10:32. In neither instance is εργον omitted or altered in B; nor in the instances of rabbinic expression involving καλα and εργα that Gundry lists (Matt 3:10; 7:17, 18, 19; 12:33) does the text of B have readings that suggest something else besides *good works* (Gundry, *Matthew*, 78), which is "an established expression" (Luz, *Matthew*, 1:252). The omission here may be a result of a scribal leap from alpha to alpha, or because it is understood in τα καλα it is omitted. The meaning of the pericope is not changed with the omission (so Nolland, *Matthew*, 211 n. e).

²⁴ Concerning a similar wording in 10:41, Gundry connects δικαιοι, a Mattheanism, with δικαιου, stating that Matthew pairs prophets with righteous men (*Matthew*, 258), but the text of B reads δικαιοι in 10:41, unlike 13:17. The scribe may have omitted και δικαιοι in 13:17, which is a portion of the subject, by homoeoteleuton, leaping ten letters from iota to iota. If it is an intentional alteration, perhaps the scribe is commenting on the nature of prophecy.

²⁵ The text of B* lacks the number εις here. Perhaps the parablepsis of epsilon (and sigma) incited a leap from εις to εστιν.

²⁶ The omission of ομ in κληρονομος may be a leap from omicron to omicron.

²⁷ The text in B* records only the epsilon of εως, perhaps because of a jump from omega to omega: εως ωρας.

²⁸ The reading in B* here is difficult to see. NT Transcripts notes that the scribe of B* omitted εν (marked as *ut videtur*), but Swanson indicates B* reads an adverb change εκειθεν > εκει here (Swanson does not distinguish *ut videtur* readings in his work). If the reading is as the NT Transcripts cites, there is a chance of homoeoteleuton, a leap from εν to εν. If the reading of B* is as Swanson cites, then such an alteration may be the result of proleptic attraction, εκει for εκειθεν (which is also the reading of 1279). Turner, *Syntax*, 226, §2. Wallace states that distinction of far/near demonstratives is not always made in the NT (Wallace, *Greek Grammar*, 318, 328), however, similar instances of εκειθεν + ανεχωρησεν in 12:15 and 15:21 (Davies and Allison, *Matthew*, 2:486) are not altered in B. In addition, Nolland notes that "the use of 'from there' with 'withdrew' links a pattern in Matthew in which a verb for moving on is used to point to the itinerant nature of Jesus' ministry" (*Matthew*, 588). Of the eight other instances of a similar pattern identified by Nolland in Matthew, never does the scribe of B change the adverb εκειθεν (cf. 4:21; 9:9, 27; 11:1; 12:9, 15; 13:53; 15:21, 29; 19:15 where προβας, παραγων, παραγοντι,

3.2.3.2. DITTOGRAPHY

There is one instance of a dittograph (21:4)[29] and a somewhat modified dittograph (26:57).[30]

3.2.4. TRANSPOSITIONS

Transpositions in B in Matthew are more frequent than most other types of singular readings, comprising 7.36% of the singular readings. In some instances, verbs are placed forward in sentences (13:39;[31] 20:27)[32] or moved back (15:15).[33] In two instances, the genitive pronoun is placed before the word it modifies (18:31;[34] 20:13).[35] One transposition may be stylistic (22:43),[36] and one corrected leap

---

μετεβη, μεταβας, ανεχωρησεν, μετηρεν, εξελθων, or επορευθη are found), but there are, however, other possible instances of the scribe creating haplography with small amounts of parablepsis; therefore, if the reading of B* here is as the NT Transcripts cites, which is probably the case, it would be in alignment with other instances of haplography.

[29] The scribe of B* leaps 20 letters, perhaps caused by pi in πληρωθη and προφητου, and repeats text.

[30] The text of B* reads οι δε κρατησαντες τον Ιησουν εφυγον at the beginning of v. 57. The addition here in B* creates a modified dittograph, in that the beginning of v. 57 is repeated, then the final word of v. 56, εφυγον, is repeated. In all, there are 6 words added: εφυγον οι δε κρα. τ. Ιησουν. If Ιησουν in v. 57 is spelled in full in the exemplar of B, then the addition is of 30 letters, but if Ιησουν is abbreviated as ιν̄ as it is in B in v. 57, then the addition involves 26 letters. (The marginal reading of G 011, not a correction of G 012 as Swanson states, is possibly a scribal notification of a variant reading, not dittography.)

[31] The verb εστιν is placed closer to the beginning of the sentence, which is good biblical Greek placement (with Hebraic influence). Cf. Turner, *Syntax*, 347–8.

[32] The text of B X 085 in Matt 20:27 resembles Mark 10:44 (especially D W f^1 565 2542, which read υμων ειναι πρωτος). The singular feature of the text of B in Matthew, however, is the transposition to predicator > adjunct > complement.

[33] The word order in B here is transposed to subject > complement > predicator.

[34] The word order is transposed genitive pronoun > subject.

[35] The singular portion of the variant in B here is the transposition within the partitive genitive complement (ενι αυτων).

[36] The text of B* Θ contain an additional αυτον than *rell*, but the word order between B* and Θ differs slightly.

may produce a reading with theological interest (6:33).[37]

In the aforementioned transpositions, construed grammar is reflected in readings that involve placing a genitive pronoun (or dative) forward in sentences (15:15; 18:31; 20:13) or placing it after the verb (20:27).[38]

3.2.5. INFLUENCE FROM CONTEXT

In some instances, the textual context seems to have some influence on readings—it seems possible that the preceding or following text has affected a reading in 6.31% of the singular readings in B in Matthew. Sometimes text is repeated from preceding text (2:13;[39] 17:15).[40] Influence from the preceding text could have produced a theologically interesting reading in another instance (12:32a).[41] There is a

---

[37] In B here, the words βασιλειαν and δικαιοσυνην are transposed. According to Metzger, the result of the reading in B "suggest[s] that righteousness is prerequisite to participation in the kingdom" (*Textual Commentary*, 16). Such an interpretation is accurate if in Matt 5:10, 20, δικαιοσυνη "represents the distinctive lifestyle of the disciples" (France, *Matthew*, 271).

The intention of the reading in 6:33 is difficult to determine because there is evidence of parablepsis with την. The two instances of την stand directly on top of each other in B, both occurring as the final word on a line. Thus, it is possible to see that after the principle την was copied, the scribe skipped to the following την and copied δικαιοσυνην out of order, then noticed his mistake and copied βασιλειαν so as to not leave it out altogether. Even if the reading is a corrected leap, Metzger's interpretation is reasonable, but it means that the reading is accidental, not intentional.

[38] Concerning pronoun placement, "Unemphatic (enclitic) pronouns and the like are placed as near the beginning of the sentence as possible;" and "Unemphatic pronouns tend to follow immediately the verb" (BDF, §473.1; §472.1.d).

[39] The prepositional phrase of v. 12, εις την χωραν αυτων, is repeated in v. 13 in B. It could have been prompted by the similar ανεχωρησαν (v. 12) and αναχωρησαντων (v. 13). The repetition occurs 36 letters (or 35 letters if not counting the nu omission at the end of a line) after its principle occurrence.

[40] The preceding μου is repeated after υιον.

[41] The addition of the negative ουκ in B* in v. 32a changes the meaning of the verse to read that it will *not* be forgiven if someone speaks against the son of man. Nolland states that the addition of ουκ in B* destroys the structure of the sentence, and results in the protection of the significance of the son of man (*Matthew*, 503 n. d). (The addition is not found in the parallel in B in Luke 12:20.) The addition

substitution of a proper noun with a pronoun, which may have been influenced by preceding text (26:51).[42] Sometimes the following text influences changes as well (15:11;[43] 25:32).[44] None of these readings result in a loss of text.

3.2.6. INEXPLICABLE READINGS

One singular omission in B in Matthew eliminates part of the subject of the sentence (26:3).[45] There is only one instance where the text of B is singular in its omission of an article (20:32).[46] In two instances, small

---

in v. 32a could have been influenced from the context, as the "synonymous parallelism" (ibid., 505) with the previous verse reads, βλασφημια ουκ αφεθησεται; and therefore, the subsequent use of αφεθησεται retained the negative.

[42] The previous reference to Jesus was by a pronoun (26:50 αυτον), which might have influenced the substitution of Ιησου for αυτου in v. 51. There is a pronoun addition in other MSS after χειρα, found in 517, 569, 954, 1424, 1675, sy[s.pesh.hier] cop[sa.bo] aeth, but this pronoun refers to "his hand", not as a substitution for Jesus as it is in B*. Hoskier notes that B* is *ut videtur* and agrees with "Hil" here, but no reference is given for a treatise of Hilarius'. Cf. H.C. Hoskier, *Codex B and its Allies: Part 1, A Study and an Indictment* (London: Bernard Quartich, 1914), 1:16. After consultation of digital images of B, it seems the distinction of *ut videtur* is not warranted.

[43] The verb in B here is simple, whereas other MSS contain a compound. The word εις that follows the verb could have influenced the change to eliminate redundancy. Or, perhaps, the scribe leaped from epsilon to epsilon in the verb, thus omitting its prefix, εισ.

[44] Several scholars note that the difference between προβατα and εριφων is not entirely clear, and why a shepherd must separate (αφοριει/αφορισει) them is even more puzzling. Cf. France, *Matthew*, 961–2; Nolland, *Matthew*, 1025–6; Luz, *Matthew*, 3:276–7. The text of B singularly reads εριφων as a diminutive in 25:32. The word in diminutive form is also found in the following verse, 25:33 εριφια, in all MSS (also, an interchange is found in Tob 2:12, 13, εριφιον and εριφος). Cf. BDAG, s.v. ἐρίφιον. The scribe could have noticed a way to distinguish προβατα from εριφια in v. 33, thus gaining clarity in v. 32 by employing a diminutive. (Interestingly, B and 𝔓[75] read εριφιον for εριφον in Luke 15:29.)

[45] The combination πρεσβυτεροι + του λαου occurs in four instances in the synoptics, all in Matthew: 21:23; 26:3; 26:47; 27:1. Only in 26:3 does the text of B not read part of the subject, του λαου.

[46] The text of B does not read the article for Ιησους here, which is found in indirect speech.

words of three letters are omitted, perhaps due to carelessness (12:48;[47] 16:17).[48] In another instance, an adjective is changed to an adverb and the word that the adjective modifies is omitted (22:39).[49]

3.2.7. ATTIC AND KOINE GREEK

Some of the singular readings in B in Matthew seem to be Atticisms, or at least more closely aligned with classical usage than Koine (5:10, 11;[50] 12:32b),[51] but a few more singular readings exemplify the Koine dialect rather than the Attic (10:16;[52] 10:25a, 25b;[53] 25:6),[54]

---

[47] The text of B* does not read μου in Matt 12:48 (nor in the parallel with codex D, Mark 3:33). The omission does not resemble typical classical or Koine usage (cf. BDF, §284.1) and is probably an accidental omission.

[48] Contrary to Swanson, 1424 does in fact read ὅτι here (f. 31v, ln. 16), which makes the omission a singular reading in B*. The omission of the causal ὅτι in B* here creates a difficult reading, but it is still grammatically construed (on causal adverbial ὅτι). Cf. Wallace, *Greek Grammar*, 460.

[49] In a comparison of Matt 22:39 to the Markan parallel (12:31), Luz states that in context in Matthew, ὁμοία, which is absent in Mark, means, "The second commandment is of equal importance with the first" (*Matthew*, 3:83). In the variation unit in Matt 22:39, the text of B reads an adverb, ὁμοίως, in place of an adjective, ὁμοία, and omits the dative pronoun (the use of dative with the adjective ὁμοιος is, however, "frequent" in the NT). Cf. Turner, *Syntax*, 220. Perhaps the change to adverb rendered the pronoun unnecessary if it is understood in context.

[50] The form ἕνεκεν, as opposed to ἕνεκα, is generally found from the third century C.E. onward. Cf. BDF, §35.3; Moulton-Milligan, 213, s.v. ἕνεκα, ἕνεκεν, εἵνεκεν; BDAG, s.v. ἕνεκα. (In the NT, ἕνεκα is found in Matt 19:5 in a few MSS including B; Matt 19:29 in few MSS; Mark 13:9 only in B; Luke 6:22 in most MSS; Luke 21:12 in codex D; Acts 19:32 in some MSS including B; Acts 26:21 in most MSS; Rom 8:36 in many MSS.) The word ἕνεκα is found in B as a singular reading in Matt 5:10, 11, when Jesus is addressing the crowds during the Sermon on the Mount (the Beatitudes). The usage here could be an attempt to add an Attic element to Jesus' speech.

[51] The construction οὐ μή + aorist subjunctive or future indicative is found in classical usage, but is considered more emphatic in the NT and is usually restricted to LXX quotes and the words of Jesus, as it is here in ℵ* B. BDF, §365. The text of B is singular, reading an aorist subjunctive rather than the future indicative as in *rell*, but the reverse is typical of the progression of classical to Koine where the subjunctive is replaced by the future. BDF, §363.

[52] The reading in B here is accusative, εἰς μέσον, rather than dative, ἐν

even though Voelz argues that the text of B in Mark has an Attic tendency.[55] There is a fluctuation of declension with the dative plural of σαββατον, which does not resemble the typical Attic form (12:1a).[56]

3.2.8. AORIST CONSTRUCTIONS

An alternate, but construed, spelling is found for an aorist form of δυναμαι (17:16).[57] In a few consecutive instances, there is a move away from the aorist tense to present in γενναω in Jesus' genealogy

---

μεσω. The preposition εις was used with verbs of rest in classical, whereas εν was used with verbs of motion (Zerwick, *Biblical Greek*, §99). In Hellenistic Greek, "the distinction between rest and motion begins to be neglected" (ibid.) which could account for the alteration in B here because εις μεσον modifies a verb of motion, αποστελλω (Zerwick, *Grammatical Analysis*, 30). Therefore, the construction in B here seems to be Koine.

[53] The text of B* reads the dative instead of the accusative in two "awkward" instances in 10:25a, 25b (McNeile, *Matthew*, 144). The accusative in Koine Greek was being phased out (Wallace, *Greek Grammar*, 138), but the change in B* here may result from contemporary usage because the dative takes the place of the classical accusative (Zerwick, *Biblical Greek*, §51) (which was the default case of the oblique cases in classical). Cf. Wallace, *Greek Grammar*, 177.

[54] The text of B reads an aorist middle γινομαι in place of a perfect active in 25:6. In some instances in the NT, the perfect replaces the aorist in narrative, which is a late classical phenomenon (BDF, §343). The narrative in Matt 25:6 is one of the places where the perfect is used where an aorist is expected in Koine, but B reads an aorist.

[55] Voelz, "The Greek of Codex Vaticanus," 228, 229

[56] Concerning the word *Sabbath(s)*, the readings in *rell* and B are both neuter plural dative, but there is a fluctuation in declension (*rell* displays a 3rd decl. and codex B has a 2nd decl.) (BDF, §52). The 2nd decl. form, σαββατοις, in the LXX is typically preceded by εν τοις (cf. Lev 26:35; Num 28:10; 1 Chr 23:31; 2 Chr 8:13; Zech 8:13; Ezek 45:17; 46:3), unlike here in B where the preposition is not found. Also, in 12:12, B 1555 read the 2nd decl.

[57] Instead of ηδυνηθησαν, the text in B reads ηδυνασθησαν, a change η > ασ (both are 3pl aorist indicative). The form in B appears to be an acceptable spelling in the LXX: Josh 15:63; 17:12; Judg 1:19; 2:14; 14:14; 2 Chr 30:3; Ezra 2:59; Neh 7:61; and Obad 7. The form ηδυνηθησαν is also found in LXX and NT: Exod 12:39; Judg 2:14; 2 Kgs 3:26; Job 32:3; Ps 129:2; Isa 7:1; Dan 5:15; Matt 17:16; Luke 9:40; and Heb 3:19.

(1:12a, 12b, 13).⁵⁸

There are instances where 1ˢᵗ aorist active endings are found on 2ⁿᵈ aorist verbs (7:25; 8:32; 9:3, 28), and the reverse (23:23). It is interesting to note that in a MS where there are changes Koine > Attic and *vice versa*, that there are also changes of 1ˢᵗ aorist > 2ⁿᵈ aorist and *vice versa*. In these exchanges, the Attic aorist constructions outweigh Koine aorist constructions (four to one), but Koine grammatical constructions are found more often than Attic (five to three in favor of Koine). Nevertheless, Koine constructions and Attic constructions are exhibited in the singular readings.

3.2.9. Synonym Substitutions

Some words are substituted for synonyms (6:32;⁵⁹ 16:4;⁶⁰ 27:13).⁶¹ Pronouns are changed to reflexive in two instances,⁶² which may be stylistic (5:28;⁶³ 13:24).⁶⁴ These substitutions account for 5.26% of the singular readings in B in Matthew.

---

⁵⁸ Of the 38 occurrences of the aorist γενναω in the genealogy of Jesus in Matthew (1:1–16), the text of B reads a present tense in three instances, 1:12a, 12b, 13. The alterations all occur consecutively at the start of the third list of generations (1:12–16), but the regular employment of εγεννησεν resumes after the three occurrences of γεννα.

⁵⁹ The text of B* contains a verb substitution, from χρηζω (*have need of*) to χραομαι (*make use of*), which the latter is "a common multivalent term" (BDAG, s.v. χράομαι). The reading of B* is a mere difference of the omission of -ζε- in the verb χρηζετε. The connection to 6:8, χρειαν, *need* (Davies and Allison, *Matthew*, 1:659; France, *Matthew*, 270), is now disconnected with the verb change in B* in v. 32.

⁶⁰ The verb read in B* here, αιτει, is a contextual synonym for επιζητει.

⁶¹ The interrogative pronouns ποσα (so *rell*) or οσα (so B*) in 27:13 are used as an exclamation, and are both characteristic of NT Greek as opposed to classical (BDF, §304; Turner, *Syntax*, 50).

⁶² Reflexive pronouns in B in Mark are also found, but Voelz is not precise here, noting that they occur in 5–10 instances ("The Greek of Codex Vaticanus," 213).

⁶³ The text reads a reflexive pronoun here in place of αυτου. In v. 28 in B, the epsilon of εν occurs almost directly above the epsilon of εαυτου, which could have influenced the epsilon addition of αυτου if it was unintentional.

⁶⁴ The text of B reads a reflexive in place of αυτου (but in a close parallel, 13:31, εν τω αγρω αυτου, the scribe does not change the pronoun to reflexive).

3.3. Conclusion

3.3.1. Scribal Habits in General

None of the singular readings in B in Matthew seem to consist of conflation of variants or harmonizations to remote parallels.[65]

In several instances in B in Matthew, groups of ten letters either produce or result in singular readings, which could suggest that the exemplar had ca. 10 letters per line.[66] This is slightly different from what Hort posits, stating that the exemplar had about 12 to 14 letters per line.[67] According to Metzger, there are approximately 16–18 letters per line in Vaticanus the NT,[68] which means if the exemplar had ten letters per line, then the scribe of B would not have been copying his exemplar exactly line for line. Since there are so few examples that could suggest the exemplar's line length, not much more can be made of this.

There are two instances where singular readings result in theological changes (6:33; 12:32a), but both have evidence that could indicate error rather than intention.

There does not seem to be a one-sided preference for either Attic or Koine readings in B in Matthew since there are instances of both (cf. §3.2.7). Of the changes to Koine or Attic dialects, typically only a few

---

[65] This is in agreement with what Pisano notes: "harmonizations and conflate readings, which are found frequently in later manuscripts, are generally absent from B" ("The Text of the New Testament," 34). In a comparison of B to $\mathfrak{P}^{75}$, Porter states that "a large number of textually insignificant variations (spelling, itacism, confusion of vowels and consonants with like sounds, nu-movable, confusion of the endings of the first and second aorist forms)" are found. These same types of variations, that are found in B when compared to $\mathfrak{P}^{75}$, also exist in the singular readings of B in Matthew. Porter does not, however, state *how many* insignificant differences there are between B and $\mathfrak{P}^{75}$ in his comparison (Calvin L. Porter, "Papyrus Bodmer XV (P75) and the Text of Codex Vaticanus," *JBL* 81.4 [1962]: 367–68).

[66] There are two omissions consisting of ten letters (10:4 and 13:17). One addition is of a multiple of ten letters (21:4) and another readings is an addition of a word that occurs ten letters previous (17:15).

[67] Fenton John Anthony Hort, *The New Testament in the Original Greek: Introduction and Appendix* (Cambridge: Macmillan, 1881), 233–34.

[68] Bruce M. Metzger, *Manuscripts of the Greek Bible: An Introduction to Greek Paleography* (New York: Oxford University Press, 1981), 74.

letters of existing words are modified, giving the impression of subtlety.

There are at least three patterns of consecutive changes where the scribe shows consistency. First, in 1:12a, 12b, and 13, there are changes to γεννα from εγεννησεν; second, the multiple Ιωαννης > Ιωανης changes (which cover all the singular readings in Matthew chapter 11); and third, the 1ˢᵗ aorist active endings that are found on 2ⁿᵈ aorist verbs in four singular readings (7:25–9:28). As the readings within these groups all occur essentially back-to-back, this gives the impression of intentionality, or at least consistency.

A number of changes give the impression of a scribal concern to improve the text—be it the three aforementioned groups of consistent changes or dialectical changes, but these rarely indicate a willingness to make *drastic* changes to the text. Overall, the singular readings seem to elicit a scribal tendency to create small changes, often where only a few letters are modified.

About a scribal tendency in Vaticanus, Hort states, "it remains to be considered whether its singular readings, which alone are relevant, include such and so many omissions as to indicate a characteristic habit of the scribe."[69] He continues, stating that the scribe "omits slight and apparently non-essential words found in all other documents, such as pronouns and articles," and that his habit is to "drop petty words not evidently required by the sense...."[70] Of course, Hort is not considering omissions due to homoeoteleuton or other errors, but rather intentional changes. There are only a few points of agreement with Hort's hypothesis evident in the singular readings in Vaticanus in Matthew that could be intentional, i.e. the omissions in 20:32; 22:39; and 26:3. In Matthew, Hort's theory could also be extended to other types of modifications that *alter*, rather than *omit*, "petty words" or "slight and non-essential words." Omission is only one way that the scribe carries out small changes in his text.

---

[69] Hort, *Introduction*, 235–36. Cf. Carlo Martini, *Novum Testamentum e Codice Vaticano Graeco 1209 (Codex B)* (Vatican City: Bibliotheca Apostolica Vaticana, 1968), xxi–xxii.

[70] Hort, *Introduction*, 236.

3.3.2. LONGER AND SHORTER READINGS

Of the 95 singular readings, 10.52% are omissions and 6.31% are additions, but contrary to the frequency, there are more words added in B than omitted (cf. APPENDIX 17). There are 10 instances of *omission*, compared to 6 additions, but 13 omitted words compared to 18 *added* words. On the one hand, there are more instances of omissions, but overall, more words are added in Matthew than omitted. This is one example where a distinction between frequency of additions/omissions and number of words added/omitted is necessary when documenting longer and shorter readings.

Of the readings that affect length, several are inexplicable, but others (both omissions and additions) have evidence of parablepsis (cf. §3.2.2). There are only a few that involve influence from context, *all of which are additions* (cf. §3.2.5), which is similar to the tendency in Codex Sinaiticus (cf. §2.4.2).

CHAPTER 4
CODEX EPHRAEMI

4.1. The Scribe and Extent of Matthew in Ephraemi

One scribe (scribe A) is responsible for the initial transcription of the NT portion of the codex and there are two correctors (scribes B and C).[1] Two verses of Matthew (1:1–2) and eight leaves containing 5:15–7:5; 17:26–18:28; 22:21–23:17; 24:10–45; 25:30–26:22; 27:11–46; 28:15–end, are lacunose.[2] Therefore, Ephraemi contains 806 of 1,071 possible verses of Matthew (which is 75.25% of the gospel).

4.2. The Singular Readings in Ephraemi in Matthew

Scribe A produces 75 singular readings in Matthew, which amounts to one singular reading per 10.74 extant verses.[3] This is the fewest amount of singular readings of our MSS in Matthew—which is certainly affected by the non-extant portions of text—but singulars occur only *slightly* more frequently here than in Vaticanus in Matthew (Vaticanus has one singular for approximately every eleven verses).[4]

---

[1] Robert W. Lyon, "A Re-Examination of Codex Ephraemi Rescriptus" (Ph.D. diss., The University of St. Andrews, 1958), 16–8, 19–26.

[2] Ibid., 10. See also C 04 in *Codices Graeci et Latini*, in the NA^{28}, 799.

[3] See APPENDIX 4 for a list of singular readings. Of the 64 test passages in Aland *et al.*, *Text und Textwert*, Codex C is reported to have one singular reading in 10:3, which is marked as *ut videtur* in the study and not counted as singular. Both Constantine Tischendorf (*Codex Ephraemi Syri Rescriptus sive Fragmenta Novi Testamenti e Codice Graeco Parisiensi Celeberrimo Quinti ut Videtur Post Christum Seculi* [Leipzig: Bernh. Tauchnitz, 1843], 14, 312) and Lyon ("Re-Examination," 330) are not certain of the original reading, although one possibility they give is aligned with the suggestions in *Text und Textwert*.

[4] Hernández states that his conclusions of scribal habits in C in Revelation "cannot be considered incontrovertible proof of a particular scribal tendency" due to the six absent leaves, yet he could still discern some scribal habits (*Scribal Habits*, 135). Ephraemi has 62.22% of the text of Revelation extant, or 252 verses. There is more than three times the amount of verses extant in C in Matthew than Revelation.

Itacistic and orthographic changes each occur less often than the most frequent type of alteration, haplography. Of the readings that result in a shorter text, haplography (cf. §4.2.7) and what is considered "inexplicable changes" (cf. §4.2.9) comprise all of the instances of omissions. Dittography is the primary cause of readings that result in a longer text, though influence of context and stylistic/editorial changes are also a significant factor. It is significant that Ephraemi is the only MS in this study in which there is a the greater number of additions than omissions; yet overall there are the same number of words omitted as added, thus portraying an entirely new set of scribal behaviors that, for one, has never been documented, and two, has never been theoretically conceived.

4.2.1. Orthography and Spelling

The orthography in C reflects some of the same changes recorded by Hernández in C in Revelation,[5] but there are *more* and *different* spelling variations in C in Matthew than C in Revelation. This may not only suggest a lack of standardization in the historical context which produced this MS, but also a lack of standardization within Ephraemi itself (at least between the books of Matthew and Revelation, that is, if the differing methods here and Hernández's are comparable).

4.2.1.1. Itacisms

There are not many itacistic spellings in C in Matthew, the most frequent being ι > ει (11), followed by the reverse, ει > ι (3), then ε > αι (2) and its reverse, αι > ε (1).[6]

---

[5] Hernández found that 15.58% of the singulars in the text of Revelation in Ephraemi are orthographic variations that are comprised of "consonantal confusion (1); vowel replacement (8); and consonantal duplication (3)" (Hernández, *Scribal Habits*, 138). Apart from itacistic spellings, he discovers seven different changes: α > ε (1), ε > α (1), ει > η (1), ιει > ι (1), ο > α (1), ου > ω (1), and ω > ου (2) (Hernández, *Scribal Habits*, 139–40).

[6] See APPENDIX 14.

4.2.1.2. VOCALIC ORTHOGRAPHY

Outwith itacisms, changes involving vocalic orthography account for 10.66% of the singular readings in C in Matthew. These changes include αι > α (9:15), αι > ει (8:31), εη > η (17:15), ει > ε (14:4), η > ε (3:10), η > ι (24:4), ο > α (15:11), and ο > ε (8:32).

4.2.1.3. CONSONANTAL ORTHOGRAPHY

Few changes in C in Matthew involve consonantal orthography. There is one lingual change (4:21a) and one labial change (16:12).

4.2.2. LETTER OMISSIONS

Omissions of single letters occur surprisingly often in comparison to other types of changes, comprising 10.66% of the singular readings. When there is no evidence of parablepsis and the reading is unlikely to be an orthographic spelling, there are instances where words are shortened by one letter (8:5;[7] 11:21; 20:19; 27:64).[8] There are two aberrant spellings that occur more than once, Ιωσαφατ > Ιωσαφα (1:8[1], 8[2]) and των > τω (13:44;[9] 26:51).

4.2.3. LETTER ADDITIONS

There are several instances where words are lengthened by one letter (16:22;[10] 22:10a;[11] 26:50; 27:58),[12] and sometimes the addition is

---

[7] The change from masculine to neuter is nonsense in context. It is unlikely an instance of a moveable nu because it does not occur at the end of a line in C.

[8] The variant in 27:64 is an aphaeresis of epsilon. Cf. Gignac, *Grammar*, 1:319.

[9] The variant in 13:44 is an omission of final nu before a word beginning with a rough breathing on the vowel. Cf. ibid., 1:112.

[10] The change from verb, επιτιμαν, to noun, επιτιμιαν, is the difference of a single letter, iota, and could be accidental repetition influenced from the repetitious iotas in the verb.

[11] The "curious usage" of αγαμος in C here could be translated as *unmarried [person]* (BDAG, s.v. ἄγαμος). Such a translation, however, produces nonsense: *the unmarried person was filled with guests*. If αγαμος means *single estate*, then the reading in C is grammatically construed, but still nonsense in context (Liddell-Scott, s.v. ἀγάμετος). Perhaps the alpha of αγαμος was accidentally influenced by the preceding αγα of αγαθους. Tischendorf states that the reading of C here is *vitiose*, or faulty.

a final sigma (4:2; 4:21b; 7:9).

4.2.4. OMISSION AND ADDITION OF SYLLABLES

In some instances, words are shortened by one or two syllables (4:14; 12:4, 12:7; 15:2; 22:10b),[13] and one instance where a word is lengthened by a syllable (26:67).

4.2.5. OTHER SPELLINGS

There are several misconstrued spellings in Ephraemi. There are word-ending conflations (7:16;[14] 12:6;[15] 23:26)[16] and inexplicable spellings (2:16;[17] 8:21;[18] 16:3).[19] In 9:30, the verb ανοιγω has been triple augmented in some MSS (ηνεωχθησαν),[20] but the text of C* retains the οι of the present stem (instead of εω). In one instance, there

---

[12] Lyon writes for this particular variant in 27:58, "What the scribe [of Codex C] thought he was writing is certainly not clear" ("Re-Examination," 404).

[13] There is an omission of –με– in 22:10b, which is similar to Rev 6:2 in C. Cf. Hernández, *Scribal Habits*, 216.

[14] The reading of C appears to be a nonsense conflation of plural and singular accusative noun endings. Lyon states that scribe A "conflated his two choices" ("Re-Examination," 328). Tischendorf writes that the ending is "yolked together" (*coniunxit*).

[15] Lyon suggests that the reading is μειζοων, but is unsure ("Re-examination," 330). Tischendorf notes that there is something, perhaps an omicron, before the omega in μειζων (*Codex Ephraemi*, 312).

[16] Lyon states that the scribe "combined suffixes" ("Re-Examination," 332).

[17] Lyon records β̄λεεμ as a *nomen sacrum* for Βηθλεεμ (ibid., 9). This is the only instance of such a spelling in Ephraemi in all of the other occurrences of Βηθλεεμ in the MS. In Tischendorf's transcription (*Codex Ephraemi*, 5, ln. 23), there is no bar over βλεεμ as other *nomina sacra* have in Ephraemi and Lyon makes no note of an error in Tischendorf here. The word βλεεμ in Matt 2:16 is unique in that omissions of more than one letter in C in Matthew usually comprise a complete syllable, but not here, which is the omission of ηθ. It is difficult to determine if it is a *nomen sacrum* that occurs nowhere else or a misspelling that occurs nowhere else.

[18] The spelling may be influenced by the similar letters of μαθητων, which precedes three words earlier in C.

[19] The change χειμων > χειχων could be due to the graphical similarity of the majuscule mu and xi (though that may be a little far fetched).

[20] Zerwick, *Grammatical Analysis*, 27–28.

may be graphical confusion (24:3b).[21]

4.2.6. NOT CONSTRUED IN CONTEXT

Some singular readings in C in Matthew create nonsense in context (5.33% of the singular readings). These readings here seem to be modifications of existing words, rather than whole word omissions or additions of new words (20:32;[22] 21:17a;[23] 21:23;[24] 21:28a;[25] 23:24),[26] all of which involve verbal endings, except 21:28a. In all instances, the word created is a real word, but in context, it does not make sense.

4.2.7. PARABLEPSIS

Omissions and additions involving parablepsis are one of the

---

[21] The text of C reads τοτε instead of the interrogative ποτε. The change could have been accidental due to the graphical similarity of pi and tau. The interrogative is needed with τοτε for grammatical construal. Tischendorf calls the change *vitiose*.

[22] A change from 2pl to 2s creates nonsense in C.

[23] In 21:17a, C* reads the aorist passive 3pl form of αυλιζομαι instead of the 3s form as in *rell*. The change in verbal number from singular to plural makes the reading inconsistent with the 3s context: *Jesus* left them (καταλιπων αυτους) and *he* went forth (εξηλθεν) to Bethany and *he* lodged there (ηυλισθη)—not *they* lodged (ηυλισθησαν). Furthermore, the next verse begins with the singular (επαναγων and επεινασεν); thus the reading in C* here is grammatically inconsistent within the context.

[24] The reading of C here, a plural nominative participle, is not a grammatically construed genitive absolute as is the reading in ℵ B D *et al*., but it could refer to the subject, οι αρχιερεις και οι πρεσβυτεροι του λαου. Following ελθοντες, C still reads the genitive pronoun, αυτου, of the genitive absolute; thus the reading of C does not seem to be grammatically construed.

[25] The text of C reads ειπεν in place of ειχεν. The result is nonsense in context, mainly because the following complement (τεκνα δυο) could be expected to be in the dative case if the man (ανθρωπος) were speaking to the two children. There are also occurrences of ειπαν and ειπεν nearby (21:27, 28 respectively) that might have influenced an unintentional alteration.

[26] With the change from active participle to indicative in C*, the article, οι, functions as a personal pronoun, *they*, and οι δε would be needed for grammatical construal. The mood change eliminates consistency with the other participle in context (καταπινοντες).

most common types of changes the scribe makes, accounting for one quarter (25.33%) of the singular readings. Dittography (of letters or words) alone accounts for 14.66% of the singular readings. When letters or words are added, sometimes the repetition begins a new line of text in the MS (2:20; 7:22; 17:4).

4.2.7.1. WITHIN WORDS

In some instances, there is evidence of parablepsis where words are shortened by two letters (8:13;[27] 19:1;[28] 21:28b;[29] 26:57).[30] In other instances, words are lengthened by one letter (7:22;[31] 10:20),[32]

---

[27] The change from γενηθητω to γενητω (seemingly from passive to middle) in C could result from a leap from eta to eta. The passive verb form of γινομαι + dative used in similar contexts to 8:13, such as Matt 9:29 and 15:28 (Davies and Allison, *Matthew*, 2:32), is not altered in C, but there are other instances where words are truncated where there is evidence of parablepsis.

[28] The omission of the syllable in C, resulting in ετελεν, may be due to parablepsis. The letter epsilon is found in eight instances in three consecutive words (ετελεσεν being the final of the three words), which may have contributed to oversight due to repetition.

[29] The scribe of C may have leaped from omega to omega, transcribing πρω instead of πρωτω. Four of the preceding nine letters are omega (προσελθων τω πρωτω), which may have created confusion for the scribe.

[30] The singular reading in C here omits a syllable in απηγαγον, creating απηγον.

[31] The text of *rell* contains a question beginning with ου, but the text of C contains a statement that, if construed, begins with ουτως. The sentence has the same essential meaning, regardless of whether it is a statement or a question. The singular reading in C, ουτως, is the final word of a page (f. 9) and then the following σω begins a new page (f. 10). The alteration may be a dittograph of the letter sigma, similar to 2:20 where dittography is produced at the end of a line of text. There are instances, however, where a *final sigma* is added without evidence of parablepsis onto a number (4:2 τεσσερακοντας), a name (4:21b Ζεβεναιους), and a verb (7:9 αιτησεις), all of which result in nonsense. Regarding 7:22, it is not certain what can be gained in context by changing the question into a statement. Given that there are multiple other instances in C of manipulation within a word, and that this additional letter is found at the start of a folio, it seems that it is more likely simply an unintentional letter addition rather than an intentional grammatical change from a question to a statement. Hernández notes one occurrence of letter repetition in C in Revelation, the repetition of epsilon in 3:7 ουδεις > ουδε εις, which is nonsense in context

two letters back-to-back (8:17;[33] 27:49),[34] or three letters back-to-back (17:4).[35] Such confusion possibly resulted from letter repetition within the same word. Most of these singular readings here (8:13, 8:17; 21:28b; 26:57; 27:49) result in either the addition or omission of a syllable but, unlike the omission and addition of syllables above, here there is evidence of parablepsis. Nonetheless, the large number of readings that witness an omission or addition of syllables (11 in total), no matter their perceived cause, is striking.

4.2.7.2. Whole Words

Parablepsis is also found when entire words are omitted (13:3–4;[36] 13:15;[37] 15:30;[38] 15:36)[39] or added (2:20;[40] 12:47;[41] 20:11;[42]

---

and occurs in the middle of a line of text (f. 294), not different lines as it is in Matt 7:22 (Hernández, *Scribal Habits*, 142, 216).

[32] The additional lambda of αλλλα is nonsense.

[33] In C here, there is the repetition of αι. The preceding ια of δια may have contributed to carelessness while transcribing Ησαιου.

[34] The scribe repeats σω in the word σωσων.

[35] The line of text ends with σκη, and the following line begins afresh with σκηνας.

[36] The scribe of C could have jumped from σπειρειν in v. 3 to σπειρειν in v. 4, which would account for the omission. Regarding the omission in C, Tischendorf states, "*a σπειρ. ad σπειρ. transiliens*" (*Novum Testamentum Graece*, 1:68). The word σπειρειν in C begins a new line of text.

[37] The predicator, ακουσωσιν, is omitted due to parablepsis. In the verse, the repetition of καρδια, ωσιν, and οφθαλμους create parablepsis, but this possible instance of haplography would be caused by ωσιν. The omega of ωσιν ends line 25 and –σιν begins line 26 (folio 22).

[38] The *prima manus* of C could have jumped from τους to τους, thus omitting παρα τους by haplography. The omission is found at the end of a verse that contains many words ending in –ους.

[39] If Lyon's correction of Tischendorf is accurate here, the text of C* does not read ευχαριστησας ("Re-Examination," 331, 404). According to the text of C*, then there is no mention of Jesus giving thanks (ευχαριστησας) before he distributed the bread and fish to the crowd. Perhaps the parablepsis of ας in ιχθυας and ευχαριστησας prompted the scribe to omit by homoeoteleuton.

[40] The first την is written τη̄ at the end of a line in C, then the second την begins the next line.

26:39;⁴³ 26:65;⁴⁴ 27:56).⁴⁵

4.2.8. Influence of Context

Few singular reading seem to be influenced from the textual context (4% of the singular readings). One reading may have been influenced from nearby context (22:20),⁴⁶ where as two other readings may have been influenced by context a few verses away (5:10;⁴⁷ 25:6).⁴⁸ Hernández found that in four out of five times the textual con-

---

⁴¹ The text of C reads αυτω twice.

⁴² The κατα του is repeated.

⁴³ The text reads επεσεν twice back to back. Perhaps the parablepsis of επ in επι and επεσεν caused the scribe to commit dittography.

⁴⁴ The reading is difficult to see in C, but Lyon deciphers the writing after λεγων in 26:65 as τι, not οτι as posited by Tischendorf ("Re-Examination," 333). There is a τι following εβλασφημησεν, which could have been duplicated after λεγων if the scribe jumped from the nu endings of the words.

⁴⁵ The singular portion of the reading in C here is the addition of και, which occurs as the first word of a line of text, preceding the first instance of Μαριαμ. It is possible that the parablepsis of Μαριαμ (or even ην/νη Μαριαμ) caused the repetition of και. Including 26:65, these are the only singular instances in C* in Matthew where the reading precedes the cause of the error in the text; though this is rare, it seems to be caused by parablepsis.

⁴⁶ The text of C contains a conjunction substitution and adds a relative pronoun. This particular introduction of discourse, ο δε λεγει, is not common in the gospels (there are four occurrences of ο δε λεγει in the Gospels: Matt 17:20; Mark 6:38; 16:6; John 6:20), but a similar ο δε ειπεν or especially ειπεν δε is found more often throughout the gospels. A few words earlier, in v. 19, is οι δε, which may have influenced the alteration in v. 20 in C.

⁴⁷ Here is the only singular reading in Matthew in C when an article is added where there is no evidence of parablepsis. The addition is perhaps influenced from 5:6, την δικαιοσυνην, where *righteousness* "is a future object for which men hunger," whereas in v. 10, *righteousness* is "a quality for which they are persecuted" (McNeile, *Matthew*, 53). In this portion of text in C, each of the nine Beatitudes (5:3–12) begins a new line of text, each line starting with μακαριοι.

⁴⁸ Throughout the LXX and NT, the grammatical construction εις + απαντησιν/ υπαντησιν/ συναντησιν is used interchangeably with a noun/pronoun in an oblique case. In Matt 25:6, the text of C contains the grammatical construction εις + συναντησιν with a dative pronoun. A few verse earlier, in 25:1, the text of C reads εις + υπαντησιν with a dative noun (the phrase in 25:1 contains a dative in C

text had influenced the scribe of C in Revelation to create singular readings, but that is certainly not the case here in C in Matthew.[49]

4.2.9. INEXPLICABLE READINGS

There is one omission of a pronoun in the singular readings of C in Matthew (12:48).[50] Another reading is the substitution of ειπεν for λεγει, though there does not seem to be a need for the substitution (15:32).[51] There are a few readings that could be mere oversights (13:57;[52] 21:17b;[53] 24:45),[54] one of which is the omission of an adjec-

---

157, υπαντησιν τω νυμφιω, as opposed to the genitive in *rell*, του νυμφιου). Although there may be a preference for the dative case in 25:1 (with 157) and 25:6 (with ⁄13 ⁄63), the singular portion of the reading, απαντησιν > συναντησιν, produces a grammatically construed reading since it is a familiar Koine Greek construction.

[49] Hernández, *Scribal Habits*, 144 n.70.

[50] Here is the only instance where the original text of C singularly omits a personal pronoun in Matthew, if the reading is certain (Lyon, "Re-Examination," 331). The omission creates inconsistency with the parallelism involving μου that follows (οι αδελφοι μου) in v. 48, as well in v. 47 where the pronoun σου is used with η μητηρ. The omission, however, creates consistency with the absent pronoun of η μητηρ preceding in v. 46, but is still, perhaps, an arbitrary omission.

[51] The reading of C in Matthew here contains the same verb in the Markan parallel (Mark 8:1, λεγει). The word λεγει occurs frequently in the NT, which perhaps aided in its substitution in place of ειπεν, and is probably not an attempt to harmonize the texts because the substitution makes little of meaning in the text. (Codex C is lacunose in the Markan parallel.)

[52] The omission of ει eliminates the idiom, ει μη, and results in a difficult, but grammatically construed, reading.

[53] In 21:17b, the omission of εκει, a Mattheanism (Gundry, *Mathew*, 415), in C* may be a simple oversight. Its inclusion is implied in context.

[54] The word εαυτου in 24:45 in C occurs as the first word on the first line of text on a page (folio 43), following a missing folio. The context in Matthew lends itself naturally to the use of a reflexive pronoun, as found in C. Hernández found two instances of changes to reflexive pronouns in C in Revelation, but noted both were "switched arbitrarily," which may be the case here as well. The change αυτων > εαυτων occurs in Rev 3:4; 18:19a. Weiss notes that the scribe of C has an "unjustified preference" for the reflexive (Hernández, *Scribal Habits*, 152, 152 n.120, 216, 218). The only singular occurrence of a change to reflexive in Matthew in C is here in 24:45.

tive where other MSS read two adjectives (12:22).[55]

4.2.10. TEXTUAL IMPROVEMENT

Two singular readings may improve the text (9:2;[56] 21:1).[57]

4.2.11. HARMONIZATION TO MARK

Perhaps the most interesting singular reading in Ephraemi in Matthew is the parallel wording in Matt 24:3a to Mark 13:3. The Markan text is certainly identical to that found in C in Matthew here, but it may not be an intentional harmonization.[58] The addition in C provides

---

[55] The reading of C* in Matt 12:22 bears close resemblance to parallels (Matt 9:32; Luke 11:14), which make no mention of τυφλον. The material that is harmonized is small, which is only the omission of τυφλος και in C* in Matthew. The parallels, including Mark, are similar and have many commonalities, such as casting out a demon (Matt 9:33; 12:22; Luke 11:14) by the name of demons/Beelzebul (Matt 9:34; 12:24; Mark 3:22; Luke 11:15), the people were amazed (Matt 9:33; 12:23; Luke 11:14); and the statements about a kingdom divided against itself and Satan against himself (Matt 12:25–26; Mark 3:25–26; Luke 11:17–18), which make it easier to include an unintentional harmonization. Cf. Holmes for possibilities on what constitutes an intentional harmonization ("Early Editorial Activity," 137–39).

The omission of τυφλον creates an inconsistency later in v. 22 when Jesus heals the one who is both τυφλον *and* κωφον, not just κωφον as earlier in the verse. On the other hand, the presence of parablepsis (the kappas and the –ος endings), could have caused homoeoteleuton, but, less plausibly, that would require two leaps, from –ος of δαιμονιζομεν<u>ος</u> to –ος of τυφλ<u>ος</u>, then κ– of <u>και</u> to κ– of <u>κωφος</u>.

[56] Matthew has eliminated the historic present here (Davies and Allison, *Matthew*, 2:87). The Markan parallel, 2:3 (as well as Luke 5:18), reads the present participle φεροντες. The conative imperfect (προσεφερον, read in all MSS for Matt 9:2), which is present in function, is actually changed to present in form in C (προσφερουσιν). Cf. Zerwick, *Grammatical Analysis*, 25.

[57] The nonsingular addition of και Βηθανιαν (so C Φ f^{13} 33 *et al.*) is harmonized from Mark 11:1 and Luke 19:29; but the additional και that follows the harmonization in C is a singular reading (and is the only singular addition of a conjunction in Matthew in C). The inclusion of και Βηθανιαν is somewhat jarring, but the additional και improves the flow of the narrative, which was interrupted by the harmonization, and therefore the additional και in C may have been intentional because it improves the flow of the text.

[58] On the one hand, this may witness an intentional harmonization because it

details of the whereabouts of the Mount of Olives—it is *opposite the temple*. All other MSS leave out this detail in Matthew. Codex C and most MSS agree together on reading ορος των ελαιων κατεναντι του ιερου in Mark 13:3. Commenting on Mark, Cranfield states that the location of the Mount of Olives "commanded a view of the Temple across the Kedron valley," because "it was from the Mount of Olives that the full grandeur of the Temple could be best seen."[59] The addition, κατεναντι του ιερου, is the longest singular addition in Ephraemi in Matthew and in fact, besides the instances of dittography, this is the only singular reading where more than one word is added to the text of Ephraemi. This may be the only singular reading in all five of our MSS that obviously contains material supplied from another gospel.

4.3. Conclusion

4.3.1. SCRIBAL HABITS IN GENERAL

With the exception of a few readings, there is no evidence of a systematic editing preference in the singular readings in C in Matthew.[60]

The orthography in C in Matthew agrees with contextual stand-

---

is a lengthy addition: it is not the mere omission of a word that brings harmony to Matthew and Mark here, but three words—a complete phrase—that is included *verbatim* from Mark. On the other hand, it could be *unintentional* because the parallels contain the same story (Jesus telling his disciples about End Times signs) and many textual details are similar, such as the prediction about all of the Temple stones being thrown down (Matt 24:2; Mark 13:2); the prediction about many coming in his/Christ's name (Matt 24:5; Mark 13:6); the prediction about hearing of wars and rumors of wars (Matt 24:6; Mark 13:7), etc. Because of the vast similarities of the parallels, it is possible to consider that, as the scribe was transcribing such similar material, a detail was recalled and placed in an appropriate location. If the scribe was familiar with Mark, it is even more plausible that such a detail was recalled from memory. It is not possible to determine with certainty, however, if the addition was intentional or not, but nonetheless it is an addition in Matthew that reads parallel Markan wording.

[59] Cranfield, *Mark*, 393.

[60] Similarly, Hernández notices that C in Revelation "exhibits almost no editorializing and certainly no clear theological changes among its singular readings" (*Scribal Habits*, 154).

ards in that it hardly deviates from normal Koine usage (cf. §4.2.1). The scribe makes no attempt at Atticizing, revealing himself to be a product of his colloquial environment.

A number of variants result in haplography and dittography. There are many instances where, as opposed to omitting/adding entire words, single-words are shortened or lengthened by one (or two) *syllable(s)* (11),[61] as well as instances where words are shortened (8)[62] or lengthened by *one letter* (7).[63] The scribe does not typically create errors consisting of many consecutive words.

There are a few instances where it seems that two variants are combined into one word, but these create nonsense (7:16; 12:6; 23:26).

Because generally most singular readings in Ephraemi consist of only minor changes, it is surprising to find a obvious harmonization in 24:3a to the Gospel of Mark. This instance is seemingly contrary to the other patterns of readings in C in Matthew, which could potentially be an instance where Ephraemi agrees with an unknown source or non-extant MS. Considering the few small differences that could be attempts to improve the text (9:2; 21:1), it would be very difficult to characterize the scribe (by these singular readings) as one who made deliberate attempts to edit the text of Matthew. Rather, other than the few aforementioned exceptions, the scribe typically makes very small changes, ones that do not drastically transform the text.

4.3.2. Longer and Shorter Readings

There is an interesting phenomenon found in C that is not documented in the singular readings of our other MSS: a greater frequency of additions than omissions (cf. APPENDIX 17). There are 8 instances of omission and 10 instances of *addition*, but the number of words added and omitted is *the same* (13 each). Neither of these scenarios are found in C in Revelation (according to Hernández), as Ephraemi exhibits more omissions there, both in frequency and quantity of words.[64]

---

[61] 4:14; 8:13, 17; 12:4, 7; 15:2; 21:28b; 22:10b; 26:57, 67; 27:49.
[62] 1:8^1, 8^2; 8:5; 11:21; 13:44; 20:19; 26:51; 27:64.
[63] 4:2, 21b; 7:9; 16:22; 22:10a; 26:50; 27:58.
[64] Concerning singular readings in Ephraemi in Revelation, 11.63% are ad-

In addition to Vaticanus, the scribal activity in C in Matthew is another example where a distinction between frequency of additions/omissions and quantity of words added/omitted is necessary.

Among the readings that affect the length of the text, most have evidence of parablepsis (cf. §4.2.7), whereas only one seems to have been influenced from the nearby context (cf. §4.2.8).

---

ditions (ibid., 143), which is somewhat less than the 13.33% of additions in Matthew. A greater disparity, however, exists between the percentages of omissions in the singular readings: in Revelation, Hernández records 48.84% omission (ibid., 145), which is quite outstanding, but a relatively mere 10.66% of the singulars are omissions in Matthew.

CHAPTER 5
CODEX BEZAE

5.1. The Scribes and Extent of Matthew in Bezae

One scribe is responsible for the initial text of Codex Bezae. Eighteen other scribes are responsible for corrections and/or lectionary notes, ranging in date from the fifth to seventh centuries; and the supplemental folios were added in the ninth century.[1]

The majority of Bezae is intact, but there are several lacunae in Matthew: 1:1–20; 6:20–9:2; and 27:2–12. There is a supplementary folio for 3:7–16, but its contents are not included for this study since the *prima manus* of the codex is not responsible for it. These eleven missing folios of the original codex contain 121 verses. There are 948 extant verses of the original transcription of Matthew in D.

5.2. The Singular Readings in Codex D in Matthew

There are 252 singular readings in Matthew in D. One singular reading occurs for every 3.76 verses, which is the highest rate of singular readings per verse and, by far, the greatest number of singular readings in the Gospel of Matthew in our MSS.[2]

---

[1] David C. Parker, *Codex Bezae: An Early Christian Manuscript and its Text* (Cambridge: Cambridge University Press, 1992), 48–49.

[2] See appendix five. Some readings are, however, difficult to see due to erasure or other factors in the MS. One particular reading that is difficult, but not impossible, to determine is in 2:21, where the original text of the MS is either την Ισραηλ or γην Ισραηλ (the *d* text is lacunose here). Both Swanson and Scrivener posit that the reading of D* in 2:21 is την, and was changed to γην by a corrector (Swanson, *Matthew*, 20; Frederick H. Scrivener, *Bezae Codex Cantabrigiensis: Being an Exact Copy, in Ordinary Type, of the Celebrate Uncial Graeco-Latin Manuscript of the Four Gospels and Acts of the Apostles, Written Early in the Sixth Century, and Presented to the University of Cambridge by Theodore Bezae, A.D. 1581. Edited with a Critical Introduction, Annotations, and Facsimiles* [Cambridge: Deighton, Bell, and Co., 1864], 5, 428). In Bezae, the majuscule gamma normally has a

This large number apparently does not correlate with the number of readings that witness to a longer or shorter text, as Codex Sinaiticus exhibits more, that is 164 readings in this category, while Bezae has approximately half of that, 87, that result in either a longer or shorter text.

There is a high number of orthographic changes, which could stem from the scribe using Greek as his second language. As in our other MSS, many changes are grammatical, and there are several changes from Koine to Attic and *vice versa*, but in Bezae there are also many instances where Latin has influenced a change. And overall, it seems the Western element that the MS is known for is absent from the singular readings in Matthew.³

5.2.1. ORTHOGRAPHY

5.2.1.1. ITACISMS

The change ι > ει (264) is the most common itacistic spelling in D in Matthew, greatly outnumbering the other itacistic spellings: ε > αι (23), ει > ι (12), and αι > ε (9).⁴

---

slight serif on the top left side of the top bar, and the underside of the right portion of the top bar has a slight arch. In the situation of 2:21, the initial letter of την/γην does not have the arch (as other gammas do), but rather a straight and level line that resembles other taus. Therefore, consistent with Swanson and Scrivener, 2:21 is not recorded as a singular reading in D in the study here, but is recorded as as την Ισραηλ which is in agreement with the majority of MSS.

Of the 64 test passages in the Gospel of Matthew in *Text und Textwert*, Codex D is reported to have singular readings in 5:11 (which I have found Latin support); 10:3 (which is not singular for witnessing Λεββεος, and the following και is supported by Latin witnesses, cited as 10:4a here); 10:23 (but has support with 0171 and some Latin witnesses); 12:36 (which is accurate); 13:1 (which is accurate, cited as 13:1c here); and 19:17 (but 579 agrees in the omission of του before αγαθου).

³ For a brief overview of D and its commonly referred to "Western" traits, see Bruce M. Metzger and Bart D. Ehrman, *The Text of the New Testament: Its Transmission, Corruption, and Restoration*, 4th ed. (New York: Oxford University Press, 2005), 70–73.

⁴ See APPENDIX 15. In a study of D by Ángel Urbán, its orthography in Mark is compared to the NA²⁷. It is documented that ι > ει occurred most frequently (233 in-

5.2.1.2. VOCALIC CHANGES

Vocalic changes are among the most types of singular readings in D in Matthew (accounting for 9.12% of the singulars).[5] The singular readings in D in Matthew witness thirteen types of vocalic changes: α > ε (2:6, 8c; 11:25; 18:15b; 25:22), α > ο (17:8), ε > α (10:8; 11:8; 17:18), ε > ει (24:9), ε > η (19:12), ε > ι (12:20b), η > ε (2:8a, 16a; 6:12), ει > ε (12:41a), ο > α (16:4), ο > ω (21:31), ω > α (2:16b), ω > ο (26:13), and ω > οι (4:13). In two separate instances, the change ε > η occurs in the verb ερχομαι (12:43; 13:1b).

5.2.1.3. CONSONANTAL ORTHOGRAPHY AND OTHER SPELLINGS

The following changes are found in single instances, some of which are identifiably colloquial: interchange of final nu and sigma (13:1a),[6] the Attic form ρρ instead of ρσ (14:27),[7] a reduplicated rho (9:36),[8] medial sigma omitted before a stop (15:1),[9] omission of gamma before a front vowel (12:41b),[10] omission of final nu before a word beginning with a vowel (21:28),[11] the addition of a vowel between two consonants, i.e. anaptyxis (26:23b), which is more frequent in "the colloquial nature of the language of the papyri in comparison with the

---

stances), followed by ε > αι (76), ει > ι (51), and αι > ε (34). Ángel Urbán, "Bezae Codex Cantabrigiensis (D): Intercambios Vocálicos en el Texto Griego de Marcos," *CCO* 4 (2007): 245–68. The same itacism exchanges are also found in the same order, from most frequent to least frequent, in the singular readings in D in Matthew.

[5] There is some disparity of non-itacistic vocalic changes in D in Matthew compared to D in Mark (against the NA[27]). Urbán documented ten similar types of changes: α > ε (5), α > ο (2), ε > α (6), ε > ει (2), ε > η (7), ε > ι (2), η(η) > ε (5), ο > α (8), ο > ω (5), and ω > ο (4). Eighteen other types of changes were not in the singular readings in D in Matthew: α > αι, αα > α, α > η, αι > ε, ε > ο, η > α, η > ει, η(η) > ι, ι > α, ι > ε, ι > η, ι > οι, ο > ε, οι > υ, ου > ο, υ > ι, υ > ου, and ω > ου). But there are three types of changes are not found in Urbán's study that are found in D in Matthew: ει > ε, ω > α, and ω > οι. Urbán, "Bezae Codex Cantabrigiensis (D)," 245–68.

[6] Cf. Gignac, *Grammar*, 1:131–2.
[7] Cf. ibid., 1:142.
[8] The rho has been reduplicated in an Ionic or Hellenistic fashion. Cf. BDF, §68.
[9] Cf. Gignac, *Grammar*, 1:130.
[10] Cf. ibid., 1:72.
[11] Cf. ibid., 1:112.

formal nature of inscriptional and other literary or monumental evidence,"[12] and a full spelling of απο (25:32a).[13]

Other spellings that result in a singular reading are a non-itacistic spelling of πειν (27:34¹, 34²),[14] one instance of metathesis (23:33),[15] and a misspelling of υγιης that involves both υ > η and ι > υ (12:13).

5.2.1.4. CONSONANT CHANGES

Like vocalic changes, consonantal changes are also among the most frequent type of change found in the singular readings in D in Matthew (accounting for 13.88% of all singulars). The nasal substitution of μ > ν occurs often in words beginning with εμπ (11:26; 15:14b; 17:2; 18:14; 23:13; 25:32b; 26:70; 27:29, 30, 41)[16] and συμ (18:6, 19a; 19:10). There are two other instances of μ > ν (4:15; 15:16). The change γ > ν occurs when gamma precedes a palatal mute or xi (15:32a; 18:15a; 18:27), especially when the palatal mute is another gamma: γγ > νγ (3:2; 4:17; 11:10; 13:49b; 15:35; 24:33; 26:18; 27:48). Other changes involve linguals (10:10; 13:41,[17] 52), palatal mutes (10:36; 17:24¹; 22:44), labials (15:37), smooth mutes (27:13), and letters that produce similar sounds, σ > ζ (12:20c).

---

[12] Cf. ibid., 1:311.

[13] Cf. ibid., 1:315.

[14] Codices ℵ* and D contain the same reading, except that ℵ* is an itacism of what D reads. The "vulgar" form πειν is "overwhelmingly attested in papyri of the Roman age" (Moulton-Milligan, s.v. πίνω).

[15] The word εχιδνα is found in five instances in the NT (Matt 3:7; 12:34; 23:33; Luke 3:7; Acts 28:3), one of which, 23:33, D reads εχνιδων, perhaps resulting from metathesis.

[16] The fourth/fifth century 𝔓¹⁹ reads ενπροσθεν along with D in 10:32¹, 32², 33¹, and 33². Unfortunately 𝔓¹⁹ is lacunose for other occurrences of εμπροσθεν.

[17] In 13:41, D reads συνλεξουσιν for συλλεξουσιν. The lambda that is replaced with the nu (συλλ > συνλ) reflects an augmented spelling, but without the augment (imperfect: συνελαλουν). In the previous verse, there is the same λ > ν interchange in D (συνλεγονται) which resembles the Latin and matches the plural noun τα ζιζανια.

5.2.2. Letter Additions

In one instance, nu is added after eta (13:34). There are other letter additions: iota (12:40) and sigma (12:4a; 26:45).

5.2.3. Letter Omissions

There are a few instances of sigma being dropped before an ει ending where it is unexpected or not construed (5:41; 9:2; 12:19).[18] There are also omissions of alpha (19:29), iota (9:20; 13:38[1]), and nu (15:22a).

5.2.4. Syllable Omissions

There are two separate instances of syllable omissions (2:22; 27:54).

5.2.5. Not Construed in Context

One gender change of an adjective does not match the head noun (4:16a).[19] Some case changes do not create grammatically construed sentences (4:18;[20] 6:18b;[21] 17:20).[22]

5.2.6. Inexplicable Readings

Some singular readings seem to be inexplicable, such as the spelling αποκρεις for αποκριθεις, which occurs in two instances

---

[18] Holmes notes that the reading of 12:19 "is likely a scribal error" ("Editorial Activity," 218). Similar omissions are found in Codex W in Matthew: 21:41a; 23:14.

[19] In 4:16a, the text of D* reads a masculine adjective in place of a neuter that modifies the neuter φως.

[20] The noun here is the direct object and should be accusative for grammatical construal. Perhaps the final sigma on previous word, βαλλοντες, influenced a change in D*.

[21] The transcription of κρυφια in 6:18b is difficult to see due to chemical agents on the page (folio 16v). The text of D* probably read κρυφια, which was corrected to κρυφαιω by D^A. The plural accusative form of κρυφιος would be nonsense in context, and should be singular dative to be grammatically construed as it is found in other MSS.

[22] The reading in D*, κοκκος, a nominative instead of an accusative, is nonsensical in context.

(21:21; 26:23a). Conjunctions are sometimes omitted (4:16b;[23] 5:25a;[24] 13:25)[25] or added (13:1c),[26] without any apparent reason. One name is declined which is not normally declinable (24:15).[27]

5.2.7. PARABLEPSIS

There are omissions (11) and additions (12) in D in Matthew that could have resulted from parablepsis. These account for 9.12% of the singular readings in D in Matthew.[28] Interestingly, more words are added than omitted due to parablepsis, which does not resonate with the overall tendency in Bezae to omit more text than to add.

---

[23] The text in Matthew here is an OT quote. In the source of the quote, LXX Isa 9:1, the και is omitted in the text of Constantine Tischendorf, *Vetus Testamentum Graece* (Lipsaie: F.A. Brockhaus, 1869) and the BHS, but not in Alfred Rahlfs, ed., *Septuaginta: Id est Vetus Testamentum graece iuxta LXX interpretes*, Duo volumina in uno (Stuttgart: Deutsche Bibelgesellschaft, 1979). The Göttingen LXX edition (ed. Ziegler) notes the omission of και in ℵ* B 534* 544 (for Isa 9:2). The conjunction is omitted in D* *d* in Matthew.

[24] In the five occurrences of εως + οτου in the NT (Matt 5:25a; Luke 12:50; 13:8; 22:16; John 9:18), only in John 9:18 does the text of D offer a variant: εως ου (also $\mathfrak{P}^{66}$* 1071). The omission of εως in Matt 5:25a is perhaps an oversight by the scribe of D*.

[25] The και in *rell* aids in separation of clauses, but its omission in D* creates a difficult reading.

[26] The context in Matthew never states that Jesus is *in* a house, but states only that he went *out* of a house (although the word εξω may imply a house in 12:46. McNeile, *Matthew*, 187). The omission in D *a b d e f ff*$^{1.2}$ *g*^{1} *k* Sy^s eliminates such an inconsistency, but the text of D *d* adds a conjunction, which may smooth the text.

[27] The text of D* seems to read a declined form of Δανιηλ, which is not normally declinable. This may be harmonized with the genitive that follows, του προφητου, but the form Δανιηλος is actually attested elsewhere, in the Epistle of Aristeas 49, and Δανιηλου is witnessed in Josephus (*Ant.* 10, 193) (BDAG, s.v. Δανιήλ).

[28] There is no reason to believe that the codex was written by dictation rather than by eye, because, as Parker states, "The evidence for this lay in the high number of readings where the copyist's eye had been distracted by groups of letters near to those he was attempting to copy" (*Codex Bezae*, 30). Indeed, both letters and words are repeated in the singular readings in D in Matthew that would support Parker's claim.

5.2.7.1. HAPLOGRAPHY

Most of the omissions that have evidence of parablepsis result in a truncated word (10:34², [29] 12:1c; [30] 12:41c; [31] 13:30; [32] 18:25; [33] 21:46), [34] or lack a portion of the beginning or end of a word (2:9; [35] 15:29; [36] 26:1; [37] 26:16), [38] rather than resulting in an entire word omission (21:22). [39] Only one or two pairs of identical letters ever facilitate

---

[29] The misspelling in D*, ειρην, could result from a leap from ην to ην within ειρηνην.

[30] In D, there is an addition of a nonsensical genitive article for the accusative σταχυας, but perhaps if the exemplar of D read as U W *et al.* rather than *rell*, then the scribe could have leaped from the sigma of τους to the initial sigma of σταχυας.

[31] A leap from alpha to alpha (κατακρινουσιν) would account for the omission of letters within the word in D*.

[32] It could be possible that the scribe leaped from eta to eta (αποθηκην), thus creating a nonsense reading.

[33] The omission of δο in D* in αποδοθηναι could have resulted from a leap from omicron to omicron within the word.

[34] The scribe of D could have leaped from eta to eta (προφητην), which would explain the misspelling.

[35] The ending of ακουσαντες is not transcribed in D* here. It is possible that the scribe leaped from the tau of ακουσαντες to the tau of του. The word ακουσαν as it stands in D* is a neuter singular participle, which is nonsense in context.

[36] The scribe writes only one of the consecutive omicrons of το ορος.

[37] Zerwick notes that "all five Great Discourses in Matt conclude w[ith] this same formula: και εγενετο οτε ετελεσεν ... ([7:28;] 11:1; 13:53; 19:1; 26:1)" (*Grammatical Analysis*, 21). The text of D is lacunose in 7:28, but agrees with the concluding formula in 11:1 and 13:53. In 19:1, however, the D text and some Latin witnesses read ελαλησεν in place of ετελεσεν, and here in 26:1, the D* text reads ο τελεσεν in place of οτε ετελεσεν.

Grammatically, the reading in D* is either a nominative articular future infinitive without a governing preposition, or an aorist active indicative with a personal pronoun. Neither option, however, is entirely construed in context: the former option would place a future tense verb in a past tense context, and the latter option has an article functioning as a pronoun, which is odd because it is not used in a δε or μεν construction. See Wallace on the article used as a personal pronoun (*Greek Grammar*, 211–2). The reading of D* could have resulted from a leap from οτε to ετελεσεν.

[38] The misconstrued reading in D of the preposition and conjunction, απο τε, could result from a leap from οτ to οτ in απο τοτε.

[39] In 21:22, the inclusion of αν renders the statement indefinite (Zerwick,

an omission (in contrast to Sinaiticus where many letters facilitate omissions, e.g., Matt 9:15).

5.2.7.2. Dittography

Sometimes words are repeated back-to-back (4:6a;[40] 13:38a;[41] 23:3;[42] 23:6)[43] resulting from dittography, and in one instance they are repeated out of order (21:3).[44]

Perhaps as a tendency opposite to the truncating of words (cf. the previous section), letters are sometimes repeated within a word (6:20;[45] 26:12;[46] 27:60),[47] or on the front or end of a word (10:15;[48] 11:24a;[49] 13:22;[50] 21:29).[51]

Grammatical Analysis, 68), but the omission of αν in D only slightly minimizes emphasis on the indefiniteness. The omission of this small word may be explained as haplography, as there is parablepsis of alphas: οσα αν αιτησητε.

[40] The text of D* reads a dittograph of θεου in place of the article του. Only the latter θεου in D* here has a bar over the top (θῡ) indicating *nomina sacra*. The former θεου is contracted without the bar (θυ).

[41] This is a peculiar reading in D*. The scribe repeated lettering, της βασ, which was later erased (the top bar of the tau was erased, only leaving a vertical line, which then acts as the missing iota in υιο, see 13:38¹). An explanation can become convoluted, involving the scribe mistaking the vertical line of the missing final iota of υιοι as the vertical line for the tau of της, then continuing on to copy της βασ, then becoming confused and recopied της βασιλειας.

[42] The D* text reads a dittograph of two words. The addition of παντα ουν is not grammatically construed.

[43] The text of D* repeats the article, την, for πρωτοκλεισιαν.

[44] The scribe may have leaped (from nu to nu of αυτων χρειαν) and copied εχει out of place, then copied the missing χρειαν and continued onto copy εχει again.

[45] The letters –ους are repeated in θησαυρους in D*.

[46] In D* here, ματος is repeated in the word σωματος. This could result from a leap back from the mu of μου to the mu of σωματος.

[47] The text of D* reads a dittograph of –λισας within προσκυλισας (the text of *d* reads a participle rather than an indicative as in the Latin).

[48] The *prima manus* of D may have copied the eta of ημερα twice, or perhaps changed εν to ενη. As such, it is not counted as a word addition (as a definite article) regarding shorter/longer reading preferences.

[49] The dative of γη is needed here, rather than γης as in D. Perhaps the scribe merely copied the sigma of Σοδομων twice.

[50] The text of D* here reads a plural accusative πλουτους rather than the

5.2.8. TRANSPOSITIONS

Most transpositions seem to result from a preferred grammatical sequence, rather than word emphasis (though the latter occurs as well). Sometimes the genitive pronoun is placed before the word(s) it modifies (4:24),[52] or after (5:29).[53] Sometimes words are transposed to verb > subject (5:18),[54] or similar (12:4b);[55] or the reverse: subject > verb (26:26;[56] or similar (12:1b).[57] Sometimes the word order of noun > adjective creates a singular reading (18:28).[58] One transposition may be for word emphasis, rather than for purely grammatical reasons (16:22).[59]

5.2.9. SYNONYM SUBSTITUTIONS

In one instance in Matthew, a word is replaced with a more

---

singular genitive πλουτου in *rell*. The reading of D* does not fit the context or the definite article του. Perhaps the initial sigma of συνπνειγει was copied twice, and therefore, the mistake is the result of dittography.

[51] The *prima manus* of D repeats the prepositional prefix of μεταμεληθεις, possibly by leaping back from the second instance of με in the prefix.

[52] The word order in D here within the subject is transposed to genitive pronoun > noun.

[53] In the transposition in D, the σου does not interrupt the attributive position of ο οφθαλμος and ο δεξιος as in *rell*. The transposition of words occurs within the subject and results in the word order of noun > adjective > genitive pronoun.

[54] The word order in D *d* here is predicator > subject.

[55] The order of the two predicators is rearranged in D so that the complementary participle, εξον, follows the verb, ην.

[56] Following the genitive absolute in 26:26, in D the word order reads subject (ο Ιησους) > verb (λαβων), rather than verb > subject as in other MSS.

[57] The transposition in D of τιλλειν and σταχυας is complement > predicator.

[58] The text in D *d* is transposed within the complement to noun > adjective. The number εκατον (100) is abbreviated as ρ̄ in D here. There is no abbreviation here in *d*.

[59] The context of the pericope is a "remarkable act" by Peter to "reprove" Jesus (Hagner, *Matthew*, 2:480). The τουτο refers to the suffering Jesus must undergo, made explicit in 16:21. The words τουτο and σοι are transposed in D (D also reads an orthographic spelling of εσται). The emphasis seems to fall on the final element, σοι. Thus in Bezae the sentiment is not that *this* (τουτο) suffering could not happen, but it could not happen *to this person* (σοι), i.e. Jesus.

common word (2:8b).⁶⁰ Some words are substituted with words that are better suited for the context (10:28;⁶¹ 15:27a;⁶² 16:3).⁶³ One pro-

---

⁶⁰ The word επαν is a *hapax legomenon* in Matthew (Davies and Allison, *Matthew*, 1:245) and occurs in only two other instances in the NT (Luke 11:22, 34). In one of those instances (Luke 11:34), the text of D reads επαν with the majority of MSS, whereas in the other instance (Luke 11:22), the text of D reads εαν in place of επαν. The result of the singular reading in 2:8b (and Luke 11:22) is that an uncommon word is replaced with a word that occurs more frequently in the NT.

⁶¹ The verb σφαζω is used to describe brutal homicide as well as murder in sacrificial contexts, but the context of 10:28 is within admonishments about persecution. In particular in the NT, the verb σφαζω is used with *lamb* (αρνιον) in Rev 5:6, 12; 13:8. BDAG, s.v. σφάζω. In LXX Zech 11:4, 7, the noun σφαγη is used with προβατα: τα προβατα της σφαγης (BDAG, s.v. σφαγή). The use of σφαζω with ψυχη is only found in Rev 6:9, which refers to martyrs, τας ψυχας των εσφαγμενων δια τον λογον του θεου. If σφαζω + ψυχη alludes to martyrdom, then the scribe of D* in Matt 10:28 has chosen specific wording to emphasize the surrounding context of persecution in Matthew because the D text reads the combination of σφαζω + ψυχη.

⁶² The reading of D here is ψειχων, rather than the diminutive ψ(ε)ιχιων in *rell*. Holmes notices that in all three occurrences of the diminutive ψιχιον in the NT, Matt 15:27a; Mark 7:28; and Luke 16:21 (ψιχιων is omitted in 𝔓⁷⁵ ℵ* B L it sy^{s.c} sa^{mss} bo^{pt} Cl NA²⁸), the D text always reads the non-diminutive ψιξ ("Editorial Activity," 183). Outside of the NT, the diminutive form is found in the work of Archigenes (second century C.E.) referring to "stomach residue after emesis" (Liddell-Scott, s.v. ψιχίον), but its use by Eustathius (twelfth century C.E.) is, however, more inline with the context in Matthew here: "like a crumb, minute" (Liddell-Scott, s.v. ψιχιώδης). The non-diminutive form is found works by Plutarch (first–second centuries C.E.); Aretaeus (second century C.E.); Alexander of Aphrodisias (third century C.E.); and Hesychius (fifth(?) century C.E.), referring to breadcrumbs (Liddell-Scott, s.v. ψίξ), which is a better fit to the context in Matt 15:27a than the diminutive. Therefore, the non-diminutive in D seems to be a better fit for the context than the diminutive that seems to have a rare occurrence regarding gastronomy and in another late instance (twelfth century C.E.) instance, "like a crumb."

⁶³ In 16:1–4, the word ουρανος is found in four instances. In the third instance (16:3), the text of D reads αηρ instead of ουρανος (*d* and the Latin witnesses read *caelum*, which can be translated as *sky* or *heaven*). Because the context of vv. 2–3 concerns notions of sky and the weather, this could have prompted the scribe of D to substitute ο ουρανος with the more precise ο αηρ, signifying *atmosphere* or *sky*. As it stands in *rell*, there is "a deliberate play on the word 'heaven/sky' as it occurs in the request, v.1" (Hagner, *Matthew*, 2:455), but the D text exposes the *double en-*

noun is replaced with the noun it represents (15:14a).[64] One adjective is replaced with a similarly spelled adjective (20:10),[65] and another one is substituted with a dissimilarly spelled word (10:16).[66] Another substitution is found with a proper noun (23:39).[67]

5.2.10. Definite Articles

Alterations involving definite articles account for 11.5% of the singular readings in D in Matthew. In many instances the omissions seem inexplicable.[68] The article is omitted in a few instances in front of names such as *Jesus* or *Magdalene*, otherwise both omissions and ad-

---

tendre with the reading of ο αηρ.

[64] The reading of *rell* has αυτους referring to either πασα φυτεια in 15:13 or the Pharisees in v. 12 (Hagner, *Matthew*, 2:436). The reading in D *d*, however, records τους τυφλους instead of an ambiguous pronoun; thus, this reading refers to "the blind leaders of the blind" subsequent in 15:14a. The alteration may result from parablepsis of the forms of τυφλος in proximity (although *d* contains the same variant without parablepsis), or this might be an attempt at clarifying the text. Even though the Pharisees are being referred to as *blind* in v. 14, it is not until after αυτους that Jesus makes the comparison (τυφλοι εισιν); therefore, this would be a preemptive clarification.

[65] In 20:10, the comparative adjective is πλειον in some MSS, but is replaced in D with πλειω, an indeclinable form (Moulton-Milligan, s.v. πλείων). The form πλειω is also found in Matt 26:53 in ℵ* B D.

[66] Instead of ακεραιος (*harmless*), the text of D links απλοτης (*guileless*), with doves, which Davies and Allison commend as a "good interpretation" (*Matthew*, 2:181). Commenting on the text represented in *rell*, Luz states, "The dove's purity fits well with the sheep's nonviolence" (*Matthew*, 2:88). The connotation of doves with purity/guileless works well in context. The Latin reads *simplices*, which is closer in meaning to the reading of D than ακεραιος is.

[67] This is the only singular reading in Bezae in Matthew where another noun is substituted for θεος or κυριος (the text reads a *nomen sacrum*, and therefore it is a difference of one letter in Greek, κυ > θυ, or two letters in Latin, *dmo > dei*). This portion of 23:39 is from Ps 118:26, *blessed is the one coming in the name of the Lord*. In other occurrences of Ps 118:26 in the NT, e.g., Matt 21:9; Luke 13:35; 19:38; John 12:13, Bezae reads *Lord*. The words θεος and κυριος can be used interchangeably here without altering the meaning of the text, so perhaps the substitution was merely used to be specific, as opposed to a theological heightening.

[68] Turner states, "Codex Bezae will often omit the art[icle] in an arbitrary way, perhaps through Latin influence" (*Syntax*, 173).

ditions are found with both nouns and verbs, the majority of which are omissions. In Bezae, omissions of articles are the most common type of omission; likewise, additions of article are the most common type of addition.

5.2.10.1. Proper Nouns

In one instance, an article is omitted from the land Israel (9:33).[69] In three instances each, the nominative articles for Jesus (14:31; 27:46; 28:16) and Magdalene (27:56;[70] 27:61a;[71] 28:1) are omitted. Only in two instances are articles added to proper names, both of which are genitive (12:42;[72] 15:39b).[73]

5.2.10.2. Common Nouns

There are many instances where articles for common nouns are omitted (5:3;[74] 5:48;[75] 6:18a;[76] 6:18c;[77] 10:13^2;[78] 10:35;[79] 12:1a;[80] 13:16;[81] 19:28b;[82] 21:13;[83] 24:21),[84] and in several instances an article

---

[69] The scribe omits the masculine singular dative article for Ισραηλ.

[70] The text of D* does not read the article for Μαγδαληνη.

[71] The text of D* does not read an article for Μαγδαληνη, which is also the reading in the Markan parallel in D (Mark 15:47).

[72] The genitive article is supplied in D* with the first occurrence of *Solomon* in 12:42.

[73] The text of D reads the feminine singular genitive article with Μαγαδαν.

[74] The neuter singular dative article is omitted in D* for πνευματι.

[75] The text of D* does not read the plural dative article for ουρανοις.

[76] The reading of D* does not include the article for κρυφια (changed to κρυφαιω by D^A). The article is added by D^{CorrC}.

[77] As in 6:18a, τω is omitted in D for κρυφαιω in 6:18c.

[78] The D* text does not read the feminine singular nominative article for ειρηνη.

[79] The masculine singular genitive article is omitted before πατρος, but is retained before μητρος in the same verse.

[80] The text of D does not contain the neuter plural dative article for σαββασιν here. Although there is evidence of parablepsis that could have facilitated a leap (from the final sigma of Ιησους to the sigma of τοις or the initial sigma of σαββασιν, thus passing over τοις), the reading seems to have more in common with other omissions of articles rather than omissions due to parablepsis since the latter almost always involves truncated words rather than omissions of entire words.

[81] The text of D does not read the neuter plural nominative article for ωτα.

is added (11:11a;⁸⁵ 11:11b;⁸⁶ 11:16;⁸⁷ 12:12;⁸⁸ 18:19b;⁸⁹ 27:15).⁹⁰

5.2.10.3. Verbs

In one instance, the article is supplied with an equative verb (27:16).⁹¹ In another instance, the article is omitted when it belongs to a substantival participle (23:16).⁹²

5.2.10.4. Genitive Absolute Construction

In one instance of a genitive absolute, the text of D reads an articular genitive absolute (13:6).⁹³

5.2.11. Attic, Koine, Hebraic, and Latin Constructions

Read-Heimerdinger notices that there are "conflicting conclusions" as to whether the language in D is more colloquial (so Parker) or classical (so Delebecque).⁹⁴ As far as singular readings in Matthew

---

[82] The reading in D* here omits the feminine plural accusative article for δωδεκα.

[83] The D* text does not include the nominative article for οικος here.

[84] The neuter singular genitive article is not witnessed in D. In *rell*, it is used as a substantive with the adverb, rendering the translation of εως του νυν as *until the present*. Cf. Wallace, *Greek Grammar*, 231–2. The preceding phrase, απ αρχης, does not have an article in all MSS, which is a common omission in prepositional phrases—even more, it is especially common for prepositional phrases not to have an article when the genitive follows, as it does here. Cf. Zerwick, *Grammatical Analysis*, 79. Perhaps the omission of the του in D following απ αρχης is somehow influenced from preceding construction of prepositional phrase + genitive.

[85] The text of D* reads a masculine plural dative article for γεννητοις here.

[86] The text of D* reads an article for γυναικων here.

[87] Of the MSS that read the feminine singular accusative αγορα (as opposed to the plural dative αγοραις), D is the only one that includes an article.

[88] The D* text reads a neuter singular genitive article for προβατου here.

[89] The neuter singular genitive article is read with πραγματος in D*.

[90] The article for εορτην is read in D here.

[91] The text of D reads the article with the equative verb (see Wallace, *Greek Grammar*, 436, for uses of equative verbs).

[92] The text of D* does not read the article for substantival participle λεγοντες.

[93] The grammatical construction in D here is an articular genitive absolute. The text of D reads the masculine singular genitive article with the noun *sun* (ηλιου).

[94] Jenny Read-Heimerdinger, *The Bezan Text: A Contribution of Discourse*

are concerned, there are instances of both, Koine (5) and classical (4), features in D, but there are more instances where Latin seems to have influenced a change (9).

Sometimes there is a de-Atticization of the Greek in the singular readings (27:1;[95] 28:2),[96] but some grammatical constructions are more classical than Koine (13:46;[97] 14:25;[98] 19:28a;[99] 24:19).[100] There

---

Analysis to Textual Criticism, JSNTSup 236 (London: Sheffield Academic, 2002), 175 and n. 4.

[95] The word ωστε in 27:1 is "normally consec[utive, but] here final" (Zerwick, *Grammatical Analysis*, 91). The conjunction ωστε, a "favorite" of Matthew's (Gundry, *Matthew*, 552), is replaced with ινα in D and the verb is future indicative (also 69[mg]) rather than aorist infinitive. The use of ωστε + infinitive is found in classical Greek and in 27:1 would mean to suggest an intended result. Cf. BDF, §391.1–3. In the NT, however, "a ινα-clause so often serves as periphrasis for the infinitive," and the future indicative has been "introduced to a very limited degree in the very places where it would *not* have been permissible in classical, i.e. after ινα and final μη" (BDF, §369.1–2). Thus, here the text of D manifests Koine grammar (ινα + future indicative) rather than Classical (ωστε + infinitive).

[96] The D text reads απο instead of εκ in *rell*. The meaning is essentially the same in D (*descended from heaven*) and *rell* (*descended out of heaven*). The change from εκ to απο is a de-Atticization of the Greek (Gignac, *Grammar*, 1:44).

[97] The reading in D is a different verb and tense than in *rell*. The perfect tense verb in *rell*, πιπρασκω, "has no active aorist" (Zerwick, *Biblical Greek*, §289), but in context, the aorist is found "wanting" in the verb (Zerwick, *Grammatical Analysis*, 44). The scribe of D has changed to a different verb, πωλεω, and altered the tense to aorist. The change from a perfect form of πιπρασκω to an aorist form of πωλεω in D reflects an older grammatical familiarity "because the perfect in later Greek use lost its specific sense and became a simple narrative tense like the aorist" (Zerwick, *Biblical Greek*, §289). In addition, the BDF states, "There are scattered traces of the late use of the perfect in narrative" (§343).

[98] The change from dative to genitive agrees with της νυκτος that follows. Now the whole phrase is in the genitive of time. Cf. BDF, §186.

[99] The word δεκαδυο is found in Ptolemaic papyri in place of δωδεκα (Moulton-Milligan, s.v. δεκαδυο; BDF, §63.2). Though it is written in full here in D, the second occurrence of δωδεκα in D (and א) in 19:28 is abbreviated, ιβ̄.

[100] The present active participle of *rell* is in the middle voice in D, which forms a *hapax legomenon* in the LXX and NT (except D and 28 in the gospel parallels, Mark 13:17 and Luke 21:23, read θηλαζομεναις). The verb is used transitively in Matthew, which is similar to the use found in P.Lond 951 (late third century C.E.),

are instances where aorist subjunctives are replaced with future indicatives, which is a Koine characteristic[101] (5:25b;[102] 5:25c;[103] 27:64),[104] two of which are modified by μηποτε (5:25b and 27:64). One singular reading creates a Hebraicism (5:40).[105]

While some singular readings seem grammatically Attic, Koine, or Hebraic, Latin seems to influence spelling rather than grammar. In two instances, proper names in the genitive case are spelled with – ους endings when the Latin forms end with an *s* (2:1;[106] 11:12).[107] Several other singular readings resemble Latin spellings (2:11; 3:4;

θηλαζειν, but there it is active in voice (Moulton-Milligan, s.v. θηλάζω). The verb is, however, used in the middle voice by Aristotle (fourth century B.C.E.), ου συλλαμβανουσι θηλαζομεναι (Liddell-Scott, s.v. θηλάζω). The use of the middle voice in D in 24:19 seems to be classical.

[101] Cf. BDF, §363.

[102] Instead of an aorist subjunctive form of παραδιδωμι, the text of D reads a future indicative. The conjunction μηποτε usually modifies a subjunctive (as seen in the parallel, Luke 12:58, κατακρεινη in D), but in Matt 5:25b (and Heb 3:12) it modifies a future indicative (cf. μηπως which modifies a perfect indicative in Gal 4:11). Cf. BDF, §370.

[103] Davies and Allison state that one of several ways Matthew alters Q differently than Luke (in Luke 12:58) in Matt 5:25 is that Matthew constructed the sentence so that the verb in 5:25b, παραδω, is implicitly read into v. 25c after ο κριτης instead of being explicitly stated (Davies and Allison, *Matthew*, 1:519–20). Codex D reads the future indicative form of παραδιδωμι in both v. 25b and 25c rather than the aorist subjunctive. (The Latin *d* is aligned with the majority of Latin MSS, reading the subjunctive *tradat* in both v. 25b and 25c, as opposed to reading a future with D.)

[104] The aorist subjunctive ειπωσιν in 27:64 is a future indicative in D. The conjunction μηποτε modifies κλεψωσιν and ειπωσιν in v. 64, but only ειπωσιν is changed to a future indicative.

[105] In 5:40, the nominative participle in D (ο θελων) followed by a dative pronoun is "in the Hebraic manner," McNeile states, "which is possibly the true reading" (*Matthew*, 69–70). In addition, "anacoluthon (without a relative clause) following an introductory participle [e.g., 5:40] is Semitic," and "a comparable usage is found in classical" (BDF, §466.4). Cf. Davies and Allison, *Matthew*, 1:454.

[106] The spelling of Ηρωδου in D as Ηρωδους could have been influenced from the nominative form, Ηρωδης, or perhaps the Latin *Herodes*.

[107] The reading in D*, Ιωαννους, should be genitive to be grammatically construed.

13:44a; 21:9¹, 9², 15; 26:6).[108]

5.2.12. Influence from Context

The influence from context seems to be the most common cause of alteration in the singular readings in D in Matthew (accounting for 12.3% of the singular readings). With a few exceptions, these changes never result in a gain of text; and without exception, there is never in a loss of text among these singular readings. The pattern displayed here, of primarily additions and no omissions, is not congruent with the overall tendency in Bezae to omit more often than add.

In many instances, singular readings seem to be influenced from preceding text (5:10;[109] 5:12;[110] 5:24;[111] 5:36;[112] 11:3;[113] 12:26;[114]

---

[108] In 26:6, the spelling is probably influenced from the Latin, *leprosi* (so BDAG, s.v. λεπρός). The spelling in D* is a *hapax legomenon* in the NT and LXX. The word is also used adjectivally in the parallel, Mark 14:3, but D reads λεπρου.

[109] The verb in D here, εστε in place of εστιν, is probably an orthographic spelling of the 3s future indicative εσται rather than a 2pl present indicative form of ειμι (i.e. εστε). The orthographic change αι > ε is found in εσται in other instances in D as well as other verbs (cf. 1:23; 9:2; 16:19², 22; 19:27; 21:37; 22:28 in appendix fifteen. In addition, the verb in *d* here is 3s future indicative, *erit*). The change from present, εστιν to future, εσται in D fits well in context of the Beatitudes, and would imply a future reward of heaven: "Blessed are the persecuted for sake of righteousness, because theirs *will be* the kingdom of heaven" (emphasis added). All but one of the preceding Beatitudes (5:3) imply future rewards (5:4, 5, 6, 7, 8, 9), and therefore, the text of Bezae here could have been influenced by the previous futuristic context.

[110] The change from accusative υπαρχοντας to genitive υπαρχοντων could be due to influence from the ending of the preceding word, υμων.

[111] The imperative verbs in *rell* and D here are synonyms, translated as *be reconciled*. The short parables in 5:23–24 and 5:25–26 pertain to reconciliation and so the verb in D fits well in context (France, *Matthew*, 202). The preposition κατα is found in the previous verse, which could have influenced a change of the verbal prefix, δια– to κατα–, in D.

[112] The word transposition in D is also found in *d k* Cyp[178] Aug[semel]. The singular element of the D* text here is the present infinitive verb, ποιειν, in place of an aorist infinitive, ποιοσαι, that is found in most MSS. A present tense indicative verb (δυνασαι) precedes the singular reading and could have influenced the *prima manus* of D to continue with the present tense in his transcription of the following verb.

[113] The noun εργα from the previous verse could have influenced an unin-

12:28;[115] 12:34;[116] 13:48a;[117] 13:49a;[118] 18:22;[119] 19:6;[120] 21:39;[121]

tentional change in D* in 11:3, ερχομενος > εργαζομενος.

[114] The "synonymous expressions" in 12:25, ερημουται and ου σταθησεται, are not as synonymous in D* as they are in most MSS because in D* they are not all in the same verbal voice (in 12:25, στησεται is read in D* f^{13} 174 230 788 826 828 983) (Hagner, *Matthew*, 1:342). The reading in the following verse in D, 12:26, is a singular reading, στησεται, a change from passive to middle, which could have been influenced from the same verb στησεται in v. 25 in D* f^{13} *et al*.

[115] The verbal number in D* does not fit the grammatical context. There are no other verbal ending changes such as this in D* that are singular readings. Therefore, in D* here, this may be a scribal slip from 3s to 3pl, influenced from the previous plural noun, τα δαιμονια.

[116] The addition of αγαθα clarifies the text since both αγαθα and πονηροι are mentioned previously in the verse (cf. *ff*² where the opposite of αγαθα is used, i.e. *mala*).

[117] The reading in D here is an aorist indicative, as opposed to an aorist participle in *rell*. The reading in *d* is also indicative, but future tense as opposed to the present participles (*educentes*, *ducentes*) or perfect indicatives (*eduxerunt*, *duxerunt*, *posuerunt*, *imposuerunt*) in the Latin variants. The verb αναβιβαζειν (used only here in the NT) is mainly classical (McNeile, *Matthew*, 204). The reading in D could have been influenced from the preceding word, an aorist indicative (επληρωθη).

[118] The phrase uttered at the end of 13:40, in which συντελεια (του) αιωνος is repeated from v. 39 (Nolland, *Matthew*, 560), is identical to the phrase in *rell* that begins 13:49: ουτως εσται εν τη συντελεια του αιωνος (ibid., 569; Gundry, *Matthew*, 280). In D in 13:49 however, the "common eschatological term" αιων is substituted with κοσμου (ibid., 272), which the latter "is a broad term for both the created universe ... and for human society in general" (France, *Matthew*, 535). The nearest use of κοσμος before v. 49 in D is within the same eschatological context in v. 38 (though in different parables). The κοσμος in v. 38 may refer to "the widespread extension of the kingdom through evangelism" (Gundry, *Matthew*, 272), which "points to a time when missionary activities had spread much further" than Palestine (McNeile, *Matthew*, 200). The text of D contains a variant due perhaps to the physical, earthly, terms of the preceding verses (vv. 47–48), terms that have more consonance with κοσμος than αιωνος, e.g., *a net cast into the sea* (σαγηνη βληθειση εις την θαλασσαν), *bringing onto the shore* (αναβιβασαντες επι τον αιγιαλον), *put the good into the vessels* (συνελεξαν τα καλα εις αγγη), and therefore the scribe could have been influenced by the preceding context.

[119] The D text reads an adverb, επτακις, instead of the adjective επτα, which may have been influenced by other words ending in –τακις in vv. 21–22, such as ποτακις, επτακις (twice), and εβομηκοντακις.

24:30b;[122] 27:59;[123] 27:61b).[124]

There are few instances where the inclusion of articles is probably influenced from the previous words (13:48b;[125] 24:30a).[126] One addition could be a harmonization with the following context

---

[120] The preceding verb in context, συνεζευξεν, is compounded. The verb change χωριζετω > αποχωριζετω in 19:6 in D parallels the previous compound verb naturally because they are antonyms. The text of D may have been influenced from the grammatical context with the change to compound here in 19:6. The simple verb in 19:6 in *rell*, χωριζετω (*separate*), is, however, more commonly used in the context of divorce than the compound. Cf. BDAG, s.v. χωρίζω and s.v. ἀποχωρίζω.

[121] The verb ending –αν in εξεβαλαν in D is a 1st aorist ending; but a 2nd aorist ending, –ον, would be expected on the 2nd aorist stem εξεβαλ–. Perhaps the ending of the previous aorist verb, απεκτειναν, influenced a change in the following verb, εξεβαλον, in D. (The word order in D, as well as Θ *a b c d e ff*[2] *h r*[1.2] geo Iren[int] Lucif Iuvenc, is transposed so that απεκτειναν is placed before εξεβαλον/εξεβαλαν.)

[122] The text of D reads dative plural (ουρανοις) instead of singular (so *rell*), but *d* remains dative singular. The Latin in 24:30, *caelo*, may attest to a harmonization (Parker, *Codex Bezae*, 203). Of the four occurrences of ουρανος/*caelum* in vv. 29–30, *d* always reads a singular (either *caelo* or *caeli*), where D reads two singulars (ουρανοις, ουρανου) and two plurals (ουρανων, ουρανοις). Only in one instance do D and *d* agree here (του ουρανου and *caeli* in v. 30). The previous occurrence of ουρανος in v. 29 is plural, which could have influenced a change following in v. 30 to plural. Parker states that D was influenced by the context (ibid., 202), which he must be referring to the former των ουρανων.

[123] The text of D reads a compound verb as opposed to the simple verb in *rell*. (The text of *d* reads a cognate of the Latt reading.) The preceding Greek verb, αποδοθηναι two words earlier (in 27:58), is compound, which could have influenced the scribe of D to substitute λαβων with the compound παραλαβων, thus creating a connection between the two words.

[124] Gundry states that there is an intended parallel in the Matthean text between κατεναντι (in B D) in 27:24a and απεναντι (in *rell*) in 27:61b (*Matthew*, 582). The text of D creates a stronger link between the two passages than the wording in *rell* because the word κατεναντι is supplied in both instances, 27:24a and 27:61b.

[125] The text of D reads a neuter plural accusative article with αγγια (αγγη in NA[28]) where no other MSS contain an article. The prior noun (καλα in *rell*; καλλιστα in D 700 *et al.*) has a neuter plural article with it, which could have possibly influenced an addition for the following noun (i.e. τα αγγια).

[126] The του in D before εν is probably unintentional, due to unconscious repetition or dittography of the definite articles in του υιου του ανθρωπου, which immediately precede it (Holmes, "Editorial Activity," 227).

(15:22b).[127] Only two, however, seem to be influenced from following text (12:18a;[128] 26:53).[129]

Some substitutions are influenced from the word it replaces (11:22;[130] 11:24b;[131] 14:24;[132] 15:27b;[133] 20:15;[134] 26:15),[135] three of which are ην > η (11:22, 24b; 14:24); most, however, do not seem to

---

[127] The additional preposition and pronoun (οπισω αυτου) in D d are not foreign to the context since the similar κραζει οπισθεν ημων is found in the following verse. The addition in Bezae could be a pre-harmonization.

[128] The following non-singular variant in D in 12:18 (εν ω in place of εις ον) is caused by "assimilation" of Matt 3:17 and 17:5 (Holmes, "Editorial Activity," 168). The text of D in 12:18 then contains a parallel involving the combination of a preposition with a relative pronoun: εις is supplied with ον and then εν with ω.

[129] The plural accusative form of the noun λεγιων is a singular genitive in D*. The noun then agrees with the following genitive, αγγελων, but it should be plural to be grammatically construed with the preceding δωδεκα.

[130] The text of D reads the relative pronoun ην in place of the comparative particle η. The reading of D* here is not construed with the comparative ανεκτοτερον (more tolerable).

[131] As in 11:22, the text of D* reads a relative pronoun in 11:24b where all other MSS read a comparative particle. The pronoun υμ(ε)ιν, read by D M^mg 124 659 1424 it vg^mss sa^ms bo^pt arm^(cdd) Ir^int278 is retained from the plural subject from earlier in the sentence.

[132] The reading in D* of either a conjunction or article, rather than a verb, is not grammatically construed.

[133] The reading of D here is a diminutive form of *dogs* (which occurs earlier in the verse), rather than the word for *masters* as in *rell*. The reading in D is perhaps influenced from the similar spelling of κυριων and the να of the κυναρια that occurs earlier in 15:26 and 27. The non-diminutive form of *dogs*, κυων, has a figurative use, which can imply "those who were unbaptized and therefore impure" (BDAG, s.v. κύων). The change *masters* > *little dogs* could make sense in context if there is an implication that masters are unbaptized/impure, but the figurative implication is more closely associated with κυων rather than κυναριον. In addition, there seems to be other instances where a singular reading in D closely resembles the word it replaces—these instances typically do not make sense in context.

[134] The singular reading in D* is a substitution of εξεστιν, *it is lawful*, for εστιν, *it is*, which does not make sense in context.

[135] The plural article in *rell*, which functions as a nominative pronoun, is a plural dative relative pronoun in D. The reading in D is nonsensical because a nominative is needed to modify the verb εστησαν.

be construed in context. In one instance, a substitution with a definite article, της, resembles the word it replaces, ης (24:38).¹³⁶ Some verbs are replaced with synonyms that are spelled very similarly (9:10;¹³⁷ 26:55;¹³⁸ 27:53).¹³⁹

5.2.13. Agreement Between the Greek and Latin Columns

Clark states that, most likely, an old-Latin MS was utilized to produce text where *d* and D disagree, thus "The consequence was that readings of this MS. were mixed up with [the scribe's] own literal

---

¹³⁶ In D*, the addition of the feminine singular genitive article could be a careless error due to the similarly spelled pronoun ης, or influenced from the preceding εν ταις ημεραις.

¹³⁷ The verb in D* is from συγκειμαι, which is a synonym for what it replaces, συνανακειμαι (so BDAG, s.v. σύγκειμαι).

¹³⁸ The text of D reads the verb καθημαι, rather than the synonym καθεζομαι as in *rell* (or *sum* in *r*¹·²). The verb employed in D is often, but not exclusively, used with *throne* (θρονος) in the NT in contexts of the Divine sitting on a throne and judging, protecting, or being worshiped (cf. Matt 19:28; 23:22; Luke 22:30; Rev 4:2, 3, 4, 9, 10; 5:1, 7, 13; 6:16; 7:10, 15; 19:4; 20:11; 21:5). Jesus is the subject of the verb in Matt 26:55 but instead of sitting on a *throne*, he is sitting *in the temple* (εν τω ιερω). Perhaps the substitution in D is meant to conjure divine/kingly imagery, but it does not seem realistic that such a small change could be so strikingly theological, especially considering that this change resembles other synonym substitutions that are spelled similarly yet are not theological.

¹³⁹ Gundry comments that the word ενεφανισθησαν here in Matthew "connotes juridical appearance for the purpose of testimony" (*Matthew*, 577), which fits well in the *Sitz im Buch*. The context in Matthew here is when Jesus dies on the cross and the earth shook, tombs opened, the bodies of saints were raised, and after Jesus' resurrection, they appeared (ενεφανισθησαν) to many people in the holy city. There are no direct parallels of the Matthean text (cf. Mark 16:9, 12—the text of *d* is lacunose in Mark here). The text of D* in Matt 27:53 reads a simple verb, φαινω, which is a cognate of εμφανιζω in *rell*. In *d* in Matthew, the text reads *paruerunt*, rather than the compound *apparuerunt* in Latt (both are inflected forms of the verbal root *pareo*). Though the verbal substitution in D* *d* occurs in a theologically difficult context, i.e. the resurrection of the dead occurring before Jesus' own resurrection (France, *Mathew*, 1082), the difference in meaning between D* *d* and *rell* does not solve any theological problems.

translation from the Greek."[140] There are, actually, two singular readings that could suggest *d* was translated from D (15:32b;[141] 22:24).[142] In another instance, however, the text of D and *d* do not agree on de-

---

[140] Albert C. Clark, *The Acts of the Apostles: A Critical Edition with Introduction and Notes on Selected Passages* (Oxford: Clarendon, 1970), xliv.

[141] The omission in D* *d* * is of a phrase that is "unique to this pericope" (cf. Mark 8:1–3) (Hagner, *Matthew*, 2:450). The sentence is still construed without the final clause of the verse and could, perhaps, be a paraphrastic omission. The omission was added by the *prima manus* in small text between two lines.

It is interesting to discover that the Latin text also omits the phrase. The omission in D* in could be explained by parablepsis, a leap from θελω to οδω (or ΘΕΛΩ to ΟΔΩ) (so Hagner, *Matthew*, 2:447 n. c), but there is no evidence of parablepsis in *d**. If it was established that some portions of the Latin text were transcribed as a translation of the Greek column, than the reading here in both D* and *d* * would support such a claim: first, the Greek was transcribed with an instance of haplography, then the Latin was translated from the Greek side. The reading alone, however, does not prove that *d* was translated from D, but could support such a claim.

[142] The reading in Bezae in Matt 22:24 lacks the phrase *his wife* (though it is found in the parallels Mark 12:19; Luke 20:28 in D), and therefore it is not explicitly stated that Moses said (Deut 25:5) that a brother *must marry his brother's widow* to raise up children for his deceased brother, only that *he must marry* and raise up children. The parablepsis of αυτου could have resulted in haplography of the complement phrase (*his wife*, την γυναικα αυτου) by the *prima manus* of D. Holmes attributes the omission to homoeoteleuton ("Editorial Activity," 129–30 n. 30).

Apart from homoeoteleuton, there are some interesting features in Bezae in this spot: (1) where normally the sense lines of D and *d* are parallel with each other, on two lines of folios 75b and 76a the text is not parallel—this occurs where the omission of *his wife* would be in both columns (on folio 76r, the words *fratri suo* end ln. 2, but on folio 75v, ο αδελφηος αυτου begins ln. 3); (2) the word *semen* is left unfinished by the *prima manus* of *d**, written as *sem*; and (3) up until *ut ducate/nubat*, the *d* text is in agreement with Latin MSS (Latt reads: *ut ducate frater eius uxorem illius et suscitet semen fratri suo*; and *d** reads: *ut nubat fratri suo et excitet sem fratri suo*), but the D text agrees with the majority of Greek MSS for the *entire* verse, except for the omission of την γυναικα αυτου, which *d* is also lacking (admittedly, this third feature of Bezae in 22:24 may have nothing to do with the scribe but perhaps merely how the exemplar read). One possible explanation for the omission in *d* is that it could have been translated from D, but an explanation for the unaligned sense lines in the columns (cf. f. 75b ln. 3 and f. 76r ln. 2) is still wanting. Nevertheless, the reading in Bezae, both in D* and *d**, is construed in context.

tails in the story (14:6).[143]

5.2.14. NOUN AND ADJECTIVE CHANGES

There are three types of changes here; one reading creates a construed gender change (19:4),[144] the preposition and nominal case of a prepositional phrase is changed (14:14),[145] and a change is made from singular to plural (23:17).[146]

5.2.15. USE OF PRONOUNS

Some pronouns are replaced with another pronoun (12:39;[147] 22:12),[148] one of which may have been influenced from text following

---

[143] There is confusion in MSS in the Markan parallel (Mark 6:22) whether the dancing girl is Herodias' daughter, αυτης της Ηρωδιαδος (so A C W M f¹ plu), or Herod's daughter Herodias, αυτου Ηρωδιαδος (so ℵ B D pc NA²⁸) (for a concise explanation see Cranfield, *Mark*, 211–2). Instead of the genitive Ηρωδιαδος, D reads the nominative Ηρωδιας and states that the girl dancing is Herod's daughter Herodias. The text of *d*, however, states the other variant, that the girl dancing is Herodias' daughter (*filia Herodiadis*).

[144] The word in this portion of 19:4 is within a quote from LXX Gen 1:27 where the adjective θηλυς is neuter (θηλυ), but the text of D reads a masculine, θηλυν (*d* with the Latin read a feminine noun, *feminam*).

[145] The prepositional phrase in D is plural genitive rather than plural dative in *rell*. The meaning of επι with dative is similar to the meaning of the genitive περι in context here. None of the Latin variants resemble D here, which are plural accusative (*super eos*), plural dative (*de eis, illis*), or singular genitive (*eius*).

[146] The comparative adjective in D is neuter plural accusative, rather than neuter singular accusative as in *rell* (cf. 20:10).

[147] Instead of αυτη, the text of D* reads σοι. Holmes states that *the scribes and Pharisees* (12:38) are identified as the evil and adulterous generation in D* because σοι refers to them ("Editorial Activity," 219). Grammatically, however, *scribes and Pharisees* are plural and σοι is singular, so σοι in D*, just as αυτη in *rell*, still refers to γενεα πονηρα και μοιχαλις (evil and adulterous generation). In addition, the plural αυτοις, which *explicitly* refers to *the scribes and Pharisees* is used in 12:39 in D and *rell*, so the referent σοι is not construed even in the same sentence—it merely refers to γενεα as did αυτη.

[148] The nominative article in 22:12 refers to εταιρε, which occurs in the previous sentence (but the same verse). Turner states, "In class[ical] Attic ὁ δέ rarely refers to the subject of the preceding sentence," but is frequently employed in the NT

the replacement (27:44).[149] There is an instance where prolepsis is created (12:45).[150] One pronoun is omitted, perhaps due to oversight (19:20).[151] In one instance, the article is omitted when it functions as a pronoun (16:23).[152]

5.2.16. Textual Improvement

Some singular readings improve the text by aiding in narration (12:23;[153] 21:36)[154] and eliminating asyndeton (25:38).[155] In one in-

---

to reference the previous subject (*Syntax*, 37, §1[b]). The text of D reads the relative pronoun, ος, in place of the nominative article here, and is a grammatically construed alternative to the reading of *rell*. Cf. ος δε > ο δε in Mark 15:23 (BDF, §251).

[149] The αυτοι in D* matches the gender, number, and case of the following οι λησται (*the robbers*). Thus the pronoun no longer functions as an identical adjective in D* (as in *rell*) and is translated, "But this, they, even the robbers ... "

[150] The reading in D* *d* here is an instance of a proleptic pronoun being followed by a resumptive noun. Turner states that "the proleptic pronoun followed by resumptive noun is an Aramaic peculiarity," and that "it appears particularly in codex Bezae" (*Syntax*, 41), but this is the only instance in Matthew in D that is a singular reading.

[151] The addition of *from my youth* (εκ νεοτητος μου) in 19:20 in some MSS is harmonized from the synoptic parallels, Mark 10:20; Luke 18:21 (Metzger, *Textual Commentary*, 40). In Matthew, the singular portion of the reading of D is the omission of μου (and is omitted Luke 18:21 in D as well, but not Mark 10:20). The omission of the pronoun may be a simple oversight in Bezae or thought unnecessary.

[152] The reading of D omits the neuter plural accusative article τα, which functions as a pronoun in context (the Latin MSS read the pronoun *ea*, except for *d*). This is the second occurrence of the article τα (functioning as a pronoun) in the verse.

[153] The addition in D* introduces indirect speech and is grammatically construed.

[154] The text of D reads ουν following παλιν, which, in context, aids in the continuation of the narrative (Liddell-Scott, s.v. οὖν, II.). None of the gospel parallels (Matt 22:4; Mark 12:4; Luke 20:11) read the same ουν as in D in 21:36.

[155] Davies and Allison notice parallelism between 25:35–36 and 25:37–39, stating, "Each question consists of ποτε + σε + ειδομεν + condition of sufferer (+ και + verb ending in –μεν) + η + condition of sufferer + και + verb ending in –μεν" (*Matthew*, 3:428). The text of D reads και in place of the Matthean conjunction η in 25:38 (Gundry, *Matthew*, 514). The D text now reads και three consecutive times in v. 38, producing "the impression of extensiveness and abundance" (BDF, §460.3). The και is used in the same manner just prior, in 25:35–36, which grosses six instances, and could have influenced the substitution in the subsequent parallel in v. 38

stance, a mathematical calculation is not performed (25:28),[156] which could be considered a concession for a reader/hearer who cannot perform mathematical addition, but no other such mathematical concessions are performed in the singular readings in D in Matthew.

Few singular readings go deeper than grammatical changes. Two singular readings involve a Christological statement (16:16)[157] and another theological statement (19:26).[158] Both of these, however, could be unintentional alterations. One reading hints at the disciples' ignorance of Jesus (26:1–2).[159]

(though not in *d*).

[156] The variant in Bezae refers to the same person as in *rell*, but is "representing the original amount [of talents] given" in the parable, as Nolland states about D. (*Matthew*, 1011–2 n. m). In the text, there are five (25:16) and five (25:20) talents, which are added together in *rell* in v. 28, equaling ten (δεκα) talents, but the text of D does not add the talents together.

[157] The text of D* reads το σωζοντος in 16:16, which calls Christ Son of the *Saving* God, rather than του ζωντος, Christ Son of the *Living* God. The singular reading in D* contains an article that is not grammatically construed (it should be masculine to agree with θεος, not neuter το). The variant in D* might preserve an Aramaic saying: יי, *to live*; and perhaps ייחד, *who lives*, was misread as יחמד, *who saves* (so Matthew Black, *An Aramaic Approach to the Gospels and Acts*, 2nd ed. [Oxford: Clarendon, 1954], 180; Holmes, "Editorial Activity," 83. See also ibid., 223, 231, where the reading is listed under "Christological Variants"). The similarity in spelling between ייחד and יחמד is not necessarily more confusing than the spelling difference between ζωντος and σωζοντος. (The Latin *d** reads *saluatoris* and was corrected to *viventis*, which are not similarly spelled, and therefore confusion does not seem to stem from the Latin text.) It is not easy to determine exactly what the cause of the reading is, but nonetheless, the text of D* and *d** still state that Christ is the Son of the *Saving* God.

[158] The reading in D* of δυνατον ... δυνατα, destroys all "(antithetical) parallelism" and sense of the verse (Davies and Allison, *Matthew*, 3:53). The text in D* states that all things are possible for men *and* God, rather than other MSS that state it is *impossible* for men and *possible* for God. The reading may be theological as it could place God and man on the same omnipotent plane, or at least may speak of cooperation between the two. The cause of the reading could have been from the latter occurrence of δυνατα in the verse.

[159] In 26:1–2, both D and *d* do not read αυτου οιδατε/*suis scitis* (and *l*47 does not read αυτου, but does read οιδατε). The majority of Latin MSS read *discipulis suis scitis quia,* and the omitted text in *d, suis scitis*, may be due to the parablep-

5.2.17. USE OF VERBS

The tense, voice, or prefix of some verbs has been changed, though the difference is only one letter (4:6b;[160] 5:22;[161] 6:7;[162]

sis of *-is*, but Parker does not identify any instances of haplography in one column of Bezae that has influenced an omission in the other column (i.e. it is never recorded that haplography in *d* influenced a change in D); therefore the omission in *d* (even though there is parablepsis) probably did not give rise to the omission in D (see Parker's discussion on omissions, *Codex Bezae*, 89ff).

The singular portion of the variant in Bezae is the omission of the verb οιδατε/*scitis*. The Greek verb is either an indicative (*you know*) or imperative (*know you that*), and the Latin verb is either indicative or a participle (Davies and Allison, *Matthew*, 3:437; Hagner, *Matthew*, 2:754). Luz states that οιδατε is indicative because the disciples are already aware of what οιδατε refers to (*Matthew*, 3:330). Gundry states that Matthew employs οιδατε, which "is a favorite of his," to portray "the disciples as those who understand" (*Matthew*, 517). The gospel parallels, Mark 4:1 and Luke 22:1, do not contain οιδατε, which McNeile comments, "Mt. alone relates that the Lord reminded the disciples of the date, introducing a reference to His death, already thrice predicted" (*Matthew*, 372). If οιδατε was interpreted as either an indicative or imperative, it could have been omitted in Bezae because it seemed redundant because the disciples "would hardly need to be informed about the calendar, and Jesus has already repeatedly told them about his approaching death" (France, *Matthew*, 969 n. 2). Along these lines, the word οιδατε is substituted in Acts 3:17 in Bezae in a variant that Epp identifies as an eradication of the ignorance motif of the Jews (Eldon Jay Epp, *The Theological Tendency of Codex Bezae Cantabrigiensis in Acts*, SNTSMS 3 [Cambridge: Cambridge University Press, 1966], 42ff). Though the "ignorance motif" in Luke-Acts pertains to the Jews, in Mark the "ignorance motif" is connected to the disciples. Nolland states that in *Matthew*, "the Markan ignorance motif, especially when it shows the disciples stuck in their ignorance ('they were afraid to ask him'), does not suit Matthew" (*Matthew*, 720). Indeed, instances of the disciples' ignorance are not as common in Matthew as in Mark, so it is interesting that the variant in Bezae could possibly change the narrative to highlight such ignorance. This single instance does not, however, *create a motif* of ignorance, but perhaps the prevalence of ignorance motifs in other biblical books, i.e. Luke-Acts and Mark, influenced a change in another book, i.e. Matthew. In other words, perhaps an extra-Matthean motif spilled over into Matthew.

[160] The context in Matthew here is a quote from LXX Ps 90:12. The verb αιρω is formed with an iota only in the present tense (cf. William D. Mounce, *The Morphology of Biblical Greek* [Grand Rapids: Zondervan, 1994], §31.5d, such as found in D here: αιρουσιν). The verb in *rell* is in the future tense, αρουσιν, as well as the previous verb in the quote, εντελειται, but αιρω in D does not agree in verbal

12:18b;[163] 17:5)[164] or two letters (4:7;[165] 12:36;[166] 20:3;[167] 24:12).[168] One

---

tense within the context (there are no singular α > αι orthographic changes in D to suggest that this is an orthographic variant). This may, however, be merely an instance of incorrect word formation where the iota is mistakenly retained from the present tense stem, and not a deliberate attempt to alter the verbal tense.

[161] In 5:22, the text of D* reads an antonym for what *rell* reads. The change from οργιζω (*make angry, provoke to anger, irritate*) to οργαζω (*soften, knead, temper*) is nonsensical and is the difference of a change from iota to alpha, which could result from a scribal slip (Liddell-Scott, s.v. ὀργίζω; s.v. ὀργάζω). Furthermore, there does not seem to be any metaphorical or idiomatic use of οργαζω that might fit the context of anger.

[162] The word βατταλογεω is an onomatopoetic word meaning to *stammer* or *stutter*, and is identical in meaning to the more common βατταριζω (Liddell-Scott, s.v. βαττολογέω; s.v. βατταρίζω; BDAG, s.v. βατταλογέω). In 6:7, E G 700 *et al.* read the omicron stem, βατ(τ)ο–, where as ℵ B W and other MSS read the alpha stem, βαττα–. Little is certain about the origins of the word, and the TDNT capitulates that "such words sometimes defy exact linguistic analysis" (TDNT, s.v. βατταλογέω). The word in D* contains a stem with lambda, βλα–, which is a hapax legomenon in the NT. The D text resembles the Latin *blatero* in regards to the lambda, but no Latin MSS read *blatero* in 6:7 (the Latin MSS instead read the synonym *loquor*). If Latinization occurred here, "it must lie somewhere in the complex history of the Bezan text itself" (Moulton-Milligan, s.v. βαττολογέω).

[163] The context of 12:18b is a quote from Isa 42:1–4, which is probably Matthew's "independent translation of the Hebrew" and has some "influence from the LXX and targum" (Davies and Allison, *Matthew*, 2:323). The singular reading in D is in the present tense rather than the future tense as in *rell*. It is, however, merely the difference of an additional lambda in D, which could have been duplicated if the double gammas (preceding) somehow influenced a letter repetition, but nevertheless there are no other singular readings that witness a double letter formation similar to this. The reading in D is grammatically difficult because it is a present tense verb surrounded by future tense verbs (θησω and ερισει).

[164] The imperfect tense in D* here fits the context appropriately. The reading in *d*, however, is future tense (as opposed to perfect in other Latin MSS) and is not grammatically construed in context.

[165] The variant here is part of an OT quote (LXX Deut 6:16 or Isa 7:12) that is spoken by Jesus to the devil. The εκ prefix adds a perfective nuance that is lost in the simple verb in D (Zerwick, *Grammatical Analysis*, 8). Instead of, *you will not put the Lord your God through a test*, D is translated as, *you will not test the Lord your God*. The "key word (εκ)πειραζω [4:7] appears again in 16:1," which is simple in both D and *rell* (Luz, *Matthew*, 1:188).

verb is changed from 3s > 2s (12:20b).[169] Some verbal tense changes seem unnecessary because they do not match the tense of the surrounding verbs (10:25;[170] 15:39a).[171] The pluperfect tense in D seems to be appropriate in two close instances (11:20, 21).[172] In another instance, the individual is emphasized with a change from passive to the middle voice (25:29).[173] One verbal change lessens the connection be-

---

[166] The reading in D *d* is in present tense, unlike ℵ B C *et al.* which read the future tense, or aorist subjunctive in *rell*, or perfect participle in it$^{(pler)}$ vg. Holmes acknowledges the possibility that the variant in D (and *d*) could refer to the "'careless words' which were being spoken at that [present] time by Jesus' opponents, the Pharisees ..." rather than their *future* words having to be accounted for in the day of judgment (εν ημερα κρισεως) ("Editorial Activity," 218). The following verb, αποδωσουσιν, is still in the future tense, so the change in D *d* to present does not eliminate *all* futuristic thought.

[167] The verb in *rell* is an "echoing" of εξηλθεν in 20:1 and reappears in vv. 5 and 6 (Gundry, *Matthew*, 396). The verb in D, however, loses some of the connection with its other forms in the pericope because it is now a (double) compound verb.

[168] The text of D reads an aorist active infinitive (and *d* reads a perfect passive participle), as opposed to the aorist passive infinitive in *rell*, the perfect active indicative in most Latin MSS, or the present active indicative in *a*. The following accusative, την ανομιαν, is still the subject of the infinitive πληθυναι in D.

[169] In 12:20b, the verb καταγνυμι in D* *d** here is 2s, but is 3s in *rell* and D^F d^G. The verse is a portion of the Isa 42:1–4 quotation.

[170] The change from aorist to present in D *d* is construed in context even though the previous verb is aorist (γενηται).

[171] The change to the present tense in D creates inconsistency with the tenses of the surrounding aorist verbs, απολυσας and ηλθεν.

[172] The "catch word" in 11:20, εγενετο (aorist), is changed to γεγονεισαν (pluperfect), in D, which is similar to the change in 11:21 (εγενοντο > γεγονεισαν in D) (Luz, *Matthew*, 2:151). Luz interprets the pericope (Matt 11:20–24) stating, "The issue here is not that these cities [Chorazin and Bethsaida] are self-righteous or have a false awareness of their own election. It is simply that they did not recognize the 'mighty deeds' [δυναμεις] that Jesus performed as a call to repentance" (ibid., 2:153). The alteration to a pluperfect tense in D in 11:20 and 11:21 could intend to emphasize how the δυναμεις that were performed in the past have an enduring effect on the cities of Χοραζαιν and Βεθσαειδα (cf. BDF, §347.2, 3).

[173] In the context of 25:29, Hagner states, "The future passive verbs [περισσευθησεται and αρθησεται] imply God as the acting subject" (*Matthew*, 2:736). In D, the former verb is changed to middle voice and the latter verb remains

tween words (or phrases) (15:3).[174] There is one instance of *constructio ad sensum* where a verb is changed to singular to agree with the singular collective noun (27:27).[175]

5.2.18. OTHER OMISSIONS

In one instance, the omitted text can still be implied in context (2:3).[176] There is one instance where a detail of John the Baptist's death is omitted (14:8).[177] In another instance, a direct object is omitted

---

passive. (In the Latin, the former verb is active and the latter is passive.) The Greek and Latin variants are all in the future tense, and are still aligned with Hagner's interpretation, but the text of D perhaps nuances the text by emphasizing the individual with the middle voice employed in περισσευσεται: *he will have abundance (for himself)* (cf. Luke 15:17 περισσευονται).

[174] The verb in this portion of 15:3 in D is infinitive (παραβαιναι), rather than indicative in *rell* (παραβαινετε). Though the verb occurs elsewhere in the LXX and NT, as an infinitive it is a *hapax legomenon*. McNeile notices a connection between και υμεις παραβαινετε in v. 3 and the indicative παραβαινουσιν in v. 2, which replaces Mark's καλως αθετειτε (Mark 7:9) (*Matthew*, 222). The connection is not as clearly perceptible in Matthew in D because of the different verbal moods in παραβαιναι and παραβαινουσιν, but such a connection is still present in D.

[175] The change from 3pl to 3s in D may derive from the subject, ολην την σπειραν, comprised of singular nouns that are collective in meaning. Cf. BDF, §134.

[176] In all of Matthew, *Jerusalem* is neuter plural (except maybe 3:5), but here in 2:3 πασα Ιεροσολυμα is feminine. Davies and Allison state that the omission of πασα in D (and the omission of *omnis* in *d*) "restores consistency" with the neuter gender (*Matthew*, 1:237 n. 36). (France notices a connection of 2:3 to 21:10 where *all the city* will be *stirred up* by Jesus; and therefore it is appropriate that *all* Jerusalem "is already perturbed at the prospect of a dynastic revolution" [*Matthew*, 70]. On the other hand, Luz remarks that because "Herod was so unpopular with the Jerusalem inhabitants ... that news of the birth of a royal child or especially a messianic child would have caused great joy" [*Matthew*, 1:135].) The inclusion of *all* Jerusalem can still be implied even though the text of Bezae lacks πασα.

[177] The request by Herodias' daughter to have John's head presented on a platter, and Herod's subsequent acquiescence to her wish, "underlines the degradation of the royal court" (Hagner, *Matthew*, 2:413). The detail of how the head will be presented, *on a platter* (επι πινακι), is omitted in Bezae. Holmes states that the omission in D in 14:8 is simply "an insignificant late scribal slip" ("Editorial Activity", 191), but there may be more to it than that. Interestingly, the mention of people who have been beheaded (πεπλεκισμενων) is omitted in Codex Alexandrinus in

(12:20a).[178] In one instance, one of two subjects is omitted (13:44b).[179]

An interesting reading in 15:37–38 does not mention the number of people Jesus fed (which was four thousand, according to other MSS in Matt 15:38), and it states that everyone was filled *apart from women and children*. It seems that the *prima manus* caught the omission and corrected it himself.[180]

5.3. Conclusion

5.3.1. SCRIBAL HABITS IN GENERAL

Codex Bezae is often characterized as a free text, abounding with additions and harmonizations due to the nature of the Western text type to which it belongs.[181] Many singular readings in D in Mat-

---

Rev 20:4 and replaced with those who have been in war (πεπολεμημενων). About the substitution in Codex A, Hernández states, "the exchange [πεπλεκισμενων > πεπολεμημενων] offers a more euphemistic term to replace the graphic depiction of beheaded Christians standing before God's throne!" (*Scribal Habits*, 118 n. 104). The phrase επι πινακι is graphic, i.e. a "hideous touch" state Davies and Allison, (*Matthew*, 2:473), and perhaps if it were considered *too* graphic it was omitted, but this is unlikely since the same notion in v. 11 is subsequently not omitted in Bezae.

[178] In 12:20a, the direct object, *bruised reed* (καλαμον συντετριμμενον), of the verb καταγνυμι is omitted in D* d*, and the following *smoldering wick* (λινον τυφομενον) takes its place as the direct object. The Latin portion of Bezae contains the same omission of the direct object, *harundinem quassatam* (with no evidence of parablepsis). The verses are a portion of the Isa 42:1–4 quotation.

[179] The reading in Bezae does not contain the noun ανθρωπος, but does read τις (along with MS 892, which reads both τις and ανθρωπος), which can stand in place of the omission as the subject. The omission in D no longer echoes the previous uses of ανθρωπος in 13:25 or v. 31 (Gundry, *Matthew*, 276, 277). Origen does not read either τις or ανθρωπος here, but has ο ευρων as the subject.

[180] In one of the few explanations of variant readings made by Swanson in his work, he states that a line of text in D was erased and the text from και το in v. 37 through ανδρες in v. 38 was converted into two lines, which probably comprised three lines of the exemplar (Swanson, *Matthew*, 152; Parker, *Codex Bezae*, 90). Indeed, it appears that line 4 (folio 52v) was made into lines 4 and 5, completed in smaller than normal lettering. The scribe must have skipped the text from και το through ανδρες and probably continued with χωρις and the following before noticing.

[181] On harmonizations, not limiting his study to singular readings, Parker

thew are not remarkable and it seems that the singular readings are in fact distinctly *non*-Western. Some changes are minute, the difference of one or two letters, and others are influenced from previous text, which are not exactly harmonizations. The dearth of singular harmonizations in D in Matthew, however, suggests that the scribe himself was not involved in creating the characteristic Western harmonizations in his copy; rather, he copied them from his exemplar.

At this point, it seems that any possible deliberate "editing" of the text resulted in minute changes. Most changes do not suggest a clear desire of the scribe to adjust for awkwardness, as Holmes argues.[182] Rather, many changes occur due to contextual influence, with and without parablepsis (cf. §5.2.7; 5.2.12), as well as a different spelling standard (cf. §5.2.1). In fact, none of our other MSS witness so many consonantal exchanges. The singular readings that seem to have actually improved the text are few and could possibly be unintentional, but on the other hand, the majority of singulars do not consist of nonsensical readings.

---

notes that the D text is harmonized with the context and parallel passages in all the gospels (*Codex Bezae*, 248, 256), but states that there are more harmonizations in the Latin column than the Greek (ibid., 203).

Heinrich Vogels argues that D was influenced by Tatian's Diatessaron, stating, "Der Evangelientext des Codex Cantabrigiensis ist durch eine Evangelienharmonie—ein Diatessaron—stark beeinfluß: das ist die These dieser Arbeit" (Heinrich Joseph Vogels, "Die Harmonistik im Evangelientext des Codex Cantabrigiensis: Ein Beitrag zur Neutestamentlichen Textkritik," TUGAL 6 no. 3, ed. Adolf Harnack and Carl Schmidt [Leipzig: J. C. Hinrichs'sche Buchhandlung, 1913] 2; 1, 7). Vogels lists 220 points of variation that are harmonizations in Matthew (he has determined that D contains 1,278 harmonizations in all four gospels, but that number includes non-singular variants as well—see Parker, *Codex Bezae*, 189), but Vogels' criteria for what qualifies as a harmonization embraces a multitude of readings which are by no means singular and are often no more significant than an omission of the most common conjunctions, e.g., οτι in 27:47, or a substitution of a και for a δε in 12:26 and 27 (cf. Vogels, "Die Harmonistik," 63–71).

[182] Concerning deliberate editing by the scribe of D, Holmes states, "A number of Bezan variants entail changes, usually in the word order or syntactical structure, the effect of which is to produce a text that reads more smoothly than it previously did. That is, the original contains some feature or aspect felt to be awkward which has been altered in the Bezan text" ("Editorial Activity," 189).

5.3.2. Longer and Shorter Readings

Considering that D accumulates the most singular readings of our MSS, it is counterintuitive to find that these variants do not produce the greatest number of readings that affect the length of the text. Of the 252 singular readings in D, 21.42%, involve creating a longer or shorter text (cf. appendix seventeen). Overall, Codex D produces a shorter text and witnesses more omissions than additions. There are 31 instances of *omission* and 23 instances of addition, and 54 words *omitted* and 26 words added. There are almost two words omitted for every instance of omission, but approximately one word added for every instance of addition, signaling again another way in which the scribe has a greater tendency to omit.

Interestingly, there are two types of readings in Bezae in Matthew that witness more additions (both in number of words and in frequency) than omissions: changes involving parablepsis (cf. §5.2.7) and influence of context (cf. §5.2.12). The most common omission is of definite articles, and the most common addition is likewise of definite articles (cf. §5.2.10).

In the vast majority of instances, the longer/shorter readings consist of merely one word (85.18%), thus providing some substantial clarification about the extent of alteration the scribe had a tendency to create. This clarification is especially telling given the characteristically "wild" nature of the Western text to which Bezae belongs which is hardly, if at all, evident in the longer/shorter readings.

CHAPTER 6
CODEX WASHINGTONIANUS

6.1. The Scribe and Extent of Matthew in Washingtonianus

There are at least eight hands discernible in Codex Washingtonianus.[1] The *prima manus* is responsible for transcribing the entirety of the gospels in W except for one quire of John.[2] Matthew contains 1,071 verses in Codex with no lacunae.[3]

6.2. The Singular Readings in Washingtonianus in Matthew

There are 112 singular readings, which amounts to one singular for every 9.56 verses.[4] Many of these readings are influenced from the context and some are synonymic substitutions. The singular readings display consistent sensical readings. Also, this is the only one of our MSS that shows a preference for Atticisms over changes to Koineisms. Washingtonianus witnesses more omissions, both in frequency

---

[1] Sanders, *New Testament Manuscripts*, 38.

[2] The first quire of John, which is the first 16 pages of the gospel, begins with 1:1 and goes up to κραβαττον σου και περιπατει in 5:12. This quire was probably produced in the eighth century, independently of the rest of the MS. The three hands found here are not found elsewhere in the codex. Cf. Dennis Haugh, "Was Codex Washingtonianus a Copy or a New Text?" in *The Freer Biblical Manuscripts: Fresh Studies of an American Treasure Trove*, ed. Larry Hurtado, TCSt 6 (Atlanta: SBL Press, 2006), 167; Ulrich Schmid, "Reassessing the Paleography and Codicology of the Freer Gospel Manuscript," in *Freer Biblical Manuscripts*, 231; James R. Royse, "The Corrections in the Freer Gospels Codex," in *Freer Biblical Manuscripts*, 186; and Sanders, *New Testament Manuscripts*, 38.

[3] There are, however, three missing leaves outside of Matthew. Two of the missing leaves contain John 14:25 from ο δε παρακλητος to 16:7 including ελευσεται προς υμας. One missing leaf contains Mark 15:13 from οι δε παλιν to 15:38 including εσχισθη εις δυο. Cf. Sanders, *New Testament Manuscripts*, 27, and *Facsimile of the Washington Manuscript of the Four Gospels in the Freer Collection* (Ann Arbor: University of Michigan, 1912), vii.

[4] See APPENDIX 6. Codex W is not reported to have any singular readings in the selection of test passages in Aland *et al.*, *Text und Textwert*, which is accurate.

and number of words omitted, than additions. With the exception of haplography, omissions stem from stylistic and editorial changes.

Additions in Washingtonianus likewise result from stylistic and editorial changes, but unlike the rest of our MSS, no additions have evidence of parablepsis.

6.2.1. Orthography

6.2.1.1. Itacisms

The most common itacistic changes are ι > ει (43) and ε > αι (26), then their reverse ει > ι (19)[5] and αι > ε (17). There is one change οι > υ.[6]

6.2.1.2. Other Vocalic Changes

Vowel changes, other than itacisms, are among the most common type of change found in the singular readings in W in Matthew, accounting for 11.6% of the singular readings. There are nine types of (non-itacistic) vocalic changes, most only occur once. There is α > η (25:34),[7] α > ι (26:67), αι > α (3:5^2; 12:50; 24:18),[8] ει > η (16:27), ο > α (3:6;[9] 27:44), ο > ε (8:16); ο > ω (20:29), ου > η (27:55),[10] and ου >

---

[5] In 12:40, the word τρεις occurs four times and Codex W is the only MS that consistently contains the change ει > ι. The change is found in ℵ only in the first three occurrences (the fourth occurrence is written as a numerical sign: γ̄) and is found in N (022) only in the first occurrence. Therefore, only 12:40^4 is counted as a singular reading for W.

[6] See Appendix 16.

[7] The change, seemingly imperative to subjunctive, is a change α > η perhaps caused by the adjacent etas (so Royse, "Corrections in the Freer Gospels Codex," 195–96).

[8] The only singular instances of αι > α changes are with the conjunction και, which may result from faulty diphthong pronunciation (Sanders also refers to the same change in Matt 12:50, but perhaps that should be labeled as *videtur*), although in two instances, the letter following the alpha begins with a vertical stroke, thus the vertical stroke of the iota could have been unintentionally subsumed in the letter (for example, καιπασα becomes καπασα in 3:5^2) (Sanders, *New Testament Manuscripts*, 25).

[9] The change in 3:6, ο > α, "looks like a cursive gloss" (ibid., 46).

ω (21:41b; 24:9).

6.2.1.3. CONSONANT ORTHOGRAPHY

The substitution of consonants is the most frequent type of change found in the singular readings in W in Matthew, apparent in 16.07% of the singular readings. Several changes in W resemble spellings in the Roman and Byzantine papyri in Gignac's study, such as a change with liquids λ > ρ (26:41),[11] omission of nu or nasal (5:22[2];[12] 12:12;[13] 27:41;[14] 27:58), and various omissions of sigma (3:12;[15] 5:44;[16] 21:41a; 23:14; 25:46).[17] Perhaps the omitted sigma, as seen in 21:41a and 23:14, is also a reoccurring phenomenon of the historical context of the scribe because it is also found in the orthography in Codex D in Matthew (cf. 5:41; 9:2; 12:19 in D). There is one singular instance of letter doubling to σσ (9:20),[18] and one instance of simplification ρρ > ρ (26:65). There are two instances of epsilon omission (27:4;[19] 27:47).[20]

---

[10] The change ου > η in διακονουσαι may be a "syntactical confusion of the correct form of διακονεω" (so Royse); although Gignac notes such a change in one instance stating that is not related to syntactical form (Royse, "Corrections in the Freer Gospels Codex," 204; Gignac, *Grammar*, 1:217).

[11] The change could have been influenced by ερχεται in 26:40 (so Royse); but Gignac found similar liquid interchanges in the MSS in his study (Royse, "Corrections in the Freer Gospels Codex," 189; Gignac, *Grammar*, 1:102–4).

[12] Cf. ibid., 1:112.

[13] Omission of nu before a stop. Cf. ibid., 1:111–12.

[14] Sanders believes that if φαρισαιω was the last word of the line in the exemplar of W, then there was a bar over it indicating a contraction of nu; if there was something written above the bar, then the bar became "obscured" and therefore the scribe of W would have been unaware of the nu, hence its omission (Sanders, *New Testament Manuscripts*, 47). The word in W here is not the final word of a line.

[15] Omission of sigma before a labial. Cf. Gignac, *Grammar*, 1:130.

[16] The sibilant omission occurs before a word beginning with a vowel. Cf. ibid., 1:125.

[17] The omission of the final sigma is before a word beginning with a consonant. Cf. ibid., 1:124.

[18] Gignac states that in the Roman and Byzantine papyri he analyzes, "Nouns tend to be spelled with –σσ– unless specifically Attic or late" (ibid., 1:148).

[19] The false elision may be a slip due to the adjacent epsilons. Cf. ibid., 1:318.

In addition, there is a lingual change (18:27), labial change (18:34), nasal change (14:32), and an omission of a delta (14:3).

6.2.2. OTHER SPELLINGS

The form of ανοιγω in 20:33 in W is not found elsewhere in the NT.[21] There is one instance of metathesis (2:16).[22] There are some nonsense spellings (26:72), two of which add an iota before an omicron (13:46; 20:1). There is an instance of an omission of a fricative intervocalic gamma (1:9).[23] Verbal endings are conflated in one instance (23:37).[24]

6.2.3. NOT CONSTRUED IN CONTEXT

A change from singular to plural (26:18)[25] and one change *vice versa* (21:32b)[26] are a difference of one letter and are not construed in context. Rarely, verbal changes are not entirely construed (17:24;[27] 21:30).[28]

---

[20] This may be an instance of aphaeresis of the epsilon. Cf. ibid., 1:319.

[21] The text of W reads ανεωχθωσιν in 20:33, which is also found in Joannes Damascenus, *Theol. et Scr. Eccl. Sacra Parallela* (PG 96:56, ln. 12). The augmentation of ανοιγω "has become very involved" (see ἀν-οίγειν in BDF, §101).

[22] The nonsensical substitution of *wise men* for *wedding* may result from confusion in letters: μαγ > γαμ.

[23] Of the many instances of the verb εγεννησεν in the genealogy of Matthew, this is the only instance in W where it is missing the gamma (Gignac, *Grammar*, 1:68ff; Royse, "Corrections in the Freer Gospels Codex," 202).

[24] In 23:37, the scribe may have attempted to write an aorist, influenced from 21:35 ελιθοβολησαν (cf. ibid., 195), but there is no augment in W in 23:37 and the previous use in 21:35 is quite removed from 23:37, both textually and contextually. The word in W here conflates endings, combing –ησαν with –ουσα, creating λιθοβολησουσα.

[25] Though the article for πασχα is neuter plural here in W, it is not found elsewhere in Matthew with a plural article (e.g. 26:2, 17, 19). The word πασχα is never plural in the TLG. Sanders notes that the number change in v. 18 is a mistake (*New Testament Manuscripts*, 24).

[26] Perhaps the singular subject of the previous clause (Ιωαννης) influenced the change from 2pl to 3s. The result is nonsense in context.

[27] The phrase in 17:24 should retain the verb τελει for grammatical construal, but it is omitted in W. Perhaps the reading in W is an incomplete spelling of the verb τελει (instead τε) or a substitution of negation words, ου for ουτε with an

6.2.4. PARABLEPSIS

6.2.4.1. HAPLOGRAPHY

Some omissions have evidence of parablepsis that could have facilitated a leap of text. These account for 7.14% of the singular readings. In some instances, parablepsis results from two letters (2:17;[29] 7:17;[30] 27:46)[31] three letters (8:28;[32] 18:4;[33] 19:1;[34] 26:1),[35] or eleven

---

omission of the verb.

[28] The text of W* reads an indicative verb instead of a participle. The ο δε + indicative is construed, but would need και επιεν following. Royse states that the scribe caught part of the mistake and changed the eta of απεκριθη to ει *in scribendo*, but did not correct the augment ("Corrections in the Freer Gospels Codex," 189).

[29] The omission of του προφητου is a leap from ου to ου (ibid., 202).

[30] The scribe leaps from ον to ον, thus omitting αγαθον (ibid.). The adjective should be included for the doublet to match noun and adjective: δενδρον αγαθον ... σαπρον δενδρον.

[31] In place of λιμα (λεμα in NA²⁸), the text of W reads μα. The words before μα in W are ηλι ηλι, which create parablepsis. Thus, ηλι ηλι λιμα σαβαχθανει becomes ηλι ηλιμα σαβαχθανει in W.

[32] A portion of the adjunct has been omitted in W (a leap from περαν to χωραν), perhaps by homoeoteleuton. In Matthew, the region in which the story takes place is somewhat disputed in MSS, evident by the number of textual variants for Γαδαρηνων (there are similar variants in the parallels, Mark 5:1 and Luke 8:26). See Metzger, *Textual Commentary*, 18–19. The omission in W of εις την χωραν, does not, however, resolve any matter concerning the location of the story (and is not omitted in the textual parallels in W).

[33] Sanders posits that the scribe of W has written του ουρα (the beginnings of του ουρανου) instead of εν τη βασιλεια, but Royse argues for τουτου here because the scribe "leapt back from μειζων to παιδιον, which would likely have stood (as in W) more or less directly above in the exemplar" (Sanders, *New Testament Manuscripts*, 156; Royse, "Corrections in the Freer Gospels Codex," 188–89). Though Royse's argument for the reading of W* is convincing, his explanation for the *cause* of the leap is not accurate if the exemplar resembles W because in W the final nu of μειζων is below the initial pi of παιδιον. If this were a straightforward instance of homoeoteleuton, perhaps the final nu of μειζων should stand below the final nu of παιδιον, not six letters prior as it is. Sanders' theory that the exemplar of W contained ca. twenty letters per line is perhaps a more plausible explanation of the cause of the leap (i.e. that in the exemplar the leap would comprise a full line) rather than Royse's theory which involves a six-letter discrepancy. The leap from μειζων

letters (16:2b–3).³⁶ Five of these readings result in a loss of text (2:17; 7:17; 8:28; 16:2b–3; 18:4), one is a word substitution (19:1), and the remaining two readings contain truncated words (26:1; 27:46). These singular readings indicate, then, that error due to parablepsis never results in a gain of words in W in Matthew.

Another interesting possibility that these readings could bring to light is the line length of the exemplar of W. Sanders proposes that the exemplar of Washingtonianus had either about twenty or forty letters per line.³⁷ Two instances of leaps in Matthew could support his claim: the leap of twenty letters (18:4) and the leap that consists of thirty-nine letters (16:2b–3). Of course this is indirect evidence and, apart from these instances, there does not seem to be further evidence among any of the singular readings that could indicate an exemplar of ca. twenty or forty letters per line.

6.2.5. TRANSPOSITIONS

Transpositions account for 4.46% of the singular readings in Matthew in W. There is one instance where a verb is moved forward in

---

to παιδιον is of twenty-two letters, which would involve approximately a two-letter discrepancy, and in that case, could support the theory that the exemplar of W had ca. twenty letters per line.

³⁴ Royse states that the leap from της to της "probably stood more or less directly above in the exemplar (as in W)" (ibid., 189). If the exemplar is ca. twenty letters per line, Royse's explanation is somewhat off because the leap is of twenty-nine letters. It is possible, however, the leap is *still* a result of parablepsis because the words της and της do stand almost directly on top of each other in the MS itself, and therefore the error in copying Γαλιλαιας a second time could be due to parablepsis in W itself (rather than in the exemplar).

³⁵ The surrounding occurrences of –ους perhaps influenced the scribe to write τους in place of τουτους.

³⁶ Both Sanders and Legg state that the omission in W in 16:3 is due to homoeoteleuton (a leap from πυρραζει γαρ to the same) (Sanders, *New Testament Manuscripts*, 26).

³⁷ Cf. Sanders, *New Testament Manuscripts*, 27; *Facsimile of the Washington Manuscript*, vi; also Jack Finegan, *Encountering New Testament Manuscripts: A Working Introduction to Textual Criticism* (London: SPCK, 1975), 145.

the sentence (19:8),[38] and other similar instances (9:6;[39] 23:8).[40] In one transposition, the subject is placed further back in the sentence and the complement is moved forward (12:27).[41]

Hurtado notes that the scribe of W in Mark prefers to transpose possessive pronouns *before* nouns rather than *after* nouns.[42] In the few instances of transpositions involving a genitive pronoun (12:27; 19:8; 23:8), only once (27:39)[43] does a singular reading in W in Matthew align with the evidence that Hurtado extracts from W in Mark. There are more singular readings in W in Matthew than Mark where the genitive pronoun in placed *after* the noun rather than *before*.[44]

---

[38] The text of W is transposed here to subject > predicator > adjunct (and, though not a singular reading, does not read the complement υμιν in W*). Royse notes that the transposition in W* may be stylistic, moving the verb forward in the sentence. Royse states that the omission of υμιν—also omitted in 892 Chr—may intend to "generalize the applicability of the law" ("Corrections in the Freer Gospels Codex," 203). (The transposition and omission of υμιν agree with the parallel Mark 10:4–5, but the transposition may be coincidental to Mark since the change does not seem to be significant.)

[39] In W here, the predicator (αφιεναι) is prior to the adjunct (επι της γης), which occurs within the larger complement (εξουσιαν εχει ο υιος του ανθρωπου επι της γης αφιεναι αμαρτιας). Thus, the order in W is subject (ο υιος του ανθρωπου) > predicator > adjunct > complement (αμαρτιας). Sanders notes that the transposition in 9:6 is harmonized with *rell* in the Markan parallel (*New Testament Manuscripts*, 61). Indeed, W in Matt 9:6 resembles the reading of many MSS in Mark 2:10 (though not the transposition in ℵ C D L M 700 *plu* [επι της γης αφιεναι αμαρτιας], or Β Θ 157 [αφιεναι αμαρτιας επι της γης], or in W itself which omits επι της γης and is a singular reading). There are other singular readings in W where the verb is placed forward in the sentence, so perhaps, rather than being a harmonization to a word order that may be insignificant, the transposition may be coincidental because of a desire to move αφιεναι forward in the sentence.

[40] The transposition within the complement (υμων ο καθηγητης) results in the nominative being placed next to the verb it modifies (εστιν).

[41] In W here, there is a transposition of word order to adjunct > complement > predicator > subject > complement.

[42] Hurtado, *Text-Critical Methodology*, 80.

[43] The word order in W has been modified within the complement.

[44] The non-singular reading in 24:20 in W in Matthew, however, agrees with Hurtado's findings.

6.2.6. INFLUENCE FROM CONTEXT

Readings that seem to be influenced by context are found in 9.82% of the singular readings in W in Matthew, which are the most frequent type of readings apart from orthographic changes. Some modifications could be influenced from preceding text (7:8;[45] 10:5;[46] 18:15;[47] 19:9a;[48] 20:12;[49] 20:15;[50] 21:23;[51] 24:11).[52] Some changes may

---

[45] The scribe could have been influenced by the preceding ο αιτων λαμβανει to change ζητων to αιτων. The verbs in context, αιτεω, ζητεω, and κρουω, "have a religious dimension in Jewish-Christian usage: one asks or seeks God, one knocks on the 'gate of mercy'" (Luz, *Matthew*, 1:421). The substitution in W* weakens the effectiveness of the verbal triumvirate, unless for some reason *asking* should be emphasized over *seeking*.

[46] The text in W reads a compound verb here. Perhaps the –εκα ending of the previous word, δωδεκα, influenced an addition of a similar sound, εκ–, or εξ–, to απεστιλεν.

[47] The text of W reads a 2nd aorist imperative ending here rather than the 1st aorist imperative ending supported by *rell*. Perhaps the scribe was influenced by the preceding word υπαγε.

[48] The change to plural agrees with the number of the preceding subject υμιν, rather than the 3s generic subject introduced with ος αν. Cf. Wallace, *Greek Grammar*, 478.

[49] The change to singular is nonsense, possibly influenced by the nu of the preceding word, which is ημιν in W (so Royse, "Corrections in the Freer Gospels Codex," 195).

[50] The relative pronoun is changed to a comparative particle in W, perhaps influenced by the ως in the preceding verse: ως και σοι. In BDAG, there is an example for the comparative use of ως, similar to ως in W here: "γενηθήτω σοι ὡς θέλεις *let it be done (=it will be done) for you as you wish*" (s.v. ὡς 1.b.β).

[51] The verb in W here is 3s, as opposed to 3pl in *rell*. The verb is surrounded by 3s phrases, which could have, perhaps, influenced the 3s change in προσηλθον. Prior to προσηλθεν in W is a 3s dative construction (which is a genitive absolute is some MSS), ελθοντι αυτω, and following προσηλθεν is W is another 3s dative construction, αυτω διδασκοντι. The verb in W, προσηλθεν, creates nonsense in context.

[52] The text of W reads υμας instead of πολλους. In the pericopes surrounding the variant here, The False Christs (24:3–5), Wars, Rumors of War, Famine, and Earthquake (24:6–8), and Tribulation, Hate, Death, and Betrayal (24:9–13), πολυς is used in six instances as a pronoun and υμεις is used in three instances. A form of the verb πλαναω is used in three instances, twice with πολυς and once with υμεις (in the majority of MSS, Matt 24:4 contains υμας πλανηση; 24:5 contains πολλοι and

be due to an influence from subsequent text (13:2;[53] 24:49),[54] or be merely repetition of a previous word with possible temporal implications (13:20)[55] (cf. 24:32b and 25:19 below).

Hurtado identifies fourteen variants where the scribe of W in Mark harmonizes to other gospels.[56] Although the harmonizations have support with other MSS, Hurtado maintains they can in fact be attributed to the scribe of W because "these kinds of harmonizations mean little for textual relationships without overall agreement in a majority of all readings."[57] These relatively "small variants," states Hurtado, were harmonized to "the more popular Gospels" in order to "improve or clarify the Markan text."[58] Thus, the popularity of Matthew could account for the almost non-existent harmonizations here to other gospels; at best, the only harmonization would be Matt 6:30 (cf. §6.2.9).

πολλους πλανησουσιν; 24:9 contains υμας and υμας; 24:10 contains πολλοι; 24:11 contains πολλοι and πλανησουσιν πολλους; and 24:12 contains πολλων). The scribe may have recalled υμας πλανηση of v. 4, and due to the mixture and interchangeability of πολυς and υμεις throughout the surrounding pericopes, the scribe committed the unintentional alteration of πλανησουσιν πολλους > πλανησουσιν υμας in v. 11.

[53] The text of W reads a singular, *a large crowd*, in place of a plural, *many crowds*. This is a possible pre-harmonization to the singular ο οχλος in the final clause of the verse.

[54] The verb in W here is in the future tense rather than present. The text of W is still grammatically construed, retaining a substantival participle, but the verbal change creates a difficult reading with the future tense. There is a future indicative verb immediately following (24:51, ηξει), which, perhaps, influenced a preemptive unintentional change in των μεθυοντων to the same tense.

[55] The addition of και in W in 13:20 may be an unintentional repetition of the previous και, as it is in the textual vicinity. If 24:32b and 25:19 are an indication of the scribe's concern about temporality, and if the και is an intentional addition, then the reading here may also shows such a concern. The addition in W, then, could emphasize that it is *both* immediately *and* with joy that one should receive the word of the kingdom (Matt 13:19, τον λογον της βασιλειας).

[56] Hurtado, *Text-Critical Methodology*, 69–71.

[57] Ibid., 71.

[58] Ibid.

6.2.7. ATTIC AND HEBRAIC INFLUENCE

There is only one instance where a singular reading involves (an elimination of) a grammatical Hebraicism in W (2:6).[59] More common though, are the instances where singular readings seem to display the Attic dialect. Some singular readings create classicisms (12:20;[60] 13:38;[61] 26:14),[62] and if not a classicism, a good grammatical construction is created (12:4).[63] There is a verbal change, future indica-

---

[59] The use of γη with Ιουδα is a Hebraicism (as in *rell*), which would otherwise be a definite article. Cf. BDF, §261.4. The text of W reads a locative dative article in place of γη.

[60] Zerwick states that the ου μη construction "is never used by the Evangelists (or by Luke in Acts) in their own narrative but only in quoting the spoken word" (*Biblical Greek*, §444). The addition of μη following ου in W in 12:20 not only occurs in a LXX quote (Isa 42:1–4) but also with a future indicative (κατεαξει) which creates a classicism. Cf. BDF, §365.

[61] The text of W has a singular verb, as opposed to a plural, with a neuter plural subject (Royse, "Corrections in the Freer Gospels Codex," 194), which is an Attic feature (BDF, §133).

[62] Hagner points out that "Matthew will not have the reader miss the irony that it was εις των δωδεκα, 'one of the twelve,' which the evangelist moves to the beginning of his sentence, who actually betrayed Jesus" (*Matthew*, 2:761). In general, the form δεκαδυο (W) is found instead of δωδεκα in Ptolemaic papyri and may be more of a classical spelling than Koine (cf. Moulton-Milligan, s.v. δεκαδυο; BDF, §63.2). Cf. 19:28a in Codex D. The words, *one of the twelve*, here refer to Judas Iscariot, who is "new actor on stage" (Luz, *Matthew*, 3:345). Interestingly, Head notices in a different MS, Sinaiticus, that in Mark the number twelve is written in *plene* as opposed to the typical abbreviation when it is associated with Judas, but does not make much of it, saying, "I could be more persuaded that there was something in this view if there were more consistency in other regards" (Head, "The Gospel of Mark in Codex Sinaiticus," §27). There are, however, no other singular readings in W in Matthew that could suggest a perceived scribal stigma with Judas.

[63] In Matthew here, the πως, which is found in all MSS except W, is indirect and (a weakened) interrogative (Zerwick, *Grammatical Analysis*, 35). When the conjunction ως (found in W in place of πως) is used temporally, it "is most frequently followed by the aorist indicative," which is the construction found in W in Matt 12:4 (and the Lukan parallel, Luke 6:4): ως + εισηλθεν (Robert W. Funk, *A Beginning-Intermediate Grammar of Hellenistic Greek*, Sources for Biblical Study 2 [Missoula, MT: Scholars Press, 1973], §866.1). (In W in the Markan parallel, Mark 2:26, πως is employed and a participle, εισελθων, follows instead of an indicative.) The

tive > aorist subjunctive (26:15),[64] which resembles classical usage. The spelling of γινωσκω with an additional gamma, γιγνωσκω (11:27[1], 27[2]; 16:3a; 24:15; 24:32a) is influenced from the Attic,[65] but it is a spelling that resurges during the Byzantine period.[66]

The instances of α > ο (10:40, 11:17a; 14:35; 28:11) are a change from 1st aorist forms to 2nd aorist forms.[67] If preference for the 2nd aorist is an Attic feature, and if the possible Atticisms (mentioned in this section) are in fact Attic, then it is possible that Atticization may be one of the most frequent types of alteration found in the singular readings in W in Matthew, almost eclipsing the amount of singulars that witness consonantal orthography.

While Sanders notes a "decided tendency toward Attic or other old forms" in Washingtonianus,[68] Hurtado contends, "Nearly all the scribal changes in Codex W seem prompted by a similar kind of concern to produce a copy of Mark in a style of Greek familiar to the reader of that day."[69] A critical question, then, is whether or not these Attic and old forms were familiar in the scribe's context. The findings of Sanders and Hurtado could both hold in W in Matthew, in some instances, where the singular orthography in W displays older forms that have resurged at a later date. Though there are several instances where an Attic construction is created, none of the singular readings seem to make the text more Koine than it already is, if that were possible. This

---

text of W in Matt 12:4 then reads a common temporal construction instead of an uncommon one. Cf. BDF, §396.

[64] The text of W here reads an aorist subjunctive (παραδω) and *rell* reads a future indicative (παραδωσω). The text of W also reads an aorist subjunctive in the gospel parallels: Mark 14:10 (παραδοι is a variant spelling of a second aorist subjunctive) and Luke 22:4 (Zerwick, *Grammatical Analysis*, 154). Sanders states that the W and *d* read the same here in Matthew (*New Testament Manuscripts*, 60), but *trado* in *d* is present indicative. The change may be a classicism. Cf. BDF, §363.

[65] Sanders, *New Testament Manuscripts*, 23.

[66] Gignac states, "the older orthography γιγν– becomes more common in the Byzantine period" (*Grammar*, 1:176).

[67] Sanders, *New Testament Manuscripts*, 23.

[68] Ibid., 26.

[69] Hurtado, *Text-Critical Methodology*, 81.

is not true for the orthography, where readings are aligned with *both* Koine and Attic dialects. This interesting mixture of dialects could benefit from further probing in W in the NT.

6.2.8. Synonym Substitutions

There is an instance where a word is substituted with a synonym that is spelled very similarly (14:36).[70] There are some other conjunction/particle substitutions (16:9).[71] There is one preposition substitution, απεναντι > επι (27:61).[72] Some substitutions are with synonyms and may be stylistic in nature (9:15;[73] 21:18),[74] two of which (24:32b;[75] 25:19)[76] concern temporality. The inferential conjunction

---

[70] In 14:36, the change σ > λ in διεσωθησαν > διελωθησαν may result from a stem change to διαλωφαω, a synonym, rather than an orthographic lingual change.

[71] The reading in W, ουτε, is similar to *rell*, ουδε, possibly resulting from oral confusion.

[72] The alteration to επι (*near*) in W may place Mary Magdalene and the other Mary closer to the tomb than the reading of *rell*, απεναντι (*opposite of the tomb*). Perhaps a close physical proximity to the tomb intends to give their witness even more authority.

[73] The itacistic reading in W (αφαιρεθη > αφερεθη) is from the "very common" verb αφαιρεω (Moulton-Milligan, s.v. ἀφαιρέω), which is a contextual synonym of the verb in *rell*, απαιρω.

[74] The text of W reads a form of υπαγω instead of επαναγω or παραγω, which are synonyms in context.

[75] Both εγγυς (*rell*) and ευθυς (W) can be used to indicate temporal proximity (BDAG, s.v. ἐγγύς 2.a; s.v. εὐθύς 1). The word εγγυς is not uncommonly used in an eschatological sense, cf. Phil 4:5; Rev 1:3; 22:10 (Davies and Allison, *Matthew*, 3:366), so it may not be for theological reasons that the text of W reads ευθυς instead since both seem to be able to be used interchangeably in an eschatological context.

[76] In the pericope here, Matthew is referring to the parousia (so C.G. Montefiore, *The Synoptic Gospels, Edited with an Introduction and Commentary* [London: Macmillan, 1909], 2:748; Davies and Allison, *Matthew*, 3:407; Hagner, *Matthew*, 2:735). France suggests that the "'imminent' *parousia* will not be *immediate*" (*Matthew*, 954). Perhaps concerned with the temporality of the passage, the text of W then connotes an indefinite amount of time, τινα (BDAG, s.v. τὶς 1.b.γ), instead of a long time, πολυν (BDAG, s.v. πολύς 2.a.α.א).

ουν is used as a replacement (14:25;[77] 26:19).[78]

6.2.9. DOUBLETS/TRIPLET

Some readings seem to have a common thread woven through them, namely the creation of doublets (21:26;[79] 22:7)[80] or a triplet (27:51).[81] There may be one remote gospel harmonization, but perhaps is more clearly aligned with how other doublets are created (6:30).[82]

6.2.10. TEXTUAL EMPHASIS

Some singular readings emphasize the illustrative quality of the

---

[77] In W here, ουν is found in place of δε (cf. John 6:19). If the replacement of δε with ουν is intentional, perhaps it is a stylistic alteration.

[78] The word order in W is modified to accommodate the replacement of και with an inferential ουν. BDAG, s.v. οὖν.

[79] The verse in Matthew here is part of a deliberation between the chief priests and elders. They are considering how to respond to Jesus' question of John's baptism: did it come from *heaven* (ουρανου) or from *man* (ανθρωπων)? The text of W contains a singular reading here, recording ανθρωπου instead of ανθρωπων. The grammatical change from plural to singular is insignificant in context as the meaning in context stays the same. The change could have been influenced by the preceding singular ουρανου.

[80] The text of W (though it is difficult to read here) repeats the verb υβριζω from the preceding verse, which results in a doublet.

[81] Instead of the earth being *shaken* (εσεισθη), the text of W reads that the earth was *split* (εσχισθη). With this in W in 27:51, the verb σχιζω is read in three instances (as opposed to two instances in most MSS): the shrine was split, the earth was split, and the rocks were split. The verb in W here, εσχισθη, is repeated from earlier in the verse.

[82] In W in 6:30, the noun ο αγρους is read twice. It is found in all MSS before σημερον and only in W is it found again after σημερον. The first occurrence of the word in the verse (του αγρου) could have simply influenced the scribe to repeat it in another instance (εν αγρω). On the other hand, Sanders notes that the singular addition in W here is harmonistic, suggesting with Luke 12:18 (*New Testament Manuscripts*, 61). But Luke 12:28 is a closer parallel, as it is aligned verbatim: ει δε τον χορτον εν σημερον εν αγρω οντα in M U W Ψ f^{13} 33 1071; and ($\mathfrak{P}^{75}$) ℵ B L NA[28] read ει δε εν αγρω τον χορτον οντα σημερον. The result of the addition in W is a doublet: εν αγρω doubles εις κλιβανον, which is then, "The grass of the field being *in the field* today and tomorrow being thrown *into an oven*" (emphasis added).

text (14:30;[83] 24:39).[84]

6.2.11. Various Editing

Some of the singular readings seem stylistic, though the intent of them is not always entirely clear. One addition fits naturally in place, but is not necessary (17:25).[85] There is an instance where omit-

---

[83] The context of 14:30 is the dramatic story of Peter walking on water, which encourages both sympathy and empathy on the part of the reader. Sympathy occurs when Jesus calms their fears, invites Peter to walk on the water, and when he reaches out his hand when Peter cries for help. Empathy is evoked by several factors: Peter dares to get out of the boat, there is a natural fear of wind, the description of what Peter saw and felt, Peter cried, "Lord save me", and the episode ends with the disciples worshiping Jesus as the Son of God (Timothy Wiarda, *Peter in the Gospels: Pattern, Personality and Relationship*, WUNT2, 127, ed. Martin Hengel and Otfried Hofius [Tübingen: Mohr Siebeck, 2000], 93–94). The text of ℵ B* *et al.* states that Peter saw *the wind* (ανεμον) and *was afraid* (εφοβηθη). The text of *rell* states that Peter saw *the strong wind* (ανεμον ισχυρον) and *was afraid* (εφοβηθη), which contains an additional word that "heighten[s] the dramatic effect" (Metzger, *Textual Commentary*, 30). The text of W states that Peter saw *the strong wind* (ανεμον ισχυρον) and *was exceedingly afraid* (σφοδρα εφοβηθη) *to continue on* (ελθειν), which contains two more words than *rell*.

[84] The αν in W is probably meant to be compounded with the verb ηλθεν rather than used as a separate particle following εως. The combination εως (conjunction) + αν (particle) never occurs in the NT with an indicative (normally with a subjunctive). Cf. Turner, *Syntax*, 110, 111. When attached to the verb ηλθεν, creating ανηλθεν in W, the verb is better suited to modify ο κατακλυσμος. Instead of "until the flood came," as *rell* is translated, W is translated as "until the flood rose." Though McNeile states that "flood" is commonly found in apocalyptic literature to signify the final destruction of the world (*Matthew*, 357), the change in W does not seem to have a theological motive but rather nuances the imagery of water rising.

[85] Inclusion of ο Ιησους at the beginning of 17:25 is a singular reading in W, which is written as a *nomen sacrum* with an article, ο ις̄. Royse suggests that the addition may have been either a misreading of a duplicated εις for οις, or just a natural addition due to the frequency of the "presence of 'Jesus' as subject" ("Corrections in the Freer Gospels Codex," 195). Royse's latter option is more viable than the former as long as the exemplar contained a similar letter formation as W: the epsilons in W are more angled than lunate (i.e., *E* rather than ε), and the omicrons are typically smaller in size than other letters, which could suggest that the letters epsilon and omicron as not easily confused for each other than if they were both rounded and the same size. The name *Jesus* occurs later in the same sentence as the subject, so the

ted text is understood in context (21:8).[86] One omission may be a mere oversight (17:8).[87] One pronoun is changed from reflexive to personal (16:24).[88] Some verbal changes may be stylistic in nature (11:17b;[89] 12:33¹;[90] 16:3b;[91] 21:32c).[92] There are omissions of conjunctions

---

singular addition in W earlier in the sentence is not necessary.

[86] The term κλαδους (*branches*) may connote "something fitting a religious procession" (Davies and Allison, *Matthew*, 3:123). Cf. Mark 11:8; Luke 19:36; John 12:13. If κλαδους "is a more natural word than Mark's hapax legomenon," i.e., στιβαδας, *straw*, *grass*, or *reeds* (Gundry, *Matthew*, 410), then perhaps the text of W omits the adjunct phrase (απο των δενδρων) because it is a detail that is understood in context.

[87] All Greek MSS for Matt 17:8 contain either the article τον or the intensive pronoun αυτον (or both in C* 33), but the reading of W is singular, witnessing neither variant: Ιησουν μονον (cf. Luke 9:36). If αυτον was in the exemplar, perhaps some emphasis is lost in W; and if τον was in the exemplar, it could have been omitted due to oversight. Hurtado finds only one pronoun in Mark (Mark 6:10) to be omitted because it is unnecessary, otherwise there are no pronoun omissions (Hurtado, *Text-Critical Methodology*, 75).

[88] The text of W reads αυτον in place of εαυτον. Though confusion of αυτος and εαυτος is a common scribal phenomenon (Royse, "Corrections in the Freer Gospels Codex," 194), the verb απαρνεισθαι + a reflexive pronoun "is a new linguistic creation" in the Markan parallel, 8:34 (Luz, *Matthew*, 2:383). Perhaps the grammatical construction, if unfamiliar to the scribe, prompted the mistake.

[89] The text of W reads an infinitive form of κλαιω as opposed to either a 2pl indicative κοπτω in *rell*, an infinitive κοπτω in Θ 1071, or a 2pl indicative κλαιω in 1424ᶜ. The form εκλαυσασθαι read in W is not found in the NT or LXX. The doublet in 11:17, ηυλησαμεν υμιν και ουκ ωρχησασθε with εθρηνησαμεν (υμιν) και ουκ εκοψασθε, is not as strongly tied together in W because the second 2pl indicative verb (εκοψασθε) is replaced with an infinitive from a different root verb (εκλαυσασθαι).

[90] Concerning the composition of 12:33–35 by Matthew, Montefiore states that they "are not here in their original connection" (*Synoptic Gospels*, 2:196). He continues, noting that the 2pl aorist active imperative ποιησατε is "rather obscure" and the original would have been indicative (ibid.). The text of W may read a 3s aorist middle subjunctive in its place, or an Ionic (α > η) (cf. Goodwin, *Greek Grammar*, §147) and itacistic (ε > αι) spelling of the same imperative in *rell*, but it is not entirely clear what the scribe of W intends here.

[91] The text of W reads an aorist infinitive of δοκιμαζω instead of either a present infinitive (as in G M N *et al.*), present indicative (as in L), or an aorist infinitive of γιγνωσκω (as in al^mu it^pl vg). Perhaps the change in W is stylistic here, prefer-

(19:9b;[93] 21:32a),[94] but one singular reading eliminates asyndeton (13:41),[95] which may be similar to what Hurtado noted in Mk 1:9 as a concern to avoid asyndeton.[96] One omission in W is probably due to a desire for elimination of redundancy (6:7).[97]

6.2.12. CONCERNING PHARISEES

One singular reading in W portrays the Pharisees, along with the chief priests and elders, as ones who conspired to arrested Jesus (26:3), which aligns with Hurtado's findings in W in Mark.[98]

---

ring a punctiliar tense instead of durative. Cf. BDF, §338, §335.

[92] The text of W here reads the article τω instead of του with the infinitive, both neuter in gender (there is no governing preposition in W). If the του + infinitive construction was wanting in some aspect (conceivably because a high-Koine construction was not desirable), perhaps the change, τω + infinitive, produced a low-level construction (the τω + infinitive construction is, however, very rare, occurring only in 2 Cor 2:13). Turner states the του + infinitive construction "belongs to a higher level of the Koine" (*Syntax*, 141). Cf. BDF, §400. Another possibility is that the scribe wanted to produce a causal construction (τω + infinitive) instead of a consecutive infinitive construction (Zerwick, *Grammatical Analysis*, 68; *Biblical Greek*, §351). Cf. Turner, *Syntax*, 142. Still, another possible reason for a change is that the verb takes the dative here, which prompted the scribe to create a dative construction. Nevertheless, there is little difference in meaning with the change and could be a simple oversight on the part of the scribe.

[93] The text of W does not read the connective και between the two clauses, μη επι πορνεια and γαμηση αλλην.

[94] The omission of the particle ουκ here is by oversight (so Royse, "Corrections in the Freer Gospels Codex," 203).

[95] The addition of και before αποστελει in W here smoothes over asyndeton.

[96] Hurtado, *Text-Critical Methodology*, 73.

[97] The γαρ is a causal connector (cf. BDF, §452), and therefore the following οτι may have felt unnecessary or redundant to copy. Royse notes that the scribe of W took "οτι as inferential and redundant after γαρ" ("Corrections in the Freer Gospels Codex," 202, 202 n.49).

[98] In 26:3, most MSS read two subjects, *the chief priests and elders*, who conspired to arrest Jesus. Other MSS read an additional, third subject—either, *the scribes* (found in the Majority text, minuscules, and several versions), or, *the Pharisees* (W). The Markan parallel (Mark 14:1) reveals an interesting reading in W, where *Pharisees* is read in place of *scribes* (in the other gospel parallels, Luke 22:2 and John 11:47, W reads the same subjects as most MSS). On the variant in Mark,

6.2.13. CONFLATIONS

One singular reading is a conflation of textual variants (23:25).[99] Two separate conflations manifest actions of Jesus (8:29;[100] 12:15–16).[101]

Hurtado posits that the *prima manus* of W holds the "opinion" that the *Pharisees* were "the real culprits and not the scribes" (*Text-Critical Methodology*, 80). Hurtado mentions that throughout Mark (barring the passion narrative), the Pharisees are a main opposition of Jesus and the singular reading in Mark 14:1 is therefore aligned with the rest of the gospel. Perhaps this belief takes wider hold in Mark, but it seems to be found here in Matthew in W as well. When Jesus is actually arrested, however (Matt 26:47), *the Pharisees* are not found—only *the chief priests and elders* in W.

[99] At the end of 23:25, the word ακρασιας is "replaced" by "various scribes" (Metzger, *Textual Commentary*, 50). All MSS read one noun following the και except for W (*wrong doing, injustice*), aeth (*inequality, greed*), and sy[hl] (*excess and inequality*), which read two nouns. The reading in W contains both of the well-attested variants, ακρασιας and αδικειας, but they are not connected with a conjunction (as is found in sy[hl]). Sanders states that "the scribe [of W] copied his original so accurately that he did not add the connective necessary to make a conflate reading" (*New Testament Manuscripts*, 47). In other instances of conflate readings in W (8:29; 12:15–16), the text contains a connective so that the text reads smoothly.

[100] In 8:29 in text of ℵ* 713* vg[mss] bo[pt], demoniacs ask Jesus if he will *destroy* them (cf. Luke 4:34), but in the text of *rell*, the demoniacs ask Jesus if he will *torture* them. The text of W combines the two variants with a conjunction (*destroy and torture them*), which is the addition of two words (και and either απολεσαι or βασανισαι, depending on his exemplar), perhaps by copying a correction in his exemplar (so Sanders, *New Testament Manuscripts*, 46). The conflation in W results in two signs of Jesus' power: he has the ability to destroy *and* torture the demoniacs, rather than merely one or the other of these abilities. But is the reading in W intended to magnify Jesus' power, or does the scribe merely want to preserve the readings in his exemplar? The other conflations in W, and Sanders' opinion, seem to point to variant preservation rather than a theological motive of the scribe.

[101] The reading of *rell* states that Jesus *healed all of the crowd* (εθεραπευσεν αυτοις παντας) and *warned them* (επετιμησεν αυτοις) not to make him known. The reading of D *et al.* states that Jesus *healed them* (εθεραπευσεν αυτοις), *and all whom he healed* (παντας δε ους εθεραπευσεν), *he rebuked them* (επεπληξεν αυτοις) not to make him known. The text of W contains a conflation of two variants, incorporating the readings of *rell* and D *et al.*, which state, Jesus *healed them* (εθεραπευσεν αυτοις), *and all whom he healed* (παντας δε ους εθεραπευσεν), *he rebuked them* (επεπληξεν αυτοις) and *warned them* (επετιμησεν αυτοις) not to make him known. The result of the conflation in W is

6.3. Conclusion

6.3.1. SCRIBAL HABITS IN GENERAL

The number of singular readings that seem to make sense in context, e.g. asyndeton/syndeton, conflations, emphasis of text, stylistic alterations, and creations of doublets and a triplet, could suggest that the scribe continually found places to improve the text. That is, the scribe repeatedly changed the text of Matthew, not so that it is *dramatically* re-presented, but so that it comes across a little more polished than, perhaps, what is found in other MSS. These changes are not a systematic overhaul, but are rather small changes that occur frequently enough throughout Matthew that, when focusing on the changes that are construed in context, the text of Matthew in W seems to be a more deliberately unified text, especially considering the assimilations to the nearby context. The paucity of nonsense readings could suggest that when the scribe *did* create singular readings, that they were intentional more often than not. But irrespective of the scribe's intentionality, the result is the same: the singular readings in W in Matthew often make sense in context and, on the whole, make the text and flow of Matthew a little more resilient, perhaps, than the exemplar was. In addition, as to be expected with scribal behavior, there are a few types of readings that show both consistency (e.g. concerning Pharisees, cf. §6.2.12) and inconsistency (e.g. concerning transpositions, cf. §6.2.5) with Hurtado's, and other studies, of W in the gospels.[102]

---

two negative actions of Jesus rather than only one: he warns the crowd *and* rebukes them. Sanders believes that the scribe of W incorrectly copied a correction in his exemplar, resulting in a conflation (*New Testament Manuscripts*, 46).

[102] See also Haugh, "Codex Washingtonianus," 172–78. Haugh devotes much attention to intentional verbal changes in W in John (11 noted instances), specifically changes from aorist to perfect (5 instances). (In general concerning the Gospel of John, the perfect tense occurs more frequently than Matthew. John contains 1/8th of all perfects in the NT. Cf. Enslin "The Perfect Tense in the Fourth Gospel," 121, in Haugh, "Codex Washingtonianus," 174.) Haugh notes that the alterations from aorist to perfect in John in W were not altered by the scribe of W but were probably transcribed from the exemplar of W (ibid., 178). Although Haugh begins by categorizing such alterations as intentional on the part of the scribe, he concludes by

6.3.2. LONGER AND SHORTER READINGS

Among the 112 singular readings, 17.85% result in either word loss or word gain (cf. APPENDIX 17). There are more instances of omissions than additions as well as more words added than omitted. The scribe omits in 11 instances and adds in 9 instances (a close reversal of Codex Ephraemi), accounting for 24 words omitted and 15 words added. Though on the average the scribe adds approximately two words for every instance of addition and omits two words for every instance of omission, there is a slightly higher omission rate, both in instances (i.e. frequency) and words (quantity), than addition.

Overall the singular readings show that the scribe omits more than adds. It is, however, unique in two particular aspects compared to our other MSS: first, no additions seem to have resulted from parablepsis (i.e. only omissions were the result, cf. §6.2.4), whereas our other MSS witness both additions and omissions. Second, influence from context seems to have resulted in omissions as well as an addition (cf. §6.2.6), where none of our other MSS display omissions that were influenced from the context.

---

stating that the alterations do not express the same motives of the scribe that Hurtado noted in his study of W in Mark. Therefore, Haugh believes such changes are not attributable to the scribe (ibid.). The singular readings in W in Matthew do not display changes from aorist to perfect, which could, perhaps, support Haugh's analysis that they were not created by the scribe.

CHAPTER 7
CONCLUSION

This study has drawn its data from the singular readings of five Greek MSS in the Gospel of Matthew, offering explanations for textual changes in an attempt to discover scribal habits. Through an examination of several hundreds of singular readings across Codex Sinaiticus, Vaticanus, Ephraemi, Bezae, and Washingtonianus, a number of scribal habits have come to the fore.

In each of the five main chapters, I have already offered conclusions about scribal activity pertaining to the MS under consideration. In this chapter, therefore, I offer a comparison of habits from all five MSS based on the conclusions of the preceding chapters, attempting to show from another angle how certain characteristics are unique to different scribes. Following discussions of several categories of readings (orthography, Greek dialects, influence from context, harmonizations, conflations, and theological readings), I discuss the longer and shorter singular readings, noting that not all of our scribes have a greater tendency to omit than add. The amount of singular readings created by each scribe compared to the amount of text added and omitted also gives a unique impression of the work of each scribe. The chapter concludes with a summary of the study, including mention of some areas for further study.

7.1. Comparisons of Scribal Habits via Singular Readings

7.1.1. ORTHOGRAPHY

In our MSS, no other category of singular reading (e.g. haplography, transposition, etc.) is more common than itacistic changes, which should be no surprise (cf. §2.2.1.1; 3.2.1.1; 4.2.1.1; 5.2.1.1; and 6.2.1.1). In Sinaiticus and Bezae, the itacistic singular readings outnumber the non-itacistic singular readings, but in Vaticanus and

Ephraemi, the non-itacistic singular readings outnumber the itacisms. In Washingtonianus, the number of itacistic changes is almost identical to the non-itacistic singular readings.

TABLE 7.1. NON-ITACISTIC SINGULAR READINGS COMPARED TO ITACISTIC SINGULAR READINGS

	ℵ 01	B 03	C 04	D 05	W 032
Non-Itacistic Singulars	158	95	75	252	112
Itacistic Singulars	539	73	17	394	106

There are many orthographic changes in our MSS that occur only once, but one hitherto undocumented (in sources I am aware of) orthographic change that occurs in more than once in more than one MS is the omission of sigma before ει found in codices D and W.[1] Perhaps the small pattern is due to a type of spelling familiarity; but while W favors classicisms, D contains singulars that witness both Koine and classical constructions. Perhaps this pattern could be due to the geographic locale of the scribes, but on account of both the quite debatable and uncertain provenance of these two MSS and their drastically different paleographic features (most obvious are the style of the hands and that Bezae is a diglot—though one similarity is that they both have the gospels in the Western order), arrival at a strong point of agreement is problematic.

7.1.2. ATTIC AND KOINE DIALECTS

With the exception of Ephraemi, our MSS display changes towards Atticisms and/or Koineisms. Also, there seems to be some flux in aorist forms in some MSS, changing 1st aorist endings to 2nd aorist and *vice versa*. However, there seems to be a connection between these two phenomena in our MSS. Sinaiticus, which features a preference for Koine in its singular readings, also prefers 1st aorist verbal endings.

---

[1] In D, 5:41; 9:2; 12:19; and in W, 21:41a; 23:14.

Washingtonianus, which prominently features Atticisms, prefers 2nd aorist verbal endings (cf. §6.2.7). But the MSS that feature both Attic and Koine dialectical changes in their singular readings, i.e. Vaticanus (cf. §3.2.7) and Bezae (cf. §5.2.11), either display both changes, from 1st aorist to 2nd aorist and the *versa* (though in Vaticanus there is more of a preference for 2nd aorist verbal endings) or no distinction at all in aorist forms (so Bezae).

7.1.3. INFLUENCE FROM CONTEXT

All of our MSS are influenced in one way or another by context; and in Sinaiticus, Bezae, and Washingtonianus, it is one of the most common contributors to creating a singular reading. In Sinaiticus, many readings are either affected by preceding text or following text, or in some instances there is evidence of text both before and after the variant that could have influenced a change (cf. §2.2.6). Apart from orthographic singulars, in both Bezae (cf. §5.2.12) and Washingtonianus (cf. §6.2.6), readings that are influenced from the context are actually the most common type of reading. In both codices, most of these readings are influenced from preceding text. But unlike the other MSS, Vaticanus (cf. §3.2.5) and Ephraemi (cf. §4.2.8) have only a few readings that could have been influenced by context. More often than not, preceding text could have influenced a change, but there are a couple instances in Vaticanus where text following a singular reading seems to have affected the scribe's transcription.

7.1.4. REMOTE GOSPEL HARMONIZATIONS

There is hardly a noticeable preference for gospel harmonizations in the singular readings of our MSS in Matthew. Many of the singular readings seem to have been influenced by the preceding text, rather than remote gospel harmonization, but 24:3a in Ephraemi seems to be the exception in all of the singular readings gathered in the study. Furthermore, other agreement between remote gospel parallels seems coincidental (cf. א 20:31a; א 27:15; C 15:32; D 27:61a; W 6:30; W 9:6; W 19:8).

7.1.5. CONFLATIONS

In ℵ 14:29, W 8:29, W 12:15–16, and W 23:25, the texts have evidence of conflated readings. In all instances except W 23:25, the scribes have combined two variants *with their own addition or substitution* to smooth the fusion. In most instances, the conflation concerns Jesus—either his teaching or a narrative where he is featured as one of the main characters. In these instances, instead of choosing, for example, variant A or B, the scribes seemingly chose to combine them. The conflation evident in ℵ 14:29, for example, was probably carried out by the scribe in an effort to combine variants rather than risk inclusion of the wrong variant—but without corroborating evidence, this can only be a suggestion. Both scribe A of ℵ and the scribe of W smooth their conflations with helping words (except W 23:35), thus not merely copying two variants, but forging a grammatical connection between them.

7.1.6. THEOLOGICAL READINGS

Some of the singular readings have potential to be theological in nature, especially those that occur in already existing theological contexts (i.e. ℵ 12:46; ℵ 14:29; ℵ 15:5; ℵ 21:42; ℵ 28:5a; ℵ 27:54a and 54b; B 6:33; B 12:32a; D 19:26; D 22:39; D 26:1–2; D 27:53; W 24:32b; W 24:39). However these are more readily explained as other types of phenomena since these readings are either rare within each scribe's work, have more in common with other types of tendencies, or are easier explained on other grounds such as error. It remains that, even if these readings do provide nuanced theological implications, by no means do they consistently, or drastically, re-present the Gospel of Matthew.

7.2. Longer and Shorter Singular Readings

In certain instances, each of our MSS displays singular readings that are either shorter or longer than any similar reading at that location in other MSS (cf. APPENDIX 17).

TABLE 7.2. TOTAL OMISSIONS/ADDITIONS IN THE SINGULAR READINGS IN MATTHEW[2]

MS SRs	ℵ 01 158		B 03 95		C 04 75		D 05 252		W 032 112	
	Inst.	Wrds.	Inst.	Wrds.	Inst.	Wrds.	Inst.	Wrds.	Inst.	Wrds.
Om.	50	114	10	13	8	13	31	54	11	24
	\/	\/	\/	/\	/\	||	\/	\/	\/	\/
Add.	24	27	6	18	10	13	23	26	9	15

The singular readings of Sinaiticus (scribe A)[3] and Bezae in Matthew confirm more omissions than additions (both in instances and number of words). It is evident that both Sinaiticus and Bezae omit more than they add, but between the two MSS, the rate of omissions points to disparate copying practices since Sinaiticus omits almost twice as often and certainly twice as much text as Bezae—this is especially striking considering that Bezae elicits almost *one hundred more* singular readings than Sinaiticus and yet records far fewer omissions in comparison. Codex Washingtonianus also omits more than it adds. It is interesting to note, however, that the number of instances of omissions and additions is relatively close.

Two of our MSS do not fit neatly into either category of "omitting more than adding" or *vice versa*: Vaticanus, concerning *quantity* of added words; and Ephraemi, concerning *frequency* of additions. Vaticanus, *gains more words* than it loses, but there are more *instances* of omissions than additions among its singular readings. The ratio fa-

---

[2] Data compiled from APPENDIX 17. Key to table:
    MS = Manuscript
    SRs = Total number of (non-itacistic) singular readings
    Om. = Omissions
    Add. = Additions
    \/ or /\, \|\| = greater than or less than, equal to
    Inst. = Instances of omissions/additions
    Wrds. = Number of words omitted/added

[3] The data for scribe D of Sinaiticus is extremely limited: scribe D omits in two instances (for a loss of 3 words) and adds in one instance (for a gain of 1 word).

vors word gain to word loss, but there is a greater frequency of omissions than additions. Therefore, it is not possible to say that Vaticanus adds more than it omits (or omits more than it adds) because a distinction of between frequency and quantity is found wanting.

In Ephraemi, the singular readings in Matthew record more instances of additions than omission, but there are just as many words omitted as added, which is not consistent with Hernández's findings in Ephraemi in Revelation. In Matthew, there are more instances of additions than omissions in Ephraemi, and the same amount of text is added as omitted—this is certainly a rare result.

Most of our MSS create a greater number of shorter readings than longer readings: Sinaiticus, Vaticanus, Bezae, and Washingtonianus. Remarkably, one of our MSS displays the inverse tendency by creating a greater number of longer readings: Ephraemi. Furthermore, it was also discovered that the frequency of omissions does not always correlate to a shorter text, as Vaticanus has more instances of omissions but adds more words than it omits. Another situation occurs in Ephraemi where it adds the same number of words that it omits, even though it has a higher frequency of additions than omissions. Interestingly, none of our five MSS contain more word additions than omissions *as well as* a greater frequency of additions than omissions.

Thus, a contribution of this study is to express that when looking at the singular readings, without discarding the nonsense readings or others arising from obvious mistakes (e.g. haplography), it is not possible to say that all our scribes unequivocally omitted more than they added, nor is it possible to say that they added more than they omitted, without qualifications. I have provided examples of hundreds of singular readings across five MSS to substantiate this claim. Nevertheless, the majority of our MSS (three out of five) does in fact omit more text as well as omit more often than add.

While it was indeed expected that the scribes would display different habits and that they would all add and omit text, surprising was the *frequency* of additions/omissions compared to the *quantity* of words added/omitted. This unexpected discovery in our MSS demands an important and necessary distinction between frequency of words added/omitted and quantity of words added/omitted.

7.3. Summary and Areas for Further Research

The study has focused on five of the earliest (near) complete copies of the Gospel of Matthew. In each of the selected MSS, I determined where a spelling, word, clause, phrase, sentence, or group of sentences was different from other MSS. These singular readings were collected in order to shine light on what they can tell us about the MS or the tendencies of the scribe responsible for the MS. The identification of longer and shorter singular readings also provided a useful strategy to portray scribal habits.

The examination of singular readings has illumined a number of identifiable patterns in each of our MSS. Types of readings that span all five MSS in Matthew include orthographic exchanges, haplography, transpositions, and changes resulting from contextual influence. While these types of readings are ubiquitous throughout, they are not always carried out in precisely the same manner from MS to MS. For example, concerning orthography, there are many nasal *exchanges* in Bezae, but nasals are not exchanged in Washingtonianus and are instead *dropped out*; instances of haplography in Sinaiticus sometimes begin a new line of text, but in Vaticanus text lines do not seem to factor into haplography; several transpositions in Sinaiticus could have resulted from correcting leaps, but there do not seem to be corrected leaps in Ephraemi, Bezae, nor Washingtonianus; there are several possible instances in Sinaiticus where subsequent text has influenced a change, but Ephraemi seems not at all affected by text following a singular reading, but rather is affected by preceding text. The utilization of the singular reading method seems to have been effective in elucidating unique characteristics of our MSS that might otherwise not be noticeable through a study of non-singular readings. The effect of these readings on the length of the text also sheds light on scribal behavior.

Identifying the longer and shorter readings of our MSS exposes further traits—this was an unforeseen benefit of studying the length of changes made to the text. When the readings that result in no word loss or gain are sifted away, it is possible to perceive clearly what happens when the scribe omits or adds text. For example, influence from the context results in *additions* in our MSS except for Washingtonianus where a *loss* of text typically occurs. Distinguishing frequency of omissions/additions from quantity of words omitted/added exposes still further characteristics of our MSS. For example, it was discovered that on average Vaticanus adds three words per addition, whereas no other of our MSS witness such a large rate of words added per instance of addition.

The present study has also potentially revealed something about homogenous copying practices throughout a single codex. Codex Ephraemi is a good example of this since it omits more than it adds in Revelation, based on the data from Hernández's study, but the same is not found in Matthew (cf. §4.3.2). In Codex Sinaiticus, unlike the anti-Arian tendency Hernández argued for in Revelation, a theological tendency in this MS in Matthew is unclear (cf. §2.2.14), yet the scribe does display similarities in Matthew with other portions of the codex (cf. §2.2.6). Further, Washingtonianus in Matthew displays some similar and some different copying tendencies compared to what Hurtado and others found in Mark (cf. §6.3.1). Perhaps this non-uniformity, or non-homogeneity, is indicative of fourth and fifth-century copying practices, but more research is needed to demonstrate this claim. Exploring the singular readings in the later Byzantine MSS, where the text is perceived to be more uniform, could help to shed light on copying practices carried out in a different historical context, and if a comparatively tamed tradition can still produce untamed and diverse scribal habits.

While the vast landscape of scribal tendencies will likely remain uncharted for some time, hopefully the data from this study contributes to the exploration of that territory and expresses the continuing need for empirical studies of Greek NT MSS. It seems that singular readings can still play an important role in establishing scribal habits in individual MSS. Accordingly, I cannot offer conditions that would satisfy all nuances that our MSS bring to the table, and I cannot foresee how the remaining thousands of Greek NT MSS not included in the study here add or omit text—surely there must be vast differences.

APPENDICES

APPENDIX 1
SELECT DETAILS OF II–V/VI CENTURY GREEK MANUSCRIPTS CONTAINING THE GOSPEL OF MATTHEW[1]

G-A	Publication Number and/or Artifact Number	*Liste* Date	Current Location	Matthean Contents	Percent of Matt Extant
𝔓¹	P. Oxy 2/ E 2746	III	University of Pennsylvania Museum of Archaeology and Anthropology, Philadelphia	1:1–9, 12, 14–20	1.5
𝔓¹⁹	P. Oxy 1170	IV/V	Bodleian Library, Oxford University	10:32–11:5	1.4
𝔓²¹	P. Oxy 1227/ Theo. Pap. 3	IV/V	Muhlenberg College, Allentown	12:24–26, 32–33	0.4
𝔓²⁵	Inv. 16388	IV	Staatliche Museen, Berlin	18:32–34; 19:1–3, 5–7, 9–10	1.0
𝔓³⁵	PSI 1	IV(?)	Biblioteca Medicea Laurenziana, Firenze	25:12–15, 20–23	0.7
𝔓³⁷	Inv. 1570/ P. Mich. 3.137	III/IV	University of Michigan, Ann Arbor	26:19–52	3.1
𝔓⁴⁵	P. Chester Beatty I; P. Vindob. G. 31974	III	Chester Beatty Library, Dublin; Österreichische Nationalbibliothek, Wien	20:24–32; 21:13–19; 25:41–26:39	5.6
𝔓⁵³	P. Mich. 6652	III	University of Michigan Library, Ann Arbor	26:29–40	1.1

---

[1] See p. 3 n. 13 for an explanation of this table.

G-A	Publication Number and/or Artifact Number	Liste Date	Current Location	Matthean Contents	Percent of Matt Extant
𝔓⁶²	P. Osloensis 1661	IV	Universitetsbiblioteket, Iniversitetet, Oslo	11:25–30	0.5
𝔓⁶⁴	Gr. 17	c.a. 200	Magdalen College, Oxford	3:9, 15; 5:20–22, 25–28; 26:7–8, 10, 14–15, 22–23, 31–33	1.7
𝔓⁶⁷	P. Barc. 1		Fundació Sant Lluc Evangelista, Barcelona		
𝔓⁷⁰	P. Oxy 2384/ PSI inv. CNR 419, 420	III	Ashmolean Museum, University of Oxford/ Ist. Pap., Firenze	2:13–16; 2:22–3:1; 11:26–27; 12:4–5; 24:3–6, 12–15	1.7
𝔓⁷¹	P. Oxy 2385	IV	Ashmolean Museum, University of Oxford	19:10–11, 17–18	0.3
𝔓⁷⁷	P. Oxy 2683	II/III	Ashmolean Museum, University of Oxford	23:30–39	0.9
𝔓⁸⁶	Inv. Nr. 5516	IV	Institut für Altertumskunde, Köln Universität	5:13–16, 22–25	0.7
𝔓¹⁰¹	P. Oxy 4401	III	Ashmolean Museum, University of Oxford	3:10–12; 3:16–4:3	0.7
𝔓¹⁰²	P. Oxy 4402	III/IV	Ashmolean Museum, University of Oxford	4:11–12; 4:22–23	0.3
𝔓¹⁰³	P. Oxy 4403	II/III	Ashmolean Museum, University of Oxford	13:55–56; 14:3–5	0.4
𝔓¹⁰⁴	P. Oxy 4404	II	Ashmolean Museum, University of Oxford	21:34–37; 21:43–45	0.6
𝔓¹⁰⁵	P. Oxy 4406	V/VI	Ashmolean Museum, University of Oxford	27:62–64; 28:2–5	0.6
𝔓¹¹⁰	P. Oxy 4494	IV	Ashmolean Museum, University of Oxford	10:13–15; 10:25–27	0.5
ℵ 01	Add. 43725	IV	British Library, London	Complete	100
A 02	Royal 1 D. VIII	V	British Library, London	25:7–end	18.7

APPENDIX 1: SELECT DETAILS OF MANUSCRIPTS CONTAINING MATTHEW 137

G-A	Publication Number and/or Artifact Number	Liste Date	Current Location	Matthean Contents	Percent of Matt Extant
B 03	Vat. gr. 1209	IV	Biblioteca Vaticana, Vatican City	Complete	100
C 04	Gr. 9	V	Bibliothèque Nationale, Paris	1:3–5:14; 7:6–17:25; 18:29–22:20; 23:18–24:9; 24:46–25:29; 26:23–27:10; 27:47–28:14	75.2
D 05	Nn. 2. 41	V	University Library, University of Cambridge	1:20–6:20; 9:2–27:2; 27:12–end	93.1
W 032	06.274/ Washington MS III	IV/V	Smithsonian Institute, Washington, D.C.	Complete	100
058	Pap. G. 39782	IV	Österreichische Nationalbibliothek, Wien	18:18–19, 22–23, 25–26, 28–29	0.7
071	P. Oxy 401/ Mus. Inv. 3735	V/VI	Semitic Museum, Harvard University, Cambridge	1:21–24; 1:25–2:2	0.6
0160	P. 9961	IV/V	Staatliche Museen, Berlin	26:25–26, 34–36	0.4
0170	P. Oxy 1169/ Pap. 11	V/VI	Speer Library, Princeton Theological Seminary	6:5–6, 8–9, 13–15, 17	0.7
0171	PSI 1.2 + PSI 2.124; P. Berlin inv. 11863	c.a. 300	Biblioteca Medicea Laurenziana, Firenze; Staatliche Museen, Berlin	10:17–23, 25–32; Lk 22:44–56, 61–64	1.4

G-A	Publication Number and/or Artifact Number	*Liste* Date	Current Location	Matthean Contents	Percent of Matt Extant
0231	P. Ant. 11	IV	Ashmolean Museum, Oxford	26:75–27:1, 3–4	0.3
0242	71942	IV	Egyptian Museum, Cairo	8:25–9:2; 13:32–38, 40–46	2.4

APPENDIX 2
SINGULAR READINGS IN SINAITICUS IN MATTHEW[1]

1. Scribe A

1:14¹ ⌜Σαδωκ rell ℵ^S1 |⌜Σαδωχ ℵ* |⌜Ζαδδωκ W |⌜Ζαδωδ Θ |⌜Sadoch g¹ |⌜Saddoch b c f |⌜Saddoc aur ff¹ q |⌜Sadoc a d vg

1:14² ⌜Σαδωκ rell ℵ^S1 |⌜Σαδωχ ℵ* |⌜Ζαδδωκ W |⌜Sadoch g¹ |⌜Saddoch b c f |⌜Saddoc aur ff¹ q |⌜Sadoc a d vg

1:18 ⌜μνηστευθεισης rell | ⌜μνησστευθισης ℵ* | ⌜μνηστευθισης ℵ^S1 C P |⌜μνητευθησις L* |⌜μνηστευθησις L^c |⌜μνηστευθησης Θ 2 565 |⌜μνηστευθησεις 579

1:21 ⌜καλεσεις το ονομα αυτου Ιησουν rell ℵ^S1 |⌜καλεσει L* (g¹ Arm) |⌜καλεσουσι 1241
καλεσεις το ονομα Ιησουν   ℵ*

1:23 ⌜καλεσουσιν το ονομα °αυτου Εμμανουηλ rell |⌜καλεσεις D 2* 1391 *l*184 d bo^MSS Epiph Or Eus |°ℵ*

2:2 τον αστερα εν   rell ℵ^S1
     τον αστεραν   ℵ*

2:9 ⌜προηγεν rell (προῆγεν ℵ^S1) |⌜προηγον ℵ*

3:15 ⌜ημιν rell ℵ^S1 ℵ^ca |⌜ημας ℵ*

---

[1] Readings 27:56(a) and 27:56(b) are counted as one singular reading. Matt 27:54a and 27:54b are counted as separate singular readings though the variation units overlap.

4:8 ⌜δεικνυσιν rell |⌜δικνυει ℵ |⌜δικνυσειν C |⌜εδειξεν D 372 |⌜δικνυσιν P W Δ Θ

4:12 οτι Ιωαννης (rell) ℵ^S1 ℵ^ca NA²⁸ | 21 ℵ*

4:18 τον ⌜λεγομενον   rell
τον ⌜καλουμενον   ℵ^S1 21 27 28 348 476 726 1071 1573 1579 1604 al. Eus |⌜λουμενον ℵ* |⌜επικαλουμενον E 892

4:23a εν °ολη τη Γαλιλαια (B) C k sy^{c.s.p.h} sa bo mae NA²⁸ |°ℵ* ολην την Γαλιλαιαν rell ℵ^S1

4:23b διδασκων^T rell ℵ^S1 |^Tαυτους ℵ*

4:24a και ⌜¹βασανοις ⌜²συνεχομενους   rell ℵ^S1 |⌜¹βασανους ℵ* |⌜¹om. E* 2 |⌜²συνεχομενοις U Δ 28
και βασανιζομενους   1424

4:24b °και ⌜δαιμονιζομενους □και σεληνιαζομενους` rell (δαιμονιαζομενους ℵ^ca) |°B C* Δ f¹³ 892 Eus |⌜σεληνιαζομενους ℵ* |⌜δεμονιαζομενους ℵ^S1 |⌜δεμονιζωμενους 1071 |⌜om. M Δ 280 566 1588 1604 sy^s |□253 475 1346 1424
και   71 692

5:33 ⌜επιορκησεις rell | ⌜εφιορκησεις ℵ |⌜επειορκησις D |⌜εποιρκισεις 118 |⌜επιορκισης 1346

5:39 ⌜αντιστηναι rell |⌜αντισταθηναι ℵ

5:41 ⌜αγγαρευσει rell |⌜ενγαρευση ℵ |⌜αγγαρευει D |⌜αγγαρευση E G K V Θ Σ 13 543 33 157 243 471* l49 |⌜ανγαρευση W 124 788 |⌜αγγερευση Δ 33 892* 1071 1424 |⌜αγκαρευσει 59 66 483 484 |⌜αγγαρευσει l844

5:45 αγαθους ᵀ ⌐και ⌐βρεχει επι δικαιους και αδικους⌐ rell
|ᵀκαι βρεχει επι πονηρους και αγαθους E* |ᴼℵ* |⌐βρεχι ℵᴬ Θ
|⌐βρεχη L

6:6 συ δε οταν ⌐προσευχη rell ℵ^corr |⌐προσευχης ℵ*

6:9 πατερ ημων ᴼο εν ⌐τοις ουρανοις⌐ rell ℵ^S1 |ᴼℵ* |⌐τω ουρανω
mae Didache

6:14 ⌐αυτων rell ℵ^S1 |⌐υτων ℵ*

6:16a ᵀοταν δε rell ℵ^S1 |ᵀκαι ℵ*

6:16b αμην ᵀ rell ℵ^ca |ᵀγαρ ℵ*

6:28 αυξανουσιν ου ⌐ κοπιωσιν ουδε νηθουσιν   rell   ℵ^S1
|⌐κοπιουσιν B 33
    ου ξαινουσιν ουδε νηθουσιν ουδε κοπιωσιν   ℵ*
    αυξανουσιν ου νηθουσιν ουδε κοπιωσιν   Θ sy^c
    αυξανει ου κοπια ουδε νηθει   𝔐 K L M
N^vid W Γ Δ Π 0281 *f*^13 565 579 700 788 892 1241 1424 *l*844 *l*2211

7:21 το θελημα του πατρος   rell ℵ^S1
    τα θεληματα του πατρος   ℵ*

7:22 δαιμονια ᵀ rell ℵ^S1 |ᵀπολλα ℵ*

7:25 ⌐προσεπεσαν ℵ^S1 B C E X Z Δ *f*^1.13 237 238 242 245 543 700
788 892 1071 1346 *l*47 syr^p mg gr Cyr^es77 Chr Dam NA^28 |⌐προσεπεσεν
ℵ* |⌐προσεπεσον K L M S U V Π Φ Ω 22 157 565 *al. pler.*
|⌐προσεκρουσαν W 54 234 Philo^enarr in cant |⌐προσερρηξαν Θ Σ 579 *pc*
Eus |⌐προσεκοψον 33 252 259 1424 *pc* (Eus^ps367) |⌐*inruerunt ff*^1 *g*^2 *l* aur
vg^(pler) (sy^c.pesh.hl cop) |⌐*impegerunt c f k m q* vg^(1ms) Aug^epist Cyp
|⌐*offenerunt a b g*^1 *h* |⌐*inciderunt m* |⌐*uenerunt* vg^(1ms) |⌐*percusserunt* geo^1
|⌐*corripuerunt* geo^2

7:26 και πας ᵀ ⸀ο ακουων⸃ rell ℵ^S1 |ᵀ[και?] πας ℵ* |⸀οστις ακουει Θ f^13

7:27a ⸀ηλθον rell |⸀ηλθαν ℵ

7:27b οι ποταμοι και ◻επνευσαν οι ανεμοι ºκαι⸃ ℵ^ca |◻ℵ* |ºℵ^S1

7:28 ⸀οι οχλοι⸃ επι τη διδαχη αυτου rell ℵ^S1 ℵ^ca |345612 ℵ* |⸀παντας οι οχλοι Δ Θ f^1 22 697 1278 (vg^ms) sy^hier Or |⸀παντας 998 Eus |⸀om. sa

8:3 και ºευθεως εκαθαρισθη rell (B* E L N X Π 2) |ºℵ* | 21 566

8:7 λεγει αυτω ᵀ ℵ^ca B 892 k sy^s cop bo NA^28 |ᵀακολουθι μοι ℵ* |ᵀο Ιησους rell |ᵀαποκριθεις ο Ιησους 1093*^vid

8:15a ⸀ηγερθη rell ℵ^S1 |⸀εγερθις ℵ*

8:15b ο πυρετος και ... ºκαι rell ℵ^S1 |ºℵ*

8:26 θαλασση rell |⸀θαλλασση ℵ

8:28 των ⸀Γαδαρηνων B C* M Θ 4 21 (59) 174 251 273 399 pc sy^s.p.h.txt geo^1 Epiph Or NA^28 | ⸀Γαζαρηνων ℵ* | ⸀Γεργεσηνων rell ℵ^ca |⸀Γεργεσηνων C^c L Ω f^13 565 579 788 |⸀Γαδαρινων 59 147 |⸀Γερασηνων 892^c latt sy^hmg sa mae |⸀Γαραδηνων Δ

9:6 ⸀υπαγε rell ℵ^ca |⸀πορευου ℵ* |⸀περιπατει 1071

9:9 ºκαι λεγει rell ℵ^S1 |ºℵ*

9:12 ⸀ιατρου rell |⸀ιατρων ℵ* ℵ^ca

APPENDIX 2: SINGULAR READINGS IN SINAITICUS IN MATTHEW 143

9:15   εστιν ο νυμφιος ⸆ελευσονται δε ημεραι οταν απαρθη απ αυτων ο νυμφιος` (rell) ℵ^A |⸆ℵ*

9:20   ⸂αιμορροουσα rell |⸂αιμαροουσα ℵ* |⸂αιμοροουσα ℵ^ca W Ω |⸂αιμορρουσα K |⸂αιμορουσα L

9:27   ⸂κραζοντες rell |⸂κραυγαζοντες ℵ

9:28a   αυτοις °⸆ο Ιησους` rell ℵ^ca |°ℵ* |⸆18 35 66 150 201 222 246 251 252* 253 479 484 740 1328 1329 1330 1334 1339 2726 sy^s

9:28b   δυναμαι ^T1 τουτο ποιησαι ^T2 rell ℵ^S1 ℵ^ca b d | 213 B N 892 q vg^ed | 132 C* geo^1 |^T1υμιν ℵ* |^T2υμιν it

9:30   ⸂αυτων °οι οφθαλμοι rell ℵ^ca |⸀om. ℵ* |⸂αυτω E* |°700 |231 D it vg

9:35a   αυτων °και κηρυσσων rell ℵ^S1 |°ℵ*

9:35b   μαλακιαν ^T rell ℵ^S1 |^Tεν τω λαω C^3 E F G K M U X Y Γ Θ Π 118^2 579 700 pm c vg^mss (gat al^3) sy^h aeth arm geo |^Tκαι πολλοι ηκολουθησαν αυτω a b h
    μαλακιαν εν τω λαω και ^T ηκολουθησαν αυτω ℵ* |^Tπολλοι L Φ f^13(exc.124) 7 262 273 348 517 543 566 713 1010 1187 1293 1346 1424 1574 g^1 Tat

10:4   ^T1Ιουδας ^T2 rell ℵ^S1 |^T1ο ℵ* |^T2ο ℵ* B D K M S Δ Π f^1 33 pc Chr NA^28

10:9   χρυσον ⸆ ⸂1μηδε αργυρον` ⸂2μηδε rell ℵ^S1 |⸆ℵ* |⸂1&2μητε D L F f^13 7 157 273 543 892 |⸂1μητε Θ 4 28 1424 |⸂2μητε 565 700 |⸆η 2145

10:21   αδελφος ⸂αδελφον rell ℵ^ca |⸂αδελφος ℵ*

10:39 ᵒο ευρων την ψυχην αυτου απολεσει αυτην ᵒκαι˹ ο απολεσας *rell* ℵ^(ca) (D) |ᵒℵ^D |ᵒℵ*

10:40 και ο *rell* ℵ^(ca) (om. 579 *haplography*)
     ο δε   ℵ*

11:19 εσθιων ᵀ και *rell* ℵ^(S1) (B) |ᵀκαι ℵ*

11:23 ˹σοι *rell* ℵ^(S1) |˹υμιν ℵ*

12:11 ˹¹αυτο και ˹²εγερει   *rell* |˹¹αυτω K L Θ 2* 59 700 1071 1424 *l*184 |˹¹om. U |˹¹αυτον f^13 13 471* 475* |˹²εγειρει C D G 13 124 174 230 826 828 788 983 1093 1424 1515 1689 sy^(cu) et^(utr) |˹²εγειρι L 828 |˹²εξεγερει 247
      ᵀ εγερει αυτο   ℵ |ᵀκαι c ff^(1.2) h vg^(pler) sy^(c.s.p) sah bo

12:22 ˹αυτον *rell* ℵ^(ca) |˹αυτους ℵ*

12:33 αυτου ˹καλον *rell* ℵ^D |˹αλον ℵ* |˹αγαθον ℵ^A

12:34 ˹γεννηματα εχιδνων *rell* ℵ^(S1) |˹γεννημα ℵ* |˹γενηματα Δ

12:37 ᵒσου καταδικασθηση (*rell*) NA^28 |ᵒℵ

12:44 εξηλθον και ˹ελθον ευρισκει *pler* ℵ^D NA^28 |˹om. ℵ* |˹εξελθον U |˹ηλθον Δ

12:46 εξω ᵒζητουντες ˹αυτω λαλησαι˹ (*rell*) ℵ^A [NA^28] |ᵒℵ* | *1243* D L Θ Φ f^13 7 33 174 230 349 517 659 788 826 828 983 1346 1424 1689 d f l aur vg^(pler) sy^(p.h) bo aeth arm Or^(Matt.XI.4) |˹αυτον 28 |˹σοι 487

12:49 ˹χειρα ᵒαυτου *rell* |˹χειρας 28 |˹χιρα ℵ^(S1) |ᵒD 124 a b ff^1 g^1 k q vg Or^(3,480) Aug
      χιραν   ℵ*

APPENDIX 2: SINGULAR READINGS IN SINAITICUS IN MATTHEW 145

13:25 ⌜επεσπειρεν ℵ^{S1} ℵ^{ca} B N Θ 0281^{vid} f^1 33 1241 it^{pler} vg Aug NA^{28} | ⌜επσειρεν C D E F K L W Γ Δ f^{13} 565 579 700 892 1424 𝔐 e k q sy$^{c.s.p.hl.}$ sah bo aeth arm geo Ir^{gr} Chr | ⌜επεσπαρκεν ℵ*

13:28 ⌜αυτα rell ℵ^{S1} |⌜αυτατα ℵ*

13:39 διαβολος ⸌ο δε θερισμος συντελεια ⸆ αιωνος εστιν⸍ οι δε θερισται rell ℵ^{S1} |⸌ℵ* |⸆του ℵ^{ca} C K L W Γ Δ 0106 0233 0250 f^1 565 579 700 892 1241 1424 l844 𝔐

13:44 κεκρυμμενω ⸌εν °τω αγρω⸍ ⸌ον ευρων rell ℵ^{S1} |⸌ℵ* |°D N 700 1071 1424 |⌜ο Θ

13:54 ⌜πατριδα rell ℵ^{S1} |⌜αντιπατριδα ℵ*

14:1 εν εκεινω ⸆^{1} τω καιρω ηκουσεν ⸆^{2} Ηρωδης rell ℵ^{S1} ℵ^{ca} |5612 3 4 ℵ* |⸆^{1}δε D 122 157 300 d sy$^{s.c.p.}$ bo |⸆^{2}ο X

14:7 ⌜μεθ ορκου rell| ⌜μετ X Θ Σ 124 |⌜μετα ℵ

14:17 ⌜ωδε ει μη πεντε αρτους rell (79^{vid}) ℵ^{ca} |1 5 2 3 4 ℵ* |⌜δε 2766*

14:23 και ⸌απολυσας τους οχλους⸍ ανεβη rell ℵ^D |⸌ℵ*

14:29 τα υδατα και ⌜ηλθεν προς τον Ιησουν   B C* 21 399 700 1010 1293 1355 1555 1604 sy$^{c.s}$ (sa) arm geo NA^{28} |⌜ηλθε 700^c

    τα υδατα ⌜ελθειν προς τον Ιησουν   rell |⌜ελθην Θ

    τα υδατα ελθιν ⸌ηλθεν ουν⸍ προς τον Ιησουν   ℵ* |⸌ℵ^{ca}

15:5 ωφεληθης⸆ rell ℵ^{S1} |⸆ουδεν εστιν ℵ*

15:11 το στομα⸆ rell ℵ^{ca} |⸆τουτο ℵ* |⸆του ανθρωπου 713

15:12 ⌜λεγουσιν B D Θ $f^{1.13}$ 33 579 700 pc (ff¹) ⌜ειπον C K L N W
Γ Δ 0106 565 892 1241 1424 𝔐 lat sy^h ⌜ειπαν ℵ

18:12 εννεα ᵀ επι τα ορη °και ⌜πορευθεις   L 15 579
NA²⁸ |ᵀπρο E*(?) |°rell (G L S U) ℵ^S1 |⌜πορευμενος D
       εννεα □προβατα επι τα ορη και ⌞ πορευθεις   B Θ $f^{13(exe}$
⁽¹²⁴⁾ 543 517 788 954 1346 1424* 1675 sa^mss mae arm |□ℵ*

18:18 λεγω °υμιν ⌜οσα rell ℵ^S1 |°700* |⌜ως 579 |⌜ος ℵ*

18:19 ⌜¹αιητησωνται ⌜²γενησεται αυτοις B D |⌜¹αιτησονται rell
1346 |⌜²δοθησεται 33 |⌜²γενησονται 346 1346 | 132 ℵ

18:20 °η τρεις rell ℵ^S1 |°ℵ*

18:30a ⌜αλλα rell ℵ^ca |⌜και ℵ* |⌜αλλ F Y Δ f^1 16 71 477 485 983 1223
1279 1473 1579 1588

18:30b ⌜αποδω rell ℵ^ca |⌜αποδη ℵ*

18:31 ⌜¹και ⌜²ελθοντες rell |⌜¹οι δε ℵ |⌜²απελθοντες Θ f^{13} 33 565
788 1346

19:1 ᵀ και ηλθεν rell ℵ^S1 ℵ^ca |ᵀκαι ηλθεν ℵ*

19:10 οι μαθηται ᵀ °ει ουτως 𝔓⁷¹ ℵ^S1 ℵ^ca B Θ e ff¹ g¹ sa^ms mae
[NA²⁸] |ᵀαυτου rell [NA²⁸] |°ℵ*

19:15 ⌜αυτοις rell |⌜επ αυτους ℵ |⌜αυτου 118 |⌜επ αυτα 483 484

19:18 ου φονευσεις ᵀ ου °¹μοιχευσεις ου °²κλεψεις ου rell ℵ^S1 |
1452367 1446 | 1236547 2786 |ᵀτο 184 348 829 2726 |°¹61 555 740
979 |°²579 1336
        ου φονευσεις ου ℵ*

19:21 ⌜εξεις rell ℵ^S1 |⌜εξετε ℵ* |⌜εξης Ε Γ

19:26 °αυτοις ⸂παρα ανθρωποις⸃ rell ℵ^S1 |°Θ l183 sah |⸂ℵ*

20:7 οτι ουδεις °ημας εμισθωσατο rell ℵ^S1 |°ℵ*

20:13 ⌜ουκ rell |⌜ουχ ℵ

20:14a τουτω ⌜τω εσχατω rell ℵ^S1 |⌜ω ℵ* | 231 D 1071

20:14b ως και ⌜σοι rell |⌜συ ℵ

20:18 αυτον °θανατω   rell |°B aeth
       αυτον εις θανατον   ℵ
       αυτου θανατον   700

20:19 σταυρωσαι °και τη τριτη rell ℵ^S1 ℵ^ca |°ℵ*

20:31a ⌜μειζον rell |⌜πολλω μαλλον ℵ |⌜πλεον U |⌜μειζονα 184 348 555 829 952 1421 1579 2726 |⌜περισσως 1071 |⌜μειζων f^13 124 157 788 |⌜μειζονως 851 1273 1424 1506

20:31b υιος Δαυιδ   rell (om. 124)
       υιου Δαυιδ   ℵ*
       υιε Δαυιδ   𝔓^45vid ℵ^ca C D L N O Σ Φ 085 0281 4 16 33 61 130 174^c 176 184 222 233 348* 372 489 517 555 579 659 713 740 807 829 863 892 954 990 1219 1230 1241 1293 1295 1329 1421 1424 1528 1555 1579 1606 1675 1692 2680 2726 it vg Or

20:34 ⌜αυτων rell ℵ^S1 |⌜αυτου ℵ* |⌜om. Θ 2546

21:7a ⌜επεκαθισεν B C F M S U V X Z^vid Γ Δ f^13 pler it^pler sy^utr.cu sa pc Or pc NA^28 |⌜εκαθισαν ℵ* |⌜επεκαθισαν ℵ^ca 4 16 245 291 892 |⌜εκαθητο D 700 |⌜επεκαθησεν H 118 1071 |⌜εκαθησεν K Θ

⌐επεκαθησαν L 579 ⌐εκαθισεν N Y Π Σ 1241 ⌐εκαθεισεν W ⌐επεκαθισε 69

21:7b επανω ⌐αυτων rell NA²⁸ ⌐αυτον ℵᶜᵃ L 892 ⌐αυτου D Θ *l*27 itᵖˡᵉʳ syʰ ⌐αυτης 2ᶜ
    επανω επ αυτων ℵ*

21:19 ουδεν °ευρεν ▫εν αυτηˋ rell ℵˢ¹ (692) |°ℵ* |▫945 990 1424 *ff*¹ geo¹

21:25 ποθεν ⌐ην rell ℵᶜᵃ (om. 999 1012) ⌐εστιν 28 *d e* ⌐η ℵ*

21:30 ⌐¹ωσαυτως ▫ο δε ⌐²αποκριθεις ειπενˋ rell ⌐¹ως αυτο Δ |▫ℵ* ⌐²αποκριθις ℵᶜᵃ ⌐²αποκρειθεις D ⌐²απεκριθη W* ⌐²απεκριθεις Wᶜ ⌐²αποκριθης 579 ⌐²απηλθε Y 118 157

21:34–35 γεωργους ᵀ ⌐λαβειν του καρπους αυτου ²¹:³⁵ και λαβοντες rell ℵˢ¹ (D) |ᵀτου 157| ᵀεκεινους 1424 ⌐και λαβον ℵ*

21:39 ⌐εξεβαλον εξω rell ⌐εβαλον ℵ ⌐εξεβαλαν D ⌐εξεβαλλον Z ⌐om. 69

21:42 παρα ⌐κυριου rell ℵᶜᵃ ⌐κυριω ℵ*

21:43 ⌐καρπους rell ℵᶜᵃ ⌐καρκαρπους ℵ*

22:1 °¹ειπεν °²εν rell ℵˢ¹ ℵᶜᵃ |°¹E syᵖ |°²ℵ*

22:9 των ⌐οδων rell ℵᴬ ℵᴰ ⌐υδατων ℵ*ᵛⁱᵈ

22:15 ⌐¹συμβουλιον ⌐²ελαβον rell ℵᶜᵃ ⌐¹συνβουλιον D K Θ ⌐²om. ℵ* ⌐²εποιησαν 1574

22:16 ⌐ει rell ℵᶜᵃ ⌐ε ℵ* ⌐η 28

22:21 ⌜λεγουσιν rell |⌜λεγουσι ℵ |⌜οι δε ειπον 1604

22:30 ⌜γαμουσιν rell |⌜γαμουσι ℵ |⌜γαμουνται f^{13} 579

22:32a ο θεος Ισαακ rell
       θεος ⌜Ισακ   ℵ* |⌜Ισαακ ℵ^{ca}

22:32b και °ο θεος Ιακωβ rell (om. 69) |°ℵ

22:42 °του Δαυιδ rell |°ℵ*

23:4   φορτια^T rell |^{T}μεγαλα ℵ

23:11 ⌜¹υμων ⌜²εσται °υμων διακονος rell |⌜¹εν υμιν Θ 477 1279 1473 1579 a c h $r^{1.2}$ sy$^{c.s.p.h}$ sa bo |⌜¹om. vg^{2mss} |⌜²εστω G 241 246 252 253 258 495 566 6923 983 1093 1355 1391 1573 1574 1604 2145 r^1 geo |°ℵ | 1243 a ff^1 g^1 l m q vg$^{(pler)}$ sy^h

23:16 ⌜¹οδηγοι ^{T} ⌜²τυφλοι °οι λεγοντες rell ℵ^{corr} D^{CorC} |^{T}οι ℵ* |⌜¹οδιγοι Δ* 2 565 1346 |⌜²τυφλων Θ |°D*

23:34 ⌜σταυρωσετε °και ⌐εξ αυτων⌐   rell ℵ^{ca} (om. D a d Lucif)
|⌜σταυρωσητε Σ |°q |⌐b f h ff$^{1.2}$ g^1 r^2 vg
       σταυρωσετε εξ αυτων και   ℵ*

23:37 ⌜επισυναγαγειν rell ℵ^{ca} |⌜επεισυνα[ξ]αι 𝔓^{77} |⌜επισυναγειν ℵ*

24:10a ⌐και αλληλους ⌜παραδωσουσιν⌐ ^{T} rell |⌐aeth |⌜παραδωσωσιν Σ Φ |^{T}εις θλιψιν ℵ |^{T}εις θανατον Φ 124 495* 1093

24:10b ⌐και ⌜μισησουσιν αλληλους⌐ rell |⌐ℵ |⌜μισωσιν Φ

24:15 ⌜Δανιηλ rell ℵ^{S1} D^A |⌜ιηλ ℵ* |⌜Δανιηλου D* |⌜Daniele Latt |⌜Danielum d

24:17 ⸆αραι ⸉¹τα⸊ ⸉²εκ rell ℵ^ca (om. 2 homoeoteleuton) |⸆1010 1293 |⸉¹το ℵ* |⸉¹τι D Θ f¹ 28 33 565 700 1424 1582 l2211 arm aeth latt sy^p.h arm geo Epiph Hipp^anit Cyp Caes^dial bis Isid^1,210 Ir^lat Or^int2,224 |⸉¹om. sy^s |⸉²επι 047

24:22 ⸉κολοβωθησονται °αι ημεραι εκειναι rell ℵ^ca |⸉εκολοβωθησαν ℵ* |°E

24:24 γαρ ⸉ψευδοχριστοι rell ℵ^S1 (l184 c) |⸉ιψευδοχριστοι ℵ* |⸉ψευδοχρειστοι B D |⸉ψευδοχρηστοι 69 157 |⸉om. Δ 565 ff² h δ geo¹

24:28 ⸉οπου rell |⸉που ℵ* |⸉οποι Δ

24:35 ⸆ο ουρανος και η γη παραλευσεται οι δε λογοι μου ου μη παρελθωσιν⸊ (rell) ℵ^ca NA²⁸ |⸆ℵ*

26:15a ⸉τι rell ℵ^S1 |⸉ι ℵ*

26:15b ⸉δουναι rell |⸉δωνε ℵ

26:21 ⸉ειπεν ⸋¹αμην ⸋² ⸆λεγω υμιν⸊ rell |⸉λεγι ℵ |⸋¹eis sy^s.h bo geo¹ |⸋¹iesus vg (mm) geo² |⸋²αμην l48 Eus^dem |⸋²δε V |⸆692

26:33 ⸋¹ °ει ⸋² παντες rell |⸋¹και 1424 c f ff¹ g^1.2 h l aur vg sy^p.h aeth arm Aug^cons |°ℵ* |⸋²και ℵ^ca F K W Y Π 71 482 517 579 697 700 1241 sat mu^vid it⁵ vg syr^ut arm aeth Or^4,412 et437 Bas^2,159 Epiph Hil

26:44 ⸆°εκ τριτου⸊ τον αυτον λογον ℵ^ca B 𝔐 L 4 262 273 566 1170 1187 1555 1573 NA²⁸ |⸆𝔓³⁷ A D K Π Φ f^1(exe 118) 71 157 265 472 489 565 1219 1295 1346 1424 1515 1574 1582 y^scr a b d ff² r^1vid |°E* | 34125 ℵ*

26:46 ⸉παραδιδους rell ℵ^ca |⸉παραδιδων ℵ*

26:65 ⌜μαρτυρων rell |⌜μαρτυριων ℵ

27:3 ⌜μεταμεληθεις rell |⌜μεταμεληθη και ℵ* |⌜μεταμεληθις ℵ^ca

27:11 °ο ηγεμων rell ℵ^S1 ℵ^ca (om. W Θ sy^s geo¹) |°ℵ*

27:15 ον ⌜ηθελον rell ℵ^ca |⌜παρητουντο ℵ*

27:16 ειχον δε ⌜τοτε δεσμιον rell ℵ^S1 |⌜τον τε ℵ* |⌜om. b ff² h r¹ vg^(3MSS) sy^s.p.hl.

27:23 ⌜περισσως rell ℵ^ca |⌜περισσω ℵ* |⌜περισσοτερον Σ f¹ 118 1582

27:24 υμεις ^T οψεσθε rell ℵ^ca |^Tδε ℵ*

27:33 °λεγομενον rell ℵ^ca |°ℵ*

27:48 εις ⸆εξ αυτων⸄ rell |⸆ℵ

27:53a ⌜εισηλθον εις την αγιαν rell |⌜om. ℵ |⌜ηλθον D it vg sy^s.h sah bo

27:53b πολιν °και rell |°ℵ

27:54a θεου υιος ⌜ην rell ℵ^ca |213 B D^gr 69 102 b h l r² aur vg^ed sy^hl.h sah bo (aeth) geo Or^int et^4,298 | 23του1 ℵ* {transposition} |⌜εστιν C f g¹ go Aug^ioh Vig

27:54b ^Tθεου rell ℵ^ca |⌜του ℵ* {article}

27:56(a)   ην ⌐r1Μαρια °η ⌐r2Μαγδαληνη και⸄ Μαρια   rell ℵ^ca |⁰ℵ* |⌐r1Μαριαμ L f¹ sa^mss |°D* |⌐r2Μαγδαλινη Σ 124 346 543 28 348 474 565 579 788 1279 l184

           ην ^T Μαριαμ η Μαγδαληνη και Μαριαμ C^Corr.C Δ Θ 713 sy^omn arm geo |^Tκαι C*

27:56(b) ⸀η του ⸂Ιακωβου ᵀ¹ και ᵀ²⸀Ιωσηφ ᵀ³ ⸀μητηρ και η μητηρ rell |⸀E 71 348 692 1424 1515 1573 1574 1604 *l*184 |ᵀ¹του μικρου *l*183 |ᵀ²η ℵ^{ca} |⸀Ιωσητος D¹ *l*844 |ᵀ³η 90 157 |⸀Ιωσητος D^c |⸀Ιωση 28 892 |⸀om. it

η του Ιακωβου και η Μαρια η Ιωσηφ και η Μαρια η ℵ*

27:64 ⸀κλεψωσιν rell |⸀κλεψουσιν ℵ

28:2–3 αυτου ²⁸:³ ⸂ην °¹δε °²η ⸀ειδεα αυτου⸃ rell ℵ^{S1} B^{c2} |⸂ℵ* |°¹geo |°²66 *l*47 |⸀ειδε B* |⸀ιδεα F G K L S U V W Γ Δ Θ Π Σ Φ f^{1.13} 33 69 157 565 788 1071 1241 1346 *l*844 |⸀ιδε L 579

28:5a ειπεν ⸂ταις ⸀γυναιξιν⸃ rell (ℵ^{S1}) ℵ^{cb2} |⸂ℵ* |⸀γυναιξι S Y U Ω f¹ 69 28 118 157 700

28:5b μη ⸀φοβεισθε rell |⸀φοβηθηται ℵ* |⸀φοβισθαι ℵ^{ca} Θ |⸀φοβεισθαι C D L W 579

28:7 ιδου ⸀ειπον rell ℵ^{ca} |⸀ειπα ℵ* |⸀ειπαν B*

28:10 τοις ⸀αδελφοις °μου rell ℵ^{ca} |⸀μαθηταις 157 1555 *l*2211 |°ℵ*

28:12 ⸀συμβουλιον τε λαμβοντες αργυρια rell |⸀συβουλιον W συμβουλιον τε ⸀εποιησαν ᵀ αργυρια ℵ* |ᵀκαι λαβοντες ℵ^{S1} ℵ^{cb2} |⸀λαβοντες ℵ^{ca} συβουλιον λαμβοντες αργυριον D

28:13 λεγοντες ειπατε °οτι rell | *132* ℵ |°33

2. Scribe D

16:13 λεγουσιν οι ανθρωποι ειναι NA²⁸ pler | *1423* f¹ ff¹ vg^{(1MS)} οι ανθρωποι λεγουσιν ειναι ℵ^{ca} D 579 700 a b e g² q r^{1.2} sah geo² Ir^{int210} | *1243* ℵ*

16:17 ⸀αλλ rell | ⸀αλλα ℵ

Appendix 2: Singular Readings in Sinaiticus in Matthew 153

16:19¹ επι της γης   *rell* ℵ^ca
        επι την γην   ℵ*

17:8   αυτον Ιησουν μονον B* Θ 700 NA²⁸ | *213* ℵ* ℵ^ca
       °τον Ιησουν μονον   *rell* B^c² |*312* D it^pler vg arm |°W

17:10 ⌜επηρωτησαν *rell* ℵ^S1 |⌜πηρωτησαν ℵ* |⌜επερωτησαν C 2^c
|⌜επηρωτισαν E |⌜επιρωτησαν L 2* |⌜ηρωτησαν 1689

17:17 αποκριθεις °δε ο Ιησους ειπεν   *rell* |°Ω 1071 *b gl
l r²* vg^(pler) geo
       ο δε αποκριθεις ειπεν αυτοις   ℵ*
       τοτε αποκριθεις ο Ιησους ειπεν αυτοις   ℵ^ca Z 579 892 *l184*
aur vg^(1MS) y^scr semel for aeth bo

18:3   ⌜εισελθητε *rell* ℵ^S1 |⌜εισελθηε ℵ* |⌜εισελθηται M W Θ 2*
579

18:8   ⌜εκκοψον *rell* ℵ^ca |⌜εξελε ℵ*

24:37 ⌐του υιου⌐ του ανθρωπου *rell* ℵ^ca |⌐ℵ*

24:39 ^T1εως^T2 ⌜ηλθεν ο κατακλυσμος *rell* ℵ^S1 ℵ^corr |^T1ο ℵ* |^T2εως Y*
|^T2ου Γ Δ 6 33 157 Chr |^T2οτου 346 |⌜εισηλθεν 16 544 692 1093 1293
|⌜ανηλθεν W

24:49 συνδουλους ^T K M U V W Γ Δ Π Σ 𝔐 2 28 346 565 579
1071 geo² sl^cdd Thph Or^int Hil Iren^int Bas^eth cdd |^Tαυτου *rell* |^Tεαυτου ℵ

25:16 ⌜ταλαντα *rell* ℵ^S1 |⌜αλαντα ℵ* |⌜τα K

25:22 °κυριε *rell* |°ℵ

25:36 προς ⌜με *rell* |⌜εμε ℵ

25:44a αποκριθησονται ᵀ¹ °και αυτοι ᵀ² λεγοντες   rell   ℵ^ca
|°ℵ^S1 21 1515 cop^dz |^T1αυτω f ff² h m r² vg^(pc) gat mm emm ing |^T2αυτω
f¹ 1 22 1582* 118
    αποκριθησονται αυτω οι λεγοντες   ℵ*

25:44b ου ⌜διηκονησαμεν   rell ⌜διακονησαμεν A ⌜διεκονησαμεν
B* Δ ⌜διηκονισαμεν 565
    ουκ ηδιηκονησαμεν ℵ

APPENDIX 3
Singular Readings in Vaticanus in Matthew

1:12a Ιεχονιας ⌜εγεννησεν rell (K) |⌜γεννα B

1:12b ⌜εγεννησεν τον Ζοροβαβελ rell (Δ 157 1071) |⌜γεννα B

1:13 ⌜εγεννησεν τον Αβιουδ rell ℵ^{S1} (Αβιουτ ℵ*) |⌜γεννα B

2:13 ⌐ °ιδου αγγελος rell |⌐εις την χωραν αυτων B |⌐τον μαγον C³ D³ (2ᶜ) 248 349 506 517 892 |°sy^{c.s.p}

3:4 ⌜Ιωαννης rell | ⌜Ιωανης B

3:12 ⌜ασβεστω rell B^{c2} (om. 𝔓^{101}) |⌜ασβετω B* |⌜αβεστω W

4:21 ⌜Ιωαννην rell |⌜Ιωανην B

5:10 ⌜ενεκεν rell |⌜ενεκα B

5:11 ⌜ενεκεν rell |⌜ενεκα B

5:16 ιδωσιν υμων τα καλα °εργα rell B^{c1} |°B* | 1345 346 | 13 425 28 246 482 483 1093 1355

5:28 ⌜αυτου rell |⌜εαυτου B

6:19 ⌜και βρωσις rell |⌜κα B

6:32 ⌜χρηζετε rell B^{c1} |⌜χρητε B* |⌜χρηζεται W 13 2* 33 579 |⌜χρηζητει Δ |⌜χριζεται 1071 |⌜χρειζετε 1424

6:33   την βασιλειαν ᵀ ᵒτου θεου ` και την δικαιοσυνην αυτου *rell* [NA²⁸] |ᵒℵ g¹·² k l m^semel am vg³ᵐˢˢ cop Eus^pr12,16 Ps-Ath²,³⁷⁸ Tert [NA²⁸] |ᵀτων ουρανων 301 Clem^579.lib242 Chr^txt.com Iust |ᵀαυτου 236 440 cop aeth v^cantscr Aph¹⁰⁵

        την δικαιοσυνην και την βασιλειαν αυτου   B

7:16   ⌜συλλεγουσιν *rell* B^c |⌜συλλεγουσι B*

7:25   ⌜ηλθον *rell* |⌜ηλθεν 1071 |⌜ηλθαν B

8:32   εξελθοντες ⌜απηλθον *rell* |⌜απηλθαν B

9:3   ⌜ειπαν B NA²⁸ |⌜ειπον *rell* |⌜ειπεν 346

9:28   ⌜προσηλθον *rell* |⌜προσηλθαν B

10:14   ⌜¹ος ⌜²αν ⌜³μη ⌜⁴δεξηται υμας *rell* |⌜¹οσοι L |⌜²εαν C 𝔐 M Δ Θ f¹ pc |⌜³μην B^c1 |⌜⁴δεξονται L

        ος αν μας   B*

10:16   εν μεσω   *rell*
        εις μεσον   B
        εμμεσω   C L Φ Ω

10:19   ⌜μεριμνησητε *rell* B^c2 |⌜μεριμνησετε Γ Θ 253 *l*54 |⌜μεριμνησειτε 579 |⌜μεριμησητε B*

10:22   ⌜υπομεινας *rell* B^c2 |⌜υπομενας B*

10:25a τον ⌜οικοδεσποτην   *rell* B^c2 |⌜δεσποτην 470
        τω οικοδεσποτη   B*

10:25b τους ⌜οικιακους   *rell* B^c2 |⌜οικειακους C D Y M U W f¹ 22 157 1582 *al.*
        τοις οικιακοις   B*

11:2   ⌜Ιωαννης rell |⌜Ιωανης B

11:4   ⌜Ιωαννη rell |⌜Ιωαννει D W Δ |⌜Ιωαννην E |⌜Ιωανη B^c |⌜Ιωανει B*

11:7   ⌜Ιωαννου rell |⌜Ιωανου B

11:11 ⌜Ιωαννου rell |⌜Ιωανου B |⌜Ιαννου Y*

11:12 ⌜Ιωαννου rell |⌜Ιωανου B |⌜Ιωαννους D*|⌜Ιαννου E 565

11:13 ⌜Ιωαννου rell |⌜Ιωανου B |⌜Ιαννου C 124

11:18 ⌜Ιωαννης rell |⌜Ιωανης B

12:1a ο Ιησους ᵀ °τοις ⌜σαββασιν rell |ᵀεν W 238 |°D* |⌜σαββατοις B |⌜σαβασι K |⌜σαββασι M U f^1 124^c 28 157 700 |⌜σαβασιν 565

12:1b ⌜οι δε μαθηται rell B^{c1} |⌜ο B*

12:32a ανθρωπου ᵀ αφεθησεται rell B^{c1} (ℵ K L Θ*) |ᵀουκ B*

12:32b ουκ αφεθησεται αυτω ουτε rell
       ⌜ουκ αφεθησετε αυτω ουτε ℵ^{S1} ℵ^{ca} L |⌜ου μη ℵ*
       ου μη αφεθη αυτω ουτε   B

12:33 ⌜σαπρον rell B^{c1} |⌜απρον B*

12:48 αδελφοι °μου rell B^{c1} |°B*

13:14 ⌜ακουσετε ℵ B^{c2} C L Δ Π f^1 pc NA^{28} |⌜ακουσατε B* |⌜ακουσεται D 579

13:15 ⌜τοις ωσιν rell B^{c1} |⌜τοι B*

13:17 πολλοι προφηται ⸆και δικαιοι` rell B^cl |⸆B*

13:24 εν τω αγρω ⸂αυτου   rell |⸂εαυτου B
εν τω ιδιω αγρω   D Eus^es.bis
εις τον αγρον αυτου 1424

13:30² ⸂αυτα rell B^cl |⸂αυτας B* |⸂om. D it^(excfk) vg

13:39 εχθρος ο ⸂σπειρας αυτα εστιν rell | 15234 B |⸂σπειρων L 2 1346

13:48 ⸂αιγιαλον rell B^cl |⸂αγιαλον B* |⸂εγιαλον W

14:3 Ἰωαννην rell |Ἰωανην B

14:4 Ἰωαννης rell | Ἰωανης B

14:8 Ἰωαννου rell |Ἰωανου B

14:10 Ἰωαννην rell |Ἰωανην B

14:13 ανεχωρησεν ⸂εκειθεν ⸆°εν ⸆ πλοιω` rell B^cl |⸂εκιθεν ℵ |⸂εκει 1279 |⸆Γ sy^s.c |°B*^vid |⸆τω 485

15:11 το ⸂εισερχομενον   rell |⸂εισπορευομενον 157 238 |⸂ερχομενον B

15:15 ο Πετρος ειπεν ⸂αυτω rell | 1243 B |4123 Θ 124 788 l349 | 3412 124 |⸂αυτοις 579 |⸂om. 659 954 1424 ff¹ sah

15:32 ⸂τους μαθητας rell B^cl |⸂του B*

16:4 ⸂επιζητει rell (om. 700) B^cl |⸂ζητει D* Θ b c e |⸂αιτει B*

16:17 °οτι rell B^cl |°B*

APPENDIX 3: SINGULAR READINGS IN VATICANUS IN MATTHEW 159

17:15   ελεησον μου τον υιον ⊤ *rell* B^{c2} |⊤μου B*

17:16   ⌜ηδυνηθησαν (*rell*) NA²⁸ |⌜ηδυνασθησαν B |⌜ηδυναντο Z |⌜ηδυνηθεισαν 2* |⌜εδυνηθησαν K Π 265 489 892 1219 1346 *l*184

17:23   ⌜τριτη ημερα *rell* B^{c2} |⌜τρι B* |⌜τρις 1346^c
        τρεις ημερας D it sy^s bo

18:9   ⌜σκανδαλιζει *rell* |⌜σκανδαλει B |⌜σκανδαλιζη F L Δ |⌜σκανδαληζη 2 |⌜σκανδαλησει 579

18:31   οι συνδουλοι °αυτου *rell* | *312* B |°482 *l*184

19:12   ⌜δυναμενος *rell* B^{c2a} |⌜δυνομενος B* B^{c2b}

19:17   °¹εις εστιν °²ο αγαθος   ℵ B^{c1} L Θ 892* 1582* 1424^{mg} *a d* lat sy^{s.c.hmg} mae bo Or NA²⁸ |°¹B* |°²D 1 22 700 791 2372 Iren Iust Valent Marcos Naass
        ουδεις αγαθος   *rell* (892^c)

20:13   αποκριθεις ενι αυτων °ειπεν   ℵ D Θ 085 124 700 1573 it^{pler} vg sy^{s.c} arm geo Or^{3,705} Chr NA²⁸ | *1324* B |°1346 | *1423 rell*
        αποκριθεις ειπεν μοναδι ενι αυτων Δ

20:17   ⌜κατ ιδιαν *rell* B^{c2} |⌜καθ B*

20:27   ⸆εν υμιν⸅ °ειναι πρωτος   *rell* |⸆sy^{pesh(1MS)} |°L
        ειναι υμων πρωτος   B | *213* X 085
        εν υμιν πρωτος ⌜ειναι   W 1241 1515 it^{pler} vg arm |⌜γενεσθε 28

20:32   °ο Ιησους *rell* (om. 1574 1594 *r²*) |°B

21:4 γεγονεν ινα πληρωθη το ρηθεν ⌜δια του ᵀ¹ προφητου ᵀ²
λεγοντος rell B^{c1} |⌜υπο L Z Γ Θ f^{13} 69 482 543 544 700 788 892
|^{T1}πληρωθη το ρηθεν δια του B* |^{T2}Ζαχαριου M^{mg} 42 a c h bo^{1MS}
Chr Hil^{psal.cxlv.1} |^{T2}ησαιου r² vg^{3MSS} bo^{1MS} aeth

21:17 ⌜Βηθανιαν rell B^{c2} |⌜Βηθανια B* |⌜Βιθανιαν Ω 1071
|⌜Βηθανειαν D

21:26 ⌜Ιωαννην rell |⌜Ιωανην B

21:32 ⌜Ιωαννης rell | ⌜Ιωανης B

21:33 ⌜εξεδετο ℵ* C* L NA^{28} |⌜εξεδετε B* |⌜εξεδοτο rell B^{c2}

21:38a ⌜εαυτοις rell B^{c2} |⌜αυτοις L | ⌜εαυτος B*

21:38b ⌜κληρονομος rell B^{c2} |⌜κληρονος B*

21:41 ⌜αποδωσουσιν rell B^c |⌜αποδωσουσι B* |⌜αποδωσωσιν W
|⌜αποδοσουσιν Θ

21:46 ⌜κρατησαι rell B^{c2} |⌜εκρατησαι B*^{vid} |⌜κπατεισαι E*
|⌜ποιησαι f^{13} 1346

22:39 ομοια ⌜¹αυτη ⌜²αγαπησεις rell |⌜¹αυτης Δ 0102 0138 176
238 807 1295 |⌜¹ταυτη D* Z^{vid} 692 it vg sy^{omn} bo aeth arm geo
|⌜²αγαπησις ℵ W |⌜²αγαπησης E
        ομοιως αγαπησις   B

22:43 καλει αυτον κυριον   B^{c2} D 0107^{vid} 0281 33 1093 *l*2211
latt sy^{(c).p.(hier)} (sa bo) arm geo² NA^{28} | *321* rell |*132* ℵ L Z 892 |*312* 69
sy^{hl} | *31* 1424 |*231* 0161 954 1424 | om. aeth
        καλει αυτον αυτον κυριον   B* | *1243* Θ

23:23 ⌜αφηκατε rell B^{c2} |⌜αφηκετε B*

23:25 ⌐γραμματεις *rell* |⌐γραμματις ℵ W |⌐γραματεις B

25:6 κραυγη ⌐γεγονεν *rell* |⌐εγενετο B

25:10 και ⌐εκλεισθη *rell* B^c |⌐ηκλεισθη B*

25:32 τα προβατα απο των ⌐εριφων   *rell* |⌐εριφιων B
       τα προβατα απ αγγηλων   700*

26:3 οι πρεσβυτεροι ⌐του λαου⌐ *rell* B^c1 (1071) |⌐B*

26:14 ⌐αρχιερεις *rell* B^c2 |⌐αρχιερις ℵ |⌐αρχιιερεις B*

26:51 εις °των μετα ^T Ιησου   *rell* |°𝔓^37 |^Tτου L 4 273 472 544
1010 1354 1396 *l*53 *l*184 |^T *discipulorum* sy^s
       εις των μετ αυτου   B (Hil?)

26:53a ⌐δυναμαι *rell* B^c2 |⌐δυνομαι B*

26:53b ⌐λεγιωνας B* NA^28 |⌐λεγιωνων ℵ* ℵ^S1 L |⌐λεγαιωνων ℵ^ca
|⌐λεγεονων A Δ 788 |⌐λεγεωνας *rell* B^c2 |⌐λεγεωνων C K Θ Π *f*^13 33
565 700 1071 |⌐λεγειωνης D* |⌐λεγειονας D^D |⌐λεγεονας E^c |⌐om. *ff*^2

26:57 οι δε ^T1 κρατησαντες ⌐τον Ιησουν⌐ ^T2 απηγαγον ^T3 *rell* B^c1
|^T1στρατιωται 1241 |⌐αυτον 157 sy^s[c] |^T2 οι δε στρατιωται
κρατησαντες τον Ιησουν G^mg |^T3αυτον 700 *c r*^2
       οι δε κρατησαντες τον Ιησουν εφυγον οι δε κρατησαντες
τον Ιησουν απηγαγον B*

26:59 εζητουν ⌐ψευδομαρτυριαν *rell* B^c2 |⌐ψευδομαρτυραν B*
|⌐ψευδομαρτυρειαν D

26:63 του ⌐ζωντος *rell* B^c2 |⌐ζωτος B*

27:1 ⌐γενομενης *rell* B^c2 |⌐γομενης B*

27:13 ουκ ακουεις ⌜ποσα rell B^{c1} |⌜οσα B* |⌜τοσα D* |⌜πωσα M

27:45 ⌜εως ωρας rell (D) |⌜ε B*

28:2–3 αυτου ^{28:3} ⌐ην ^{o1}δε ^{o2}η ⌜ειδεα αυτου⌐ rell ℵ^{S1} B^{c2} |⌐ℵ* |^{o1}geo |^{o2}66 *l*47 |⌜ειδε B* |⌜ιδεα F G K L S U V W Γ Δ Θ Π Σ Φ $f^{1.13}$ 33 69 157 565 788 1071 1241 1346 *l*844 |⌜ιδε L 579

28:11 τινες της ⌜κουστωδιας rell |⌜κουστωδειας A |⌜σκουστωδιας B* |⌜κουστοδιας 69 157 |⌜κωστουδιας 2

APPENDIX 4

Singular Readings in Ephraemi in Matthew[1]

1:8[1] ⸀Ιωσαφατ *rell* |⸀Ιωσαφα C*

1:8[2] ⸀Ιωσαφατ *rell* |⸀Ιωσαφα C*

2:16 εν ⸀βηθλεεμ *rell* |⸀βλεεμ C |⸀βεθλεαιμ D* |⸀βηθλεεμ D^{B} |⸀βιθλεεμ L Ω 349 1071

2:20 την ⸆ ψυχην *rell* |⸆την C

3:10 ⸀ηδη *rell* |⸀ηδε C

4:2 ημερας ⸀τεσσερακοντα ℵ B* L P Δ 33 NA^{28} |⸀τεσσαρακοντα *rell* |⸀σερακοντα 579 |⸀τεσσερακοντας C |⸀μ̅ D

4:14 ⸀προφητου *rell* |⸀φητου C

4:21a του ⸀Ζεβεδαιου *rell* (om. M W 33 *haplography*) |⸀Ζεβεναιους C {nu} |⸀Ζεβεδεου L

4:21b του ⸀Ζεβεδαιου *rell* (om. M W 33 *haplography*) |⸀Ζεβεναιους C {sigma} |⸀Ζεβεδεου L

5:10 ⸆ ⸀δικαιοσυνης *rell* |⸆της C |⸀δικαιοσυνην 13

7:9 ⸀αιτησει ο υιος ℵ* B L Δ Θ 2 28 157 1424 NA^{28} |⸀αιτηση *rell* |⸀αιτησεις C

---

[1] The spelling of Ζεβεδαιου in 4:21a and 21b is counted as two singular readings though it concerns one word.

7:16 απο ακανθων ⌜σταφυλας rell C^A ⌜σταφυλην E G K L M S U V W X Δ Θ Π f¹³ 565 579 700 1241 1424 *l*844 arm aeth Lcif Aug^semel ⌜σταφυληνας C*

7:22 ου τω σω ονοματι   rell
     ουτως σω ονοματι   C

8:5 παρακαλων ⌜αυτον rell C^c ⌜αυτο C*

8:13 επιστευσας ⌜γενηθητω rell ⌜γεννηθητω G Π* 1424 ⌜γενητω C

8:17 ⌜Ησαιου rell ⌜Ισαιου L Θ 2 ⌜Ησαιαιου C

8:21 ⌜αυτω rell ⌜ματων C | om. 399 1579

8:31 οι δε ⌜δαιμονες rell ⌜δειμονες C ⌜δεμονες L

8:32 και ⌜απεθανον εν τοις υδασιν rell ⌜απεθαναν ℵ^c ⌜απεθανεν C

9:2 και ιδου ⌜προσεφερον rell ⌜προσφερουσιν C

9:15 ⌜δυνανται rell ⌜δυναντα C ⌜δυνατε N ⌜δυναται Δ ⌜δυναντε 579

9:30 και ⌜ηνεωχθησαν B D N Σ 33 NA²⁸ ⌜ανεωχθησαν rell ⌜ηνοιχθησαν C* ⌜ανεοχθησαν C^Corr.C L

10:20 ⌜αλλα rell ⌜αλλλα C

11:21 ⌜οτι rell ⌜οτ C

12:4 ⌜προθεσεως rell ⌜προσεως C ⌜προσθεσεως D

12:6 ⌜μειζον rell |⌜μιζον ℵ N? W Θ |⌜μειζοων C* |⌜μειζων Cᴬ L N? Δ Φ f¹³ 2 13 22 118 124 157 209 346 440 543 565 788 1010 1071 1200 1346 1424 lat

12:7 ⌜κατεδικασατε rell |⌜κατεσατε C |⌜καταιδικασαται L |⌜καταδικασατε Δ |⌜τεδικασατε 33* |⌜κατεκρινετε 1574 2145

12:22 °δαιμονιζομενος ⌐τυφλος και⌐ κωφος rell Cᴮ |°1071 |⌐C* δαιμονιζομενον τυφλον και κωφον⊤ B 0281ᵛⁱᵈ 1424 1675 sy⁽ˢ·ᶜ·ᵖ⁾ cop aeth geo |⊤et surdus b (vg²ᴹˢˢ) |⊤et surdus et mutus (ff¹) h

12:47 ειπεν δε τις ⌜αυτω ⊤ rell [NA²⁸] |om. verse ℵ* B L Γ 126 225 238 400* 443 1355 1093 ff¹ k syᶜ·ˢ sa [NA²⁸] |⌜των μαθητων αυτου ℵᴬ |⌜των μαθητων αυτου προς αυτον 892 bo |⊤αυτω C

12:48 μητηρ °μου rell Cᴮ |°C*ᵛⁱᵈ

13:3–4 σπειρων °του ⌜σπειρειν ¹³:⁴ ⌐και εν τω σπειρειν⌐ αυτον rell |°D |⌜σπιρε ℵ |⌜σπειραι D L M W Θ f¹·¹³ 33 700 892 |⌜σπειραι τον σπορον αυτου 28 579 |⌐C

13:15 και τοις ωσιν ⊤ °ακουσωσιν rell |⊤αυτων ℵˢ¹ 157 |°C

13:44 ⌜των rell |⌜τω C

13:57 °ει μη rell Cᴮ |°C*

14:4 ⌜εχειν rell Cᶜ |⌜εχιν ℵ |⌜εχεν C*|⌜γαμησαι syˢ

15:2 ⌜μαθηται rell |⌜μαθητε ℵ Θ |⌜μαται C

15:11 εις το ⌜στομα rell |⌜σταμα C

15:30 αυτους ⸀παρα τους⸀ ποδας rell C^B |⸀C*
αυτους ⸀υπο τους ποδας   D b |⸀μακροθεν εμπροσθεν αυτου προς 1424

15:32 ⸀ειπεν rell |⸀λεγει C

15:36 ιχθυας ⸀°¹και ευχαριστησας⸀ °²εκλασεν και rell C^B |°¹𝔐 K L* M N P W Γ Δ 157 1241 *l*2211 f ff¹ sy^h |⸀C*vid |°²a g¹

16:3 ⸀χειμων rell |⸀χειχων C |⸀χιμων N Θ

16:12 ⸀φαρισαιων rell |⸀φαρεισαιων ℵ B |⸀παρισαιων C |⸀φαρισεω Θ*

16:22 ⸀επιτιμαν rell C^B |⸀επιτειμων B 346 |⸀επιτιμιαν C* |⸀επειτειμαν D 283 |⸀επιτιμα 579 |⸀πειτιμαν Θ

17:4 ⸀σκηνας rell |⸀σκησκηνας C

17:15 ⸀ελεησον rell |⸀ελησον C |⸀ελεησων Θ

19:1 ⸀ετελεσεν rell |⸀ετελεν C |⸀ελαλησεν D a b c e ff^{1.2} g¹ r¹ bo^{2MSS} Hil

20:11 κατα του ⸆ οικοδεσποτου rell |⸆κατα του C

20:19 ⸀σταυρωσαι rell |⸀σταυρωσε ℵ |⸀σταυρωαι C |⸀om. X

20:32 τι ⸀θελετε rell |⸀θελε 1071 |⸀θελεις C

21:1 εις ⸀Βηθφαγη ⸆ (rell) NA²⁸ |⸆και Βηθανιαν και C |⸆και Βηθανιαν Φ f¹³ 33 543 1346 sy^h

21:17a και ⸀ηυλισθη   rell C^{Corr.C} |⸀υλισεν U
       και ηυλισθησαν   C*

21:17b °εκει *rell* C^{Corr.C} |°C*

21:23 ⌐ελθοντος ℵ B D L Θ Φ $f^{1.13}$ 33 372 543 700 788 892 1346 Or NA²⁸ |⌐ελθοντες C |⌐εισελθοντι K Π 1241 1424 *l*48 |⌐ελθοντι *rell* |⌐προσελθοντι 1241

21:28a ⌐ειχεν *rell* C^B |⌐ειπεν C*

21:28b τω ⌐πρωτω *rell* |⌐πρω C

22:10a αγαθους και επλησθη ο ⌐γαμος *rell* (K) |⌐νυμφων ℵ B* L 0120 892 sy^{hmg} *pc* |⌐γαμος υμων D Θ f^{13} 124 700 788 1346 |⌐αγαμος C

22:10b ⌐ανακειμενων *rell* |⌐ανακιμενων ℵ |⌐ανακεινων C |⌐ανακειμενου K |⌐ανακημενων 2*

22:20 ⌐και λεγει αυτοις *rell* |⌐ο δε C |⌐om. D 69 it *b e ff*¹ ² *g*² *h* sah sy^{s.c} mae

23:24 °οι ⌐διυλιζοντες τον κωνωπα   *rell* C^c |°ℵ^{ca} B D* L sa^{mss} |⌐διυλιζονται C*
       ουδε υλιζοντες τον κωνωπα   579

23:26 ⌐Φαρισαιε τυφλε *rell* C¹ |⌐Φαρεισαιε B |⌐Φαρισαιοιε C*

24:3a ορους ⌐των ελαιων   *rell* |⌐τω K
       ⌐ορους των ελεων   ℵ D L 2 |⌐ορου Θ
       ορους των ελεων κατεναντι του ιερου   C

24:3b ⌐ποτε ταυτα *rell* |⌐τοτε C

24:4 ⌐πλανηση *rell* |⌐πλανησι C |⌐πλανησωσι U |⌐πλανησει Θ 2* 28 579 |⌐πλανησουσι 118

24:45 ⌐¹αυτου °του ⌐²δουναι ℵ B I L U Δ *al*³⁰ fere Bas^eth Chr NA²⁸ | ⌐¹εαυτου C |°D *al pc* Chr Ephr |⌐²διδοναι E F G H K M S V W Γ Π *al pl* Ephr

25:6 εις ⌐¹απαντησιν ⌐²αυτου *rell* [NA²⁸] |⌐¹υπαντησιν Z Θ Σ 157 Cyr |⌐²om. ℵ B Z 700 [NA²⁸] |⌐²αυτω *l*13 *l*63
εις συναντησιν αυτω C

26:39 επεσεν ᵀ επι προσωπον *rell* C^B |ᵀεπεσεν C*

26:50 ⌐εταιρε *rell* |⌐εθταιρε C* |⌐ετεραι D 579 |⌐ετερε E* W Θ

26:51 ⌐των *rell* |⌐om. 𝔓³⁷ |⌐τω C*

26:57 ᵀ¹⌐¹Ιησουν ⌐²απηγαγον ᵀ² προς *rell* |ᵀ¹αυτον 565 |⌐¹αυτον 157 sy^s[c] |⌐²ηγαγον 579 |⌐²απηγον C |ᵀ²αυτον 700 *c r*²

26:65 λεγων ᵀ εβλασφημησεν τι ετι χρειαν ℵ^ca B C^B D L Z Θ 090 0281 33 700 892 latt NA²⁸ |ᵀοτι *rell* |ᵀτι C*^vid
και ⌐λεγει °ιδε εβλασφημησεν τι ετι χρειαν ℵ* |°sy^sch |⌐λεγων sy^p pers^p aeth

26:67 ⌐εκολαφισαν *rell* |⌐εκολαφιλασαν C |⌐εκολαφησαν E F K Θ Ω 2 13 124 579 788 1424

27:49 ⌐σωσων *rell* |⌐σωσαι ℵ* Θ 69 1010 1071 1241 1293 *l*184 |⌐σωσωσων C |⌐σωσει D 1 209 1582* |⌐σωσον F Y K 2* 28 157 700* |⌐σωζων W

27:56 ην ⌐¹Μαρια °η ⌐²Μαγδαληνη και ` Μαρια *rell* ℵ^ca |⌐ℵ* |⌐¹Μαριαμ L *f*¹ sa^mss |°D* |⌐²Μαγδαλινη Σ 124 346 543 28 348 474 565 579 788 1279 *l*184
ην ᵀ Μαριαμ η Μαγδαληνη και Μαριαμ   C^Corr.C Δ Θ 713 sy^omn arm geo |ᵀκαι C*

27:58 ⌜εκελευσεν *rell* |⌜εκενλευσεν C

27:64 ⌜εσχατη *rell* |⌜αισχατη D |⌜σχατη C |⌜εσχατι 2*

APPENDIX 5
Singular Readings in Codex D in Matthew[1]

2:1   Ηρωδου   rell (*Herodis* Latt)
      Ηρωδους   D (*Herodes* d)

2:3   και ⌈πασα ᵀ Ιεροσολυμα μετ αυτου rell ⌈om. D d ⌈πασσα L ⌈ᵀη N Z Σ 248 280 692 Eus^dem

2:6   ⌈ποιμανει rell ⌈ποιμανι ℵ ⌈ποιμενει D

2:8a ⌈Βηθλεεμ rell ⌈Βεθλεεμ D ⌈Βιθλεεμ L Ω 349 *l*48

2:8b ⌈επαν rell ⌈οταν D ⌈εαν Prot^cdd6

2:8c ⌈απαγγειλατε rell ⌈αναγγειλατε 124 ⌈επαγγειλαται D* ⌈απαγγειλαται D^B

2:9   ⌈ακουσαντες ᵀ του βασιλεως rell D^CorrC ⌈ακουσαν D* ⌈ᵀπαρα 1071

2:11 ⌈θησαυρους rell ⌈θηνσαυρους D ⌈*thensauros a b d f ff*¹ *k q*

2:16a εν ⌈βηθλεεμ rell ⌈βλεεμ C ⌈βεθλεαιμ D* ⌈βηθλεεμ D^B ⌈βιθλεεμ L Ω 349 1071

2:16b ⌈ηκρειβωσεν rell ⌈ηκρειβασεν D ⌈ηκριβωσε 1424

2:22 ⌈εφοβηθη rell D^Corr.C ⌈εφηθη D*

---

[1] The singular readings recorded as 12:1b and 12:1c overlap textually, but are counted separately. This is also the case for the readings marked as 15:37–38 and 15:37—they overlap but are counted as separate readings.

APPENDIX 5: SINGULAR READINGS IN CODEX D IN MATTHEW 171

3:2 ⌜ηγγικεν *rell* |⌜ηνγικεν D |⌜ηγγεικεν W Δ |⌜ηγγικε f^1 157 788 1346

3:4 ⌜καμηλου *rell (d lacunae)* |⌜καμηλλου D |⌜καμιλου 28 565 |⌜*camelli* k sy$^{hl.hier}$ geo |⌜*cameli* q |⌜*camellorum* it^{pler} vg sy$^{c.s.pesh}$ cop aeth arm Eus Aug

4:6a ⌜του θεου *rell* D^A |⌜θεου D*

4:6b ⌜αρουσιν *rell* |⌜αιρουσιν D

4:7 ουκ εκπειρασεις   *rell*
     ου πειρασεις   D
     non ⌜*tentabis*   Latt |⌜*temptauis* d* |⌜*temptabis* d^G

4:13 ⌜κατωκησεν *rell* |⌜κατοικησεν D |⌜κατοκησεν E* | om. sy^s

4:15 ⌜Νεφθαλιμ S L W Ω 2 28 565 579 NA^{28} |⌜Νεφθαλειμ *rell* |⌜Νεφθαλειν D

4:16a ⌜μεγα *rell* D^c |⌜μεγαν D* |⌜*magnam* Latt (*magnum* d)

4:16b και ⌜σκια   *rell* D^B |⌜σκηα L
       σκεια   D* d

4:17 ⌜ηγγικεν *rell* |⌜ηνγικεν D |⌜ηγγηκεν L |⌜εγγεικεν W 1071 |⌜ηγγικε 13 118 157 788

4:18 ⌜αμφιβληστρον *rell* D^B (*rete* Latt) |⌜αμφιβληστρος D* |⌜*retiam* d

4:24 η ακοη °αυτου *rell* |°Δ |3*12* D

5:3 °τω πνευματι *rell* D^{CorrC} |°D*

APPENDIX 5: SINGULAR READINGS IN CODEX D IN MATTHEW

5:10 ⌜εστιν rell |⌜εστε D (erit d)

5:12
υμων rell |om. sy^s
υμων υπαρχοντων D*
υμων υπαρχοντας D^c d (Latt^al) sy^c bo?
υμων οι πατερες ⌜υμων U |⌜αυτων b c k syr^cu

5:18 παντα γενηται rell |21 D d

5:22 ⌜οργιζομενος rell D^D |⌜οργαζομενος D*

5:24 ⌜διαλλαγηθι rell |⌜καταλλαγηθι D

5:25a °εως ⌜οτου rell D^A |°D* |⌜ου 13 28 124 543 788 1241 l184

5:25b μηποτε σε ⌜παραδω rell D^c |⌜παραδωσει D* |132 Cl

5:25c ο κριτης ⊤   𝔓^64vid ℵ B 0275 f^1.13 16 59 265 372 892 1473 1579 1588 k sy^hier aeth arm geo^B Aug^serm.387 Clem Alex^strom.IV.14.95 Hil |⊤σε παραδωσει D |⊤σε παραδω K L W Γ Δ Θ Π Σ 33 157 346 565 579 700 1241 1424 l844 𝔐 it vg sy^c.pesh.hl cop geo^1 et A|om. 1346
    ο κριτις παραδω   700

5:29 °ο οφθαλμος σου ο δεξιος rell (1071) |°S 157 | 12453 D

5:36 ου δυνασαι μιαν τριχα λευκην ποισαι °η μελαιναν   ℵ^S1
B W Θ 33 892 l844 lat NA^28 |12634578 f^1 209 k sy^hier cop |12346578 0250 f^13 124 543 700 788 1071 h |12348756 238 |12634875 sy^c.s.pesh Aph^500 Tat^diat |1264578 Clem^262 |°L
    ου δυνασαι μιαν τριχαν λευκην ποισαι η ⌜μελαιναν   ℵ*
⌜μελαναν W |12345786 E 157 1346
    ου δυνασαι ⌜ποιειν τριχα μειαν λευκην η μελαιναν   D*
⌜ποιησαι D^B.D
    ου δυνασαι ποιησαι τριχα μιαν λευκην η μελαιναν   d k
Cyp^178 Aug^semel

ου δυνασαι μιαν τριχα λευκην η ⌜μελαιναν ποισαι   𝔐
K M U Δ Π^c Σ 2 22 28^c 118 157 346 565 579 1241 1424 *l*844 sy^h
|⌜μελεναν 28* |⌜μελαινα 579 |⌜μελαναν Π*

5:40 τω θελοντι σοι   *rell*
      ο θελων σοι   D
      τον θελοντα σοι   Δ 485

5:41 ⌜αγγαρευσει *rell* |⌜ενγαρευση ℵ |⌜αγγαρευει D |⌜αγγαρευση
E G K V Θ Σ 13 543 33 157 243 471* *l*49 |⌜ανγαρευση W 124 788
|⌜αγγερευση Δ 33 892* 1071 1424 |⌜αγκαρευσει 59 66 483 484
|⌜αγγαρευσει *l*844

5:48 ο ουρανιος τελειος εστιν   *rell* D^B
      ο °¹εν °²τοις ουρανοις τελειος °³εστιν   E² K M S Δ Θ Π
22 565 579 700 *al. pl. b c d g*¹ *h k* sy^{cu.sch.pesh.hier} Aug^{aliq} Clem^{792allud} Lcif
Tert |°¹geo² |°²D* |°³*d k* geo^{1(2)}

6:7 ⌜βατταλογησητε ℵ B *f*¹³ NA²⁸ |⌜βαττολογησητε *rell*
|⌜βλαττολογησηται D* |⌜βλατταλογησηται D^D |⌜βατολογησητε E
G 1241 *l*183 sy^p ^{(mg gr)} |⌜βατταλογειται W 59 471 1604
|⌜βατγολογησητε 517 892 |⌜βατтολογειτε 700 |⌜βατολογησητε
1424

6:12 ⌜οφειληματα *rell* |⌜οφιλεματα D |⌜οφεληματα K L |⌜οφειλην
Didache |⌜παραπτωματα Or

6:18a τω πατρι σου τω εν °τω *rell* D^{CorC} |°D*

6:18b ⌜κρυφαιω και ℵ B D^A *f*¹ 22 660 NA²⁸ |⌜κρυφια D*^{vid} |⌜κρυπτω
rell

6:18c ο ᵀ βλεπων εν °τω ⌜κρυφαιω ℵ B *f*¹ 22 600 NA²⁸ |°D |ᵀσε 273
|⌜κρυπτω *rell*

6:20 ⌜θησαυρους *rell* D^c ⌜θησαυρουσους D*

9:2   ⌜θαρσει *rell* D^{p.m.} ⌜θαρει D* ⌜θαρσε L ⌜θαρσι Θ 579

9:10 ⌜συνανεκειντο *rell* D^{Cor.C} ⌜συνεκειντο D*

9:20 ⌜ιματιου *rell* ⌜ματιου D ⌜ηματιου 2

9:33 °τω Ισραηλ *rell* D^{CorrC} |°D*

9:36 ⌜ερριμμενοι *rell* ⌜εριμμενοι ℵ B C D^c S Σ 22 21 280 349 990 1574 1606 *l*184 ⌜ρεριμμενοι D* ⌜ερημενοι L ⌜ερρηγμενοι M ⌜ερρημενοι X Ω 471 ⌜ερριμενοι Γ Δ 209 ⌜περιεριμμενοι 1093 |om. Bas

10:8 ⌐νεκρους ⌜εγειρετε⌐ *rell* |⌐C³ K L X Y Γ Θ Π 59 118 124 209 245 251 482 485 517 579 700^{txt} 1278 1424^c 𝔐 *f* sy^{pesh.hier} sa aeth^{(2cdd)} arm geo^{1etB} Eus ⌜εγειρατε D

10:10 χιτωνας *rell* ⌜χειθωνας D* ⌜χειτωνας D^H ⌜χειτονας L ⌜χιτονας Θ

10:13² °η ειρηνη *rell* D^B |°D*

10:15 εν ^T ημερα *rell* |^Tη D* |^Tτη D^H

10:16 ⌜ακεραιοι *rell* ⌜απλουστατοι D ⌜*simplices* Latt

10:25 ⌜επεκαλεσαν *rell* ℵ^{ca} (*vocaverunt* Latt) ⌜επεκαλεσαντο ℵ* L N 4 59 *pc* ⌜εκαλεσαν Θ 0171 *f*¹ 2 124 700 1424 Epiph ⌜καλουσιν D (*uocant d*) ⌜απεκαλεσαν Y U 157*

10:28 το σωμα την δε ψυχην μη δυναμενων ⌜αποκτειναι (*rell*) ⌜αποκτιναι ℵ D^P N W Θ ⌜σφαξαι D* ⌜αποκτειναντα 579

10:34² ⌜ειρηνην rell Dᴰ |⌜ιρηνην ℵ |⌜ειρην D* |⌜ηρηνην Θ

10:35 °του πατρος rell |°D

10:36 ⌜εχθροι rell |⌜εκθροι D

11:3 ⌜ερχομενος rell Dᴮ |⌜εργαζομενος D*

11:8 ⌜ημφιεσμενον rell |⌜ημφιασμενον D |⌜περιβεβλημενον 472

11:10 ⌜αγγελον rell |⌜ανγελον D

11:11a γεννητοις rell Dᶜ |ᵀτοις D*

11:11b γυναικων rell Dᶜ |ᵀτων D*

11:12 ⌜Ιωαννου rell Dᴬ (Ioannis Latt; Iohannis d) |⌜Ιωανου B |⌜Ιωαννους D* |⌜Ιαννου E 565

11:16 ⸆εν °ταις αγοραις⸌ (ℵ) B Z 1 33 892 1424 1582* l184 NA²⁸ |°rell |⸆118 1071 1582ᶜ
        εν ᵀαγορα   047 28 59 251 349 399 470 485 544 1293 1574 al. |ᵀτη D

11:20 ⌜εγενοντο rell |⌜γεγονεισαν D |⌜εγενετο Π* |⌜εγινοντο 692 1071
        ⌜¹factae ⌜²sunt Latt |⌜¹facti d |⌜²fuerant k

11:21 ⌜εγενοντο rell |⌜εγεγονεισαν D |⌜εγενηθησαν 33 157 517 892 1391 1424 1675 l7 l49

11:22 η ⌜υμιν   rell |⌜σοι M* | om. 1346
       ⌜ην υμειν   D* |⌜η Dᶜ

11:24a ⌜γη Σοδομων rell (L) |⌜γης D |ᵒom. 1604 ff¹ k Iren^int

11:24b η ⸀¹ ⸀²σοι   rell |⸀¹εν 21 1279 |⸀²υμιν M^{mg} 124 659 1424 it vg^{mss} sa^{ms} bo^{pt} arm^{(cdd)} Ir^{int288} |⸀²συ 157 471*
　　　⸀ην υμειν   D* |⸀η D^c

11:25 ⸀απεκαλυψας rell |⸀απεκαλυψες D

11:26 ⸀εμπροσθεν rell |⸀ενπροσθεν D

12:1a ο Ιησους ⸀¹ °τοις ⸀²σαββασιν rell D^{CorrC} |⸀¹εν W 238 |°D* |⸀²σαββατοις B |⸀²σαβασι K |⸀²σαββασι M U f^1 124^c 28 157 700 |⸀²σαβασιν 565

12:1b τιλλειν ⸀σταχυας   rell |⸀τους U W 118 28 700 sa bo
     του σταχυας τιλλειν D {transposition}

12:1c °τους σταχυας   U W 118 28 700 sa bo |°rell
     του σταχυας   D {letter om.}

12:4a ⸀προθεσεως rell |⸀προσεως C |⸀προσθεσεως D

12:4b ουκ εξον ην   rell |l32 D
     ουκ ⸀εξον   Chr^{com}et^{mo6} |⸀εξην Or |⸀εξεστιν C 16 33 118 726 1010 1375 1579 1675 |⸀εξεστι 28

12:12 ⸀προβατου rell D^c | ⸀του D*

12:13 ⸀υγιης rell |⸀ηγυης D* |⸀υγειης D^{p.m.} |⸀υγιη E* |⸀υγιεις L Θ |⸀om. l184* a b c ff^1 h vg^{1MS} sy^{c.s.pesh} aeth arm Hil

12:18a ιδου °ο παις μου ⸀ον ηρετισα rell |°Δ |⸀εις D

12:18b ⸀απαγγελει rell |⸀απαγγελλει D |⸀απαιτελει L |⸀αναγγελει 348 700 788 1187 |⸀επαγγελει 248 485

12:19 ⸀ακουσει rell |⸀ακουει D |⸀ακουση 28 476 l184

12:20a ⸆καλαμον συντετριμμενον ⸆ rell (B) D^F |⸆D* d*
⸆arundinem quassatam   Latt |⸆harundinem d^G

12:20b ⸆κατεαξει rell |⸆κατιαξεις D* (confringes d*) |⸆κατεαξεν D^F d^G

12:20c ου ⸆ σβεσει   rell (ℵ Δ 1071) |⸆μη 713
ου °μη ζβεσει D* |°D^c

12:23 ⸆μητι ⸆ rell D^c |⸆μη 258 945 990 |⸆οτι D*

12:26 ⸆σταθησεται rell D^{Corr.C} |⸆στησεται D*

12:28 ⸆εφθασεν rell |⸆εφθασαν D*

12:34 λαλει ⸆ rell D^D |⸆αγαθα D* d |⸆mala ff²

12:36 ⸆λαλησουσιν ℵ B C Θ 4 21 33 273 700* 713 945 1093 1223 1354 1391 1555 NA²⁸ |⸆λαλουσιν D (locuntur d) |⸆λαλησωσιν rell |⸆locuti it^{(pler)} vg

12:39 ⸆αυτη rell D^D |⸆σοι D* |⸆αυτοις Iust

12:40 ωσπερ γαρ ην Ιωνας   rell |1243 047 252 892
      ωσπερι γαρ Ιωνας   D*
      ωσπερ °γαρ Ιωνας   D^c c^{scr} |°472
      ωσπερ γαρ εγενετο Ιωνας   Θ 7 517 954 1391 1424 1675 l49
l184
      ην Ιωνας   565

12:41a ⸆Νινευιται B C L W X Δ Θ Σ 213 443 1574 2145 al. NA²⁸ |⸆Νινευειτε ℵ |⸆Νεινευεται D* |⸆Νεινευειται D^D |⸆Νηνευιται Γ |⸆Νινευιται rell

12:41b ⸆γενεας rell D^B |⸆νεας D* |⸆γεναιας E

12:41c ⌜κατακρινουσιν rell D^D |⌜κακρινουσιν D*

12:42 ᵀΣολομωνος και ιδου (rell) D^c NA²⁸ |ᵀτου D*

12:43 ⌜εξελθη rell |⌜εξηλθη D

12:45 τα εσχατα ᵀ του ⌜ανθρωπου °εκεινου   rell (ℵ) |ᵀχειρονα τω Ε |⌜ουρανου Θ |34512 1689 |°348 sy^c
       τα αισχατα ᵀ του ανθρωπου εκεινου   D^c Ω |ᵀαυτου D* d

13:1a ⌜εν rell D^c |⌜ες D*

13:1b ⌜εξελθων rell |⌜εξηλθεν D

13:1c ο Ιησους ᵀτης οικιας   Β Θ f^{1.13} 1424 Or^{3,3} NA²⁸ | ᵀεκ ℵ Z 33 892 c f h q vg Or^{int3,2} Chr(et^{mo7}) |ᵀαπο rell
       ο Ιησους ᵀ   a b e f ff^{1.2} g^1 k Sy^s |ᵀκαι D d

13:6 ηλιου °δε ⌜ανατειλαντος   rell (^s e) |°4 61 h geo |⌜ανατιλαντος ℵ N W |⌜ανατηλαντος Θ |⌜ανατελλοντος 1253 2542
       του δε ηλιου ανατειλαντος   D
       και ηλιου ανατειλαντος   735

13:16 °τα ωτα rell |°D

13:22 του ⌜¹πλουτου ⌜²συμπνιγει rell |⌜¹κοσμου 157 |⌜²συνπνειγει B* D^c |⌜²συμπνειγει B^c |⌜²συνπνιγει ℵ C L N W Δ Θ f^{13} 788 565 |⌜²συνπνηγη 2* |⌜²συμπνηγη 2^c |⌜²συμπηνγει 28 του πλουτους συνπνειγει   D*

13:25 του σιτου °και rell |°D*

13:30 ⌜αποθηκην rell D^B |⌜αποθην D* |⌜αποθηκιν Ω

APPENDIX 5: SINGULAR READINGS IN CODEX D IN MATTHEW

13:34   ταυτα παντα ⌐ελαλησεν rell D^c |⌐ελαλι ℵ^c W |⌐ελαληνσεν D*

13:38¹ οι ⌐υιοι rell D^c |⌐υιο D*

13:38a ⌐της βασιλειας rell D^c |⌐της βασ D*

13:41   ⌐συλλεξουσιν rell |⌐συνλεξουσιν D |⌐συλεξουσιν L |⌐συλλεξωιν Φ

13:44a ⌐θησαυρω rell D^c |⌐θηνσαυρω D* |⌐thensauro d

13:44b ⌐°ανθρωπος rell |⌐τις 892 |°af (Or)
        τις   D d

13:46   ⌐πεπρακεν rell |⌐επωλησεν D |⌐πεπραχεν E

13:48a ⌐αναβιβασαντες rell |⌐ανεβιβασαν D |⌐αναβηβασαντες F L Θ 13 2 579 1346 1424 |⌐αναβασαντες 118 |⌐educentes c ff¹ l vg |⌐educentes d |⌐ducentes r² vg^2MSS |⌐eduxerunt a b f ff² h q sy^omn sa bo aeth |⌐duxerunt g¹ |⌐posuerunt e |⌐imposuerunt k

13:48b εις ⌐αγγη   ℵ B C* N M* Θ f¹ 124 399 700 892* Or NA²⁸ |⌐αγγεια rell |⌐αγια L |⌐αγγια P X |⌐αγγειον 33 | om. sy^c.s
        εις τα αγγια D

13:49a του ⌐αιωνος rell |⌐κοσμου D

13:49b ⌐αγγελοι rell |⌐ανγελοι D

13:52   ⌐μαθητευθεις rell |⌐μαθητευθις ℵ |⌐μαθηθευθεις D |⌐μαθητευθη L

14:6   °της Ηρωδιαδος   rell |°W (Ηροδιαδος Θ) f¹³
        αυτου Ηρωδιας   D

14:8 ᵀ °ωδε επι ⌜πινακι την κεφαλην rell |ᵀεξαυτης 1424
|°it⁽ᵖˡᵉʳ⁾ vg⁽⁵ᴹˢˢ⁾ bo |⌜πινακος 473
   ωδε ᵀ κεφαλην   D* d |ᵀτην Dᴮ

14:14 ⌜¹επ ⌜²αυτοις rell |⌜¹εν L 485 |⌜²αυτον I 067 1253 (aur vgˢᵗ·ʷʷ)
Or³'⁵⁰⁹ |⌜²αυτους Φ 13 33 868 979 983 1331 1335 1424 1574 1689
*l*2211

   περι αυτων   D
   super eos   k syᶜ·ᵖᵉˢʰ·ʰˡ sa bo
   °*de eis*   d |°*f ff*¹ vg⁽ᵐᵘ·⁾
   ⌜*illis*   a b c g¹ h l |⌜*eius* aur vg⁽ᵖˡᵉʳᵉᵗ ᵂᵂ⁾

14:24 ⌜ην γαρ εναντιος rell Dᴷ |⌜η D*

14:25 τεταρτη ⌜δε φυλακη   rell | ⌜ουν W
      τεταρτης δε φυλακης   D

14:27 ⌜θαρσειτε rell |⌜θαρσιτε ℵ |⌜θαρρειτε D |⌜θαρσειται W Θ 2*
|⌜om. 517 954 983 1424 1675 1689

14:31 °ο Ιησους   rell |°D |om. E* vg⁽¹ᴹˢ⁾
      dominus noster   syᵖᵉˢʰ

15:1 τοτε προσερχονται rell Dᶜᵒʳ·ᶜ Orᵗˣᵗ
      τοτε ⌜προερχονται D* |⌜απερχονται Orᶜᵒᵐ

15:3 δια τι °και ⌜¹υμεις ⌜²παραβαινετε rell |°ℵ* 579 1012 1187
1365 Iren |⌜¹ημεις f¹³ |⌜²παραβαιναι D
   δια τι υμεις παραλαμβαινετε   1071

15:14a ⌜αυτους rell |⌜τους τυφλους D d

15:14b ⌜πεσουνται rell ℵˢ¹ |⌜πεσουντε ℵ* |⌜εμπεσουνται F O W Σ Φ
4 262 273 517 565 659 700 1010 1012 1293 1295 1412 1424 1675
Epiph Chr |⌜ενπεσουνται D

APPENDIX 5: SINGULAR READINGS IN CODEX D IN MATTHEW 181

15:16 ⌜ακμην rell |⌜ακνην D

15:22a ⌜εκεινων rell D^{p.m.} |⌜εκινων ℵ |⌜εκειων D* |⌜εκεινον L |⌜αυτης 349 517 659 954 1424 1675

15:22b ^{T1}λεγουσα ^{T2} rell |^{T1}αυτω 𝔐 K L M U V W X Γ Δ Π Φ 0106 0119 (om. λεγουσα f^1) 565 f ff^1 k vg^{(3MSS)} sy^{hl.p} Bas |^{T1}οπισω αυτου D d |^{T2}αυτω c ff^2 g^1 vg^{pler} Aug

15:27a ⌜ψιχιων rell |⌜ψειχιων B |⌜ψυχιων 565 1071 |⌜ψειχων D

15:27b ⌜κυριων rell D^c |⌜κυναριων D*

15:29 το ⌜ορος rell |⌜ρος D

15:32a ⌜σπλαγχνιζομαι rell |⌜σπλαγχνιζομε ℵ C W |⌜σπλανχνιζομαι D |⌜σπλαχνηζομαι K |⌜σπλαγχνιζωμε L |⌜σπλαχνιζομαιλ Δ Ω

15:32b ου θελω ⌐μηποτε εκλυθωσιν εν τη οδω⌐ rell D^{p.m.} D^D d^{p.m.} |⌜μη ℵ 1 22 1582* 700 892 2372* a b c g^1 l q aur vg sy^{omn} |⌐D* d*

15:35 ⌜παραγγειλας B f^{1.13} 33 579 788 892*^{vid} 1346 NA^{28} |⌜παραγγιλας ℵ Θ |⌜εκελευσεν rell |⌜παρανγειλας D |⌜εκευσε Y* |⌜εκελευσε Y^c M U 118 157 700 1071 |⌜κελευσας 291

15:37–38   ^{15:37}⌐και το περισσευον των κλασματων ηραν επτα ⌜1σπυριδας πληρεις ^{15:38} οι δε εσθιοντες ησαν ^T ⌜2τετρακισχιλιοι ανδρες⌐ rell (pon. ηραν a. το ℵ C K L N P W Γ Δ f^{13} 565 1241 1424 m f (ff^1) q) NA^{28} |⌐D* |⌜1σφυριδας D^{p.m.} |^Tως B Θ f^{13} 33 892 l2211 |^Tωσει ℵ 579 1241 |⌜2τετρακισχειλιοι B D^{p.m.} W Θ |⌜τετρακισχιλιας 157

15:37 ⌜σπυριδας rell |⌜σφυριδας D^{p.m.}

15:39a ⌜ενεβη ℵ B N S Φ Ω 1 18 33 35 124 184^vid 735 892 1009 1328 1334 1335 1338 1339 1342 1348 1582 1604 1661 2193^c 2372^c 2766 NA²⁸ |⌜ανεβη rell |⌜ενβαινει D

15:39b ᵀΜαγαδαν (rell) NA²⁸ |ᵀτης D

16:3 ο ουρανος °υποκριται   rell (om. verse ℵ B Y f¹³ 2* 157)
|°C W Δ 33 NA²⁸
       ο αηρ   D

16:4 ⌜σημειον ου δοθησεται rell |⌜σημιον ℵ D^c W |⌜σημιαν D*
|⌜σημιων Θ

16:16 του ζωντος   rell D^H
      ⌜το σωζοντος D* (saluatoris d*) |⌜του D^A
      ⌜uiui   Latt |⌜uiuentis d^G |⌜om. l sy^pesh(1MS*) Hil^semel.Trin.VI.36

16:22 ⌜¹εσται °σοι ⌜²τουτο rell |⌜¹εστω f¹³ 788 1071 |°a b e ff² sy^c
Hil al |⌜²τουτω L
      εστε τουτο σοι   D d

16:23 τα των ανθρωπων   rell | om. e ff² g¹ r¹
      ᵀ του ανθρωπου   D |ᵀτα d ff¹ q sy^c.(p.hl.) sah aeth

17:2 ⌜εμπροσθεν rell |⌜ενπροσθεν D

17:5 ⌜επεσκιασεν rell D^D (obumbravit Latt) |⌜obumbrabat d
     επεσκιαζεν D*

17:8 ⌜επαρεντες rell |⌜επεροντες D* |⌜επαραντες D^p.m.+D

17:18 ⌜εθεραπευθη rell |⌜εθαραπευθη D

17:20 κοκκον rell D^B |⌜κοκκος D* |⌜κοκον F Δ |⌜κοκο L |⌜κοκκω 2
|⌜κοκκο 1424*

17:24¹ τα ⌜διδραχμα (rell) ⌜διδραγματα D

18:6 ⌜συμφερει rell ⌜συνφερει D ⌜συμφερι Θ

18:14 ⌜εμπροσθεν rell ⌜ενπροσθεν D ⌜εμπροσθε 1346 ⌜om. ℵ f¹³ bo

18:15a ⌜ελεγξον rell ⌜ελενξον D ⌜ελεγξε W ⌜ελλεγξον Ω 579

18:15b ⌜εκερδησας rell ⌜εκερδησες D ⌜εκερδισας E L

18:19a ⌜συμφωνησωσιν rell ⌜συμφωνησουσιν ℵ E N L Δ Θ 078^{vid} 0281^{vid} f¹³ 33 700 788 1071 1346 1424 ⌜συνφωνησουσιν D

18:19b παντος^T πραγματος rell D^c |^T του D*

18:22 εως επτακις ⌜¹αλλα °εως εβδομηκοντακις ⌜²επτα B D^c 058^{vid} 174 2145 NA²⁸ |⌜¹αλλ rell |°d e ff¹ h |⌜²επτακις D* ⌜septies Latt |⌜septies et septies b r² vg^{2MSS} |⌜septem septem sy$^{c.s.pesh}$

18:25 ⌜αποδοθηναι rell D^A ⌜αποδοθηνε ℵ ⌜αποθηναι D* ⌜αποδωθηναι 579 1071 ⌜αποδουναι 1604

18:27 ⌜σπλαγχνισθεις rell ⌜σπλαγχνισθις ℵ ⌜σπλανχνισθεις D ⌜σπλαγχνησθεις E 2^c ⌜σπλαχνισθεις K ⌜σπλαγχνησθης 2* ⌜σπλαγχνισθης 579

18:28 εκατον δηναρια rell |21 D d

19:4 ⌜θηλυ rell D^c ⌜θηλυν D* ⌜θυλη 1346

19:6 ⌜χωριζετω rell ⌜αποχωριζετω D ⌜separet Latt ⌜separari a

19:10 ⌜συμφερει rell ⌜συμφερι ℵ Θ ⌜συνφερει D ⌜συμφερη 2*

19:12 ⌜ευνουχισθησαν rell |⌜ηυνουχισθησαν D |⌜ευνουχιθησαν G |⌜ευνουχησθησαν 28

19:20 εφυλαξα ᵀ ℵ* B L Θ *f*¹ 579 700* *ff*¹ *g*¹·² *l m* aur vg⁽ᵖˡᵉʳ⁾ Iren Cyp Ath^cod NA²⁸ |ᵀεκ νεοτητος μου rell ℵ^cb2 |ᵀεκ νεοτητος D *d*
  εφυλαξαμην εκ νεοτητος μου C W Γ Δ Σ Φ 𝔐 Minusc. *pler* Or

19:26 αδυνατον ... δυνατα rell Dᴬ
  δυνατον ... δυνατα D*

19:28a επι ⌜δωδεκα rell |⌜ιβ̄ ℵ |⌜δεκαδυο D

19:28b °τας rell Dᴮ |°D*

19:29 ⌜εκατονταπλασιονα rell Dᴮ |⌜πολλαπλασιονα B L 579 sa mae Or |⌜εκατονταπλασιον D* |⌜ποφλαπλασιονα L* |⌜πολλαπλασιωνα 579 |⌜εκατονταπλασιωνα 2* 1071

20:3 ⌜εξελθων rell |⌜διεξελθων D

20:10 ⌜πλειον B C* L N Z 085 *f*¹·¹³ 124 579 788 1346 *l*844 NA²⁸ |⌜πλιονα ℵ |⌜πλειονα rell |⌜πλειω D |⌜πλιον W Θ |⌜πλειωνα 1071 |⌜πλεων Or^semel Matt.XV.30

20:15 ⌜εξεστιν °μοι rell Dᴷ |⌜εστιν D* |°Φ
  εξον μοι εστιν 157

21:3 °αυτων χρειαν εχει rell Dᴮ |°*r*²
  ατυου χρειαν εχει ℵ Θ 544 579 1194 1241 1515
  αυτων εχει χρειαν εχει D*

21:9¹ ⌜ωσαννα rell |⌜οσσανα D* (*ossana d*) |⌜ωσσανα Dᴴ |⌜ωσσαννα F |⌜ωσανα L 2

21:9² ⌜ωσαννα rell |⌜οσσανα D* (ossana d) |⌜ωσσανα D^H |⌜ωαννα E* |⌜ωσανα L Θ 2

21:13 °ο οικος rell D^H | °D*

21:15 ⌜ωσαννα rell |⌜οσσανα D* (ossana d) |⌜ωσσανα D^H |⌜ωσανα L Θ* 2

21:21 ⌜αποκριθεις rell |⌜αποκρεις D |⌜αποκρηθεις Θ |⌜απωκριθεις 28 |⌜αποκριθης 579

21:22 οσα ⌜¹αν ⌜²αιτησητε rell |⌜¹εαν C E F G K M O S V W Y Δ Π Σ Minusc. pler. |⌜²αιτησειτε Θ |⌜²αιτησετε 28 |⌜²αιτεισθαι 1071
    οσα αιτησητε   D
    οσα εαν ⌜αιτησησθε L 4 273 482 544 945 1355 Clem
|⌜αιτησηται M W 69 |⌜αιτησειται 579

21:28 εν τω αμπελωνι ⊤ rell |⊤μου B C^B E F G H S U V W X Z Π^c Φ Ω 0102 0281 579 1241 1424 pc f l r² vg^(pler) sy^omn sa bo^pt mae Or^{3,770} Eus^luc Cyr^glaph Op
    εις το αμπελωνα   D*
    εις τον αμπελωνα ⊤ D^B a b d e ff^{1.2} h q Chr Dam^{2,809} |⊤μου 1424 c f g¹ aur vg Ps-Ath^dispu

21:29 ⌜μεταμεληθεις rell D^c (v.30 B f^13 4 174 230 238 262 273 346 543 566 700 788 826 828 983 1187 1346 1555 1573 r² vg^(2MSS) sy^hier sa^(pler) bo aeth^(2cdd) arm geo) |⌜μεταμεληθις ℵ |⌜μεταμεταμεληθεις D* |⌜μεταμελιθης 579 1071 |⌜(v.30) μεταμελληθεις Θ

21:31 ⌜δυο rell D^c |⌜δυω D*

21:36 ⊤¹παλιν⊤² rell ℵ^ca |⊤¹και ℵ* m vg^(1MS) sy^pesh(pler).sch |⊤²ουν D |⊤²δε 487 579 (vero d) vg^(1MS)
    rursus iterum ff¹
    rursus etiam   cop

21:39 ⌈εξεβαλον rell |⌈εβαλον ℵ |⌈εξεβαλαν D |⌈εξεβαλλον Z

21:46 ⌈προφητην rell |⌈προφην D

22:12 ⌈ο δε   rell |⌈ος D
       at ille   it^(pler) vg
       ⌈ille autem   sy^(s.pesh.hl) sa bo geo |⌈qui d

22:24 αυτου ⸋την γυναικα °αυτου⸍ rell |⸋D d |°vg^(1MS)

22:44 ⌈εχθρους rell |⌈εκθρους D

23:3   παντα °ουν⸆ rell D^K |°118 579 vg^(2MSS) sy^c bo aeth arm geo |⸆παντα ουν D*

23:6   την ⌈πρωτοκλισιαν   rell |⌈πρωτοκλησιαν F G Γ Δ 2* 28 69 565 579 1071 |⌈προτοκλισιαν Θ
       τας ⌈πρωτοκλισιας   ℵ^(ca) 157 713 892 a c f ff^1 g^1 h l m r^(1.2) aur vg sy^(c.s.pesh(pler).hl.hier) sa bo aeth Hil |⌈πρωτοκλησιας L f^1 33
       °την την πρωτοκλεισιαν   D* |°D^K

23:13 ⌈εμπροσθεν rell |⌈ενπροσθεν D

23:16 °οι λεγοντες rell D^(CorC) |°D*

23:17 ⌈μειζων rell |⌈μειζω D |⌈μειζον F

23:33 ⌈εχιδνων rell |⌈εχνιδων D

23:39 ⌈κυριου rell |⌈θεου D d

24:9   ⌈αποκτενουσιν rell |⌈αποκτεινουσιν D

24:12 ⌈πληθυνθηναι rell ℵ^(ca) |⌈πληθυνθηνε ℵ* |⌈πληθυναι D |⌈abundavit Latt |⌈abundat a |⌈repleta d

24:15 ⌜Δανιηλ rell ℵ^S1 D^A |⌜ιηλ ℵ* |⌜Δανιηλου D* |⌜Daniele Latt |⌜Danielum d

24:19 ⌜θηλαζουσαις rell |⌜θηλαζομεναις D |⌜ενθηλαζουσαις L |⌜nutrientibus Latt |⌜lactantibus d

24:21 απ αρχης ^T κοσμου ⌜εως °του νυν rell |^Tτου 579 |⌜μεχρι 1223 |°D |om. 660 1293 1424 Hip

24:30a ^T1 °εν ^T2   ℵ B L Θ 700 NA^28 |^T1του D |°544 1515 |^T2τω rell
        εκ των   713 sah

24:30b ⌜ουρανω rell |⌜ουρανοις D |⌜ουρανων 713 sah | om. 544 1515

24:33 ⌜εγγυς rell |⌜ενγυς D

24:38 ⌜αχρι ⌐ης ημερας⌐   rell |⌐sy^s.pesh.(2MSS) aeth |⌜αχι Θ*
      αχρει της ημερας^T   D* |^Tης D^D
      αρχις ημερας   f^13 69 124 543 788 1346

25:22 ⌜παραδωκας rell |⌜παραδωκες D |⌜εδωκας 579 c q ff sy^[sc] pa^a

25:28 ⌜δεκα rell |⌜πεντε D d

25:29 ⌜περισσευθησεται   rell |⌜περισσευσεται   D |⌜περισευθησεται X W Γ |⌜προστευθησεται Or^Iohan32.7et9 |⌜abundabit Latt

25:32a ⌜απ αλληλων rell |⌜απο D

25:32b ⌜εμπροσθεν rell |⌜ενπροσθεν D

25:38 και συνηγαγομεν ⌐¹η γυμνον °και ⌐²περιεβαλομεν ᵀ rell
|⌐¹και D |⌐²περιεβαλλομεν Δ 1424 *l*53 |⌐²περιεβαλωμεν 579 1346 |°sa
|ᵀσε 157 b c ff^{1.2} g¹ r² aur vg^{(pler)} sy^{s.pesh.hier} sa bo aeth arm geo

26:1 ⌐¹οτε ⌐²ετελεσεν rell Dᴷ |⌐¹ως U |⌐²ετελεν K
|⌐²συνετελεσεν M 248 566 954 |⌐²ελεγεν 59 |⌐²τελεσεν 579
    ο τελεσεν   D*

26:1–2 τοις μαθηταις ▫°αυτου, ²⁶:²οιδατε⸌ οτι   rell |°*l*47 |▫D d
         ▫τοις εαυτου μαθηταις⸌ ²⁶:² οιδατε οτι   Y |▫238 vg^{(1MS*)}

26:6 του ⌐λεπρου rell Dᶜ |⌐λεπρωσου D*

26:12 του ⌐σωματος μου rell Dᶜ |⌐σωματοσματος D*

26:13 ⌐ολω rell |⌐ολο D

26:15 ⌐οι δε εστησαν rell Dᶜ |⌐οις D*

26:16 απο τοτε   rell
      απο τε   D

26:18 ⌐εγγυς rell |⌐ενγυς D

26:23a ⌐αποκριθεις rell Dᴷ |⌐αποκριθις ℵ |⌐αποκρεις D*
|⌐αποκριθης 579 |⌐om. sy^s

26:23b τω τρυβλιω   plu NA²⁸
       το ⌐τρυβλιον   sa | ⌐τρυβαλιον D (*parapside* d)

26:26 λαβων ▫°ο Ιησους⸌ ᵀ αρτον   𝔓^{37.45} ℵ B C G L Z Θ f¹ 4
33 79 517 579 700 735 792 892 954 968 1012 1230 1331 1333 1343
1348 1424 1446 1451 1574 1692 1780 2680 2766 *l*844 *l*2211 co NA²⁸
|▫1375 |ᵀτον rell |*l*423 157 851 1170
       ο Ιησους λαβων αρτον   D d

APPENDIX 5: SINGULAR READINGS IN CODEX D IN MATTHEW 189

      λαβων ο Ιησους τους αρτους   2542
      λαβων °Ιησους τον αρτον   M |°Δ 1675

26:45 ⌜του rell D$^{Corr.C}$ |⌜τους D*

26:53 ⌜λεγιωνας B* NA^{28} |⌜λεγιωνων ℵ* ℵ^{S1} L |⌜λεγαιωνων ℵ^{ca} |⌜λεγεονων A Δ 788 |⌜λεγεωνας rell B^{c2} |⌜λεγεωνων C K Θ Π f^{13} 33 565 700 1071 |⌜λεγειωνης D* |⌜λεγειονας D^D |⌜λεγεονας E^c |⌜om. ff^2

26:55 ⌜εκαθεζομην rell |⌜εκαθημην D |⌜eram $r^{1.2}$

26:70 ⌜εμπροσθεν rell |⌜ενπροσθεν D

27:1 ⌜^{1}ωστε ⊤ ⌜^{2}θανατωσαι   rell |⌜^{1}οπως S | ⊤αυτον 69 |⌜^{2}θανατωσουσιν 69^{mg}
      ινα θανατωσουσιν   D (d lacunose)

27:13 ουκ ακουεις ⌜ποσα rell D^F |⌜οσα B* |⌜τοσα D* |⌜πωσα M

27:15 ⊤εορτην rell |⊤την D

27:16 ⊤λεγομενον rell (om. 1090 Got.) |⊤τον D

27:27 ⌜συνηγαγον rell |⌜συνηγαγεν D |°1344

27:29 ⌜εμπροσθεν rell |⌜ενπροσθεν D |⌜εμπροσθεεν Θ

27:30 ⌜εμπτυσαντες rell |⌜ενπτυσαντες D

27:34^1 ⌜πιειν rell |⌜πιν ℵ* |⌜πειν D |⌜om. L

27:34^2 ⌜πιειν rell |⌜πιν ℵ* |⌜πειν D

27:41 ⌜εμπαιζοντες rell |⌜εμπεζοντες ℵ W Θ Ω 69 788 |⌜ενπαιζοντες D |⌜εμπαιζονταις E* |⌜om. 348

27:44 το δ ⌜αυτο   rell |⌜αυτω Ω
       το δε αυτοι   D*
       το ⌜δε αυτο   D^c Φ |*321* 517 |⌜om. g¹ sy^p arm
       δε   sy^s sah

27:46 °ο Ιησους rell |°D |om. 2 21 349 892

27:48 ⌜σπογγον rell |⌜σπονγον D

27:53 ⌜ενεφανισθησαν πολλοις rell |⌜εφανησαν D* d |⌜ενεφανεισαν D^Cor.C |⌜ενεφανησαν 273

27:54 ⌜λεγοντες rell D^B |⌜γοντες D*

27:56 °η ⌜Μαγδαληνη rell D^B |°D* |⌜Μαγδαλινη Σ 124 346 543 28 348 474 565 579 788 1279 *1184*

27:59 ⌜λαβων rell |⌜παραλαβων D |⌜accepto Latt |⌜suscipiens d

27:60 ⌜προσκυλισας rell D^c d |⌜προσκυλισασλισας D* |⌜προσκυλησας E F 2 |⌜προσεκυλισας U |⌜προσκιλυσας 69 |⌜advolvit Latt

27:61a °η Μαγδαληνη rell D^B |°D*

27:61b ⌜απεναντι rell |⌜επι W |⌜κατεναντι D

27:64 ⌜ειπωσιν rell |⌜ειπωσι B M S U Y 69 118 157 700 788 1071 1346 |⌜ερουσιν D

28:1   °η Μαγδαληνη rell D^B |°D*

28:2   ⌜εξ rell |⌜απ D |⌜de Latt

28:16 °ο Ιησους rell |°D

APPENDIX 6
Singular Readings in Washingtonianus in Matthew

1:9 ⌜εγεννησεν τον Ιωαθαμ rell |⌜εεννησεν W*

2:6 ⌜γη Ιουδα   rell |⌜τη W
    της Ιουδαιας   D 61 *a c d f g¹ q* sy$^{s.c.p}$
    γη των Ιουδαιων   *ff¹* (sy^h) bo$^{ms(s)}$

2:16 ⌜μαγων rell | ⌜γαμων W

2:17 Ιερεμιου του προφητου   rell W$^{c2.mg}$ |⌜Ιηρεμιου D^c Π^c
|⌜Ηρεμιου D*
     Ιηρεμιου   W*

3:5² ⌜και rell |⌜κα W

3:6 ⌜ποταμω υπ αυτου εξομολογουμενοι rell | ⌜πατάμω W |⌜om.
C³ D K L Γ Π 𝔐$^{(exc.\ M)}$ *f*^{13} 565 700 892 1241 *l*844 lat mae

3:12 ⌜ασβεστω rell |⌜ασβετω B* |⌜αβεστω W*

5:22² ⌜αν rell |⌜α W

5:44 ⌜τους εχθρους rell |⌜του W

6:7 δοκουσιν γαρ °οτι rell |°W*

6:30 ει δε τον χορτον του αγρου σημερον ᵀ οντα rell |ᵀεν αγρω W

7:8 και ο ⌜¹ζητων ⌜²ευρισκει rell W^{c2} (om. 273 1579) |⌜¹αιτων W*
|⌜²ευρησει 99 732 1093 1780 2546*^{vid} *l*^{vid} Aug

7:17 δενδρον °αγαθον καρπους ⌜καλους ποιει rell W^c2 |12354 B* B^c2 vg^mss |12453 Δ ⌜αγαθους 700 |°W*

8:16 ⌜γενομενης rell |⌜γονομενης W

8:28 ⌜περαν ⁰εις την χωραν⸌ rell |⌜περα Δ |⁰W

8:29 ⁰προ καιρου⸌ βασανισαι ημας   rell |⁰sy^s[c]
     ημας απολεσαι προ καιρου   ℵ*   713* vg^mss bo^pt
     απολεσαι ημας και προ καιρου βασανισαι   W

9:6 επι °της γης αφιεναι αμαρτιας rell |41235 W |°487

9:15 ⌜απαρθη rell ⌜αρθη D f^1 71 237 g^scr al ⌜αφερεθη W ⌜παρελθη 472

9:20 ⌜κρασπεδου rell |⌜κρασσπεδου W |⌜κρασπαιδου 2 |⌜om. 1689 a b c g^1 k vg^1MS

10:5 ⌜απεστειλεν rell |⌜απεστιλεν ℵ N Θ |⌜αποστειλας F |⌜εξαπεστιλεν W

10:40 ⌜αποστειλαντα rell |⌜αποστιλαντα ℵ Θ |⌜αποστιλοντα W |⌜αποστηλαντα 2*

11:17a ⌜Ηυλησαμεν rell |⌜Ηυλισαμεν L Y 13 2 788 1346 1424 |⌜Ηυλησομεν W

11:17b ⌜εκοψασθε rell |⌜εκλαυσασθαι W |⌜κοψασθαι Θ 1071 |⌜εκλαυσατε 1424^c |⌜planxistis Latt |⌜lamentastis d k sy^cu.s sa bo

11:27^1 ⌜επιγινωσκει rell |⌜επιγινωσκι ℵ |⌜γινωσκει C 71 692 g^scr Clem^1 Iust^tr100 Eus^marc88cdd Did^tri26.72 |⌜επιγεινωσκει D |⌜επιγιγνωσκει W

APPENDIX 6: SINGULAR READINGS IN WASHINGTONIANUS IN MATTHEW

11:27² ⌜επιγινωσκει *rell* |⌜επιγινωσκι ℵ |⌜επιγεινωσκει B D |⌜επιγιγνωσκει W |⌜γινωσκει 71 692

12:4 ⌜πως εισηλθεν *rell* |⌜ως W

12:12 ⌜ουν *rell* |⌜ου W

12:15–16 αυτους °παντας ¹²:¹⁶ και ⌜¹επετιμησεν ⌜²αυτοις *rell* (B) |°Θ |⌜¹επετιμα Θ |⌜²αυτους 2 700
αυτους ¹²:¹⁶ παντας δε ους εθεραπευσεν ⌜επεπληξεν αυτοις⊤ D 1 *a b c ff*¹ (*h*) *k* it |⌜επεπλησσεν *f*¹ |⊤και επετιμησεν αυτοις W

12:20 ου ⊤κατεαξει *rell* (D) |⊤μη W

12:27 τουτο αυτοι κριται εσονται υμων ℵ B D 0281 892 1424 NA²⁸ | *12534* L 16 1579
τουτο αυτοι υμων εσονται κριται C K N Γ Δ 0233 *f*¹³ 565 579 700 𝔐 |*12354* Θ *f*¹ *pc c* vg^cl
τουτο κριται εσονται αυτοι υμων W |*15423* 348 477 1279 1473

12:33¹ ⌜ποιησατε *rell* |⌜ποιησηται W |⌜ποιησον sy^s

12:50 ⌜και *rell* |⌜κα W

13:2 οχλοι °πολλοι   *rell* |°*ab ff*²
οχλον πολλον   W

13:20 και ⌜ευθυς ⊤μετα χαρας *rell* |⌜ευθεως E U Σ 659 892 1279 1355 1424 1675 Or |⌜om. *e* sy^s |⊤και W

13:38 τα δε ⌜¹ζιζανια ⌜²εισιν *rell* (Δ) |⌜¹ζειζανια B |⌜¹ζηζανια Θ 2* 28 1346 |⌜²εστιν W* |⌜²om. M

13:41 ᵀ ⌜αποστελει rell (X) |ᵀκαι W |⌜αποστελι ℵ |⌜αποστελλει Γ 157

13:46 πολυτιμον rell |⌜πολυτειμον B D |⌜πολουτιμιον W |⌜πολυτιμων Θ

14:3 ⌜Ηρωδιαδα rell |⌜Ηρωιαδα W |⌜Ηρωδιαιδα 700*

14:25 ⌜δε rell |⌜ουν W

14:30 ανεμον   εφοβηθη   ℵ B* 073 33 vg^lms sa bo [NA²⁸]
   ανεμον ισχυρον εφοβηθη   rell [NA²⁸]
   ανεμον ισχυρον σφοδρα εφοβηθη ελθειν   W

14:32 ⌜αναβαντων ℵ B D Θ f^1 33 700 788 892 1346 1424 sy^h NA²⁸ |⌜εμβαντων rell |⌜ενβαντων W |⌜εμβαντι 1241 (it vg^s) sy^c sa^ms mae bo

14:35 ⌜απεστειλαν rell |⌜απεστιλαν ℵ N Θ |⌜απεστιλον W

14:36 ⌜διεσωθησαν rell |⌜εσωθησαν ℵ al 579 |⌜διελωθησαν W

16:2b–3 πυρραζει °γαρ °ο ουρανος ᵀ¹ ¹⁶:³και ᵀ² πρωι Σημερον χειμων πυρραζει γαρ` (rell) [NA²⁸] |°M 471 1293 e |°W |ᵀ¹και γινεται ουτος K |ᵀ²παλιν K |om. ℵ B V X Y Γ Ω* f^{13} 2* 13 124* 157 230 267 472 478 543* 579 788 826 828 1473 1573 sy^s.c sa mae bo^pt arm Or Hier^mss [NA²⁸]

16:3a ⌜γινωσκετε rell (Δ) [NA²⁸] (om. v. 3 ℵ B Y f^{13} 2* 579 788 [NA²⁸]) | ⌜γεινωσκεται D (1346) |⌜γιγνωσκεται W

16:3b ου ⌜δυνασθε ᵀ   rell [NA²⁸] |om. ℵ B L Y f^{13} 2* 579 788 [NA²⁸] |⌜δοκιμαζετε L |⌜συνιετε S 700 al⁵⁰ |ᵀγνωναι al^mu it^pl vg
   ου δυνασθε δοκιμαζειν   G M N O U Σ 33 al^mu syr^sch.p
   ου δυνασθαι °δοκιμασαι   W |°Δ

16:9 ⌐ουδε *rell* (om. ℵ X) |⌐ουτε W

16:24 απαρνησσθω ⌐εαυτον *rell* |⌐αυτον W*

16:27 ⌐αποδωσει *rell* |⌐αποδωση W

17:8 αυτον Ιησουν μονον   B* Θ 700 NA²⁸ |*213* ℵ* ℵ^ca
    °τον Ιησουν μονον   *rell* B^c2 |*312* D it^pler vg arm |°W

17:24 υμων ου τελει   *rell*
      υμων ουτε   W

17:25 ⌐ελθοντα εις την οικιαν ℵ^ca B *f*¹ 892 NA²⁸ |⌐εισελθοντα ℵ* ℵ^cb2 579 |⌐οτε ηλθον C *l27* |⌐εισελθοντι D |⌐οτε εισηλθον U syr^cu |⌐οτε εισηλθεν ο Ιησους W* |⌐εισελθοντων Θ *f*¹³ 788 1346 |⌐ελθοντων αυτων 33 |⌐οτε εισηλθεν *rell*

18:4 το παιδιον ⌐τουτο ουτος εστιν ▫°ο μειζων` εν τη βασιλεια των ουρανων *rell* (Δ) |⌐τουτον *f*¹³ |▫579 |°037 1279
    το παιδιον τουτο ουτος εστιν ο μειζων τουτου των ουρανων W*

18:15 ⌐ελεγξον *rell* |⌐ελενξον D |⌐ελεγξε W |⌐ελλεγξον Ω 579 |⌐ελεγξαι 247

18:27 το ⌐δανειον   *rell* |⌐δανιον ℵ D E L Δ Θ 2* 124 788
     το νανιον   W
     την οφειλην   1 1424 1582

18:34 ⌐βασανισταις *rell* |⌐βασανησταις E |⌐μασανισταις W

19:1 απο της Γαλιλαιας και ηλθεν ᵀ εις τα ορια της ⌐Ιουδαιας (*rell*) NA²⁸ |ᵀκαι ηλθεν ℵ* |⌐Γαλιλαιας W*

19:8 Μωυσης ⌐ προς την σκληροκαρδιαν ⌐¹υμων ⌐²επετρεψεν ⌐³υμιν (rell) |⌐μεν U |⌐¹ημων 579 |⌐²εγραψεν 1424 Eus |⌐³om. 892 Chr | 2345671 D a b c d e f g¹ h r¹ vg^lms | 1672345 W^c |162345 W*

19:9a ⌐αυτου rell |⌐υμων W*

19:9b °και ⌐¹γαμηση αλλην ⌐²μοιχαται   rell C³ |°W
|⌐¹γαμησει H S Y Γ 0211 3 28 579 713 732 752 791 827 954 968 983 1009 1093 1253 1273 1296 1326 1333 1334^c 1340 1342 1346 1446 1555 1574 1593 1692 1823 |⌐¹γαμησας 740 |⌐²μοιχατε W Δ Θ^c 579 1424 |⌐²μηχατε Θ* |1324 79

        ποιει αυτην ⌐μοιχευθηναι   ($\mathfrak{P}^{25}$) B N O 0233 1 4 33 273 566 1573 1582 2680 2766 ff¹ m^189 cop syr^hr vid bo Or^3,647sq Aug |⌐μοιχασθαι 1502

        και ⌐γαμηση αλλην ποιει αυτην μοιχευθηναι   C*   61*
555 829 1279 |⌐γαμησει 16 1528 1579 2726

20:1 ⌐ομοια rell |⌐ομυοθει C^c |⌐ομοινα M* |⌐οιμια W

20:12 ⌐αυτους rell |⌐αυτον W*

20:15 ⌐ο θελω rell |⌐ω 579 | ⌐ως W

20:29 ⌐ηκολουθησεν rell |⌐ηκολουθησαν $\mathfrak{P}^{45}$ D Γ 1241 1424 it vg^mss sy^h bo^mss |⌐ηκωλουθησεν W

20:33 ινα ⌐ανοιγωσιν B L Z Θ 13 33 69* 124 157^c 233 346 543 713 788 826 828 892 983 990 1223 1230 1253 1293 1692 2680 Or^bis pc NA²⁸ |⌐ανοιχθωσιν   rell |⌐ανεωχθωσιν   W |⌐ανυχθωσιν   Ω |⌐αναβλεψομεν 851

21:8 εκοπτον κλαδους ⌐¹απο των δενδρων⌐ rell (N) |⌐W |⌐0110

21:18 ⌐επαναγων rell ℵ^ca B^c1 |⌐επαναγαγων ℵ* B* L |⌐παραγων D it syr^c.hier Hil |⌐υπαγων W |⌐reuertens f g¹ l q aur vg sy^pesh.hl sa (bo) |⌐ascendens aeth geo¹

21:23 ⌐προσηλθον *rell* |⌐προσηλθεν W |⌐προσηλθαν 33 |⌐προσηλθων Θ 2*

21:26 ⌐ανθρωπων *rell* |⌐ανθρωπου W

21:30 ⌐¹ωσαυτως ⌐ºο δε ⌐²αποκριθεις ειπεν` *rell* |⌐¹ως αυτο Δ |⌐ℵ* |⌐²αποκριθις ℵ^ca |⌐²αποκρειθεις D |⌐²απεκριθη W* |⌐²απεκριθεις W^c |⌐²αποκφιθης 579 |⌐²απηλθε Y 118 157

21:32a °ουκ *rell* |°W*

21:32b ⌐επιστευσατε *rell* |⌐επιστευσαται D |⌐αιπιστευσαται L |⌐επιστευσατο W* |⌐επιστευσαν 1424

21:32c °¹υστερον ⌐του πιστευσαι ⊤ °²αυτω *rell* (28 r² aur) |°¹047 |⌐τω W |⌐om. Θ 124 1010 |⌐εν Θ 33 713 892 sy^{s.pesh} Or |°²c ff^{1.2} g¹

21:41a ⌐απολεσει *rell* |⌐απολεσι ℵ |⌐αναλωσει L |⌐απολει W |⌐απολεση 28

21:41b ⌐αποδωσουσιν *rell* |⌐αποδωσουσι B* |⌐αποδωσωσιν W |⌐αποδοσουσιν Θ

22:7 ⌐ωργισθη *rell* |⌐ωργησθη L |⌐υβρισθη W* |⌐οργισθη 1071 1424 *l*183 *l*184

23:8 εστιν °υμων ο διδασκαλος ℵ^ca B 33 892* NA²⁸ |°1093 *l*184 *q* εστιν υμων ο καθηγητης *rell* | 2134 659 692 700 1194 1200 1424 1604 *l*183 |*l*342 W
23:14 om. ℵ B D L Θ *pler* NA²⁸ |⌐προφασει *rell* |⌐προφαει W

23:25 αρπαγης και ⌐ακρασιας *rell* |⌐αδικιας C E F G H K S U V Γ Ω 28 157 579 700 *pm* sy^p et^{p.cod} Bas^{eth 236 cod} Chr^{mo 5} Op *pc* |⌐ακρασειας D |⌐πλεονεξιας M 1093 Chr^{montf} Dam^{par517} |⌐ακαθαρσιας O Σ 66 71 1295 1515 *l*844* Cl |⌐ακρασιας αδικειας W |⌐πονηριας 999

⌜*intemperantia* lat ⌜*intemperantiae* d ⌜*iniquitate* r² sy^pesh ⌜*incontinentia* e r¹ ⌜*iniustitia* f ⌜*immunditia* ff¹ g^{1.2} l m aur vg sah sy^s sa bo geo ⌜*iniquitate auaritia* aeth ⌜*intemperantia et iniquitate* sy^{hl}

23:37 ⌜λιθοβολουσα *rell* |⌜λιθοβολησουσα W* |⌜λιθοβολησασα W^c

24:9 ⌜παραδωσουσιν *rell* |⌜παραδοσουσιν E* Y 1424 |⌜παραδωσωσιν W

24:11 ⌜πολλους *rell* |⌜υμας W |⌜αλληλους 1241

24:15 ⌜αναγινωσκων *rell* |⌜αναγεινωσκων D |⌜αναγιγνωσκων W |⌜αναγινοσκων Θ |⌜αναγινωσκον 118 565

24:18 ⌜και *rell* |⌜κα W

24:32a ⌜γινωσκετε *rell* |⌜γινωσκεται L Θ 2* 579 |⌜γιγνωσκεται W |⌜γεινωσκεται B² D Γ 348 1187 *al.* |⌜γεινωσκετε B*

24:32b ⌜εγγυς *rell* |⌜ενγυς εστιν D (33) 482 *pc* it vg sy^{s.h.} Or^{int} |⌜ευθυς W

24:39 ^{T1}εως ^{T2}⌜ηλθεν ο κατακλυσμος *rell* ℵ^{S1} ℵ^{corr} |^{T1}ο ℵ* |^{T2}εως Y* |^{T2}ου Γ Δ 6 33 157 Chr |^{T2}οτου 346 |⌜εισηλθεν 16 544 692 1093 1293 |⌜ανηλθεν W

24:49 μετα των ⌜μεθυοντων *rell* |⌜μεθυωντων E* |⌜μεθυστων W

25:19 πολυν χρονον ℵ B C D G L Θ 074 f^{1.13} 33 245 517 543 700 788 892 954 1346 1424 1582 1675 it vg^{(1ms*)} arm cop geo sy^{hier} Or^{3,631} NA^{28} | *21 rell*
    χρονον τινα W

25:34 ⌜κληρονομησατε *rell* |⌜κληρονομησητε W*

25:46 ᵀ ⌜εις ζωην rell |ᵀει 124 |⌜ει W

26:1 τους λογους ⌜τουτους rell |⌜τους W

26:3 οι ⌜αρχιερεις ᵀ και οι πρεσβυτεροι rell |⌜αρχειερεις D |ᵀκαι οι γραμματεις 𝔐 K M U Γ Π Σ Θ 22 346 28 157 565 579 892 1006 1241 1342 1346 1506 al pler c f ff² g² h q r⁽¹⁾ sy⁽ˢ·⁾ᵖᵉˢʰ·ʰˡ Arm gat Chr Orⁱⁿᵗ³,⁸⁹¹inᵗˣᵗ (transposition 1010 1071 1293 syᵖᵉˢʰ⁽¹ᵐˢ⁾) |ᵀκαι γραμματεις S Δ Ω 1223 |ᵀκαι οι φαρισαιοι W

26:14 ⌜δωδεκα rell |⌜δεκαδυο W

26:15 ⌜παραδωσω rell |⌜παραδω W

26:18 ⌜το πασχα rell |⌜τα W

26:19 και εποιησαν rell
       εποιησαν ουν W

26:41 ⌜εισελθητε rell |⌜ελθητε 𝔓³⁷ b ff² sa bo |⌜εισελθηται ℵ D L |⌜εισερθητε W*

26:65 ⌜διερρηξεν rell |⌜διερηξεν W

26:67 ⌜εραπισαν ℵ A B C D L Z Γ Δ Θ Σ Ω 047 090 4 71 229 230 262* 273 517 544 566 659 713 726 1200 1241 1279 1295 1375 1555 1574 1579 1675 NA²⁸ |⌜ερραπισαν rell |⌜εριπισαν W |⌜εραππισαν Φ |⌜ερραπησαν 118 |⌜εραπιζον 157

26:72 ⌜¹μετα ⌜²ορκου ℵ A B C K L W Δ Θ Π* Σ Φ 33 71 565 892 1346 1402 2145 NA²⁸ | om. l184 |⌜¹μεθ rell |⌜²ρορκου W

27:4 οι ⌜¹δε ⌜²ειπαν L f¹³ 33 788 1346 NA²⁸ |⌜¹δ W* |⌜²ειπον rell

27:39 τας κεφαλας °αυτων rell |312 W |°251 544
       την κεφαλην αυτων D d bo aeth geo¹

27:41 ⌜φαρισαιων D 𝔐 K M U Δ Π Σ Φ 2 4 22 71 157 273 346 348 349 517 565 579 1071 1279 1424 1579 plu l47 ⌜om. rell |⌜φαρισαιω W

27:44 ⌜ωνειδιζον rell |⌜ονειδιζον H L 69 118 1424 |⌜ωνειδιζον Δ |⌜ωνιδιζον Θ 1346 |⌜ωνειδιζων 2* |⌜ονιδιζον 579 |⌜ωνιδιζαν W

27:46 ⌜λεμα ℵ B L 4 33 273 700 a g¹ l vg$^{(aliq.)}$ am emm for ing harl (sa) bo aeth^{pc} arm^{pc} aug Eus$^{dem486.excdd2(item490bis)etps389}$ NA²⁸ |⌜λιμα A K U Γ Δ Θ^f Π Σ Φ 090 346 471 472 475 481 483 565 692 892 l183 al. f q go sy$^{p.hl}$ Eus^{es544} Chr^{gue} Bas$^{eth\ cod}$ |⌜λειμα E F G H M S V al Bas$^{eth\ cdd}$ |⌜λαμα D Θ f¹ 22 565 al. pler a b d ff¹ h gat mm aur vg$^{(aliq.)}$ aeth^{pc} arm$^{aliq.}$ geo Eus$^{dem496ed(item490bis)}$ Bas$^{eth\ cod}$ Or^{int3,924} |⌜μα W |⌜laba vg$^{(1MS)}$ |⌜lamma c g² vg^{ed} Bas^{eth235ed} |⌜labath r² |⌜lamath vg$^{(1MS)}$

27:47 εκει ⌜εστηκοτων rell |⌜εστωτων A D 𝔐 K M Γ Δ f$^{1.13}$ 565 579 1241 1424 l844 |⌜στηκοτων W

27:51 και η γη ⌜εσεισθη rell |⌜εσισθη ℵ* ℵ^{ca} K* L Θ |⌜εσησθη E* |⌜εσχισθη W |⌜εσχισθει 2*

27:55 ⌜διακονουσαι rell |⌜διακονησαι W*

27:58 ⌜προσελθων rell |⌜προσηλθεν D lat |⌜προσελθω W

27:61 ⌜απεναντι rell |⌜κατεναντι D | ⌜επι W

28:11 ⌜απηγγειλαν rell |⌜ανηγγειλαν ℵ D Θ 565 Or Chy |⌜απηγγειλον W

APPENDIX 7
NON-SINGULAR READINGS IN SINAITICUS IN MATTHEW

1:2   ⌜Ισσακ rell |⌜Ισακ ℵ (*a b d e ff² h k r¹*) vg

1:6   ⌜Σολομωνα rell |⌜Σολομωντα W Δ Σ 472 1071 1093 *al pler* |⌜Σαλομων ℵ* 1 209 |⌜Σαλομωνα ℵ^c? |⌜Σαλωμωνα ℵ^b? |⌜Σαλωμωνα 33 692 |⌜Σολωμων 399 700 983 1689 |⌜*Solomonem g¹ k q* vg

1:7   Αβια, Αβια   *pler* NA²⁸
      Αβιουδ Αβιουδ   *f¹³ pc* it sy^hmg
      ⌜Αβεια, Αβεια   *l*183 |⌜Αβ[ει]α 𝔓¹
      ⌜Αβια Αβιας   ℵ* 131 |⌜Αβιας sah

1:13¹ ⌜Αβιουδ *rell* ℵ^S1 |⌜Αβιουτ ℵ* |⌜*Abiuth d f g¹* |⌜*Abiut c* |⌜*Abiiud q*

1:13² ⌜Αβιουδ *rell* ℵ^S1 |⌜Αβιουτ ℵ* |⌜*Abiuth d f g¹* |⌜*Abiut c*

1:14   ⌜Ελιουδ *rell* ℵ^S1 |⌜Ελιουτ ℵ* |⌜Ελειουδ E^c |⌜*Heliut d* |⌜*Eliuth f*

1:15   ⌜Ελιουδ *rell* ℵ^S1 |⌜Ελιουτ ℵ* |⌜Ελειουδ E* |⌜Ελειουδ E^c |⌜*Heliut d* |⌜*Eliuth f*

1:23   ⌜Εμμανουηλ *rell* |⌜Εμανουηλ ℵ* 472

2:6   °γαρ *rell* |°ℵ* 2

3:6   °ποταμω ⌐υπ αυτου⌐ *rell* |°D C* E K 700 788 *pc* |⌐ℵ* sy^p(1MS) Hil

3:11a μεν^T *rell* | ^Tουν 13 118 124 543 788 999 1093 1588 | ^Tγαρ ℵ 892

3:11b υμας βαπτιζω εν υδατι ℵ* B W f^1 33 124 700 788 1010 $c\,ff^1$ $l\,m$ vg$^{pler.etWW}$ NA^{28} |1342 ℵ^{S1} Or$^{4,131.132}$ | 2134 rell

4:19 ⌜αλιεις rell |⌜αλεεις ℵ* B* C |⌜αληεις L

4:22 το πλοιον ^{T} rell |^{T}αυτων ℵ* aeth | om. verse M W 33
       τα δικτυα ^{T} 126 $c\,ff^1$ g^2 $h\,l$ aur vg^{pler} |^{T}αυτων b g1 vg^{pc} sy^c sa |om. sy^s

5:30 □και μη ολον τον σωμα σου `   rell ℵ^{S1} |⌐579 |om. verse D pc vg^{ms} sy^s bo^{ms}
       η ολον τον σωμα σου   ℵ* Lucif

5:40 ⌜αυτω rell |⌜ταυτω ℵ* 892 |⌜om. Or

5:42 ⌜σε rell |⌜σοι ℵ* y^{scr}

5:46 °ουχι και οι τελωναι rell ℵ^{S1} |°ℵ* sy^s Theoph

6:15 ο πατηρ ⌜υμων rell |⌜ημων 245 579 |⌜om. f sy^c |⌜υμιν ℵ 301

6:16a °οι υποκριται rell |°ℵ* 1279

6:16b τα προσωπα rell
       το προσωπον ℵ* k syr^{sch} Aug

6:22 εαν °ουν rell |°ℵ pc lat sy^c mae bo^{ms}

6:25 τω σωματι °υμων τι rell |°ℵ* b

6:32 οιδεν ⌜γαρ^{T}ο πατηρ rell |⌜δε ℵ^c |^{T}ο θεος ℵ* mae

7:4 τω αδελφω σου ^{T} rell |^{T}αδελφε ℵ g^2 vg^{pc} sa^{lms} Gild

APPENDIX 7: NON-SINGULAR READINGS IN SINAITICUS IN MATTHEW 203

7:13a πολλοι ⸂η πυλη⸃ *rell* | ⸂ℵ* 1646 *a b c h k m* Clem^{bis} Or^{1,228} et^{2,800} et^{3,270} Eus^{ps286} Or^{int2,387} Cyp Lcif al

7:13b °εισιν *rell* | °ℵ* sah (Cl)

7:18a πονηρους ποιειν   ℵ^{S1} C L W Z Θ 0250 0281 $f^{1.13}$ 33 𝔐 latt sy Or^{pt}
   πονηρους ενεγκειν   (ℵ*) B Or^{4,221} Ad Dial⁴⁰ (Dial⁴¹ προσενεγη)

7:18b καλους ποιειν   ℵ^{S1} ℵ^{ca} B C L W Z Θ 0250 $f^{1.13}$ 33 𝔐 lat sy Or^{pt}
   καλους ενεγκειν   ℵ* Dial⁴⁰ (Dial⁴¹ προσενεγκαι) Or^{3,267}

7:22 ⸌εξεβαλομεν *rell* |⸌εξεβαλλομεν ℵ* geo Dam^{1,605} |⸌εξεβαλλωμεν L |⸌εξεβαλωμεν 565 697 |⸌εποιησαμεν 1424

7:28 ⸌εξεπλησσοντο *rell* |⸌εξεπληττοντο ℵ* Eus

8:4 ⸌λεγει *rell* |⸌επεν ℵ* *k* Cl

8:6 °κυριε *rell* |°ℵ* *k* sy^{s.c} Hil

8:11 ⸌Ισσακ *rell* |⸌Ισακ ℵ (*a b d e ff*² *h k r*¹) vg

8:12 ⸌εκβληθησονται *rell* | ⸌εξελευσονται ℵ* it^{pler} syr^{cu} et^{sch} Heracl ap Or^{4,276} Ir^{int} Cyp^{semel} Aug^{saepe} | ⸌εμβληθησονται 118

8:28 ελθοντος αυτου   ℵ^c B C Θ $f^{1.13}$ 788 (1346) NA²⁸
   ελθοντι αυτω   *rell* (Δ)
   ελθοντων αυτων   ℵ* (vg^{mss} arm)

8:29 προ καιρου βασανισαι ημας   *rell* ℵ^{S1}
       ημας απολεσαι προ καιρου   ℵ* *pc* vg^{mss} bo^{pt}
       απολεσαι ημας και προ καιρου βασανισαι W

9:5   °και *rell* |°ℵ* sah

9:10a εγενετο αυτου ανακειμενου   *rell* |132 ℵ^c C 99 544
       1093 1170 1396 Eus
       ανακειμενων   ℵ* 892 syr^{sch.pesh} Aeth

9:10b °ελθοντες *rell* ℵ^{S1} |°ℵ* 243 *l*50 *a* sa bo^{(1MS)} sy^{hl}
9:16   πληρωμα °αυτου απο *rell* (Δ) |°ℵ* *a h* sy^s

9:17   αλλα βαλλουσιν οινον νεον εις ασκους καινους *rell* (L 2*
       157) -D Δ 1071
       αλλα οινον νεον εις ασκους βαλλουσιν καινους C 21 399
       517 (892) 1010 1293 1424 *l*49 *l*844^{(*)} *l* 2211 it^{pler} vg Aug
       αλλ οινον νεον εις ασκους καινους βλητεον   ℵ 1604

9:21   εαν °μονον *rell* |°ℵ* *a* g^2 *h*

9:22   ο δε °Ιησους *rell* |°ℵ* D *a b c k q* sy^s

9:24   κατεγελων ⌜αυτου⌝ (*rell*) |⌜αυτον D* |⌜ειδοτες οτι
       απεθανεν ℵ* 61 sah^{(2MSS)}

9:31   °ολη *rell* |°ℵ* (sy^s)

10:3   Αλφαιου °και *rell* (M N) |°ℵ* 122

10:5   οδον °εθνων *rell* |°ℵ* 1424

10:11 τις εν αυτη *rell* | 231 ℵ K p^{scr}

APPENDIX 7: NON-SINGULAR READINGS IN SINAITICUS IN MATTHEW 205

10:16 °οι οφεις   rell | °L
       °οι οφις   B* K Θ f^{13} 33 157^c 579 | °157* 700 1346
       ο οφις   ℵ* Epiph Or^{3,2}

10:34 ηλθον βαλειν ειρηνην (rell) |*132* ℵ g^1 ff^1 q Tert Hil

11:8   ιδειν ανθρωπον rell ℵ^{S1} ℵ^{ca} (L) |*21* ℵ* 1355

11:27 πατρος °μου rell |°ℵ* sa^{mss} bo Iust^{tr100} Marcos ap Ir^{int93} Hil

11:29 απ εμου rell ℵ^A ℵ^D |om. ℵ* 245 1010

12:11a °εαν ⌜εμπεση rell |°D 33 124 157 234 346 700 788 1424 b sy$^{s.c}$ sa bo |⌜ενπεση ℵ^{S1} D L N W Θ 28 |⌜εμπεσει 1071 1346 |⌜πεση ℵ* Γ

12:11b ⌜κρατησει rell |⌜κρατησας ℵ ff^1 h |⌜κρατει D |⌜κρατισει L 2*

12:13 ⌜^{1}υγιης ως ^{T} ⌜^{2}η αλλη rell |⌜^{1}υγειης D^c |⌜^{1}ηγυης D* |⌜^{1}υγιη E* |⌜^{1}υγιεις Θ |⌜^{1}om. *l*184* a b c ff^1 h vg^{1MS} sy$^{c.s.pesh}$ aeth arm Hil |^{T}et a f ff^{1,2} h vg^{pc} |⌜^{2}ει 2
       υγιης   ℵ 892*
       υγιης ... λλη   C^{vid}
       ⌜^{1}υγιης ωσει ⌜^{2}αλλη   28 118 |⌜^{1}υγιεις L |⌜^{2}αλη 1424

12:31^1 ⌜αφεθησεται rell |⌜αφεθησετε ℵ L

12:32 ⌜^{1}ουκ ⌜^{2}αφεθησεται αυτω ουτε rell |⌜^{1}ου μη ℵ* B |⌜^{2}αφεθησετε ℵ L |⌜^{2}αφεθη B

12:47 ⸋ειπεν δε τις αυτω ιδου η μητηρ σου και οι αδελφοι σου εξω εστηκασιν ζητουντες σοι λαλησαι⸍ (rell) [NA^{28}] |⸋ℵ* B (L) Γ 126 225 238 400* 443 1355 1093 ff^1 k sy$^{s.c}$ (sah) [NA^{28}]
       ειπεν δε τις των μαθητων αυτου ιδου η μητηρ σου και οι αδελφοι σου εξω ζητουσιν σε   ℵ^A (892)

13:10 παραβολαις λαλεις °αυτοις *rell* ℵ^S1 |*132* ℵ* 954 Eus^dem |°vg am Tert

13:17 °γαρ *rell* |°ℵ X Φ 983 1170 1241 1689 *a b c e f ff*^{1.2} g^1 *h l* aur vg^{4mss} cop aeth arm geo Hil

13:36 ⌜ηλθεν εις *rell* | ⌜εισηλθεν ℵ Or^{3,3bis} (*a b h q abiit*)

13:57 °Ιησους *rell* |°ℵ 21

14:19 ⌜κελευσας *rell* |⌜κελευσατε B* |⌜εκελευσεν ℵ Z *e ff* ^1 Or^{3,479 b} |⌜κελευει Or^{3,509} et^{509}

14:26 οι δε μαθηται ιδοντες αυτον ℵ^S1 B D *f*^{13} 788 1346 mae NA^{28} και ιδοντες αυτον οι μαθηται C 𝔐 L W Δ 0106 33 sy^h (bo^{pt}) ιδοντες δε αυτον ℵ* Θ 700 *pc* it sa Eus^{pt}

14:28 κυριε ει συ ει *rell* |*2341* ℵ 892

15:17 ⌐αφεδρωνα *rell* |⌐τον ℵ Γ Chr

15:18–19 ▫κακεινα κοινοι τον ανθρωπον ^{15:19} εκ γαρ της καρδιας` (*rell*) NA^{28} |▫ℵ W 33^{vid} bo^{ms}

16:6 °αυτοις *rell* |°ℵ 892 *l*184 bo^{(1MS)}

16:9 ουπω νοειτε ▫⌐ουδε μνημονευετε` *rell* |▫ℵ* X ⌐ουτε W

17:11 ειπεν^T B D W 33 700 *pc* |⌐αυτοις C 𝔐 L (*f*^1) *f*^{13} 579 1424 *pler* |⌐αυτοις οτι ℵ 713

17:15 °Κυριε *rell* |°ℵ Z

APPENDIX 7: NON-SINGULAR READINGS IN SINAITICUS IN MATTHEW

17:18 °ο παις`   rell |⁰ℵ 1515*
      ο παις αυτου   1071
      ο ανθρωπος   349 517 954 1424 1675

17:24² τα ⌜διδραχμα   rell ℵ^{ca} |⌜διδραγμα 𝔐 L 118 f^{13} 28 157 565 700 1071 |⌜διδραχματα 579 |⌜διδραχμον 1093
      ⌜δειδραγμα   D |⌜διδραχα ℵ* mae bo |⌜tributum a d e f ff^1 n vg$^{(pler)}$ aeth |⌜didgrama uel censum b |⌜didgramam g^1
      το ⌜διδραγμα   W |⌜διδραχμον Cyr^{4,791}

17:25–26   απο των αλλοτριων $^{17:26}$ ᵀ rell |ᵀο δε εφη απο των αλλοτριων ℵ bo^{pt}

18:5 °εν παιδιον τοιουτο B Θ f^1 700 NA^{28} | 213 ℵ G syr^p arm |°S X Δ 2 579 al plus^{15} e sah cop syr^{sch} al

18:18 ⌜δεδεμενα rell |⌜δεδεμενον ℵ* 251

18:21 ειπεν °αυτω (rell) |°ℵ* Dam^{par828} sy^s

18:24 ⌜μυριων rell |⌜πολλων ℵ* sah cop Or^{3,621} et^{627sqq}

18:25 ⌜τεκνα rell |⌜πεδια ℵ Chr (et^{mo6})

19:8 λεγει αυτοις^T rell |ᵀο 118 |ᵀο Ιησους ℵ M Φ a b c mae

19:12 °γαρ rell |°ℵ* vg$^{(2MSS)}$ Epiph

19:21 ⌜ειναι rell |⌜γενεσθε ℵ* Clem

19:24 δια ⌜τρυπηματος ℵ^{ca} D E F G H L S V (W) X Y Z Γ Δ $f^{1.13}$ 33 579 892 1241 1424 pm NA^{28} |⌜τρηματος ℵ* B Or |⌜τρυμαλιας C K M U Θ 0281 124 157 565 700 l2211 pm

19:25 °δε rell |°ℵ* geo

20:24 οι δεκα^T rell |^Tηρξαντο αγανακτειν ℵ 253 473 1207 d^scr

20:29 °αυτω rell ℵ^S1 |°𝔓^45 ℵ*

20:30 ⌜οτι ^T °Ιησους rell ℵ^S1 ℵ^ca ⌜ο ℵ* |^To 544 1012 |°565

20:33 ⌜ημων rell ⌜υμων ℵ* Δ (Υ 118 28 579)

21:14 ⌜προσηλθον rell ⌜προσελθοντες ℵ* (bo)

21:27 και αυτος   rell
      ο Ιησους   ℵ (0293) pc (a) c e ff^1 2 h sy^c.p et^sch

21:31 υμιν °οτι οι τελωναι rell |°ℵ* 1279 1473 l184

21:33 ωρυξεν °εν rell (1071) |°ℵ* 69

21:36 παλιν   rell
      και παλιν   ℵ* syr^sch
      παλιν ουν   D*
      παλιν δε   579 (iterum vero d)
      rursus iterum   ff^1
      rursus etiam   cop

21:43 ⌜αυτης rell ⌜αυτου ℵ* 238 Or^3,705 ⌜om. ff^1 syr^cu et^sch

22:11 °εκει rell |°ℵ* Chr

22:15 ⬜°εν λογω` rell |⬜ℵ* bo^(1MS) |°517 579 1424

22:23a ^Tεν rell |^Tκαι ℵ* sy^s.h aeth

22:23b °αυτω rell |°ℵ* vg^(2MSS) sy^s

23:26 και °το ⌜εκτος rell |°Δ ⌜εντος ℵ* l183 l184 ⌜εξωθεν D Clem

APPENDIX 7: NON-SINGULAR READINGS IN SINAITICUS IN MATTHEW

22:29 αποκριθεις δε   *rell*
       και αποκριθεις   ℵ aeth

22:32 ⌜Ισσακ *rell* |⌜Ισακ ℵ (*a b d e ff*² *h k r*¹) vg

23:3 ποιησατε ⸆και τηρειτε⸇ κατα   ℵ^c B L Z Θ 124 sah cop syr^hr arm aeth Eus^ps Hil^sem NA²⁸ |⸆ℵ* *pc* sy^s mae²
    ποιειτε και τηειτε κατα   D *f*¹ 1 118 209
    τηρειν τηρειτε και ποιετε κατα   𝔐 (F) K M U Y W Δ Π 0102 0107 *f*¹³ 2 33 28 157 565 579 788 1071 1346 1424 𝔐 *q* sy^p.h (Ir^lat)
    ποιειν ποιειτε κατα   Γ
    ποιειν ποιειτε και τηρειτε κατα   700
    ακουετε και ποιειτε κατα   sy^c

23:4b ⸆και ⌜δυσβαστακτα⸇ ⸋και επιτιθεασιν επι τους ωμους *rell* (δυσβαστακτα *pro* βαρεα 544 700 1010 1293) |⸆ℵ L *f*¹ 892 1582 *a b e ff*² *h* sy^c.s.pesh bo Iren^int |⌜αδυσβαστακτα D* 700 |⌜δυσβακτα 0138 |⸋1295

23:7–8 ραββι ⸆ ²³:⁸⸋υμεις δε μη κληθητε ραββι⸇ εις γαρ ℵ^c B L *f*¹·¹³ Δ 565 (Θ) NA²⁸ |⸋ℵ* (124) sah |⸆ραββι (*rell*)

23:35 Ζαχαριου ⸆υιου Βαραχιου⸇ *rell* (D) |⸆ℵ* 6^ev 13^ev

23:37 ⸋η ⌜αποκτεινουσα τους προφητας B   *pler*   NA²⁸ |⸋659 |⌜αποκτενουσα ℵ^c Δ *f*¹³ 33 69 579 *pc* Caes^dial Cyr^es9 et⁴⁰
    τους προφητας αποκτενουσα   ℵ* Or³,¹⁶⁷

24:2 ⸋παντα *rell* ℵ^S1 |⸋ℵ* 1093

24:3 ⌜κατ ιδιαν *rell* |⌜καθ ℵ B*

24:7 εσονται λιμοι ⸆ ⸋και σεισμοι⸇ (B D) E* NA²⁸ |1432 ℵ bo |⸆και λοιμοι (*rell*) |⸋565 1573

24:9 υπο °¹παντων °²των °³εθνων rell ℵ^{ca} -579 |°¹ℵ* r² |°²D* C Ω f¹ 1 131 1424 ti* Chr Ps-Ath^{dispu} | °³C f¹ 1424 l 2211 pc 1 131 ti* (sy^s) bo^{ms} Chr Ps-Ath^{dispu}

24:14 εν ολη τη οικουμενη   rell
       εις ολην την οικουμενην   (𝔓^{70}) ℵ e h r¹

24:24 σημεια °μεγαλα rell |°ℵ W* pc ff¹ r¹ bo^{ms}

24:26 εαν °ουν rell |°ℵ* 248 geo

24:28 πτωμα rell
       σωμα ℵ* (*corpus* it vg Hil)

24:32 °τα φυλλα rell |°ℵ* 300

24:34 εως ⌜αν rell |⌜om. ℵ 1604 |⌜ου 157 209

24:48 ⌜αυτου rell |⌜εαυτου ℵ 892

25:20 πεντε °ταλαντα λαβων rell |°ℵ 506

25:24 ⌜σκληρος ει ανθρωπος   rell | ⌜αυστηρος 1 22 |132 G 124 157 579
       ανθρωπος αυστηρος ει   ℵ a b c f (ff²) g¹ h l q r^{1.2} aur vg

25:33 °αυτου τα δε εριφια εξ ευωνυμων rell | °A al³ fu^{(vid)} aeth Cyr^{mal} Bas^{se} Or^{int4,622} Cyp^{sem} Avit |234561 ℵ (cop syr^{utr})

25:43 συνηγαγετε με ^{T1} ⌐γυμνος ^{T2} και ου περιεβαλετε °με⌐ rell |^{T1}και p^{45} Θ sy^{s.p} |^{T2}ημην 𝔓^{45} h vg^{mss} sy^{s.p} |⌐ℵ* 124 21 127* 1194 1424 1604 |°ℵ^c l47

26:50 °Ιησους rell (exc. 𝔓^{37}) |°ℵ Z^{scr} l185

26:62–63   αυτω   ᵒουδεν αποκρινη τι ουτοι σου καταμαρτυρουσιν ο δε Ιησους εσιωπα και ο αρχιερευς ειπεν αυτω` (rell) |ᵒℵ* 243 983 1689 *l*183

26:65 λεγων ᵀ εβλασφημησεν τι ετι χρειαν ℵ^{ca} B C^c D L Z Θ 090 33 700 892 NA²⁸ |ᵀοτι rell |ᵀτι C*^{vid}
και ⌜λεγει ᵒιδε εβλασφημησεν τι ετι χρειαν ℵ* |ᵒsy^{sch} |⌜λεγων sy^p pers^p aeth

26:72 ορκου ⌜οτι rell |⌜λεγων D *b c ff*² mae |⌜om. ℵ 36 40

27:5 και ριψας τα ᵀ αργυρια rell |ᵀτριακοντα ℵ 122 Chr^{gue}

27:9 ⌜τοτε rell |⌜και ℵ* vg (*et tunc* am)

27:41 γραμματεων και πρεσβυτερων   rell | *321* ℵ 238 Eus^{dem498}
γραμματεων και φαρισαιων   D W 1424 *pc a b c ff² h q* gat Cassiod sy^s
γραμματεων και πρεσβυτερων και φαρισαιων   𝔐 *f* sy^{p.h} bo^{pt} arr pers^p sl Or^{int3,921} Thphyl

27:45 ᵒεπι πασαν την γην` εως   rell (B*) | ᵒℵ* 248 *l* Lactant^{4,18}
εφ ολην την γην εως   ℵ^c 1424

27:48 ⌜εποτιζεν rell ℵ^{ca} |⌜εποτιζον ℵ* Φ

27:51–52 εσχισθησαν ᵒκαι τα μνημεια ανεωχθησαν` ℵ^c B D 𝔐 700 788 *pler* NA²⁸ |ᵒℵ* 2*

27:55 ⌜εκει ᵀ rell |⌜κακει ℵ sy^{p(pler)} |⌜και D *al*¹⁰ Chr^{gue} |⌜om. 579| ᵀκαι F K L Π 33 1071

28:10a ⌜απελθωσιν rell ℵ^{ca} |⌜ελθωσιν ℵ* Latt |⌜απελθων 579

28:15 ⌜διεφημισθη rell |⌜εφημισθη ℵ Δ 33 60 Or^{1,249} et^{4,455}

28:18 ᵒαυτοις rell |ᵒℵ* 1375*

APPENDIX 8
NON-SINGULAR READINGS IN VATICANUS IN MATTHEW

1:3   ⌜Ζαρα rell |⌜Ζαρε $\mathfrak{P}^1$ B

1:12   Σαλαθιηλ Σαλαθιηλ   rell
       Σελαθιηλ Σελαθιηλ   B (g¹ k Selathiel)

1:18   °¹Ιησου °²Χριστου rell Or^{int3,965} |°¹ 71 it vg sax fr syr^{cu} pers^w Ir^{int} ^{bis} Ps-Ath^{633} Thph^{cod} Aug |°²W 74 pers^p et^{cod} Max^{dial} |21 B Or^{int3,965}

1:25   εως °ου ετεκεν rell B^{c2} |°B* 1042^{s*}

2:13   ⌜φαινεται rell |⌜εφανη B it vg Ir^{int} pp^{lat} sa mae

4:19   ⌜αλιεις rell |⌜αλεεις ℵ* B* C |⌜αληεις L

5:1   °¹αυτω °²οι μαθηται rell |°¹B pc Or^{3,496} |°²579

5:18   εως °αν παντα rell (D) |°B* l2211 pc

5:32   και °ος ⌜εαν απολελυμενην γαμηση   rell (om. D pc a b k Or^{mss}) |°348 1279 1473 |⌜αν ℵ* K* W? Σ 118 f^{13} (124) 237 349 473* 543 565 597 700 1071
       και ⌜ο απολελυμενην γαμησας   B 80 sa? Or |⌜ος 372 |⌜ος αν 245
       και ⌜¹ος ⌜²αν απολελυμενην γαμησει   Θ |⌜¹ως L |⌜²εαν 2 579

5:37   ⌜περισσον rell |⌜περισον B* Δ

6:16   ⌜αυτων rell |⌜εαυτων B Ω 485 1093 l47 l50

Appendix 8: Non-Singular Readings in Vaticanus in Matthew 213

6:18   φανης τοις ανθρωποις νηστευων *rell* | *1423* B k

6:21   εσται °και η καρδια σου *rell* |°B bo^mss

6:22   ο οφθαλμος ⊤ *rell* |⊤σου B it^pler vg^ed aeth Or^int2, 109 Hil al

6:25   τη ψυχη ⌜υμων *rell* |⌜ημων B 2

6:34   ⌜εαυτης °αρκετον *rell* B^c2 |⌜αυτης B* L Δ co? |°G* 506 692

7:8   ⌜ανοιγησεται *rell* |⌜ανοιγεται B sy^c.p.hl bo |⌜ανοιχθησετε Θ*

7:14   ⊤ στενη *rell* |⊤δε B 1582*^vid sa^(al)

7:17   καρπους καλους ποιει *rell* B^c1 -W* 700 |*231* Δ |*132* B* B^c2 vg^mss

7:18a   πονηρους ποιειν   ℵ^S1 C K L W Z Δ Θ 0250 0281 $f^{1.13}$ 33 565 579 700 892 1241 1424 *l*844 𝔐 latt sy Or^pt
        πονηρους ενεγκειν (ℵ*) B Or^4,221 Ad Dial^40 (Dial^41 προσενεγη) 𝔐

7:18b   καλους ποιειν   ℵ^S1 ℵ^ca B C K L W Z Δ Θ 0250 $f^{1.13}$ 33 565 579 700 892 1424 *l*844 𝔐 lat sy Or^pt
        καλους ενεγκειν   ℵ* Dial^40 (Dial^41 προσενεγκαι) Or^3,267

7:24   τους λογους °τουτους *rell* |°B* 1424 a g^1 k m go syr^hr mae bo^mss Cyp

9:28   δυναμαι ⊤ τουτο ποιησαι *rell* |*213* B N q vg^ed |*132* C* |⊤υμιν ℵ* (lat)

10:7   °οτι *rell* |°B sy^s

10:37 αξιος ⁰και ο φιλων υιον η θυγατερα υπερ εμε ουκ εστις μου αξιος` rell | ⁰B* D 17 243 syrᵖ cod

12:10 ⌜κατηγορησωσιν rell |⌜κατηγορησουσιν D W 1346 |⌜κατηγορησωσι B* L

12:11 τοις ⌜σαββασιν rell |⌜σαββασι B* L |⌜σαββασειν N

12:12 ⌜σαββασιν rell |⌜σαββατοις B 1555

12:22 ⌜προσηνεχθη rell |⌜προσηνεγκαν B 0281ᵛⁱᵈ 1424 1675 sy⁽ˢ·ᶜ·ᵖ⁾ etᵘᵗʳ sa bo aeth geo

12:38 των ⁰γραμματεων και` Φαρισαιων °λεγοντες rell (M Θ) | 14325 K 238 251 252 482 544 1355 1675 2145 | ⁰579 |°syᶜ
των γραμματεων λεγοντες B 59

13:5a ⌜εξανετειλεν rell |⌜εξανετειλαν B it vg syʰ (exorta/nata sunt)

13:5b βαθος ᵀ γης rell |ᵀτης B 372 2737

13:6 ⌜εκαυματισθη rell B* |⌜εκαυματωθη Bᶜ² |⌜εκαυματισθησαν D it vg syʰ copˢᵃ·ᵇᵒ |⌜εκαυμαστισθη Δᶜ |⌜εκαυμαστισεν Δ* |⌜εκαυματησθη Θ 2*

13:16 ωτα °υμων οτι rell |°B 1424 a b c ff² g¹ q Chrᵐᵒˡ Hil

13:44 και πωλει °παντα οσα εχει ℵ D f¹ 1 61 108 118 127 itᵖˡᵉʳ vg syrᶜᵘ etˢᶜʰ cop mae NA²⁸ |13452 rell (28) |°B 28 61 435 armᶜᵈᵈ bo Or³,⁴⁴⁶

14:2 και ⁰δια τουτο` rell |⁰B* a

14:5 ⌜οτι rell |⌜επιεδη N Σ |⌜επι Π |⌜επει B* 700

14:19 ⌜κελευσας rell B^{c1} |⌜εκελευσεν ℵ Z 243 1012 1295 *l*184 *e ff* ¹ sy^{c.s.pesh.} sa bo geo Or^{3,479b} |⌜κελευσατε B* 1093 |⌜κελευει Or^{3,509} et^{510}

14:36 παρεκαλουν °αυτον rell |°B* 892 *q* Or^{3,487} Chr

15:27 °γαρ rell |°B *e* sy^{s.pesh.hier} sa bo^{1ms}

15:30 χωλους τυφλους κυλλους κωφους ℵ 157 *a b ff* ² sy^s NA²⁸ | *1243* 𝔐 E G P U *pc f*^{1.13} 118 2 700 788 1071 1346 cop syr^{cu} et^{sch} arm | *1423* C K 565 *pm* | *4123* L W Δ *l q* vg^{st.ww} sy^h | *4213* 33 892 1421 *l* 844 *l* 2211 *pc* aur (*ff*¹) vg^{cl} |*1324* B 0281 *pc* sa^{mss} mae

15:31 ⌜¹θαυμασαι ⌜²βλεποντας rell | 21 B 892 |⌜¹θαυμαζειν E* |⌜²βλεποντες Δ Θ |⌜²βλεποντα 33 237 713 892

15:32 οτι °ηδη ημερα (rell) |°B 106 301 1

16:12 διδαχης των Φαρισαιων και Σαδδουκαιων rell (ℵ W) -*f*^{13} | *12543* (B) 0281^{vid}

16:14 ⌜αλλοι δε rell |⌜αλλη 1346 |⌜οι B Eus^{steph223} Chr^{(mo5)}

16:17 ο πατηρ μου ο ▫εν °τοις⸌ ⌜ουρανοις rell |⌜▫*f*^{13} 565 579 788 1346 |°B *l*184 |⌜ουρανιος 0281 *f*^{13} 565 579 788 1346

16:17 °οτι rell |°B* 1424*

16:21 ⌜δεικνυειν rell |⌜δεικνυναι B Or^{3,537}

16:21 ⌜δεικνυειν rell |⌜δεικνυναι B 892

16:22 ηρξατο επιτιμαν αυτω^T λεγων   ℵ (C) 𝔐 K L M U W Δ Π 2 118 579 1071 NA²⁸ |^Tκαι F | *1324 f*^{1.13} 124 157 700 788 1346 1424
    ηρξατο αυτω επειτειμαν και λεγειν   D (it)

                ηρξατο αυτον πειτιμαν λεγων   Θ
                ηρξατο αυτω επιτιμαν αυτω λεγων   565
                λεγει αυτω επιτειμων   B 346

16:24   °ο Ιησους   rell B^{c2} |°B* 713* 2372
        om.   118 157 205 209 348 349 487 565 1446 *l*184
sa^{ms}

17:1   ⌜κατ ιδιαν   rell B^{c2} ⌜καθ B* 𝔓^{44}
        λειαν   D *d* Eus^{dem208}

17:4   τρεις σκηνας *rell* | *21* B 0281^{vid} *e*

17:19   ⌜κατ ιδιαν *rell* ⌜καθ B* D

18:16   μετα σου °ετι ενα η δυο   rell |°579 |*345612* 𝔓^{44vid} B 0281
        μετα σεαυτου ετι ενα η δυο ℵ K L M Θ Π *f*^{1.13} 33 788 *pc*

18:28   ο δουλος °εκεινος *rell* |°B 245 arm^{zoh}

19:22a τον λογον ⊤ *rell* |⊤τουτον B 51^{ev} *a b c ff*^1 syr^{cu} et^{sch} sah

19:22b ⌜κτηματα *rell* ⌜χρηματα B Chr

19:24   δια ⌜τρυπηματος ℵ^{ca} D E F G H L S V (W) X Y Z Γ Δ *f*^{1.13} 33
579 892 1241 1424 *pm* NA^{28} |⌜τρηματος ℵ* B Or |⌜τρυμαλιας C K M
U Θ 0281 124 157 565 700 *l*2211 *pm*

20:9   και ⌜ελθοντες   *rell* ⌜ελθωντες 2*
        ελθοντες ⌜δε   B sy^c sa^{mss} bo^{mss} (arm) ⌜ουν D Θ *f*^1 33
788 1346

20:14   θελω ⌜δε ⊤ *rell* ⌜εγω B bo^{(1MS)} aeth |⊤και E 118 209 1424 *a b c
f ff*^{1.2} *g*^1 *h n r*^1 aur vg |⊤εγω sah

20:17¹ ⌜και rell |⌜μελλω δε B f¹ Or

20:17a αναβαινω rell |⌜αναβενων ℵ Θ |⌜αναβαινειν B f¹ Or |⌜αναβαινον 2*

20:17b °ο Ιησους rell |°B f¹³

20:18 °θανατον   ℵ 700 |°B aeth
       θανατω   rell

20:26 θελη εν υμιν μεγας γενεσθαι rell |*14523* C (579) 1424 pc ff¹ | *14235* B sah cop
       θελη υμων μεγας γενεσθαι L Z 892

20:34 των ⌜¹ομματων ⌜²αυτων D L f¹³ 124 788 NA²⁸ |⌜²αυτου ℵ* |*312* B Or |⌜¹οφθαλμων rell |⌜²om. Θ

21:28 τεκνα δυο rell |*21* B 142 299 1424 lat (vg Hil)

21:29 ⌜υπαγω °κυριε και ουκ απηλθεν f¹³ 700 788 1346 | ⌜εγω B 346 4 238 262 r² vg¹ᴹˢ bo aeth | °Θ

21:30 υστερον °δε μεταμεληθεις απηλθεν Θ f¹³ 69 543 700 788 1346 geo2 |°B r² vg²ᴹˢˢ (syʰ· sahᵖˡᵉʳ bo aeth arm geo)

21:31 ⌜πρωτος rell |⌜εσχατος (D) Θ f¹³ 69 238 262 543 700 788 1346 |⌜υστερος B 2ᵖᵉ sah |⌜δευτερος 4 273

23:32 ⌜πληρωσατε |⌜επληρωσατε D 118 |⌜πληρωσετε B* 60 e arᵉ arᵖ perss

23:37 τα νοσσια ⌜αυτης   ℵ* Bᵐᵍ D M W Δ 0102 33 892 1424 Clem¹⁴³ Or³,²⁹³ Eusᵈᵉᵐ etᵉᶜˡ Cyrᵉˢ⁹ et⁴⁰ Thdrt¹,⁶⁹⁸ᶜᵒᵈ NA²⁸
       τα νοσσια εαυτης   rell
       τα νοσσια   B* 700 Clemᵖᵗ Or³,¹⁶⁷ et²⁰⁶ Eusᵖˢ ¹³⁸ etᵗᵉʳ Cyp

24:3 ⌐κατ ιδιαν rell |⌐καθ ℵ B*

24:23 ⌐πιστευσητε rell |⌐πιστευητε B^c |⌐πιστευετε B* 262 Or^cdd

24:38 γαμουντες και ⌐γαμιζοντες ℵ 33 1346 NA²⁸ |⌐γαμισκοντες B 1424? 1675 |⌐εκγαμιζοντες rell |⌐γαμειζοντες D |⌐εκγαμισκοντες W 517 1424? |⌐εκγαμειζοντες Δ |⌐εκγαμηζοντες Θ |⌐εγγαμιζοντες Σ 047 13 pc

25:23 ης πιστος rell |21 B 102 h r¹ Ir^lat

25:37 ποτε σε ⌐ειδομεν rell |⌐ειδαμεν B* 067

25:40 ενι τουτων^T ◻των ⌐αδελφων μου˥ των ελαχιστων rell |^Tτων μικρων I |◻B* 0128* 1424 ff^1 2 Cl^pt et^467 Eus GrNy | ⌐ελαχιστων 118* ενι τουτων αδελφων μου των ελαχιστων   579

25:42 και °ουκ εδωκατε rell 𝔓^45c B^c2 |°𝔓^45* B*

26:4 τον Ιησουν δολω ⌐¹κρατησωσιν ◻και ⌐²αποκτεινωσιν˥ rell (M S W Y Θ f¹ pc) |⌐¹κρατησουσι 28 |◻B* 36 40 61 174 258 r² vg^1MS |⌐² απολεσωσιν 579

26:42 προσηυξατο ⌐λεγων rell |⌐ο Ιησους λεγων L Θ f¹ 69 124 788 1424 |⌐om. B 102 g¹

27:6 εις τον ⌐κορβαναν rell B^c2 |⌐κορβαν B* f g¹ q aeth |⌐κορβοναν E K M 22 f¹³ 4 229 248 273 472 517 543 544 788 1010 1071 1241 1555 pc vg^(2mss) gat Chr^ed Or^int3,914 Aug^cons3,28 |⌐κορβανα X 157 act^pil ven (sy^sch.hr) |⌐κορβονα 33 sy^s.pesh.hl |⌐Τολγοθαν 69 |⌐κορβωναν 118 Cyr^hr198 |⌐corbonam ff¹ mm |⌐corbam a (b c) d h r¹ (ff²)

27:29 εξ ακανθων ⌐επεθηκαν επι rell (33) |⌐εθηκαν K N Y W Δ Θ Π 1 69 124 al¹² |⌐περιεθηκαν B 131 pc Chr^mol

27:35 αυτον ⌜διεμερισαντο τα ιματια rell |⌜διεμερισατο B^c |⌜διεμερισαν B* Θ al.

27:40 ει υιος ει του θεου ᵀ καταβηθι   rell [NA²⁸] |ᵀκαι ℵ* A D [NA²⁸]

ει υιος θεου ει καταβηθι   B *a b c f ff*¹·² *g*¹ *h l r*¹·² aur vg aeth Or^int Aug

27:43 επι τον θεον rell
επι τω θεω   B Eus^ps82 (it^pl vg *in deo* or *domino*)

27:46 σαβαχθανι rell |⌜σαβαχθανει ℵ A W 69 700 |⌜σαβακτανει B 22 |⌜ζαφθανει D* (*zaphthani d ff*² *h*) |⌜σαφθανει D^c |⌜*sabathani r*¹ |⌜*sabactani ff*¹ |⌜*sibactani q* |⌜*zabachthani* vg^1MS |⌜*zabethani g*¹ |⌜*zaptani b* vg^3MSS |⌜*zabthani* vg^tot |⌜*zabtani* vg^1MS |⌜*zahthani a*

27:65 ⌜κουστωδιαν rell B^c2 |⌜φυλακας D*^vid arm^usc |⌜κουστουδιαν D^c |⌜σκουστωδιαν B* K |⌜κουστοδιαν 67 |⌜*custodiam ff*¹ *l* vg^(pler) (sy^s.hl sah bo arm geo¹ Aug) |⌜*custodes a b c d f ff*² *g*¹ *q* aur vg^(1ms) sy^pesh.hier (geo²) |⌜*milites h r*¹ vg^(4mss)

APPENDIX 9
Non-Singular Readings in Ephraemi in Matthew

2:10 ⌜αστερα *rell* | ⌜αστεραν ℵ* C

3:16 ερχομενον ⌜επ αυτον *rell* D^B (*d super*) |⌜προς C* E* 71 247 258 *l*48 |⌜εις D* 21 299 Eus^ps

4:19 ⌜αλιεις *rell* |⌜αλεεις ℵ* B* C |⌜αληεις L

4:23 και περιηγεν εν ολη τη Γαλιλαια   (B) NA²⁸
      και περιηγεν ο Ιησους εν τη Γαλιλαια   ℵ*
      και περιηγεν ο Ιησους ολην την Γαλιλαιαν   ℵ^c   D   *f*¹
157 33
      και περιηγεν ολην την Γαλιλαιαν ο Ιησους   *rell*
      και περιηγεν ο Ιησους εν ολην τη Γαλιλαια   C*sy^s.p.h
bo|*12567834* C^c

7:20 ⌜απο των καρπων *rell* |⌜εκ C (*ex* it^pler vg Leif Aug)

8:27 οτι °¹και °²οι ανεμοι και η θαλασσα *rell* |°¹C *a b c ff*¹ g¹ *h q* vg sah cop syr^sch aeth Hil Op |°² 124

8:32a και ειπεν αυτοις ᵀ υπαγετε *rell* |ᵀο Ιησους C *b c* g¹ *h* sy^p.sch

8:32b πασα η αγελη *rell* |*231* C* 21 399 892 1010

9:9 ανθρωπον καθημενον επι το ⌜τελωνιον *rell* |*13452* C 21 399 1010 |⌜τελωνειον 124 346 33

9:10 πολλοι τελωναι και αμαρτωλοι ελθοντες *rell* |*14325* C cop aeth Cyr^es 105 | *21345* W | *43215* 157 | *12534* 565

APPENDIX 9: NON-SINGULAR READINGS IN EPHRAEMI IN MATTHEW 221

9:27 ελεησον ημας ⊤ rell |⊤κυριε N f^{13} 13 788 pc l47 pc g^2 geo^B |⊤ο Δ 700 |⊤Ιησου C* Σ 21 399 1293

9:28 δυναμαι ⊤¹τουτο ποιησαι⊤² rell ℵ^{s1} ℵ^{ca} b d | 213 B N 892 q vg^{ed} | 132 C* geo¹ |⊤¹υμιν ℵ* |⊤²υμιν it

10:3 ⌈επικληθεις rell C^B | ⌈om. ℵ B 124 788 NA²⁸ | ⌈και C*^{vid}

10:13 μεν ⌈η rell |⌈ην C* 157

10:17 παραδωσουσιν γαρ °υμας rell |°C* 99

10:19 τη ⌈ωρα rell |⌈ημερα C* 1424 cop syr^{hr}

10:23 λεγω υμιν ⊤ ου μη rell |⊤οτι C* 245

11:13 ⌈Ιωαννου rell |⌈Ιωανου B |⌈Ιαννου C 124

11:27 και ουδεις ⌈επιγινωσκει rell |⌈επιγεινωσκει D |⌈επιγιγνωσκει W |⌈γινωσκει C 71 692 g^{scr} Clem¹ Iust^{tr100} Eus^{marc88cdd} Did$^{tri26.72}$

12:10 ⌈επηρωτησαν rell |⌈επερωτησαν C X 485 |⌈επηρωτισαν E |⌈επιρωτησαν L

12:13a και εξετεινεν και   rell C^B
       και εξετεινεν ... και   (C*^{vid}?)

12:13b ⌈¹υγιης ως ⊤ ⌈²η αλλη rell |⌈¹υγειης D^c |⌈¹ηγυης D* |⌈¹υγιη E* |⌈¹υγιεις Θ |⌈¹om. l184* a b c ff¹ h vg^{1MS} sy$^{c.s.pesh}$ aeth arm Hil |⊤et a f ff$^{1.2}$ h vg^{pc} |⌈²ει 2

       υγιης   ℵ C^B 892*
       υγιης ... λλη   (C*^{vid}?)
       ⌈¹υγιης ωσει ⌈²αλλη   28 118 |⌈¹υγιεις L |⌈²αλη 1424

13:10a και ⌈προσελθοντες ⊤ rell |⌈προσελθοντος U |⊤αυτω C cop

13:10b οι μαθηται ᵀ rell |⸀αυτου C X it^{pl} et^{sch} vg^{mss} syr^{cu.p} sa bo et^{sch} cop aeth Eus^{dem} Chr^{mo4}

13:33 αλλην παραβολην ⸀ελαλησεν rell -D |⸀παρεθηκεν C 243 1241 pc sa^{mss}

14:33 οι δε εν °τω πλοιω rell C^{Bvid} |°(C*^{vid}?)

15:20 ου ⸀κοινοι τον ανθρωπον rell (-1071 1424 haplography) |⸀κοινωνει D |⸀κοινει C l184

15:33 εν ⸀ερημια rell |⸀ερημω τοπω C cop Or^{3,510}

17:8 τους οφθαλμους °αυτων ᵀ ουδενα rell |°W |⸀ουκετι C* O Σ

17:20 λεγω υμιν ᵀ εαν rell |⸀οτι C l27 sah cop Or^{3,202}

17:25 ⸀ελθοντα εις την οικιαν ℵ^{ca} B f^1 892 NA^{28} |⸀εισελθοντα ℵ* ℵ^{cb2} 579 |⸀οτε ηλθον C l27 |⸀εισελθοντι D |⸀οτε εισηλθον U syr^{cu} |⸀οτε εισηλθεν ο Ιησους W* |⸀εισελθοντων Θ f^{13} 788 1346 |⸀ελθοντων αυτων 33 |⸀οτε εισηλθεν rell

17:26 ειποντες δε ᵀαπο των αλλοτριων ℵ B Θ 0281 f^1 700 892* pc vg^{mss} sa bo^{pt}; Chr NA^{28} | ᵀτου Πετρου 892^{mg}
    λεγει αυτω απο των αλλοτριων   D sy^s
    λεγει αυτω ο Πετρος απο των αλλοτριων ▫ειποντος δε °αυτου απο των αλλοτριων ⸍   C Cyr |°L | ▫rell (D)

19:9 °και ⸀^1γαμηση αλλην ⸀^2μοιχαται   rell C^3 |°W |⸀^1γαμησει H S Y Γ 0211 3 28 579 713 732 752 791 827 954 968 983 1009 1093 1253 1273 1296 1326 1333 1334^c 1340 1342 1346 1446 1555 1574 1593 1692 1823 |⸀^1γαμησας 740 |⸀^2μοιχατε W Δ Θ^c 579 1424 |⸀^2μηχατε Θ* |l324 79
    ποιει αυτην ⸀μοιχευθηναι   (𝔓^{25}) B N O 0233 1 4 33 273 566 1573 1582 2680 2766 ff^1 m^{189} cop syr^{hr vid} bo Or^{3,647sq} Aug |⸀μοιχασθαι 1502

APPENDIX 9: NON-SINGULAR READINGS IN EPHRAEMI IN MATTHEW 223

και ⌜γαμηση αλλην ποιει αυτην μοιχευθηναι   C*   61*
555 829 1279 |⌜γαμησει 16 1528 1579 2726

19:13 οι δε μαθηται ⌜επετιμησαν ℵ L M W 𝔐 $f^{1.13}$ 33 pc NA^{28}
|⌜επετειμησαν B |⌜επετιμων C 66 it vg

20:12 ουτοι °οι εσχατοι $rell$ |°C* H*

20:21 καθισωσιν °¹ουτοι οι °²δυο ⊤ υιοι μου $rell$ |°¹C 56 58 $a e n$
sah cop Bas$^{se181\ 133bis}$ Isid^{1,187} |°²H |⊤οι 579

21:23 και τις σοι εδωκεν $rell$
       η τις σοι εδωκεν   C ff^1 g^2

21:41 ⌜εκδωσεται $rell$ |⌜εκδοσεται 118 f^{13} 2 157 565 788 1346 1424
|⌜εκδωσει C pc Cyr^{es}

24:5 λεγοντες ⊤ εγω $rell$ |⊤οτι C* Φ 245 713 1047 1200 1579 1604
2145 l49 l184 f syr^{utr} bo geo^2 arm Or$^{int\ 3,\ 851}$

24:8 ⌜ωδινων $rell$ |⌜ωδεινων B C Δ 565 1424 |⌜οδυνων D* 1293
|⌜οδινων 13 579 |⌜$dolorum$ it vg

26:49 ειπεν ⊤ χαιρε $rell$ |⊤αυτω 𝔓^{37} C (sy^s) sa^{ms} mae bo Eus^{dem}

26:69 ησθα μετα Ιησου του ⌜Γαλιλαιου $rell$ |⌜Γαλειλαιου B D
|⌜Γαλιλεου ℵ |⌜Ναζωραιου C 047 238 252* syr^{sch} pers^p

26:73 και γαρ ⊤ η λαλια σου $rell$ -L |⊤Γαλιλαιος ει και C* Σ sy^{h**}

27:54 θεου υιος ην $rell$ |213 ℵ^c B D^{gr} 69 102 $b h l$ vg^{ed} Or^{int}
et^{4,298}
       θεου υιος εστιν   C f g^1 go Aug^{ioh} Vig
       υιος ην του θεου   ℵ*

APPENDIX 10
Non-Singular Readings in Codex D in Matthew

1:23 καλεσουσιν   *rell*
    καλεσεις   D 2* *d*** y[scr] bo[mss] Eus[dem320] Epiph[2,1,5lib] Vig

1:25 εγεινωσκεν αυτην εως   B
    εγινωσκεν αυτην εως   *rell*
    εγνω αυτην εως   D syr[sch] it Hil

2:6a ⌜γη Ιουδα   *rell* |⌜τη W
    της Ιουδαιας   D 61 *a c d f g*^{1} *q*

2:6b ουδαμως   *rell*
    μη   D (*ff*^{1} tol *numquid*, it[pl] Tert Hil al *non*)

2:9 ου ην το παιδιον   *rell*
    του παιδιου   D *b c d g*^{1} *k q*

2:11 το παιδιον   *rell*
    τον παιδα   D (565 it vg aur Aug[cons])

2:13a το ⌜παιδιον   *rell* |⌜παιδιων 2*
    τον παιδα   D (565 it vg aur Aug[cons])

2:13b ειπω σοι *rell* | *21* D al

2:13c το παιδιον   *rell* |⌜παιδιων 2*
    τον παιδα   D (565 it vg aur Aug[cons])

2:13d απολεσαι ⌜αυτο *rell* |⌜αυτω K L* 28 1071 |⌜αυτον D *a d f ff*^{1} *k* aur vg[(pler)] Aug[cons] |⌜om. *b c g*^{1} vg[(1 MS)]

2:14 το ⌜παιδιον *rell* |⌜πεδιων ℵ
      τον παιδα   D (565 it vg aur Aug^cons)

2:16 απο ⌜διετους *rell* D^B |διετειας D* (it vg *a bimatu*)

2:17 ρηθεν   *rell*
      ρηθεν υπο κυριου   D aur

2:20 το παιδιον   *rell*
      τον παιδα   D (565 it vg aur Aug^cons)

2:21a εγερθεις   *rell* (it^pler vg *surgens* vel *consurgens*)
      διεγερθεις   D (*k exsurrexit*)

2:21b το παιδιον   *rell*
      τον παιδα   D (565 it vg aur Aug^cons)

3:16a °¹το πνευμα °¹του θεου °²καταβαινον   *rell* [NA^28]
|°¹ℵ B [NA^28] |°²Ir^int
      […] καταβαινοντα εκ του ουρανου   D (Latt)
      το πνευμα του θεου ⌜καταβαινον εκ του ουρανου   372
⌜καταβαινοντα *a b c d g*¹ *h l* vg^(3mss) sy^h gat mm Hil

3:16b ⌜ωσει *rell* Eus^dem |⌜ως D Eus^ps409

3:16c ερχομενον ⌜επ αυτον *rell* D^B (*d super*) |⌜προς C* E* 71 247
258 *l*48 |⌜εις D* 21 299 Eus^ps

3:17a λεγουσα   *rell*
      λεγουσα προς αυτον   D *a b g*¹ *h* sy^c.s.

3:17b ουτος εστιν   *rell*
      συ ει   D *a* sy^c.s. Ir Aug^ioh1

4:3   προσελθων ο πειραζων ειπεν αυτω   rell | 15234 C 𝔐 L 1424 *pler*
      προσηλθεν αυτω ο πειραζων °και ειπεν αυτω   D it^cdd |°cop

4:4a   ο δε αποκριθεις ειπεν   *plu* NA²⁸
       αποκριθεις δε ο Ιησους ειπεν   D (it^mu sy^cu sax)

4:4b   ▫εκπορευομενω δια στοματος`θεοω *plu* NA²⁸ | ▫D *a b d g¹ k* Sy^hier

4:8   ⌜δεικνυσιν *rell* (C P W Δ Θ) |⌜δικνυει ℵ |⌜δικνυσειν C |⌜εδειξεν D 372 |⌜δικνυσιν P W Δ Θ

4:14   ᵀλεγοντος *rell* |ᵀτου D U

4:16a   φος ειδεν   ℵ B C W *pc* NA²⁸ | *21* E K L M P S U V Γ Δ *al pler k* vg Hipp^fragm Or^bis
        ειδον φος   D it^pm Eus^dem

4:16b   τοις καθεμενοις   *rell* NA²⁸
        οι καθημενοι   D it^pm

4:17a   τοτε ᵀ *rell* |ᵀγαρ D *d k*

4:17b   °ο Ιησους *rell* |°D 16

4:18   περιπατων   *rell*
       παραγων   D it^pler sy^s Eus

4:24   εθεραπευσεν αυτους   *rell*
       παντας εθεραπευσεν   D *a b c d g¹ h* Sy^pesh.hl

5:2   ⌜εδιδασκεν *rell* |⌜εδιδαξεν D Or

5:11a ονειδισωσιν υμας και διωξωσιν   *rell*
       διωξουσιν υμας και ονιδισουσιν   D (33) *h k* (sy^c) mae bo cop aeth

5:11b ειπωσιν παν πονηρον καθ υμων   ℵ B NA^{28}
       ειπωσιν παν πονηρον ρημα καθ υμων   C W *plu*
       ειπωσιν καθ υμων παν πονηρον   D *h k m* flor syr^{cu} et^{utr} Const^{2,8,1} Tert Lcif

5:11c πονηρον ⊤καθ υμων ψευδομενοι   ℵ B [NA^{28}] | ⊤ρημα *rell*
       πονηρον ⊤καθ υμων   [NA^{28}]
       καθ υμων παν πονηρον   D (*b c d h k* syr^s geo Tertullian *al*)

5:11d ⌜¹ενεκεν ⌜²εμου *rell* | ⌜¹ενεκα B | ⌜²δικαιοσυνης D 47 *a b c g^1 k*

5:12a τοις ουρανοις   *rell*
       τω ουρανω   D 258 it^{mu} Hil^{ter} *al mu*

5:15   ⌜αλλ επι *rell* |⌜αλλα D Σ

5:19   ⌜εαν   *rell* |⌜αν D^{CorC} 33 |⌜om. D* (it^{pl} vg pp$^{lat\,mu}$ *non exprim*)

5:19–20 ^{19}ουρανων ^{20}▫ος δ αν ποιηση και διδαξη ουτος μεγας κληθησεται εν τη βασιλεια των ουρανων. λεγω γαρ υμιν οτι εαν μη περισσευση υμων η δικαιοσυνη πλειον των γραμματεων και Φαρισαιων ου μη εισελθητε εις την βασιλειαν των ουρανων` (*rell*) (M*) | ▫D *d* vg$^{(1\,MS)}$

5:24   προσφερε   *rell*
       προσφερεις   D* *a b f* *pc*

5:29   βληθη   *plu* NA^{28}
       απελθη   D 700^{mg} it sy^{sc} (mae) bo cop

5:29–30 ²⁹γεενναν ³⁰⸋και ει η δεξια σου χερι σκανδαλιζει σε εκκοψον αυτην και βαλε απο σου συμφερει γαρ σοι ινα αποληται εν των μελων σου και μη ολον το σωμα σου ⸉βληθη εις γεενναν⸊⸌ (rell) | ⸉εις γεενναν απελθη ℵ B f^1 33 157 NA²⁸ |⸋D pc vg^{ms} sy^s bo^{ms}

5:32 μοιχευθηναι ⸋και ος εαν απολελυμενην γαμηση μοιχαται⸌ plu NA²⁸ |⸋D (0250) 64 579 a b k cdd ap sy^{s.c} sa^{ms} bo Aug

5:39 την °δεξιαν rell |°D k ar^p cdd^{lat} ap Aug^{adimant19} Dial Amb

5:40b ⸀¹αφες ⸀²αυτω rell |⸀¹δος 471 1093 |⸀²τουτο ℵ* 892 |⸀²om. Or αφησεις αυτωD d l m vg^{1MS} Bas^{bapt637}

5:41 αυτου ᵀ δυο rell |ᵀετι αλλα D a b c (ff¹) g¹ (h) k (vg^{cl} am for syr^{cu}) Chrom Ir^{int} Aug

5:42 θελοντα απο σου   rell
      θελοντι απο σου   565 700
      θελοντι   D k m Clem Cyp

6:4 η σου η ελεημοσυνη plu NA²⁸ |3241 ℵ* 33 |124 Δ |324 1071 | 3421 D it vg

6:5a φιλουσιν ᵀ rell |ᵀστηναι D a b c h k q

6:5b προσευχεσθαι   rell
      ᵀπροσευχομενοι   13 |ᵀκαι D h k

6:5c ⸀αυτων rell |⸀αυτον D* Latt

6:8   ⸀αιτησαι αυτον   rell |⸀αιτεισθαι 157
      ανοιξε το στομα   D h

6:10 °ως εν ουρανω rell D^A |°D* a b c k bo^{mss} Tert Cyp Aug^{semel}

APPENDIX 10: NON-SINGULAR READINGS IN CODEX D IN MATTHEW

6:14 αφησει και υμιν   plu NA²⁸
      αφησει υμιν και   D b c f g¹ h k q

6:17 αλειψαι   rell
      αλιψον   D al³

6:18 ⌜οπως μη φανης rell ⌜ινα D bo fa

6:19 σης και βρωσις αφανιζει   rell
      σης και βρωσις αφανιζουσιν   D* Or³,²³⁹

9:6 ⌜εγερθεις   rell ⌜εγειρε B 0281 pc lat
      εγειρε και   D a g¹ ² h k aeth Hil

9:11a °και ιδοντες rell |°arm
      ειδοντες δε   D d sah

9:11b τι μετα των τελωνων και αμαρτωλων εσθιει ο διδασκαλος υμων   pler NA²⁸
      τι ο διδασκαλος υμων μετα των αμαρτωλων και τελωντων εσθιει D b c g¹ h q

9:15a ⌜μη rell ⌜μητι D (it vg numquid)

9:15b ᵀημεραι rell (ℵ) |ᵀαι D* 59 61 1279

9:15c νηστευσουσιν   pler NA²⁸
      νηστευσουσιν εν εκειναις ταις ημεραις   D a b c g¹ h q f ff¹ k vg syrᵖ ᵐᵍ Bas²,²⁴⁷ Orⁱⁿᵗ²,²³⁹

9:17a ρηγνυνται οι ασκοι   rell
      ρησσει ο οινος ο νεος τους ασκους D g¹ k μ Syʰʳ ˢ

9:17b ⌜εκχειται rell ⌜om. D k Arn ⌜εκχυται 579

9:17c απολλυνται ℵ B *pc* NA²⁸ ⌈απολουνται L W *pc* ⌈απολλυται D *k* Arn

9:17d αλλα βαλλουσιν   *rell* (ℵ C 21 399 517 892 1010 1293 1424 1604 *l*49 *l*844⁽*⁾ *l* 2211 it^pler vg Aug)
  βαλλουσιν δε   D (*a*) *k*

9:17e ⌈συντηρουνται *rell* D^Cor.C (*f ff* ¹ aur vg sy^s.p.hl, Aug: *conseruantur*) |⌈τηρουνται D* (*a d h k q seruantur*) |⌈om. S

9:21 εαν μονον αψωμαι   *rell*
  εαν αψωμαι μονον   D *b c f ff*ᵈ *g*¹ *k* vg

9:22 °Ιησους ⌈στραφεις   *rell* |°ℵ* *pc* it sy^s |⌈επιστραφεις C L W Θ *f*¹ 𝔐
  εστη στραφεις   D *al*²

9:24 ⌈αυτου *rell* D^D |⌈αυτον D* Latt

9:25 της ⌈χειρος   *rell* |⌈χιρος ℵ
  την χειρα   D Latt

9:28a ελθοντι δε   ℵ^c B C L W *pler* NA²⁸
  ελθοντος δε αυτου   700 *pc f*
  εισελθοντι δε αυτω ℵ* N (1424 *al*)
  και ερχεται   D *a b c g*¹ *h k*

9:28b προσηλαν   B
  ᵀπροσηλθον *rell* |ᵀκαι D *a b c d g*¹ *k*

9:30 ⌈αυτων °οι οφθαλμοι *rell* ℵ^ca |⌈om. ℵ* |⌈αυτω E* |°700 | *231* D it vg

9:34 ⁰οι δε Φαρισαιοι ελεγον εν τω αρχοντι των δαμονιων εκβαλλει τα δαιμονια⸌ (*rell*) | ⁰D *a d k* Sy^s

9:38 του κυριου   rell D^D
      τον κυριον   D* Latt

10:4a ⸆ Σιμων rell |⸆ο C* |⸆και D h q syr^sch

10:4b Καναναιος   (rell)
       Χαναναιος   D a c f ff¹ vg Or^int

10:5a °λεγων   rell |°ℵ* 1424
       και λεγων   D it^pler vg^mss

10:5b Σαμαρειτων   B pc
       Σαμαριτων   ℵ L W pc NA²⁸
       Σαμαριτανων D (it vg)

10:6 ⸀πορευεσθε °δε   rell |⸀πορευεσθαι B* E W Δ 2* 1071 |°Cyr^glaph380
      υπαγετε   D d k

10:8a ⸀θεραπευετε rell |⸀θεραπευσατε D Latt

10:8b ⸀εγειρετε rell |⸀εγειρατε D Latt

10:8c ⸀καθαριζετε ⸆ rell |⸀καθαρεισατε και D (Latt om. και) |⸆om. 28 1428* |⸆και 348 k sy^s.pesh

10:8d ⸀εκβαλλετε rell |⸀εκβαλετε D F Θ 2 4 99 273 349 485 1108 1424

10:10 γαρ ⸆¹ ο εργατης της τροφης αυτου ⸆² ℵ B C L pler NA²⁸ |⸆¹εστιν D 21 399 517 544 713 945 1010 1293 1391 1396 l49 l184 vg |⸆²εστιν rell

10:11 εις ην δ αν πολιν η κωμην εισελθητε   pler   NA²⁸ |
123458 700 *f*¹ 1 118 209 *a b ff*¹ *h k* Hil *al* sy^s | *12345867* L 0281 *f*¹³
124 *pc* sah co

    η πολις εις ην αν εισελθητε εις αυτην   D 28

10:13a °και εαν *rell* |°D sy^p arm

10:13b εαν δε μη η αξια   *plu* NA²⁸
       om.   579
       ει δε μη γε   D *d* sy^s

10:13c ⌜ελθατω ℵ C N W *f*¹³ *pc* NA²⁸ |⌜99 *b*^scr* |⌜ελθετω B 𝔐 *f*¹ *pc*
|⌜εστε D *d* sy^s.p(1 MS)

10:14 ⸂της οκιας η ` της πολεως °εκεινης *rell* |⸆D arm^zoh |°D *al*⁶ it^pler vg

10:15 Γομορρων   *pler* NA²⁸
      Γομορρας   C M P 1 22 *al* plus³⁰ *ff*¹ *h k* Chr^montf et^mo6
      Γομορας   D L*

10:17 εν ταις συναγωγαις   *rell*
      εις τας συναγωγας   D 0171

10:18a ⌜ηγεμονας *rell* | ⌜ηγεμονων D 111 Or^1,158

10:18b δε και βασιλεις *rell* |om. D 111

10:18c αχθησεσθε   *rell* (ℵ P W Δ Θ 2* 33 157)
       σταθησεσθαι D 111 it^pler (0171 sy^s) Cyp Hil Or^int3,532.534

10:20 πατρος ⌜υμων *rell* | ⌜om. D (*non d*) Epiph Or |⌜ημων 479** 482
*l*184

10:28 εν γεεννη   *rell*
      εις γεενναν D (it^pler vg Ir^int Tert)

APPENDIX 10: NON-SINGULAR READINGS IN CODEX D IN MATTHEW 233

10:29a ⌜ασσαριου *rell* (L) |⌜του D* Or^{2,722}

10:29b πωλειται *rell*
πωλουνται D it vg Hil Cyp

10:30 υμων δε και αι τριχες *rell*
αλλα και αι τριχες D it^{pler} Clem^{263} Hil Ir$^{lat\ vid}$

10:32 εν αυτω *rell*
αυτον D L

10:35 ανθρωπου κατα του πατρος *rell*
υιον κατα πατρος D 42 114* it^{pler} sy$^{s.c}$

10:37 αξιος ⸂και ο φιλων υιον η θυγατερα υπερ εμε ουκ εστις μου αξιος⸃ *rell* |⸂B* D 17 243 syr^p cod

10:39 και ο απολεσας *rell*
ο δε απολεσας D Tert

10:41 λημψεται ⸂και ο δεχομενος δικαιον εις ονομα δικαιου μισθον δικαιου λημψεται⸃ (*rell*) NA^{28} |⸂D d 482 1093 *l*53

10:42a ⌜μικρον (*rell*) NA^{28} |⌜ελαχιστων D (1424 it vg go al *minimis*)

10:42b ⌜ψυχρου (*rell*) NA^{28} |⌜υδατος D it lat Sy$^{s\ c}$ co; Or Cyp

10:42c απολεση τον μισον *rell*
απολπται ο μισθος D *a b c* g^1 *h k q* cop aeth sy$^{s\ c}$ bo Cyp

11:4 και αποκριθεις *rell*
αποκριθεις δε D *a b c ff*^{1} g^1 *h*

11:5 αναβλεπουσιν ⸂και χωλοι περιπατουσιν⸃ (*rell*) |⸂D *d* 1187 1346 1355 1675 2145 [Cl?]

11:8   ανθρωπον °εν rell D^B |°D* it vg

11:12a °δε rell |°D* a sy^s bo^aliq.

11:12b ⌜βιασται rell |⌜οι D Clem^947

11:20a ⌜εγενοντο plu NA^28 |⌜γεγονεισαν D (d k)

11:20b δυναμεις °αυτου rell |°D g^1 sy^cu

11:21a ⌜Χοραζιν N U f^1 579 700 NA^28 |⌜Χοραζειν ℵ B W pc
|⌜Χωραζει 28 |⌜Χοραζαιν D (a q corazain, b ff^2 g^1 vg corozain)

11:21b ουαι ⌜σοι   plu NA^28 |⌜σου S Ω
       και   D it^pler Hil

11:21c Βηθσαιδα   C N f^1 33 pc NA^28
       Βηθσαιδαν   B W pc
       Βηδσαιδαν   ℵ K Π 565
       Βεθσαειδα   D (a c g^1 h q vg bethsaida)
       betsaida   b d f ff^1 l

11:28 πεφορτισμενοι ⌐ rell |⌐εσται D (it vg estis)

12:6   λεγω ⌜δε rell (700) |⌜om. 565 |⌜γαρ D k syr^cu

12:11a ⌜εξει rell |⌜εχει D pc c^scr it vg^mss

12:11b °τουτο rell |°D it^pl syr^cu et^sch

12:11b ⌜κρατησει plu NA^28 |⌜κρατει D k

12:18b ⌜ον ℵ* B |⌜εις ον ℵ^c C^c W pler NA^28 |⌜εν ω C* D 1424 f^1 33

12:20 ου σβεσει   rell
       ου μη ζβεσει   D* 713

APPENDIX 10: NON-SINGULAR READINGS IN CODEX D IN MATTHEW 235

12:21 ⌜ελπιουσιν *rell* D^c |⌜ελπιζουσιν D sah |⌜*credent k* aeth

12:25a πασα βασιλεια μερισθεισα καθ εαυτης   *rell*
  πασα βασιλεια μερισθεισα ⌜καθ εαυτην L 118 33 28 1424
|⌜εφ D Chr^{com.gue}

12:25b ⌜σταθησεται *rell* D^{Cor.C} |⌜στησεται D* f^{13} 174 230 788 826 828 983 |⌜συσταθησεται 482

12:26 και ει   *rell*
       ει δε και   D (*d si autem*; *b ff² g¹ q si enim*; *c ff¹ h si ergo*;
a si)

12:35 °ο αγαθος *rell* D^D |°D* Or^{semel (3,665libere)}

12:37 ⌜και εκ των λογων *rell* |⌜η D^{gr} *a c g¹* Hil Paulin

12:44 ⌜ευρισκει *rell* |⌜ευρησει 124 |⌜ευρεισκει τον οικον D (sy^{hmg})

12:45² εαυτου   *rell*
       αυτου   D E* *al pc*

12:45 ⌜χειρονα *rell* |⌜χιρονα ℵ |⌜χειρον D* *l*184 |⌜χειρωνα L 59 124 245

12:47a ⌐εξω εστηκασιν ζητουντες⌐   C 𝔐 W *pler* [NA²⁸] | ⌐ℵ B L Γ [NA²⁸]
       εστηκεισαν εξω ζητουντες   D *b c f g¹ ff² h q* syr^{utr} | *21354* 33

12:47b ⌐ζητουντες σοι λαλησαι⌐   C 𝔐 W *pler* [NA²⁸] | ⌐ℵ B L Γ [NA²⁸]
       ζητουντες λαλησαι σοι   D *b c f g¹ ff² h q* syr^{utr} | *21354* 33

12:50 ⌈αν ποιηση	ℵ B W *plu* NA²⁸ | ⌈εαν *f*¹³ 1346 |⌈om. *al pc*
⌈αν ποιησει	L *pc* | ⌈εαν 124 788
ποιει	D *d* sy^{c.s.p.} sah

13:1 εξελθων	*rell*
εξηλθεν	D it^{pl} syr^{cu} et^{sch} Or^{int3,835} Hil

13:2 ⌈ειστηκει B^c D^{c?e?} K M S U Y Γ Π Ω *f*¹ 28 118 124 157 565 579 700 788 1071 1346 1424 etc. NA²⁸ | ⌈ιστηκι ℵ |⌈ιστηκη E* |⌈ιστικει 2* |⌈ιστηκει B* C W E^c F G L W X Z Δ Θ 2 33 etc. |⌈εστηκει D*^{?c?e?} (*d stabat*) 234 (*a b c ff² h* vg *stabant*)

13:3 °του σπειρειν	B *pc* |°1424
°του σπειραι	L W *pc* |°D

13:6a ⌈εκαυματισθη *plu* NA²⁸ |⌈εκαυματωθη B² |⌈απεξηρανθη E* |⌈εκαυματισθησαν D sy^h

13:6b ⌈εξηρανθη *rell* |⌈απεξηρανθη E* |⌈εξηρανθησαν D sy^h

13:8 ⌈εδιδου *rell* |⌈εδιδουν D it vg

13:13 αυτοις λαλω	*rell* |21 N O Θ Σ *f*^{1.13} 7 33 174 230 517 543 565 788 826 828 954 1424 1555 1675 *pc* it^{(pler)} (*loquar c*) vg sy^{c.s.pesh} sa bo arm geo
⌈λαλει °αυτοις	D* |⌈ελαλει D^B |°L *c* Cyp

13:14a ⌈αναπληρουται^T	*rell*	⌈αναπληρουτε	W*
⌈αναπληρουνται Θ 579 |⌈πληρουται 1 485 1582* |^Τεπ M W^c
τοτε πληρωθησεται °επ	D |°7 517 954 1424 1675

13:14b ^THσαιου *rell* (L) |^Ττου D *l*185 |om. 126 *al*⁴ *b* Chr^{mo2}

13:14b °η λεγουσα	*pler* NA²⁸ | °S *f*¹³ *pc*
λεγουσα πορευθητι και ειπε τω λαω τουτω	D it mae Eusebius

13:16 °οι οφθαλμοι *rell* |°D M*

13:17 ουκ ⌜ειδαν   ℵ B N 33 NA²⁸ |⌜ειδον *rell*
       ουχ ⌜ιδον   Θ f^1 788 1346 |⌜ηδυνηθησαν ειδειν D *d* geo¹

13:19 αυτου   *rell*
       αυτων   D *q*

13:22 ⌜σπαρεις *rell* (*b f ff* ¹ g² *h q* vg *est seminatus*) |⌜σπειρουμενος D (*a c d* g¹ *ff* ² *k seminatur*)

13:23a ο τον λογον ακουων   *plu* NA²⁸
        ο ακουων τον λογον   D it vg syr^cu et^sch

13:23b ος δη   *plu* NA²⁸
        τοτε   D *a b c h q* (*k* et tunc*)

13:24 τω αγρω αυτου   *plu* NA²⁸
        τω ιδιω αγρω   D Eus^es.bis

13:28 οι δε δουλοι λεγουσιν αυτω   ℵ NA²⁸
        οι δε δουλοι αυτω λεγουσιν   C
        οι δε δουλοι ειπον αυτω   L W *pc*
        λεγουσιν αυτω οι δουλοι   D *a b c e ff* ² g¹ *k* syr^sch

13:29 ο δε ⌜φησιν   ℵ B C Δ 21 399 892 1010 1295 1396 1555 NA²⁸ |⌜εφη *rell* |⌜εφη αυτοις N O Θ Σ 33 1071 *a* vg^(3MSS) (sa bo^pc geo)   ⸋ο δε ⸌ λεγει αυτοις 33 659 1424 1675 *b f q ff* ^1.2 g^1.2 *l* aur vg aeth arm |⸋D *d k* (*h r*) sy^c.s

13:29 αμα ⌐αυτοις τον ⌜στιον   *plu* NA²⁸ |⌐it^pl cop syr^p |⌜σειτον Θ
        αμα και τον σειτον συν αυτοις   D (*k* syr^cu arm) | 156234 (Γ) *ff* ¹ g² vg syr^sch

13:30a συναυξανεσθαι αμφοτερα *plu* NA²⁸
      αμφοτερα συναυξανεσθαι D it vg

13:30b ⸆αυτα °εις` ℵ B *pler* NA²⁸ | °L X Δ 1 *al*⁵ *a b c g*¹·² *ff*² *q* am for em gat san mm syr^(cu)et^(sch) arm^(zoh) Chr(et^(mo6)) |⸆D *e f h k* Or^(3,135) Ir^(latvid) Epiph

13:30c ⸂συναγαγετε *rell* |⸂συνεγετε B Y* Γ 1 348 440 1689 |⸂συνλεγεται D *k* |⸂συναγαγεται W 2* 28 579 |⸂συναταγετε Δ* |⸂εισαγαγετε 1194 |⸂αγαγετε 1293

13:32 παντων °των σπερματων *rell* |°D* 124 346 543 828

13:33 ⸆ελαλησεν αυτοις⸇ B 𝔐 *f*¹ 33 *pler* NA²⁸ |⸆παρεθηκεν C |⸇λεγων ℵ L M *f*¹³ 788 *pler* | om. D 76 *k* syr^(s.c)

13:46b °παντα οσα *rell* |° 1071 *a c h* Cop^(bo(pler))
       α   D (*a c*) *d* (*h*) *ff*²

13:40 ⸂συλλεγεται *rell* |⸂συνλεγονται D it vg

13:54 τουτω ⸉ *rell* |⸉τουτα και τις W |⸉πασα D 892 *pc* sys mae aeth Eus^(steph223)et^(ps398)

13:58 την απιστιαν   *rell*
      τας απιστειας   D 892 *k*

14:2a ⸇ουτος *rell* | ⸇μητι D *pc b f h* vg^(mss) gat mm

14:2b Ιωανης ο βαπτισης ⸇ *rell* |⸇ον εγω απεκεφαλισα D *a d ff*¹ *h* vg^(mss)

14:3a και εν φυλακη απεθετο   ℵ* B* *pc* NA²⁸ |142 τη 3 *f*¹ 700 *pc* |2 τη *314* ℵ² Z^(vid)
      και εθετο εν φυλακη   C L W 0106^(c) 𝔐 it^(pl) vg syr^(omn) cop arm
      ⸆εν τη` φυλακη   D *a*^(vid) *e k* aeth Or^(3,469) |⸆61

14:3b ᵒΦιλιππου *rell* |ᵒD a c d (e) *ff*¹ *g*¹ *k l* vg⁽ᵖˡᵉʳ⁾ aug^{cons.2.92}

14:8 ᵀδος μοι φησιν *rell* | ᵀειπεν W
επιεν θελω ινα μοι δος εξ αυτης 1424
ειπεν δος μοι D 0106ᶜ 1424 it vg^{mss} syr^{cu} et^{sch} aeth

14:9 και τους συνανακειμενους *rell*
και δια τους συνανακειμενους D it^{pler} syr^{cu} aeth

14:14 τους ⌐αρρωστους *rell* (1230) (*languidos* Latt) |⌐αρρω-
στουντας D 233 372 2737 |⌐αρρωστας 3 |⌐*infirmos d* |⌐*animas* geo¹
τας νοσους 863

14:16 δοτε αυτοις υμεις φαγειν *rell*
δοτε υμεις φαγειν αυτοις D 1354 *d*

14:19a τους οχλους *rell*
τον οχλον D^{gr} 892 it^{pler} vg mae bo^{mss} arm^{zoh}

14:19b του χορτου ℵ B C* W Θ *f*¹ 33 157 565 579 NA²⁸
⌐τους χορτους Cᶜ K M P U Δ Π 2 28 118ᶜ 788 *f*¹³ 1071
1346 |⌐του L
τον χορτον D 16 61 892 (it vg syr^{cu} et^{sch} syr^{p mg} cop
arm aeth *super faenum*)

14:19c ⌐λαβων *rell* (*accptis* Latt) |⌐ελαβεν D (*accepit d*) (*e*) sy^{s c .pesh.}
cop^{sa} aeth geo |⌐λαμβων Δ

14:22 αυτον *rell*
om. D it

14:24a °ηδη σταδιους πολλους ᶜαπο της γης˸ απειχεν B f^{13} 174
230 543 788 826 828 1346 sy^hier NA²⁸ |°sy^pesh sa (bo) |ᶜ238 983 1689

°ηδη μεσον της θαλασσης ην   ℵ C F L P
W X Γ Δ Π Σ Φ 073 084 0106 f^1 33 𝔐 (lat) sy^h mae? |°28 *a b d f ff*^{1} *l*
geo |2*1345* 1555

ην ᵀ μεσον της θαλασσης   517   954
1424 1675 |ᵀεις D *d* it vg sy^hl

ηδη σταδιους της γης απειχεν ικανους   700
°ηδη απειχεν απο της γης σταδιους ικανους Θ |°sy^c

14:28 °ο Πετρος *rell* | °D 482* 544

14:33 θεου υιος ει   *rell*
       υιος θεου ει °συ D *d* aeth |°it vg sy^s sah bo arm geo

15:1   τω Ιησου   *rell*
       αυτω f^1 1424
       προς αυτον D it^pler vg aeth Hil Aug^cons2,102

15:3   ειπεν °αυτοις *rell* |°D *e* cop

15:11a ου ᵀ *rell* |ᵀπαν D *d* pers^p

15:11b στομα ᵀ κοινοι   *rell* (C) |ᵀτουτο ℵ*
       στομα κοινωνι   D (*d communicat*)

15:11c τουτο κοινοι   *rell* |om. f^1 124 1071
       εκεινο κοινωνει D (*d* Tert Aug Hier *communicat*)

15:18 κοινοι τον ανθρωπον   *rell* D^D
       κοινωνει τον ανθρωπον D* (*d communicant*) Aug^semel

15:20a ταυτα ⌜εστιν *rell* |⌜εισιν D* *e ff*^{1} *k* Aug^semel

15:20b κοινουντα   *rell* D^D
       κοινωνουντα D* (*d e ff*^1 *k* Aug^semel *communicant*)

15:20c φαγειν ου ⌜κοινοι *rell* |⌜κοινει C |⌜κοινωνει D* (*d k* Aug^semel *communicat*)

15:24 τα προβατα^T *rell* | ^Tταυτα D sy^s.c.h

15:26 εστιν καλον *rell*
       εξεστιν   D it sy^s.c Origen

15:27 ⌜εσθιει *rell* (B) |⌜εσθιυοσιν D y^scr semel

15:28a αποκριθεις ο Ιησους ειπεν αυτη *rell*
       αποκριθεις ειπεν αυτη   D Γ *al*^2 fu syr^cu

15:28b °ω γυναι *rell* |°D 259

15:30a °κωφους *rell* |°D 1207 (472) *pc d g*^2 *l*

15:30b αυτους ⸌παρα τους⸍ ποδας *rell* C^B |⸌C*
       αυτους ⌜υπο τους ποδας   D *b* |⌜μακροθεν εμπροσθεν αυτου προς 1424

15:30c εθεραπευσεν αυτους   *rell*
       εθεραπευσεν αυτους παντας   D 954 *b c ff*^2 *g*^1 it sa^mss bo^mss

15:31 ^Tτυφλους *rell* |^Tτους D 1012

15:32a οχλον^T *rell* |^Tτουτον D E^c *c f g*^2 cop Hil Chr^mo4
15:32b τρεις ^T *rell* |^Tεισιν και D (it)

15:34 ειπαν ℵ *pc* NA^28
       ειπον^T B C L W *pc* |^Tαυτω D^gr *pc* syr^omn

16:1   πειραζοντες επηρωτησαν αυτον   B *plu* NA²⁸ | *132* D 1396
       πειραζοντες επηρωτων αυτον   ℵ* *pc*

16:2   °αυτοις *rell* |°D y^scr it^mu

16:4a γενεα πονηρα και μοιχαλις   (*rell*) NA²⁸
       γενεα πονηρα   D 4 *a e ff*¹ ² Prosp

16:4b σημειον ⌜επιζητει   *rell* -700 |⌜σημιον ℵ W |⌜σιμειον 2 |⌜σημειων 1346
       σημειον αιτει   B*
       ⌜σημιον ζητει   D^H *d* |⌜σημιον Θ
       ζητει σημιον   D* *b c e quaerit signum*

16:7   οι δε διελογιζοντο *rell*
       τοτε διελογιζοντο   D 4 *a b c e ff*² sy^s Lcif

16:9a ᵀτους πεντε *rell* |ᵀοτε D Δ

16:9b των ⌜πεντακισχιλων   *rell* | ⌜πεντασχιλιων 124
       τοις πεντακισχιλειοις   D *d* (*c f ff*² *g*² *in milia quinque*) geo¹

16:10 των τετρακισχιλιων   *rell*
       τους τετρακισχιλιους   157
       τοις τετρακεισχειλειοις   D (*a b c f* g¹ ² *ff*¹ ² *q* vg Lcif *in quattuor milia*)

16:11 ⌜αρτων ειπον υμιν   *plu* NA²⁸ |⌜αρτου E F G H U V X Γ Δ it^pl vg Or³,⁵¹⁸ Amb
       αρτου ειπον ᵀ   D *a b ff*² Lcif | ᵀυμιν W *pc*

16:13a °αυτου *rell* |°D *d* arm

16:13b °τον υιον του ανθρωπου *rell* |°D bo

16:17 ειπεν °αυτω rell |°D am fu

16:18a ταυτη τη πετρα   rell | 231 E*
       ταυτην την πετραν   D (Δ) Eus^dem121 it vg

16:18b μου την εκκλησιαν rell
       την εκκλησιαν μου   D it vg Tert Cyp

16:21 τη τριτη ημερα εγερθηναι   rell
       μετα τρεις ημερας αναστηναι   D cop bo

16:22a ηρξατο επιτιμαν αυτω^T λεγων   ℵ (C) 𝔐 K L M U
W Δ Π 2 118 579 1071 NA²⁸ |^Tκαι F | 1324 $f^{1.13}$ 124 157 700 788
1346 1424
       ηρξατο αυτω επειτειμαν και λεγειν   D 283 (it)
       ηρξατο αυτον πειτιμαν λεγων   Θ
       ηρξατο αυτω επιτιμαν αυτω λεγων   565
       λεγει αυτω επιτειμων   B 346

16:26 ⌜κερδηση rell D ⌜κερδησει H L 2* 28 579 ⌜καιερδηση Θ
⌜κερδισει 1071 ⌜κερδη Latt ⌜κερδανη Or³·⁵⁴⁵

16:27 των αγγελων αυτου   rell
       των αγγελων των αγιων   C 1071 1365 b Avit
       των αγιων αγγελων αυτου   D d 047 Chr
       angelis suis sanctis   b sy^pesh

17:1a ^TΙωαννην (rell) NA²⁸ |^Tτον D* 253 Cyr^es

17:1b ⌜κατ ιδιαν   rell ⌜καθ B*
       λειαν   D d Eus^dem208

17:2a μετεμορφωθη εμπροσθεν   rell
       μετεμορφωθεις ο Ιησους εμπροσθεν   D e (sy^p)

17:2b °και ελαμψεν rell |°D d e

17:6 και ακουσαντες   rell
      ακουσαντες δε   D sah

17:7 ⌜εγερθητε rell (W) |⌜εγειρεσθαι D l33

17:8 αυτον Ιησουν μονον   B* Θ 700 NA²⁸
      Ιησουν αυτον μονον   ℵ
      τον Ιησουν μονον μεθ εαυτων   Cᶜ 33
      °τον Ιησουν μονον   B² C* L f¹·¹³ 𝔐 |°W
      μονον τον Ιησουν   D it vg

17:9 ⌜καταβαινοντων rell |⌜καταβαινοντες D d syᶜ·ᵖ
|⌜καταβενοντων W |⌜καταβαντων 655

17:11 °και αποκαταστησει rell |°D a b c e g¹ ff² sy⁽ᵖ⁾ etᶜᵘ etˢᶜʰ sah

17:12b ουτως και ο υιος του ανθροπου μελλει πασχειν υπ αυτων
       (rell)
       τοτε αυνηκαν οι μαθηται οτι περι Ιωαννου του βαπτιστου
ειπεν αυτοις D it

17:13 τοτε συνηκαν οι μαθηται οτι περι Ιωαννου του βαπτιστου
ειπεν αυτοις (rell)
       ουτως και ο υιος του ανθροπου μελλει πασχειν υπ αυτων
       D it

17:14a ⌜ελθοντων rell |⌜εισελθοντων 1424 |⌜ελθων D it vg copᵈᶻ arr (syˢ·ᶜ) boᵖᵗ Hil Aug

17:14b ⌜αυτον plu NA²⁸ | ⌜ενπροσθεν αυτου D itᵐᵘ e f ff¹ l Hil placeᵒᵐ surᶜᵘ etˢᶜʰ arm vg syrᵖ

17:16 ⌜¹ηδυνηθησαν ⌜²αυτον θεραπευσαι (rell)   NA²⁸
|⌜¹ηδυνασθησαν B |⌜¹ηδυναντο Z |⌜¹ηδυνηθεισαν 2* |⌜²εδυνηθησαν
K Π 265 489 892 1219 1346 *l*184
|⌜²αυτω 2
    ηδυνηθησαν θεραπευσαι αυτον   D it vg

17:19 ⌜κατ ιδιαν *rell* |⌜καθ B* D

17:24¹ τα ⌜διδραχα   *rell* G |⌜διδραγματα D *al. pc* |⌜διδραγμα 𝔐 L
1 118 *f*¹³ 2 28 157 565 700 1071 1346 *b ff*² am fu for gat *al.*
|⌜*didragmas q* |⌜*tributum a c d e f ff*¹ *n* vg⁽ᵖˡᵉʳ⁾ aeth |⌜*dragma g*²
    το ⌜διδραγμα W |⌜διδραχμον Cyr⁴,⁷⁹¹

17:22 συστρεφομενων δε αυτων   ℵ B *f*¹ (*f* g¹·² *q* vg) NA²⁸
    αναστρεφομενων δε αυτων   *rell*
    υποστρεγοντων δε αυτων   579
    αυτων δε αναστρεφομενων   D (*a b c ff*² *n* Hil)

17:23 τη τριτη ημερα εγερθηναι   *rell*
    τη τριτη ημερα αναστηναι   (B) 047 118 *f*¹³ (1346ᶜ) *plu*
    μετα τρεις ημερας εγερθηναι D *d* (sy^s) bo

17:24a ελθοντων δε *rell*
    και ελθοντων D it vg syr^cu et^sch

17:24b τω Πετρω και ⌜ειπον*rell* | ⌜ειπαν ℵᶜ B
    και ειπαν τω Πετρω D 27^ev syr^hr

17:24² τα ⌜διδραχμα   *rell* ℵ^ca |⌜διδραγμα 𝔐 L 118 *f*¹³ 28 157
565 700 1071 |⌜διδραχματα 579 |⌜διδραχμον 1093 |⌜*tributum a d e f ff*
¹ *n* vg⁽ᵖˡᵉʳ⁾ aeth |⌜*didgrama uel censum b* |⌜*didgramam g*¹
    ⌜δειδραγμα   D |⌜διδραχα ℵ* mae bo
    το ⌜διδραγμα   W |⌜διδραχμον Cyr⁴,⁷⁹¹

17:27 ⌜στατηρα *rell* |⌜εκει D it sy^s.c

17:26 ειποντες δε ᵀαπο των αλλοτριων   ℵ B Θ 0281 f¹ 700 892* pc vgᵐˢˢ sa boᵖᵗ; Chr NA²⁸ | ᵀτου Πετρου 892ᵐᵍ
         λεγει αυτω απο των αλλοτριων   D syˢ
         λεγει αυτω ο Πετρος απο των αλλοτριων ▫ειποντος δε °αυτου απο των αλλοτριων ˋ   C Cyr |°L | ▫rell (D) -33

18:2   ᵀεστησεν rell |ᵀεν D e syˢ·ᶜ

18:7   °πλην ᵀ ουαι τω ανθρωπω   ℵ F L f¹ 22 579 892 d g¹ aur vgˢᵗ·ʷʷ syᵒᵐⁿ saᵐˢˢ mae bo Did |°syˢ |ᵀδε D* syˢ·ᵖᵉˢʰ |ᵀdico uobis r²
         πλην ουαι τω ανθρωπω εκεινω   rell | 15234 W e ff ¹ |1δε5234 geo

18:8   ▫η δυο χειρας ˋ η δυο ποδας εχοντα   rell f q vg |▫Γ
         η δυο χεριας εχοντα η δυο ποδας   1071
         η δυο ποδας η δυο χειρας εχοντα   D itᵖˡᵉʳ Chrᶜᵈᵈ⁴

18:9a και ει   rell
         το αυτο ει και   D d syᶜ·ˢ·ᵖᵉˢʰ

18:9b γεενναν °του πυρος rell |° Δ
         γεενναν ᵀ   D d |ᵀτο σκοτος το εξωτερον 1675

18:10 των μικρων τουτων   (rell) NA²⁸ |312 L
         τουτων των μεικρων των πιστευοντων εις εμε   D b c ff ¹·² g¹·² syrᶜᵘ sah sax Hil

18:12a τιᵀ υμιν rell |ᵀδε D qˢᶜʳ a cop syrᶜᵘ

18:12b ⌜πορευθεις rell |⌜πορευμενος D (pergens d, vadens q syᵒᵐⁿ) |⌜vadit Latt |⌜vadet e h r² vg⁽ᵃˡⁱᑫ·⁾ |⌜ibit m geo

APPENDIX 10: NON-SINGULAR READINGS IN CODEX D IN MATTHEW

18:14 του πατρος μου   B N Γ Θ 078 0281 f^{13} 33 579 700 892 1241 1424 *pc* sy$^{s.h}$ co Or

       του πατρος υμων   ℵ D^B K L W Δ f^1 565 *pc* it vg sy$^{c.p.hmg}$ NA^{28}

       του πατρος ημων   D* *al pc* harl*

18:16 °μαρτυρων *rell* |°D 435 (Aug^{semel})

18:17 και$^⊤$ *rell* |$^⊤$ως D 301 *ff*^{1} syr^{cu}et^p

18:18 δησητε επι της γης □εσται δεδεμενα εν ⌜ουρανω και οσα εαν λυσητε επι της γης⌝ εσται B NA^{28} | □D* *d n* | ⌜τοις ουρανοις D^c L

18:20   ου γαρ εισιν   *rell* D^D
       οπου γαρ εισιν   ℵ* N *pc*
       ουκ εισιν γαρ   D* (g^1) sy^s

18:26 πεσων ⌜ουν *rell* | ⌜δε D y^{scr} it vg sah syr^p arm Lcif

18:29 ⌜και *rell* |⌜καγω D *d* sy^{sc}

18:34 αποδω °παν *rell* | °D y^{scr} *al pc* Chr (ita^{mo5})

19:1 ⌜ετελεσεν *rell* |⌜ετελεν C |⌜ελαλησεν D *a b c e ff*$^{1.2}$ *g*^{1} *r*^{1} bo^{2MSS} Hil

19:3 ⌜λεγοντες ℵ B C L *pc* NA^{28} |⌜λεγοντες αυτω D$^{Cor.C}$ W *pc* |⌜λεγουσιν αυτω D* *d e*

19:6 συνεζευξεν $^⊤$ ανθρωπος *rell* |$^⊤$εις εν D *a e*** *f*$^{1.2}$ *h* Aug Chrom

19:8a   λεγει   *rell*
       και λεγει   D* aeth

19:8b Μωυσης ᵀ προς την σκληροκαρδιαν ⌜¹υμων ⌜²επετρεψεν υμιν rell (C 𝔐 L Δ f¹ 2 1071) | 2345671 D a b c d e f g¹ h r¹ vg |ᵀμεν U |⌜¹ημων 579 |⌜¹om. 892 |⌜²εγραψεν 1424 Eus | 1672345 Wᶜ | 162345 W*

19:10 του ανθρωπου rell
   ανθρωπος   𝔓²⁵
   του ανδρος   D a b c ff² g¹ h m q Amb al

19:13 τας χειρας επιθη αυτοις ℵ B C L W plu NA²⁸ |1243 U it vg |3412 1424 |3124 D sah cop Or³·⁶⁵⁸

19:16 αυτω ειπεν ℵ B Θ pc f¹³ 13 157 346 700 892 pc a b c e f ff ¹·² g¹ h q sa pc Chr Op NA²⁸
   ειπεν αυτω C L M W pc f¹ 33 𝔐 syᵒᵐⁿ Or³·⁶⁶⁴ Basᵉᵗʰ²⁴² et²⁷⁹
   λεγει αυτω D (vg ait)

19:22 δε ο νεανισκος rell (33 1424)
   ο νεανισκος   D* f h
   ου νεανισκος Dᴬ

19:25 εξεπλησσοντο ᵀ rell |ᵀκαι εφοβηθησαν D a b c e ff² g² syrᶜᵘ

19:27 ⌜ηκολουθησαμεν rell Dᴮ |⌜ηκολουθηκαμεν D* Latt

19:28 ⌜αυτοις rell |⌜αυτω D al pc |⌜αυτους 1346

20:3 τριτην ωραν ειδεν rell
  ωραν τριτην ειδεν Δ
  τριτην ωραν ευρεν 1424
  ωραν τριτην ευρεν D (it) vg

20:5 εκτην και ενατην ωραν ℵ B C L W pler NA²⁸
  ωραν εκτην και εννατην D f Op Arn

20:6 ⌜εξελθων rell | ⌜εξηλθεν ℵ* | ⌜εξηλθεν και D it vg

20:10 °και ελαβον   *rell* | °f^{13} 1346
       ελαβον δε   D it vg

20:11 εγογγυζον   *rell*
       εγονγυσαν   D it^{pler} syr^{cu} et^{sch}

20:22a δυνασθε πειν το ποτηριον *rell* (W f^{13})
       δυνασθε το ποτηριον πειν D Γ aeth

20:22b λεγουσιν αυτω   *rell*
       λεγουσιν   D am sry^{cu} aeth

20:25 ειπεν   *rell*
       ειπεν αυτοις D W 238 *e* syr^{cu} et^{sch} sah cop aeth

20:28 ⌜λυτρον αντι πολλων *rell* |⌜λυτρων 579
       λυτρον αντι πολλων υμεις δε ζετειτε εκ μεικρου αυχησαι και εκ μειζονος ⌜¹ελαττον ειναι εισερχομενοι δε και παρακληθεντες δειπνησαι μη ανακλεινεσθαι εις τους εξεχοντας τοπους ᵀ μηποτε ⌜²ενδοξοτερος σου επελθη °και προσελθων ο δειπνοκλητωρ ειπη σοι ετι κατω χωρει και καταισυνθηση εαν δε αναπεσης εις τον ηττονα τοπον και επελθη σου ηττων ερει σοι ο δειπνοκλητωρ ⌜³συναγε ετι ανω και εσται σοι τουτο ⌜⁴χρησιμον D (it) vg$^{(pler)}$ sy^c |⌜¹ελαττων Φ |ᵀανακλινεσθε Φ |⌜²ενδοξωτερος Φ |°Φ |⌜³αγε Φ |⌜⁴χρησιμωτερον Φ

21:5a πραυς °και *rell* | °D 61 *a b e ff*$^{1\,2}$ *h* vg^{ed} fu san gat fr aeth Cyp

21:5b ⌜¹υιον ⌜²υποζυγιου *rell* D^K |⌜¹om. ℵ^c L Z f^1 *d g*^{1} |⌜¹υον F |⌜¹υιων 579 |⌜²πωλον νεον f^1 |⌜²υποζυγιον D* it sa

21:6   και ποιησαντες   *rell*
       εποιησαν   D it vg

21:7a ᵀ¹ηγαγον ᵀ² *rell* |ᵀ¹και D it vg |ᵀ²δε 157

21:7b επ αυτων   ℵ B L 69 NA²⁸
       επανω αυτων   C 𝔐 W pler
       αυτω   f¹³ 124 1346
       επ αυτον   D (Φ l 2211 a b e f ff¹ ² g² q Or⁴,¹⁸¹ᶜᵒᵈ)

21:7c ⌜επεκαθισεν B C f¹³ pler NA²⁸ |⌜εκαθισεν N Π |⌜εκαθητο D 700 |⌜επεκαθισαν ℵᶜ |⌜επεκαθησαν L |⌜εκαθισαν ℵ*

21:11 °ο απο rell |°D Δ

21:18 ⌜επαναγων ℵᶜ Bᶜ C pler NA²⁸ |⌜επαναγαγων ℵ* B* L |⌜υπαγων W |⌜παραγων D it syrᶜ Hil

21:21 τουτω ᵀ rell | ᵀεαν D S

21:24 ερωτησω   rell
       επερωτησω   D 482 483 484

21:24 λογον ενα ον εαν   rell
       ενα λογον ⌜ον εαν   C Dᴰ F L 118 157 28 579 1424 |⌜ο N |⌜om. D* d c e ff¹ h

21:29 απηλθεν ᵀ rell |ᵀεις τον αμπελωνα D itᵖˡᵉʳ syrᶜᵘ

21:32 ⌜ουδε B pc NA²⁸ |⌜ου ℵ C L W pc |⌜om. D (c) e ff¹* syˢ

21:37 προς αυτους rell |om. 28 e ff¹ m Or³,⁷⁸² (Cyrᵉˢ⁶⁶⁰)
      αυτοις D a b c ff² h Irⁱⁿᵗ²⁷⁷ Lcif

22:5a ος μεν B L W pc NA²⁸
       ο μεν   ℵ C pc
       οι μεν D b c ff² h Irⁱⁿᵗ²⁷⁹ Lcif

22:5b ος δε   ℵ B C* L W pc NA²⁸
       ο δε   Cᶜ 𝔐 pc
       οι δε   D b c ff² h Irⁱⁿᵗ²⁷⁹ Lcif

22:7 ο δε βασιλευς ωργισθη   ℵ B L f^1 700 NA²⁸
      και ακουσας ο βασιλευς εκεινος ωργισθη   C W X Δ Π
0102 (33ⁿⁱᵈ) 𝔐 f q syʰ Damᵖᵃʳ³⁸²
      ο δε βασιλευς ακουσας ωργισθη   Θ f^{13} 788 1346 lat
syᵖ mae boᵖᵗ Irˡᵃᵗ
      εκεινος ο βασιλευς ακουσας ωργισθη   D a b c e ff^2 Lcif

22:10 ⌜εκεινοι *rell* |⌜αυτου D 49 it vg Irⁱⁿᵗ²⁷⁹

22:11 ⌜ουκ *rell* |⌜μη Cᶜ D *al pc* (Or⁴·³⁷⁹ˡⁱᵇ)

22:12 πως ⌜εισηλθες *rell* |⌜ηλθες D b c e $ff^{1.2}$ g^1 syrᶜᵘ Irⁱⁿᵗ Aug Lcf

22:13 ⌜εκβαλετε *rell* |⌜βαλεται D it (syˢ·ᶜ) Itˡᵃᵗ Lcf

22:16a αυτω   *rell*
       προς αυτον   D a c f

22:16b εν αληθεια   *rell*
       την αληθειαν   Athᵖˢ⁸⁴¹
       επ ⌜αληθεια   D* |⌜αληθειας Dᶜ Eusᵖˢ¹⁴¹ Cyrᵍˡᵃᵖʰ¹³⁴

22:17 ▫ειπε ουν ημιν τι σοι δοκει`   *rell* ($f^{1.13}$) | ▫1424
      τι σοι δοκει   D *pc* it syˢ boᵐˢ

22:20 ⌜και λεγει αυτοις *rell* |⌜ο δε C |⌜om. D 69 it b e $ff^{1\,2}$ g^2 h sah syˢ·ᶜ mae

22:24 ᵀεπιγαμβρευσει *rell* |ᵀινα D Zᵛⁱᵈ |ᵀκαι 13 69 788 (f^{13} 1346)

22:28 των επτα εσται γυνη   *rell*
      εστε των επτα γυνη   D (c d $ff^{1.2}$ g^1 h l q $r^{1.2}$ aur vg)

22:34 επι το αυτο   *rell*
      επι το αυτω   S 579
      επ αυτον   D it syˢ·ᶜ aeth mae? Hil

22:36 εντολη ⌜μεγαλη εν τω νομω rell |⌜μιζων Θ
       εντολη εν τω νομω μεγαλη D 122

22:37 ο δε εφη αυτω   ℵ B L 33 sah cop Ot^{int3,830} NA^{28}
       ο δε Ιησους ειπεν αυτω   W Θ f^{13} 2 700 788 1346
       ο δε Ιησους εφη αυτω   0102 0161 f^1 𝔐 q sy$^{p.h}$ mae
       εφη αυτω Ιησους   D lat bo^{ms}

22:38 η μεγαλη και πρωτη   rell
       η μεγαλη και η πρωτη   L |45312 W cop
       ⌜πρωτη και μεγαλη   (D transposition) E F G H K M S
U Y Γ Π Ω 2 28 157 579 1071 1424 $d f q$ syr$^{p.hl}$ arm pers^p Op |⌜η O Δ
Θ^b Σ Φ 1070 174 237 563 565 Bas^{eth}

22:39 ομοια ⌜^{1}αυτη ⌜^{2}αγαπησεις rell |⌜^{1}αυτης Δ 0102 0138 238
1295 |⌜^{1}ταυτη D* Z^{vid} 692 it vg sy^{omn} bo aeth arm geo |⌜^{2}αγαπησις ℵ
W |⌜^{2}αγαπησης E
       ομοιως αγαπησις   B

23:3 ειπωσιν °υμιν rell |°D 4 273 280

23:11 °δε rell |°D it^{pler} vg

23:15 ξηραν ποιησαι   rell
       ξηραν του ποιησαι   Δ Θ f^{13} 788
       ξηραν ινα ποιησηται   D mae? (it^{pler} vg ut faciatis)

23:25b ⌜εξωθεν rell | ⌜εκτος 28 | ⌜εξω D 238 Clem^{282} Chr^{mo1} (X^{comm})

23:26 και °το ⌜εκτος rell | °Δ | ⌜εντος ℵ* l183 l184 |⌜εξωθεν D Clem

APPENDIX 10: NON-SINGULAR READINGS IN CODEX D IN MATTHEW 253

23:27a εξωθεν °μεν φαινονται ωραιοι rell | 2341
f^{13} 788 1346 | 2314 157 |°Δ
    εξθωεν μεν φανονται τοις ανθρωπος ωραιοι F
    εξωθεν μεν φαινεσθε τοις ανθρωπος δικαιοι 33 (mae)
    εξωθεν ο ταφος φαινεται ωραιος D Clem²⁸²
Cyr^{iulian335} Ir^{int250}

23:27b ⌜γεμουσιν rell |⌜γεμει D Clem²⁸² Cyr^{iulian335} Ir^{int250}

23:34a □προς υμας` rell |□D y^{scr}

23:34b □και εξ αυτων μαστιγωσετε` εν ταις συναγωγαις υμων και
        rell |□E
    και   D *a d* Lcif

23:37 ⌜αυτην rell |⌜σε D y^{scr} (it vg Ir^{int} Or^{in}t *te*)

24:2 ᵀου μη αφεθη rell |ᵀοτι D syr^p

24:3 της σης παρουσιας rell
    της παρουσιας σου D (it vg *adventus tui*)

24:8 ⌜ωδινων rell D^B |⌜ωδεινων B C Δ 565 1424 |⌜οδυνων D* (it vg *dolorum*)

24:11 εγερθησονται   rell (*ff*¹ vg *surgent*)
    εξεγερθησονται   D (*a d e q* Cyp Lcif *al exsurgent*)

24:17 °αυτου rell |°D *a b ff*² *q* Ir^{int} Cyp Hil

24:23 ωδε... ωδε   rell
    ωδε... εκει   D 16^{ev} Thdrt^{2,1287 ed} Ps-Ath^{dispu}

24:30 δυναμεως και δοξης πολλης   rell
    δυναμεως πολλης και δοξης   D 115 it^{pler} vg Cyp Amb *al*

24:31a σαλπιγγος ⌐μεγαλης ℵ^c L W pc NA^{28} |⌐φωνης B 𝔐 pler |⌐και φωνης D 1241 it^{pler} vg Dam^{par346} Hil

24:31b ⌐απ ακρων rell |⌐απο D X

24:38 □εκειναις °ταις προ⌐   B 472 1295 1515 aur sy$^{hl.hier.}$ arm NA^{28} |°D 44^{7petr} 697 1573 it vg geo |□L 892 l15 a e ff^1 Or
⌐ταις πορ   ℵ 𝔐 |⌐του νωε 461 1424

24:45a τις ⌐αρα εστιν rell | ⌐γαρ D y^{scr} (q Or^{int3,878} Op quis enim; it^{pler} quis nam; Hil quis namque)

24:45b ⌐^{1}αυτου °του ⌐^{2}δουναι ℵ B I L U Δ al^{30} fere Bas^{eth} Chr NA^{28} | ⌐^{1}εαυτου C | ⌐^{2}διδοναι E F G H K M S V W Γ Π al pl Ephr |°D al pc Chr Ephr

24:51 αυτου μετα των υποκριτων θησει   rell
       αυτου θησει μετα των υποκριτων   D it (exc q) vg Hil

25:3 ⌐γαρ ℵ B C L 33 NA^{28} | ⌐om. rell | ⌐δε Z Θ f^1 157 b c f ff^1 g^{12} h l q vg aeth Aug al |⌐ουν D ff^2

25:3–4 ελαιον^T $^{25:4}$αι δε φονιμοι ελαβον ελαιον εν τοις αγγειοις rell |⌐εν τοις αγγειοις αυτων D 1424^{vid} (ff^1) Arn

25:7 παραθενοι °εκειναι rell |°D 22^{ev} arm

25:10 απερχομενων δε °αυτων   rell |°Θ^{h*}
      εως υπαγουσιν   D (b c ff^2 g^2 h)

25:17a ⌐ωσαυτως rell |⌐ομοιως D sa

APPENDIX 10: NON-SINGULAR READINGS IN CODEX D IN MATTHEW 255

25:17b ο τα δυο εκερδησεν ^{T} rell |^{T}και αυτους
A C³ K M U W Δ Θ Π 𝔐 $f^{1.13}$ 2 28 *pc h* sy^h
     ο τα δυο °ταλαντα λαβων ^{T}εκερδησεν   *c* fr aeth^{ro} Op
|°253 it vg cop Or^{int3,883} |^{T}και αυτος D 1515 *d*

25:18 λαβων °απελθων *rell* |°D *al*³ it^{pler}

25:22 ⌜ιδε *rell* |⌜ιδου D 2145 it^{pler} vg^{pler} VSS *rell* |⌜ειδε W

25:24a δε και ο το εν *rell*
     δε ο το ⌜ενα   D* 1 *a b c* g²| ⌜εν D^c

25:24b ⌜οθεν *rell* |⌜οπου D W 56 (1) lat vg sa

25:25a απελθων   *rell*
     απηλθον και   D 252*^{vid} it vg aeth geo Or^{int}

25:25b ⌜ιδε *rell* |⌜ειδου D VSS^{pler} |⌜ειδε W |⌜ο δε 1515

25:33 °μεν *rell* |°D it^{pl} syr^{sch} et$^{p\ cod}$ arm aeth

25:38 δε σε ειδομεν (*rell*) NA^{28}
     δε ειδομεν σε D Clem

25:39 ποτε °δε   *rell* |°Π* 565
     η ποτε   D it (exc *ff*¹) vg cop Clem^{952} (Or^{3,890lib})

26:4 συνεβουλευσαντο   *rell*
     συνεβουλευοντο   D Chr (*d consiliabantur*)

26:7 αυτου ανακειμενου^T *rell* |^{T}αυτου D^{gr} *a b c f ff*² *h q* mm Amb Or^{int3,892}

26:14 Ισκαριωτης   *rell* vg^{ed} sah cop syr^p Or *al*
     Σκαριωτης   D Θ$^{c\ vid}$ (lat) *f*

26:15 ᵀειπεν rell |ᵀκαι D latt (sa^ms) bo

26:18 ποιω   rell
       ποιησω   D (d q Or^int3,896 faciam)

26:23 ο εμβαψας   rell
       ο ενβαπτομενος   D 579

26:24a ᵀ¹ο μεν ᵀ²υιος rell |ᵀ¹και 118 |ᵀ²ουν D Z Chr^edd5

26:24b ᵀκαλον ην rell |ᵀδια τουτο D a d

26:25 ᵀΙουδας rell |ᵀο D al pc

26:27 ▫πιετε εξ αυτου °παντες` rell |▫a c |°D b

26:28 ⌐περι πολλων rell |⌐υπερ D Or^3,194 Cyr^4,360 Chr

26:34 °εν rell | °𝔓³⁷ D a b c ff² h q fu Chr

26:40 μαθητας και ευρισκει αυτους   rell (L)
       μαθητας ⌐αυτους και ευρισκει αυτους   D* Chr |⌐αυτου
D^corr* al it vg cop sry^sch aeth Or^int3,903 Hil

26:47 °και ετι rell |°28 1293 it^pler vg (exc for) sy^s sah^(2 MSS) bo^(1 MS) Lcif |21 D d vg (1 MS) sah^(pler)

26:50a ▫ο δε °Ιησους ειπεν` °¹αυτω   (rell) NA²⁸ |▫𝔓³⁷ |° ℵ |°¹ 700
        ειπεν δε αυτω ο Ιησους   D it (exc q) vg aeth Lcif

26:50b εταιρε εφ ο παρει   (rell) NA²⁸ |▫𝔓³⁷ |° ℵ |°¹ 700
        εφ ο παρει εταιρε   D a c f syr^sch Lcif

26:51a παταξας   rell
        επαταξεν   D it^pler syr^utr Lcif

26:51b αρχιερεως ⸀T rell | ⸀Tκαι D U* it^pler syr^utr Lcif

26:54 πληρωθωσιν   rell
       πληρωθησονται   D it vg (Oros)

26:55a ειπεν ο Ιησους   rell
       ο Ιησους ειπεν   D a

26:55b εξηλθατε   (rell) NA²⁸
       ηλθατε   D (a b c ff² g² h q gat)

26:60a ουχ ευρον   A C^c 𝔐 W pc |om. ℵ B C* L pc NA²⁸
       και ουκ ευρον το εξης   D d ff² h

26:60b ⸀Tπολλων προσελθοντων ψευδομαρτυρων   ℵ B C* L
N* 1 51 102 118 124 209 23^ev* b ff¹ g^{1.2} l n vg sah cop arm pers^w
Or^{1,315} et^{4,386} Cyr^{4,855} NA²⁸ | ⸀Tκαι A C^c 𝔐 W pler
το εξης και πολλοι προσηλθον ψευδομαρτυρες   D d ff² h

26:60c ⸀προσελθοντες rell | ⸀ηλθον D it vg sy^{s.p}

26:61a ⸀ειπαν ℵ Θ 124 NA²⁸ | ⸀ειπον rell q | ⸀και ειπον D Latt

26:61b ουτος εφη   rell
       τουτον ηκουσαμεν ⸀λεγοντα   D* b c f ff² h | ⸀λεγοντος D^c
26:64 υμιν ⸀T rell | ⸀Tοτι D pc syr^sch

26:66 αποκριθεντες   rell
       αποκριθησαν παντες και   D a b c h gat sy^s
26:67 ⸀οι rell | ⸀αλλοι D (sah go)

26:71 αλλη ⸀T rell | ⸀Tπαιδισκη D a b c ff² h n q vg arm Or^int

26:72 ορκου ⸀οτι rell | ⸀λεγων D b c ff² mae | ⸀om. ℵ 36 40

26:73 και γαρ η λαλια σου δηλον σε ποιει   rell
       και γαρ Γαλιλαιος ει και η λαλια σου δηλον σε ποιει   C*
       και γαρ η λαλια σου ομοιαζει   D (a b c ff² h q gue^lect)

26:75 ειρηκοτος ▫αυτω οτι˹   rell |▫D 61 47^ev it vg aeth
       ειρηκοτος οτι   ℵ B L 0281^vid 33 892 pc lat sa^mss NA²⁸

27:1 ⌜ελαβον rell |⌜εποιησαν D a c f r² vg^5MSS sa^1MS bo^1MS

27:13 σου ⌜καταμαρτυρουσιν   rell   D^F |21   D*   geo
       |⌜κατηγορτυρουσιν 1 209

27:14 ▫προς ⌜ουδε˹ rell |⌜ουδεν L Θ f¹³ |▫D d sy^p.hl.hier aeth arm

27:22 ποιησω   rell
       ποιησωμεν   D pc a b c ff² h q Or^int3,919
27:24a ⌜απεναντι rell |⌜κατεναντι B D |⌜εμπροσθεν 544

27:24b αθωος ειμι ^T rell |^Tεγω D d it vg arm geo sah bo Aug^cons

27:28 αυτον ^T rell |^Tτα ιματια αυτου 33 pc sy^hmg sa^ms mae bo^ms
       |^Tειματιον πορφυρουν και D d 157 a b c d f ff² h (q) gat mm (Or^int sy^s)

27:31 °και απηγαγον rell D^B |°D* d sah

27:39 τας κεφαλας rell
       την κεφαλην D d bo aeth geo¹

27:41 ⌜ελεγον rell |⌜λεγων 579 |⌜λεγοντες D 7pe g^1.2

27:45 εως ωρας ενατης rell |132 D 892 d

27:46 σαβαχθανι rell |⌜σαβαχθανει ℵ A W 69 700 |⌜σαβακτανει B 22 |⌜ζαφθανει D* (zaphthani d ff² h) |⌜σαφθανει Dᶜ |⌜sabathani r¹ |⌜sabactani ff¹ |⌜sibactani q |⌜zabachthani vg¹ᴹˢ |⌜zabethani g¹ |⌜zaptani b vg³ᴹˢˢ |⌜zabthani vgᵗᵒᵗ |⌜zabtani vg¹ᴹˢ |⌜zahthani a

27:53 ⌜εισηλθον rell |⌜om. ℵ |⌜ηλθον D it vg syˢ sa bo

27:55 ⌜εκειᵀ rell |⌜κακει ℵ |⌜και D al¹⁰ Chrᵍᵘᵉ |⌜om. 579| ᵀκαι F K L Π 33 1071

27:57 °τουνομα   rell |°geo²
       ⌜το ονομα   D 482 |⌜ω l55

27:58 Πιλατω rell |⌜Πειλατω A B* (Δ) Θ |⌜Πειλατω και D it vg syˢ·ᵖ·ʰⁱ· aeth geo Orⁱⁿᵗ

27:59 το σωμα °ο Ιωσηφ   rell |°L 229 472 1515 l184
       Ιωσηφ το σωμα   D a d ff² h* r¹ syˢ·ᵖᵉˢʰ·ʰⁱᵉʳ

27:61 και °η αλλη rell |°A D d h

27:64a εως °της rell |°D L Φ 251 253 700 945 1071 1223 1391 1402 1574 1579 Chrᵐᵒ²

27:64b τριτης ημερας rell |2¹ D it vg syʰˡ Orⁱⁿᵗ³·⁹³¹

27:65 ⌜κουστωδιαν rell Bᶜ² |⌜φυλακας D*ᵛⁱᵈ armᵘˢᶜ |⌜κουστουδιαν Dᶜ |⌜σκουστωδιαν B* K |⌜κουστοδιαν 67 |⌜custodiam ff¹ l vg⁽ᵖˡᵉʳ⁾ (syˢ·ʰˡ sah bo arm geo¹ Aug) |⌜custodes a b c d f ff² g¹ q aur vg⁽¹ᵐˢ⁾ syᵖᵉˢʰ·ʰⁱᵉʳ (geo²) |⌜milites h r¹ vg⁽⁴ᵐˢˢ⁾

27:66a ησφαλισαντο τον ταφον   rell Dᶜᵒʳ·ᶜ
       ησφαλισαν τον ταφον   D* 174 1574

27:66b της κουστωδιας ⌜rell ⌜κωστουδιας A ⌜κουστουδιας D^c ⌜κουτωδιας L ⌜κουστοδιας 69 157
    των φυλακων D* arm
    ⌜*custodibus*   it vg (go hiat) ⌜om. *h* vg$^{(2mss)}$

28:7   °ιδου *rell* |°D p^{scr} *a b c ff*^{2} *h* Or^{int2,155}

28:9   αυτου τους ποδας *rell* |*231* τους ποδας αυτου D it vg Chr^{gue}

28:10 ⌜οψονται *rell* |⌜οψεσθαι D 10^{pe} *e h*

28:12a °τε *rell* |°D *al*^{2} (*a e ff*^{2} *h*)

28:12b αργυρια ικανα   *rell*
    αργυριον ικανον   D it^{pler} vg syr^{sch} arm

28:15 Ιουδαιοις ⌜μεχρι   *rell* |⌜εως ℵ* 1424 Or^{4,455} Chr(et^{mo})
    τοις Ιουδαιοις εως   D 59 270

28:18 εν ⌜ουρανω *rell* |⌜ουρανοις D Bas^{euno289}

28:19a ⌜πορευθεντες *rell* |⌜πορευεσθαι D sy$^{p.hl.}$ sah bo arm geo Or^{4,262} Cyp

28:19b ⌜ουν B W Δ Θ Π *f*^{13} 118 33 *pc* NA^{28} |⌜om. *rell* |⌜νυν D *a b h n* Victorian Hil^{ter}

28:19c °του υιου *rell* |°D 1295 Epiph

APPENDIX 11
NON-SINGULAR READINGS IN WASHINGTONIANUS IN MATTHEW

1:3   Εσρωμ Εσρωμ   *rell*
       Εζρωμ Εζρωμ   W *f*

1:14   ⌜Σαδωκ Σαδωκ   *rell* |⌜Σαδωδ Θ
       Σαδωχ Σαδωχ   ℵ g¹
       Σαδδωκ Σαδδωκ W Δ *ff*¹ *q* aur vg

1:18   °¹Ιησου °²Χριστου *rell* Or^{int3,965} |°¹ 71 it vg sax fr syr^{cu} pers^w Ir^{int bis} Ps-Ath^{633} Thph^{cod} Aug |°² W 74 pers^p et^{cod} Max^{dial} |*21* B Or^{int3,965}

2:13   φαινεται κατ οναρ τω Ιωσηφ *pler* NA²⁸ | *23145* B C K Π 33 700 892 *pc* Thph | *14523* W *l*184 *f g*¹ sy^{c.s.hl}

3:17   των ουρανων *rell*
       του ουρανου W *l*184 *h* vg sy^{c.s.p.h} Iren
       της νεφελης 118

5:36   ⌜μελαιναν *rell* |⌜μελεναν L Θ 28* *f*¹³ |⌜μελαναν W Π*

5:21   ⌜φονευσεις *rell* |⌜φωνευσεις L |⌜φονευσης W *l*184 Clem |⌜φωνευσης 579

5:43   ⌜μισησεις *rell* |⌜μεισησεις B D |⌜μισησης W Σ |⌜μησησεις M Θ 2* 13 565 |⌜μησησεις 1424

6:7   ⌜βατταλογησητε ℵ B *f*¹³ NA²⁸ |⌜βαττολογησητε *rell* |⌜βλατταλογησηται D* |⌜βλατταλογησηται D^D |⌜βατολογησητε E G 1241 *l*183 sy^{p (mg gr)} |⌜βατταλογειται W 59 471 1604 |⌜βατγολογησητε 517 892 |⌜βαττολογειτε 700 |⌜βατολογησητε 1424

6:18 ⌐¹κρυφαιω ⌐²αποδωσει °σοι   B D^A f^1 22 660 NA²⁸
|⌐¹κρυφια D* |⌐²αποδωσι ℵ Θ
   κρυπτω αυτος αποδωσι σοι W sy^pesh geo¹
   κρυπτω αποδωσει °σοι   rell |°346 1346
   κρυπτω αποδωσοι σει   579

6:20 διορυσσουσι ⌐ουδε κλεπτουσιν   B* 1 1582* 118 |⌐και ℵ 1 1582* 118
   διουρυσσουσιν ⌐ουδε κλεπτουσιν   rell |⌐ουτε 700* 1071
   διορυσσουσιν   W k

6:23 σκοτος εστιν rell | 2¹ W k

7:25 ⌐προσεπεσαν ℵ^S1 B C E X Z Δ $f^{1.13}$ 237 238 242 245 543 700 788 892 1071 1346 *l*47 syr^p mg gr Cyr^es77 Chr Dam NA²⁸ |⌐προσεπεσεν ℵ* |⌐προσεπεσον K L M S U V Π Φ Ω 22 157 565 *al. pler.* |⌐προσεκρουσαν W 54 234 Philo^enarr in cant |⌐προσερρηξαν Θ Σ 579 *pc* Eus |⌐προσεκοψον 33 252 259 1424 *pc* (Eus^ps367) |⌐*inruerunt ff*¹ *g*² *l* aur vg^(pler) (sy^c.pesh.hl cop) |⌐*impegerunt c f k m q* vg^(1ms) Aug^epist Cyp |⌐*offenerunt a b g*¹ *h* |⌐*inciderunt m* |⌐*uenerunt* vg^(1ms) |⌐*percusserunt* geo¹ |⌐*corripuerunt* geo²

8:27 εστιν ουτος ^T rell (L) |^T ο ανθρωπος W 1354 1506 Hil |^T και 788

8:29 ⌐εκραξαν rell |⌐εκραζον W 489 Epiph

8:30 ⌐βοσκομενη rell |⌐βοσκομενον 579 |⌐βοσκομενων W X *al*² it *d* cop

9:9 ⌐λεγομενον rell |⌐ονοματι S vg arm |⌐καλουμενον W 1396

9:10 °πολλοι ⌐τελωναι rell (C 21 399 892 1010 1396) |2¹ W 157 sy^s aeth Cyr^es.105 |°1675 arm |⌐τελωνε ℵ*

9:27 εκειθεν τω Ιησου rell (1071) |23¹ W 713 945 954 *d* vg

APPENDIX 11: NON-SINGULAR READINGS IN WASHINGTONIANUS IN MATTHEW

10:14 τους λογος υμων rell των λογων υμων W* 1194

10:17 °αυτων rell |°W g^2 aur*

10:21 ⌜τεκνον και επαναστησεται τεκνα rell |⌜τεκνα W 49 64 Or

10:22 τελος ⌜ουτος rell |⌜om. W sy^s Diatess |⌜ουτως M 13 472

10:33 οστις δε rell
      και οστις W sy$^{c.s}$ arm geo^2

12:1 ⌜τοις σαββασιν rell (B D* K pc) |⌜εν W 238

12:48a ⌑τω ⌜λεγοντι °αυτω⌐ ℵ B D Z Π*^{vid} 33 49^{ev} 892 1424 NA^{28}
|⌑W Z |⌜ειποντι rell |°k
      αυτω X

12:48b °εισιν οι αδελφοι rell |°W pc

13:20 τον λογον ⊤ ακουων rell |⊤μου W X Δ 245 2145 f* q syr$^{p.hl}$

13:22 τον λογον ⊤ ακουων rell |⊤μου W q

13:23 τον λογον ⊤ ακουων rell (D Ω f^{13}) |⊤μου W 245 1012 q sy^p

13:30 ⌜εως του θερισμου B D 517 659 pc NA^{28} |⌜αχρι ℵ* L |⌜μεχρι ℵ^c C $f^{1.13}$ 565 plu |⌜μεχρις W Φ

13:54 ποθεν τουτω ⊤ rell |21 Θ |⊤πασα D |⊤ταυτα και τις W 242

14:2 ⌜εστιν rell |⌜εστι K W

14:8 ⊤δος μοι φησιν rell | ⊤ειπεν W l vg$^{(3\ MSS)}$
      επιεν θελω ινα μοι δος εξ αυτης 1424
      ειπεν δος μοι D 0106^c 1424 it vg^{mss} syr^{cu} et^{sch} aeth

14:21 ανδρες ⌜ωσει rell -700 ⌜ως D Δ Θ f^1 33 1071 ⌜om. W 0161 pc lat sy$^{s.c.p}$ bo

15:18–19 ⸆κακεινα κοινοι τον ανθρωπον $^{15:19}$ εκ γαρ της καρδιας⸃ (rell) NA^{28} |⸆ℵ W 33^{vid} bo^{ms}

15:23 ⌜οπισθεν rell ⌜εμποσθεν W 245

15:32 ⌜φαγωσιν rell ⌜φαγειν W k Diatess (a b c Ambr)

17:4 μιαν και Μωυσει μιαν και Ηλια μιαν   (ℵ) C 700 f^1 pc NA^{28} | *1234576* B^c 𝔐 (pc)
μιαν και Ηλια μιαν και Μωυσι μιαν   W *l*184

17:8a °αυτων rell |°W 235 *l*44 e dimma

17:9 ανθρωπου εκ νεκρων εγερθη   B D 1604 NA^{28}
ανθρωπου εκ νεκρων αναστη   rell |*1423* W sy^c cop Diatess

17:15 πυρ και ⌜πολλακις rell (Δ)|⌜ενιοτε D Θ f^1 22 Or^{3,574item578} mae ⌜om. W 238 Hil |⌜*crebo l* aug vg |⌜*aliquotiens ff ^{2} q* |⌜*saepius d* |⌜*aliquando a b c e f ff^1 g^1 n r^1* aeth arm

17:24^1 ⌜τα rell |⌜το W Cyr^{4,791}

17:24^2 ⌜τα rell |⌜το W Cyr^{4,791}

18:4 ⌜ουν rell ⌜om. G ⌜γαρ W g^1 sy$^{c.s}$ Aphr |⌜και 13 r^2 aeth

18:7 °πλην ⸆ ουαι τω ανθρωπω   ℵ F L f^1 22 579 892 d g^1 aur vg$^{st.ww}$ sy^{omn} sa^{mss} mae bo Did |°sy^s |⸆δε D* sy$^{s.pesh}$ |⸆*dico uobis* r^2
πλην ουαι τω ανθρωπω εκεινω   rell | *15234* W e ff^1 |*1δε5234* geo

18:8 ⌜εισελθειν rell ⌜om. N W 1093 ⌜ειελθειν F* ⌜εισελθην 2 ⌜ελθειν 71* 482 544 1354 1355

18:17 °ο εθνικος *rell* |°W 33

18:19a λεγω ⌜υμιν *rell* |⌜υμειν D |*21* 𝔓⁴⁴ᵛⁱᵈ W 174

18:19b ⌜ου *rell* |⌜ο W* X²

19:5 πατερα ᵀ¹ και την μητερα ᵀ² *rell* |ᵀ¹αυτου C Y Δ $f^{1.13}$ 1424 *pc* |ᵀ²αυτου W M Γ 69 544 566 1187 1241 2145 syᵒᵐⁿ sah bo aeth geo² Orˢᵉᵐᵉˡ

19:16 ποιησω ινα σχω ζωην αιωνιον   B C* D Θ 700* Or NA²⁸

⌜ποιησας ζωην °αιωνιον κληρονομησω   ℵ L 28 33 77 157 238 372 697 892 945 990 1010 1207 1223 1293 1515 1365 *l*2211 *pc* (syᶜ·ˢ·ʰᵐᵍ) (saᵐˢ bo) aeth arm |⌜ποιησω 579 |°bo²ᵐˢˢ

ποιησω ινα εχω ζωην αιωνιον   *rell* |*l*2435 W Jᵛᵍ

19:24 δια ⌜τρυπηματος ραφιδος εισελθειν   E F H L Z Δ $f^{1.13}$ *pc* NA²⁸ |⌜τρυμαλιας C K M U 0281 157 *l*2211 |*4123* W Or Chr

δια ⌜τρηματος ραφιδος εισελθειν   ℵ* |⌜τρυπηματος ℵᶜ

δια ⌜τρηματος ραφιδος διελθειν   B |⌜τρυμαλιας Θ 124 565 700 |⌜τρυπηματος D G S V X Y Γ

19:28 ⌜Ισραηλ *rell* |⌜Ιστραηλ W (*a b ff² h n* Istrahel)

19:30 εσχατοι ᵀ πρωτοι *rell* |*21* ℵ L 21 157 579 892 vgˡᵐˢ aeth syᵖᵉˢʰ |ᵀεσονται W syᶜᵘ·ˢ Pist-Soph

20:27 ειναι υμων πρωτος εστω   B | *2134* X 085

εν υμιν °ειναι πρωτος ⌜εσται   C M Π 565 $f^{1.13}$ *plu* NA²⁸ |°L |⌜εστω 𝔐 *pc* |⌜εστε ℵ D | *12435* W 1241 1515 it⁽ᵖˡᵉʳ⁾ vg arm

21:5 ⌜ο βασιλευς *rell* (1071) |⌜α W Θ

22:38 °η μεγαλη και πρωτη   rell |°D
       η μεγαλη και η πρωτη   L |45312 W cop
       ⊤πρωτη και μεγαλη   E F G H K M S U Υ Γ Π Ω 2 28
157 579 1071 1424 *d f q* syr[p.hl] arm pers[p] Op |⊤η Ο Δ Θ[b] Σ Φ 1070 174
237 563 565 Bas[eth]

23:17 ⌐τις *rell* |⌐τι W Z

23:25 αρπαγης και ⌐ακρασιας *rell* |⌐αδικιας C 𝔐 K 579 700 *f* sy[p]
et[p cod] Bas[eth 236 cod] Chr[mo 5] Op *pc* |⌐ακαθαρσιας Σ 844* item lat 66 71 *ff*[1]
g[1.2] *l* vg sah sy[s] co; Cl |⌐πλεονεξιας M Chr[montf] Dam[par517] |⌐ακρασιας
αδικειας W (sy[h])

24:11 ⌐εγερθησονται *rell* | ⌐εξεγερθησονται D |⌐αναστησονται W
4 262

24:13 τελος °ουτος *rell* |°W sy[s] Diatess

24:14 °πασιν τοις εθνεσιν *rell* |°W Γ bo (J[1]) Or[Cels.II.13] Chr

24:20 η φυγη ⌐υμων *rell* | ⌐ημων 579 |*312* W cop Or Eus

24:24 σημεια °μεγαλα *rell* |°ℵ W* *pc ff*[1] r[1] bo[ms]

24:38 γαμουντες και ⌐γαμιζοντες ℵ 33 1346 1355 1396 NA[28]
|⌐γαμισκοντες B 1675 |⌐εκγαμιζοντες *rell* |⌐γαμειζοντες D
|⌐εκγαμισκοντες W 517 1424 |⌐εκγαμειζοντες Δ |⌐εκγαμηζοντες Θ
|⌐εγγαμιζοντες Σ 047 13 124 543 174 230 348 788 826 828 892 983
1093 1241 1346 1473 1515 1689

24:45 δουναι αυτοις   *rell*
       διδοναι °αυτοις   𝔐 K M Π 565 579 *pc* |°W *q* (*e*)

25:24 ⌐οθεν ου διεσκορπισας   *rell* |⌐οπου D 56 *pc* sa
       οπου ουκ εσκορπισας   W latt

APPENDIX 11: NON-SINGULAR READINGS IN WASHINGTONIANUS IN MATTHEW 267

25:26 οτι ᵀ θεριζω *rell* |ᵀεγω ανθρωπος αυστηρος ειμει W sy^(p (1 MS)) sah^((1 MS))

25:32 εμπροσθεν αυτου παντα τα εθνη *rell* (D) |*34512* W aeth

25:41 τοις εξ ⌜ευωνυμων *rell* |⌜ευωνυμοις W Latt

26:2 μετα δυο ημερας   *rell*
      μεθ ημερας δυο   W cop

26:12 ⌜βαλουσα *rell* |⌜βαλλουσα W Σ

26:23 ⌜ουτος *rell* |⌜αυτος 76 157 1071 1424 *pc* |⌜εκεινος W Or

26:49 προσελθων τω Ιησου ειπεν   *rell*
       προσηλθεν τω Ιησου και ειπεν   W *a r*² sy^omn bo aeth geo

26:52 ⌜αυτω *rell* |⌜αυτοις W Ω 788 |⌜αυτως 124

27:6 ουκ ⌜εξεστιν *rell* |⌜εστιν W Eus

27:43 οτι ᵀ θεου *rell* |ᵀτου W *l47*

27:49 ⌜σωσων *rell* |⌜σωσαι ℵ* Θ 69 1010 1071 1241 1293 *l184* |⌜σωσωσων C |⌜σωσει D 1 209 1582* |⌜σωσον F Y K 2* 28 157 700* |⌜σωζων W *ff*¹ *g*¹ aur vg^(pler) Aug |⌜καθελων 544 |⌜*liberare g*² vg^(3mss) sy^p.hl cop aeth arm geo |⌜*saluaren f* |⌜*liberauit a b (c) ff*² *q r*² |⌜*liberat d* vg^(1ms) sy^s |⌜*liberet l* Or^int |⌜*liberaret* vg^(1ms) |⌜*saluabit h r*¹ |⌜*liberet* sy^hier

27:50 °παλιν κραξας *rell* | °F L | *21* W 945 1396 2145 sy^h

27:60 ᵀ τη θυρα *rell* |ᵀεπι A 242 243 (1515 it vg geo Or^int Aug) |ᵀεν W 659 2145 sy^h

28:2 ⌜καταβας *rell* |⌜κατεβη W (427 482) latt Sy^r (cop) aeth

APPENDIX 12
ITACISMS IN SINAITICUS IN MATTHEW[1]

1. αι > ε

1:24; 18:25*; 19:3, 9*; 22:24, 25* ⌜γυναικα *rell* |⌜γυνεκα ℵ

2:8   ⌜παιδιου *rell* |⌜πεδιου ℵ

2:13a   ⌜παιδιον και την μητερα *rell* |⌜πεδιον ℵ |⌜παιδα D 565

2:13b   ⌜απολεσαι *rell* |⌜απολεσε ℵ

2:14   ⌜παιδιον *rell* |⌜πεδιον ℵ |⌜παιδα D it vg

2:20   ⌜παιδου *rell* |⌜πεδιου ℵ

3:1; 23:30; 24:19 ⌜ημεραις *rell* |⌜ημερες ℵ

3:1   ⌜Ιουδαιας *rell* |⌜Ιουδεας ℵ*

3:5   ⌜Ιουδαια *rell* |⌜Ιδαια L |⌜Ιουδεα ℵ*

4:6   ⌜εντελειται *rell* |⌜εντελιτε ℵ

5:15   ⌜καιουσιν *rell* |⌜κεουσιν ℵ |⌜καιουσι C K W f^1 *pler*

5:28   ⌜επιθυμησαι *rell* |⌜επιθυμησε ℵ |⌜επεθυμησαι L |⌜επιθυμισαι 1071

---

[1] Only one singular itacism is found in the work of scribe D (24:40, αι > ε), signified in bold below. The remaining are from scribe A.

6:1; 23:5 ⌜θεαθηναι rell |⌜θεαθηνε ℵ

6:18² ⌜κρυφαιω ℵᶜ B D f¹ NA²⁸ |⌜κρυφεω ℵ* |⌜κρυπτω rell |⌜κριπτω Δ

6:22 (εστιν 157); 11:24; 13:50; 24:3, 21, 27 ⌜εσται rell |⌜εστε ℵ

8:22 ⌜θαψαι rell |⌜θαψε ℵ

8:23; 12:1; 13:36; 14:15; 19:13; 21:20; 24:1 ⌜μαθηται rell |⌜μαθητε ℵ

9:4 ⌜καρδιαις rell ℵᶜᵃ |⌜καρδιες ℵ*

9:10; 21:31, 32 ⌜τελωναι rell | ⌜τελωνε ℵ*

9:10, 37; 23:1; 26:26* ⌜μαθηταις rell |⌜μαθητες ℵ

9:34; 12:28 (δεμωνια Θ) ⌜δαιμονια rell |⌜δεμονια ℵ

10:3 ⌜Ματθαιος B* D NA²⁸ |⌜Ματθαιος rell |⌜Ματθεος ℵ |⌜Ματθεος L

10:26a ⌜αποκαλυφθησεται rell |⌜αποκαλυφθησετε ℵ |⌜αποκαλυψθησεται Δ

10:26b ⌜γνωσθησεται rell |⌜γνωσθησετε ℵ |⌜αποκαλυφθησεται E | om. 1071

10:30 ⌜ηριθμημεναι rell |⌜ηριθμημενε ℵ |⌜ηρηθμημεναι L |⌜ηριθμηνται 28 1424 |⌜απηριθμεναι 482 |⌜ηριθμιμεναι 579

10:41² ⌜δικαιου rell |⌜δικεου ℵ

10:41² (ληψεται 𝔐 K M U Π f¹·¹³ 2 33 28 157 565 579 700 788 1071 1346 1424 |λιψιται 28); 19:29 (λεψεται 𝔐 K M S U Δ Ω f¹·¹³ 2 69 118 157 565 700 788 1071 1346 1424) ⌜λημψεται rell |⌜λημψετε ℵ

11:16 ⌜ταις B Z 1 33 892 1424 1582* *l*184 NA²⁸ |⌜τες ℵ* |⌜τη D | om. rell

11:16 (αγορα D 047 28 *pc* |om. 118 1071 1582ᶜ); 23:7 ⌜αγοραις rell |⌜αγορες ℵ*

11:18 ⌜δαιμονιον rell |⌜δεμονιον ℵ* |⌜δαιμονιων Θ |om. *parablepsis* 579

11:19 ⌜εδικαιωθη rell |⌜εδικεωθη ℵ |⌜εδικαιοθη L

11:27 ⌜αποκαλυψαι rell |⌜σποκαλυψε ℵ

11:27 ⌜ψυχαις rell |⌜ψυχες ℵ

12:19 (om. 700 954); 22:40 (om. M); 23:6, 7, 30 ⌜ταις rell |⌜τες ℵ*

12:31² ⌜αφεθησεται rell |⌜αφεθησετε ℵ

12:37 ⌜δικαιωθηση rell |⌜δικεωθηση ℵ |⌜δικαιοθησει L |⌜δικαιωθησει 2* 13 28 579 1071 *l*187

12:41a ⌜Νινευιται B C L W X Δ Θ Σ 213 443 1574 2145 al. NA²⁸ |⌜Νινευειτε ℵ |⌜Νεινευεται D* |⌜Νεινευειται Dᴰ |⌜Νηνευιται Γ |⌜Νινευιται rell

12:41b ⌜αναστησονται rell |⌜αναστησοντε ℵ |⌜αναστισονται K |⌜αναστησωνται 579

12:42; 20:19 (αναστησεται B Cᶜ D 𝔐 W Θ *pler*); 24:7 (εγερθησονται L |εγερθησσεται Θ) ⌜εγερθησεται rell |⌜εγερθησετε ℵ

12:42 ⌜ακουσαι rell |⌜ακουσε ℵ |⌜ινα ακουσει 28 |⌜ινα ειδη 1071

12:43 ⌜διερχεται rell |⌜διερχετε ℵ |⌜διανοιδρων 579

13:2 ⌜καθησαι rell |⌜καθησθε ℵ |⌜καθησαι S Y* 1071 |⌜καθεισθαι 2 579 |⌜καθισαι 1424

13:3 °του ⌜σπειρειν rell |°D | ⌜σπιρε ℵ |⌜σπειραι D L M S W X Θ Σ Ω $f^{1.13}$ 1582 7 28 33 71 659 700 892 1241 1266 1293 1391 Or^{semel}

13:11 ⌜γνωναι rell |⌜γνωνε ℵ

13:12 ⌜περισσευθησεται rell |⌜περισσευθησετε ℵ |⌜περισευθησεται N 1424

13:13, 35 ⌜παραβολαις rell |⌜παραβολες ℵ*

13:17, 43; 23:28 ⌜δικαιοι rell |⌜δικεοι ℵ

13:30a ⌜θερισταις rell |⌜θεριστες ℵ |⌜θερησταις 1071

13:30b ⌜κατακαυσαι rell |⌜κατακαυσε ℵ

13:49 ⌜εξελευσονται rell |⌜εξελευσοντε ℵ |⌜εξελευσωνται 579 |⌜ελευσονται 346 1346

14:22 ⌜εμβναι rell |⌜εμβηνε ℵ |⌜ενβηναι D 28

15:13 ⌜εκριζωθησεται rell |⌜εκριζωθησετε ℵ

15:14 ⌜πεσουνται rell ℵ^{S1} |⌜πεσουντε ℵ* |⌜εμπεσουνται F O W Σ Φ 4 262 273 517 565 659 700 1010 1012 1293 1295 1412 1424 1675 al. Epiph |⌜ενπεσουνται D

15:31 ⌜θαυμασαι rell |⌜θαυμασε ℵ

15:32 ⌜απολυσαι rell |⌜απολυσε ℵ

15:33 ⌜χορτασαι rell |⌜χορτασε ℵ |⌜χορτασθηναι 1424

15:38 ⌜γυναικων rell |⌜γυνεκων ℵ

18:25 ⌜αποδουναι rell |⌜αποδουνε ℵ |⌜αποδουνα Y*

18:25 ⌜πραθηναι rell |⌜πραθηνε ℵ*

18:25 ⌜αποδοθηναι rell |⌜αποδοθηνε ℵ |⌜αποθηναι D* |⌜αποδωθηναι 579 1071 |⌜αποδουναι 1604

19:3; 22:15; 23:2, 25, 27, 29*⌜φαρισαιοι rell |⌜φαρισεοι ℵ |⌜φαρεισαιοι B

19:5 ⌜κολληθησεται B D E F G H S U V W Θ Ω 078 $f^{13(exc.124)}$ 2 7 22 28 157 174 230 565 788 1346 pler NA²⁸ |⌜προσκολληθησετε ℵ |⌜προσκολληθησεται rell |⌜κοληθησεται F

19:5 (γυναικει D W Θ | γυαικι L | γυναικη 2*); 26:10 (γυναικει D W) ⌜γυναικι rell |⌜γυνεκι ℵ

19:5; 20:16; 24:7 (εσοντα Δ) ⌜εσονται rell |⌜εσοντε ℵ

19:7; 20:23 ⌜δουναι rell |⌜δουνε ℵ

19:7 ⌜απολυσαι rell |⌜απολυσε ℵ

19:10 ⌜γυναικος rell |⌜γυνεκος ℵ

19:13 ⌜παιδια rell |⌜πεδια ℵ

19:25 ⌜δυναται rell |⌜δυνατε ℵ

19:25 ⌜σωθηναι rell |⌜σωθηνε ℵ |⌜σωθεναι Θ

19:30¹ ⌈εσονται rell |⌈εσοντε ℵ

20:1 ⌈μισθωσασθαι rell |⌈μισθωσασθε ℵ |⌈μεισθωσασθαι D |⌈μησθωσασθαι 2*

20:4; 23:35 ⌈δικαιον rell |⌈δικεον ℵ*

20:15; 23:15, 23 ⌈ποιησαι rell |⌈ποιησε ℵ

20:18 ⌈παραδοθησεται rell |⌈παραδοθησετε ℵ |⌈παραδοθησαιται M |⌈παραδωθησεται 579 1071

20:19 ⌈εμπαιξαι rell |⌈εμπεξε ℵ |⌈εμπεξαι C Δ 2* 28 33 565 1071 |⌈ενπαιξαι D E |⌈ενπεξαι W

20:19 ⌈σταυρωσαι rell |⌈σταυρωσε ℵ |⌈σταυρωαι C |⌈om. X

20:27 ⌈ειναι rell |⌈εινε ℵ |⌈om. L W 28

20:28 ⌈δικονησαι rell |⌈διακονησε ℵ

20:28 ⌈δουναι rell |⌈δουνε ℵ

21:5; 26:45 ⌈ερχεται rell |⌈ερχετε ℵ

21:11 ⌈Γαλιλαιας rell |⌈Γαλιλεας ℵ |⌈Γαλειλαιας B

21:13 ⌈κληθησεται rell |⌈κληθησετε ℵ |⌈γενησεται 118 209

21:16 ⌈αινον rell |⌈ενον ℵ |⌈αινων L f¹

21:21 ⌈γενησεται rell |⌈γενησετε ℵ

21:32 ⌈δικαιοσυνης rell |⌈δικεοσυνης ℵ* |⌈δικαιωσυνης Θ

21:42 ⌜γραφαις rell |⌜γραφες ℵ*

21:43 ⌜αρθησεται rell |⌜αρθησετε ℵ

21:44 ⌜συνθλασθησεται rell |⌜συνθλασθησετε ℵ

22:21a ⌜Καισαρος rell |⌜Κεσαρος ℵ

22:34 ⌜σαδδουκαιους rell |⌜σαδδουκεους ℵ |⌜σαδδουκαους Δ

22:40 ⌜ταυταις rell |⌜ταυτες ℵ*

22:40 ⌜προφηται rell |⌜προφητε ℵ*

22:41 ⌜φαρισαιων rell |⌜φαρισεων ℵ |⌜φαρεισαιων B

22:46 ⌜αποκριθηναι rell |⌜αποκριθηνε ℵ* |⌜αποκρειθηναι D

23:4 ⌜κινησαι rell |⌜κινησε ℵ |⌜κεινησαι B D Δ |⌜κηνησαι 2*

23:6, 34 ⌜συναγωγαις rell |⌜συναγωγες ℵ*

23:12 ⌜ταπεινωθησεται rell |⌜ταπινωθησετε ℵ |⌜ταπινωθησεται W Θ

23:13, 23, 25a, 27, 29 (οιποκριται 579) ⌜υποκριται rell |⌜υποκριτε ℵ

23:23 μη ⌜αφειναι B L |⌜αφινε ℵ |⌜αφιεναι rell

23:25², 25³, 26², 27, 28¹*, 28² ⌜και rell |⌜κε ℵ

23:27 ⌜φαινονται rell |⌜φενοντε ℵ |⌜φαινετε D

23:29 ⌜δικαιων rell |⌜δικεων ℵ* | om. H

24:5 |ελευσονται *rell* |ελευσοντε ℵ

24:12a |πληθυνθηναι *rell* |πληθυνθηνε ℵ* |πληθυναι D

24:12b |ψυγησεται *rell* |ψυγησετε ℵ |ψυχησεται K

24:13 |σωθησεται *rell* |σωθησετε ℵ

24:14 |κηρυχθησεται *rell* |κηρυχθησετε ℵ

24:18 |αραι *rell* |αρε ℵ*

24:19a |θηλαζουσαις *rell* |θηλαζουσες ℵ* |θηλαζομεναις D |ενθηλαζουσαις L

24:19b |εκειναις *rell* |εκινες ℵ* |εκιναις ℵ^c |εκεινες L |εκηναις 2

24:24 |ψευδοπροφηται *rell* |ψευδοπροφητε ℵ

24:28 |συναχθησονται *rell* |συναχθησοντε ℵ |συναχθηται M

24:30 |φανησεται *rell* |φανησετε ℵ |φανησηται 118

24:30 |κοψονται *rell* |κοψοντε ℵ

24:30 |πασαι *rell* |πασε ℵ*

24:30 |αι *rell* |ε ℵ*

24:30 |οψονται *rell* |οψοντε ℵ

24:32 |γενηται *rell* |γενητε ℵ

24:40 |παραλαμβανεται *rell* |παραλαμβανετε ℵ |παραλαμβανεται Δ*

26:13 ⌜λαληθησεται rell |⌜λαληθησετε ℵ

26:15 ⌜δουναι rell |⌜δωνε ℵ

26:29 ⌜καινον rell |⌜κενον ℵ

26:31 ⌜διασκορπισθησονται rell |⌜διασκορπισθησοντε ℵ* |⌜διασκορπησθησεται U 2

26:32 ⌜εγερθηναι rell |⌜εγερθηνε ℵ

26:36 ⌜προσευξωμαι rell |⌜προσευξεμε ℵ |⌜προσευξομαι D F S Θ Ω 2 28 788 1424 |⌜ευξομαι 700

26:40 ⌜γρηγορησαι rell |⌜εγρηγορησαι 𝔓³⁷ |⌜γρηγορησε ℵ |⌜γριγορησαι Θ |⌜γρηγορισαι 2 33 |⌜γρηγορεισαι 1071

26:53 ⌜απολουνται rell |⌜απολουντε ℵ* |⌜αποθανουνται 𝔐 K M W 2 69 565 579 788 1071 |⌜απουθαναουνται Δ* |⌜αποθαναουνται Δᶜ

26:54, 56 ⌜γραφαι rell |⌜γραφε ℵ*

26:54 ⌜γενεσθαι rell |⌜γενεσθε ℵ

26:69 ⌜Γαλιλαιου rell |⌜Γαλιλεου ℵ |⌜Γαλειλαιου B D |⌜Ναζωραιου C 047 238 252* syr^sch pers^p

27:37 ⌜Ιουδαιων rell |⌜Ιουδεων ℵ

27:39 ⌜λησται rell |⌜ληστε ℵ* |⌜λισται K

27:58 ⌜αποδοθηναι rell |⌜αποδοθηνε ℵ* |⌜αποδωθηναι 1071

27:61 ⌜καθημεναι rell |⌜καθημενε ℵ*

2. ε > αι

6:3   ⌜ελεημοσυνην rell |⌜ελαιημουσυνην ℵ

7:11 ⌜οιδατε rell |⌜οιδαται ℵ

10:11 ⌜εξετασατε rell |⌜εξετασαται ℵ

3. ει > ι

1:21 ⌜σωσει rell |⌜σωσι ℵ

1:23 (εξη L 1424); 12:11 (εξη Θ) ⌜εξει rell |⌜εξι ℵ

2:6   ⌜ποιμανει rell |⌜ποιμανι ℵ |⌜ποιμενει D

2:8   ⌜απαγγειλατε rell |⌜απαγγιλατε ℵ |⌜απαγγειλαται D* W |⌜επαγγειλαται D^c |⌜απαγγηλατε 2 |⌜αναγγειλατε 124

2:13 ⌜ζητειν rell |⌜ζητιν ℵ

2:15; 6:21; 12:45; 13:42, 58; 19:2; 22:13; 24:28 ⌜εκει rell |⌜εκι ℵ

2:21 (διεγερθεις D 33); 8:25a (ηγερθη rell), 26 ⌜εγερθεις rell |⌜εγερθις ℵ

3:3   ⌜ρηθεις rell |⌜ριθεις 579 |⌜ρηθις ℵ

3:3   ⌜ευθειας rell |⌜ευθιας ℵ |⌜ευθηας L

3:9a; 4:17; 11:7; 26:22 ⌜λεγειν rell |⌜λεγιν ℵ

3:9b ⌜εγειραι rell |⌜εγιραι ℵ

3:11 ⌜βαπτισει rell |⌜βαπτισι ℵ |⌜βαπτησει L |⌜βαπτισαι 579

4:6   ⌐εντελειται rell |⌐εντελιτε ℵ

4:8; 13:11, 19, 38, 41; 24:14   ⌐βασιλειας rell |⌐βασιλιας ℵ

4:10; 8:7, 22, 26; 9:9, 37; 12:13, 44 (λεγη Θ); 15:33; 18:32 (ειπεν 579); 19:8, 20; 20:8, 21, 23; 21:13, 16, 31; 22:8, 12, 20, 21, 43; 26:31, 35, 36, 40, 45; 27:13, 22 ⌐λεγει rell |⌐λεγι ℵ

4:17; 5:3, 19¹ (βασειλεια Θ); 10:7; 11:11, 12; 12:25, 26 (βασιλει E), 28; 13:24 (βασσιλεια L), 31, 44, 45, 52; 18:23; 19:14; 20:1; 21:43; 24:7 ⌐βασιλεια rell |⌐βασιλια ℵ*

5:9   ⌐ειρηνοποιοι rell |⌐ιρηνοποιοι ℵ |⌐ειρηνοποιει 13 |⌐ειρηνοπιοι 124 |⌐οιρηνοπιοι 1346

5:13, 48; 6:12 (Θ ειμεις); 10:31; 13:18; 15:16 (υμης 579); 19:27, 28; 20:4 (ειμεις K), 7; 21:13, 32; 23:8, 28, 32; 24:33; 26:31; 28:5 ⌐υμεις rell |⌐υμις ℵ

5:20; 7:21; 19:23, 24; 21:31; 23:13; 24:7 ⌐βασιλειαν rell |⌐βασιλιαν ℵ

5:26; 12:9, 15; 14:13 (εκει B*); 15:21, 29 ⌐εκειθεν rell |⌐εκιθεν ℵ

5:27   ⌐μοιχευσεις rell |⌐μοιχευσις ℵ |⌐μυχευσεις L |⌐μηχευσεις Θ* |⌐μοιχευσης 579 1071

5:29 (σκανδαλιζη L 243 244 346 1582* 1071 1346 *l*184 |σκανδαληζη 2* |σκανδαλιζη 2ᶜ), 30 (σκανδαλιζη L G Δ 471* 1071 |σκανδαληζει 2*) ⌐σκανδαλιζει rell |⌐σκανδαλιζι ℵ

5:29   ⌐συμφερει rell |⌐συμφερι ℵ |⌐συμφερη Θ

5:33   ⌐αποδωσεις rell |⌐αποδωσις ℵ |⌐αποδωσης W 1071 |⌐αποδοσεις 565

5:40; 15:26 ⌜λαβειν rell | ⌜λαβιν ℵ

5:44 ⌜ανατελλει rell |⌜ανατελλι ℵ |⌜ανατελει L 1424 |⌜ανατaλλει Δ

6:6 ⌜αποδωσει rell |⌜αποδωσι ℵ

6:14, 15 ⌜αφησει rell |⌜αφησι ℵ |⌜αφηση G Θ 1424

6:24 ⌜μισησει rell |⌜μισησι ℵ |⌜μεισησει B W |⌜μησησει L 565 1346 |⌜μισισει 33 |⌜μησισει 1071

6:24 ⌜αγαπησει rell |⌜αγαπησι ℵ* |⌜αγαπισει Δ* |⌜αηγαπηση 1424

6:27 ⌜τρεφει rell |⌜τρεφι ℵ |⌜τρεφη K L 2

6:34 ⌜μεριμνησει rell |⌜μεριμνησι ℵ |⌜μερημνησει L |⌜μεριμνηση N 579 1424

7:4* (ερις ℵ^c |λεγεις Θ 700); 27:11 ⌜ερεις rell |⌜λεγις ℵ

7:10 ⌜αιτησει B C K L N W Δ Σ f^{13} 28 33 124 157* 892 1071 1241 1424 ff ^{1} vg sy$^{c.pesh.hl}$ bo Clem^{hom} NA^{28} |⌜αιτησι ℵ |⌜αιτηση rell

7:25, 27; 10:19; 13:1; 22:23 ⌜εκεινη rell |⌜εκινη ℵ

8:15; 9:25 (χειρα D) ⌜χειρος rell |⌜χιρος ℵ

8:20a ⌜κατασκηνωσεις rell |⌜κατασκηνωσις ℵ |⌜κατασκινωσεις Θ |⌜κατασκηνωσης 2

8:20b (εχη L 579); 9:6 (εχη G); 13:12^1 (αιχει L), 12^2, 12^3, 21 (αιχει L), 27 (εχη E), 44 ⌜εχει rell |⌜εχι ℵ

8:22 ⌜ακολουθει rell |⌜ακολουθι ℵ |⌜ακολουθη L Θ Ω 2 13 1071

8:28; 9:22; 10:14; 15:28; 22:46 (εκηνης 2*); 26:29 ⌜εκεινης rell |⌜εκινης ℵ

8:31 ⌜εκβαλλεις rell |⌜εκβαλλις ℵ |⌜εκβαλεις E K* 33 1071 |⌜εκβαλης L 2 1424

9:22 ⌜θρασει rell |⌜θρασι ℵ

9:24 ⌜αναχωρειτε rell |⌜αναχωριτε ℵ |⌜αναχωρειται W 579 |⌜αναχωρηται Θ

10:13¹, 13² ⌜ειρηνη rell |⌜ιρηνη ℵ

10:18 ⌜βασιλεις rell |⌜βασιλις ℵ

10:21 ⌜γονεις rell |⌜γονις ℵ |⌜γωνεις L

10:28¹ ⌜φοβεισθε rell |⌜φοβισθε ℵ |⌜φοβηθητε B D Y N S Ω 1 28 33 118 1424 1582 |⌜φοβεισθαι C 13 1346 |⌜φοβησθε F K 349 1071 |⌜φοβηθηται W Θ |⌜φωβεισθε 2 |⌜φοβησθε 579

10:28² ⌜φοβεισθε B NA²⁸ |⌜φοβισθε ℵ |⌜φοβηθητε rell |⌜φοβεισθαι C W |⌜φοβιθητε L

10:29 ⌜πεσειται rell |⌜πεσιται ℵ |⌜πεσειτε Δ

10:31 ⌜φοβεισθε B *f*¹ 157 NA²⁸ |⌜φοβισθε ℵ |⌜φοβηθητε rell |⌜φοβεισθαι D L W |⌜φοβηθηται 2 579

10:32 ⌜ομολογησω rell |⌜ομολογησι ℵ |⌜ομολογηση E U Ω 28 1582*

10:34¹, 34² (ειρην D*; ηρηνην Θ) ⌜ειρηνην rell |⌜ιρηνην ℵ

APPENDIX 12: ITACISMS IN SINAITICUS IN MATTHEW

10:39 ⌜ευρησει rell |⌜ευρησι ℵ |⌜σωσει 118 |⌜ευρεσει 1071

11:1 ⌜διδασκειν rell |⌜διδασκιν ℵ

11:4, 25 (αποκρειθεις D |αποκριθης 579), 39 (αποκριθης 579); 14:28 (αποκρειθεις D |αποκριθει Θ |om. Sy^c); 15:13 (αποκρειθεις D |αποκρηθης Θ), 24 (αποκριθης 579); 20:22 (αποκριθης 579); 22:29 (αποκρειθεις D); 26:23 (αποκρεις D* |αποκριθης 579), 25 (αποκριθης 1346); 27:25 ⌜αποκριθεις rell |⌜αποκριθις ℵ

11:9 (ειδειν D M 124); 12:38 (ειδειν Θ) ⌜ιδειν rell |⌜ιδιν ℵ

11:10 ⌜κατασκευασει rell |⌜κατασκευασι ℵ |⌜κατασκευασοι 1346

11:20 (δυναμης Θ), 23; 13:54 (δυναμης Θ), 58 (δυναμης 2*); 14:2; 24:29 ⌜δυναμεις rell |⌜δυναμις ℵ

11:25 (εκειν Y*); 12:1; 14:1; 27:19 ⌜εκεινω rell |⌜εκινω ℵ

11:27; 20:7 ⌜ουδεις rell |⌜ουδις ℵ

11:27¹ (γινωσκει C 71 692 g^scr Clem¹ Iust^tr100 Eus^marc88cdd Did^tri26.72 | επιγεινωσκει D), 27² (επιγεινωσκει B D | γινωσκει 71 692) ⌜επιγινωσκει rell |⌜επιγινωσκι ℵ |⌜επιγιγνωσκει W

12:4; 14:16; 15:20 (φαγην E*); 26:17 ⌜φαγειν rell |⌜φαγιν ℵ

12:5 ⌜ιερεις rell |⌜ιερις ℵ |⌜ειερεις D |⌜ερεις Θ*

12:9 (χειραν L W f¹³ 118 157 788 1346); 26:23, 51 ⌜χειρα rell |⌜χιρα ℵ

12:12 ⌜διαφερει rell |⌜διαφερι ℵ

12:20 ⌜σβεσει rell |⌜σβεσι ℵ |⌜ζβεσει D* |⌜σβεσσι Δ |⌜σ...σεις 1071

12:25¹ ⌜μερισθεισα rell |⌜μερισθισα ℵ |⌜μερισθησα K L Θ 2* 565 579

12:26 ⌜εκβαλλει rell |⌜εκβαλλι ℵ |⌜εκβαλει L 349 472 |⌜εκβαλλη 348 |⌜εκβαλη 1424

12:29 (om. Δ |εισελθων 478); 19:17 (εισθειν E*), 24 ⌜εισελθειν rell |⌜εισελθιν ℵ

12:30 ⌜σκορπιζει rell |⌜σκορπιζι ℵ |⌜σκορπηζει 579

12:39 ⌜επιζητει rell |⌜επιζητι ℵ |⌜ζητει L |⌜επιζειτε 579 |⌜επειζητει 1071

12:41 ⌜κρισει rell |⌜κρισι ℵ |⌜κρεισει Θ

12:45a ⌜κατοικει rell |⌜κατοικι ℵ |⌜κατεικει 1346

12:45b ⌜εκεινου rell |⌜εκινου ℵ

12:45c ⌜χειρονα rell |⌜χιρονα ℵ |⌜χειρον D* *l*184 |⌜χειρωνα L 59 124 245

12:46 ⌜ειστηκεισαν rell |⌜ιστηκισαν ℵ |⌜ιστηκεισαν B C F G W Δ Θ 33 |⌜ιστηκασι L |⌜ιστικεισαν Δ |⌜ειστηκησαν 2* |⌜εστηκασιν 700

12:49 ⌜χειρα °αυτου rell |⌜χειρας 28 |⌜χιρα ℵ^S1 |°D 124 *a b ff* ¹ *g*¹ *k q* vg Or³·⁴⁸⁰ Aug
　　　 χιραν　　　　ℵ*

13:2 ⌜ειστηκει Bᶜ Dᴱ K M S U Y Γ Π Ω *f*¹ 28 118 124 157 565 579 700 788 1071 1346 1424 etc. NA²⁸ | ⌜ιστηκι ℵ |⌜ιστηκη E* |⌜ιστικει 2* |⌜ιστηκει B* C W Eᶜ F G L W X Z Δ Θ 2 33 etc. |⌜εστηκει D* (*d stabat*) 234 (*a b c ff* ² *h* vg *stabant*)

13:3 ⌜σπειρων rell |⌜σπιρων ℵ |⌜σπειρον K L |⌜σπηρων Θ 2*

13:11; 21:40 ⌜εκεινοις rell |⌜εκινοις ℵ

13:17 ⌜ιδειν rell |⌜ιδιν ℵ |⌜ειδειν D W |⌜ιδεινν Θ

13:19 ⌜αρπαζει rell |⌜αρπαζι ℵ |⌜αιρει 7 517 954 1424 1675

13:22 ⌜γινεται rell |⌜γινετε ℵ |⌜γεινεται B C D W |⌜γηνεται Θ

13:36 (αφης Θ); 18:12 (αφησει B L Θ f^1 788 1346 NA^{28} |αφιησι D |αφης 2*); 26:44 ⌜αφεις rell |⌜αφις ℵ

13:41 ⌜αποστελει rell |⌜αποστελι ℵ |⌜αποστέλει X |⌜αποστελλει Γ 157

13:44a ⌜πωλει rell |⌜πωλι ℵ |⌜πωλη Θ |⌜πολει Δ Ω 1 28 579 1071

13:44b ⌜εκεινον rell |⌜εκινον ℵ |⌜εκεινων 579

13:52 ⌜μαθητευθεις rell |⌜μαθητευθις ℵ |⌜μαθηθευθεις D |⌜μαθητευθη L

14:4 ⌜εχειν rell |⌜εχιν ℵ |⌜εχεν C

14:9 ⌜συνανακειμενους rell |⌜συνανακιμενους ℵ |⌜συνακειμενους G K |⌜συνανακημενους M Θ 1346 |⌜συνανκειμενους Δ

14:16 ⌜απελθειν rell |⌜απελθιν ℵ |⌜απελθην Θ

14:21; 15:38 ⌜ωσει rell |⌜ωσι ℵ*

14:27 ⌜θαρσειτε rell |⌜θαρσιτε ℵ |⌜θαρρειτε D |⌜θαρσειται W Θ 2* |⌜om. 517 954 983 1424 1675 1689

14:28 (απελθειν 346 1346), 29 (ελθην Θ |ηλθε 700ᶜ); 19:14 (ελθην 2*); 22:3 ⌜ελθειν rell |⌜ελθιν ℵ

14:35; 18:32 (εκεινη Δ) ⌜εκεινην rell |⌜εκινην ℵ

15:2 (χερσιν 1346); 19:13, 15; 22:13; 26:45, 50; 27:24 ⌜χειρας rell |⌜χιρας ℵ*

15:17 ⌜νοειτε rell |⌜νοιτε ℵ |⌜νοειται W 579

15:17 ⌜χωρει rell |⌜χωρι ℵ

15:22 (εκειων D* |εκεινον L |αυτης 349 517 659 954 1424 1675); 24:29 (εκεινον 579) ⌜εκεινων rell |⌜εκινων ℵ

15:28 (θελης M 2 565 1346 1424); 19:17 (θελης F 28 579), 21 (θελης F); 20:21 (θελης 1071 1346) ⌜θελεις rell |⌜θελις ℵ

16:1 ⌜πειραζοντες rell |⌜πιραζοντες ℵ |⌜πηραζοντες 579

18:21 ⌜αμαρτησει rell |⌜αμαρτησι ℵ |⌜αμαρτηση E H W Δ f^{13} 1346 1424

18:23; 22:2 ⌜βασιλει rell |⌜βασιλι ℵ

18:27 ⌜σπλαγχνισθεις rell |⌜σπλαγχνισθις ℵ |⌜σπλανχνισθεις D |⌜σπλαγχνησθεις E 2ᶜ |⌜σπλαχνισθεις K |⌜σπλαγχνησθης 2* |⌜σπλαγχνισθης 579

18:27 δουλου ⌜εκεινου rell |⌜εκινου ℵ |⌜om. B Θ 1 124 1582*

18:28 (om. B); 26:24; 27:8, 63 ⌜εκεινος rell |⌜εκινος ℵ

18:35 ⌜ποιησει rell |⌜ποιησι ℵ

APPENDIX 12: ITACISMS IN SINAITICUS IN MATTHEW

19:3   ⌜πειραζοντες rell |⌜πιραζοντες ℵ |⌜πειραζωντες Θ

19:5   ⌜καταλιεψει rell |⌜καταλιψι ℵ |⌜καταλιψιει C W Θ |⌜καταλυψει 13 |⌜καταληψει 579 1424

19:13   ⌜χωρειτω rell |⌜χωριτω ℵ

19:15   ⌜επιθεις rell |⌜επιθις ℵ |⌜επιθης Θ |επειθεις 124

19:29   ⌜κληρονομησει rell |⌜κληρονομησι ℵ |⌜κληρονομηση M *l*184 |⌜κληρονομησαι Θ |⌜κληρονομισει 700 |⌜κληρονομηση 1424

20:17, 18a; 21:10; 26:67 ⌜εις rell |⌜ις ℵ*

20:22   ⌜πινειν rell |⌜πινιν ℵ |⌜πιειν B G 085 245 477 482 485 579 1365 1689 2145 |⌜πεινειν D |⌜πινει 13 |⌜πινην 2* |⌜πινω 118 1424

21:15, 45; 26:59; 27:1, 20, 41 ⌜αρχιερεις rell |⌜αρχιερις ℵ

21:15 (γραματεις Θ* |γραμματοις 13 |γραμμαιτεις 1071); 23:15, 34; 26:57 (γραματεις Θ) ⌜γραμματεις rell |⌜γραμματις ℵ

21:29   ⌜μεταμεληθεις rell D^c (v.30 B *f*^13 4 174 230 238 262 273 346 543 566 700 788 826 828 983 1187 1346 1555 1573 *r*^2 vg^(2MSS) sy^hier sa^(pler) bo aeth^(2cdd) arm geo) |⌜μεταμεληθις ℵ |⌜μεταμεταμεληθεις D* |⌜μεταμελιθης 579 1071 |⌜(v.30)μεταμελληθεις Θ

21:41   ⌜απολεσει rell |⌜απολεσι ℵ |⌜αναλωσει L |⌜απολει W |⌜απολεση 28

22:7   ⌜εκεινους rell |⌜εκινους ℵ

22:10   ⌜εκεινοι rell |⌜εκινοι ℵ

22:10 ⌜ανακειμενων rell |⌜ανακιμενων ℵ |⌜ανακεινων C |⌜ανακειμενου K |⌜ανακημενων 2*

22:11 ⌜ανακειμενους rell |⌜ανακιμενους ℵ

22:16 ⌜αληθεια rell |⌜αληθια ℵ |⌜αληθειας D^c |⌜αληθηα Θ

22:16 ⌜βλεπεις rell |⌜βλεπις ℵ

22:17 ⌜δοκει rell |⌜δοκι ℵ |⌜δωκει 579

22:24 ⌜αναστησει rell |⌜αναστησι ℵ |⌜εξαναστησει F H M Θ 440 1012 1093 1194 1279 1295 1424 1515 1574 |⌜εξαναστασῃ Σ |⌜αναστασῃ 1582*

22:37 ⌜αγαπησεις rell |⌜αγαπησις ℵ |⌜αγαπησης 157 579 Cl^pt

22:43, 45 ⌜καλει rell |⌜καλι ℵ

23:13 ⌜εισερχεσθε rell |⌜ισερχεσθε ℵ* |⌜εισερχεσθαι D L W Θ 2 28 1071 |⌜εισερχεσθαι Δ |⌜ησερχεσθαι 579

23:18 ⌜οφειλει rell |⌜οφιλι ℵ |⌜οφιλει C L W Θ |⌜οφειλειν Δ |⌜οφειλῃ 13 |⌜ωφειλει 579 1424

23:22 ⌜ομνυει rell |⌜ομνυι ℵ |⌜ομνοιει L

23:29 ⌜κοσμειτε rell |⌜κοσμιτε ℵ |⌜κοσμειται C L W Δ 13 69 579 |⌜κοσμητε Θ

23:36 (εξει F); 24:14 ⌜ηξει rell |⌜ηξι ℵ

23:37 ⌜επισυναγει rell |⌜επισυναγι ℵ |⌜επισυναγαγει K

24:19b ⌜εκειναις rell |⌜εκινες ℵ* |⌜εκιναις ℵ^c |⌜εκεινες L |⌜εκηναις 2

24:22¹, 22² ⌜εκειναι *rell* |⌜εκιναι ℵ

24:29 ⌜δωσει *rell* |⌜δωσι ℵ |⌜δοσει E* |⌜δωση U 2*

24:31a ⌜αποστελει *rell* |⌜αποστελι ℵ |⌜αποστελλει H 2 1071 |⌜αποστελλη Θ

24:31b επισυναξουσιν *rell* |⌜επισυναξει 1375 1604 sy^s bo^{3mss} Hil |⌜επισυναξι ℵ* |⌜επισυναξουσιν Y M S U Ω f^1 13 69 28 157 700

26:7 ⌜ανακειμενου *rell* |⌜ανακιμενου ℵ

26:14a ⌜πορευθεις *rell* |⌜πορευθις ℵ

26:14b ⌜αρχιερεις *rell* B^{c2} |⌜αρχιερις ℵ |⌜αρχιιερεις B*

26:20 ⌜ανεκειτο *rell* |⌜ανεκιτο ℵ |⌜ανεκειτω 579

26:21 ⌜ειπεν *rell* |⌜λεγι ℵ

26:24 ⌜υπαγει *rell* |⌜υπαγι ℵ

26:35 ⌜αποθανειν *rell* |⌜αποθανιν ℵ |⌜αποθανην Θ 2* 69

26:37 ⌜λυπεισθαι *rell* |⌜λυπισθε ℵ |⌜λυπεισθε A 28 |⌜λυπισθαι W Θ |⌜λυπησθαι 579

26:42 ⌜παρελθειν *rell* |⌜παρελθιν ℵ |⌜παρελθην Θ

26:54 ⌜δει *rell* |⌜δι ℵ* |⌜εδει C 047 f^1 28 1396 Or^{Cels.II.10}

26:58 ⌜ηκολουθει *rell* |⌜ηκολουθι ℵ |⌜ηκολουθη E S Θ Ω 2 13 28 124 579 |⌜ηκολουθησαν 33

27:14 ⌜θαυμαζειν *rell* |⌜θαυμαζιν ℵ

27:24 ⌜ωφελει rell |⌜ωφελι ℵ |⌜οφελει L 69

27:34¹ (om. L), 34² ⌜πιειν rell |⌜πιν ℵ* |⌜πειν D

27:43 ⌜θελει rell |⌜θελι ℵ |⌜θελη F

27:63 ⌜εγειρομαι rell |⌜εγιρομαι ℵ |⌜εγειρωμαι E 579

27:8 ⌜απαγγειλαι rell |⌜απαγγιλαι ℵ |⌜απαγγηλαι Θ

28:20 ⌜τηρειν rell |⌜τηριν ℵ

4. ι > ει

7:12 ⌜υμιν rell |⌜υμειν ℵ

8:34 ⌜ιδοντες rell |⌜ειδοντες ℵ

9:2 ⌜ιδων rell |⌜ειδων ℵ |⌜ιδον E* 1346

16:12 απο ▫της ζυμηςˋ των αρτων   B ℵ^ca L
157 713 892 954 1241 1295 l48 e g¹ l aur vg sa bo geo^{1erB} Or |▫f¹ 517 1424 1675 Or
    απο της ζυμης ▫του αρτουˋ   rell |▫D Θ
124 346 174 565 566 788 a b d ff² sy^s arm
    απο της ζυμης των ⌜φαρεισαιων ▫και σαδδουκαιωνˋ   ℵ*
|⌜φαρισαιων 579 |▫33

21:2 ⌜κατεναντι B C D L Θ f¹³ 28 33 157 700 788 1346 NA²⁸
|⌜κατεναντει ℵ |⌜απεναντι rell |⌜κατεναντη L |⌜απεντι Δ

26:34 ⌜νυκτι rell |⌜νυκτει D

28:6 ⌜ιδετε rell |⌜ειδετε ℵ |⌜ειδεται D W |⌜om. 124* |⌜ιδεται 579 1071

5. Singular Readings with Non-Singular Orthographic Exchanges

5:13 ⌜καταπατεισθαι rell |⌜καταπατισθε ℵ |⌜καταπατισθαι W Θ 1071 |⌜καταπατεισθε 579

10:16 ⌜ακεραιοι rell |⌜ακαιρεοι ℵ |⌜ακερεοι L Θ 124 579 |⌜ακαιραιοι 33 1071

11:11 ⌜εγηγερται rell |⌜εγηγερτε ℵ |⌜εγειγερται 𝔐 2 33 124 1071 1424 |⌜αιγειγερτε L

12:24 ⌜εκβαλλει rell |⌜εκβαλλι ℵ |⌜εβαλλει Δ |⌜εκβαλι Θ |⌜εκβαλει 1424

12:39 ⌜δοθησεται rell |⌜δοθησετε ℵ |⌜δωθησετε L Θ* |⌜δωθησεται Θ^c 579 1071

12:42 ⌜κατακρινει rell |⌜κατακρινι ℵ |⌜κατακρεινι D |⌜κατακρινη L |⌜κατακρινουσιν U 346 1346

13:4 ⌜σπειρειν rell (om. C) |⌜σπιριν ℵ |⌜σπειριν D E |⌜σπιρειν W Θ

13:18 ⌜σπειραντος B 13 33 1071 1346 NA[28] |⌜σπιραντος ℵ* |⌜σπειροντος rell |⌜σπιροντος N |⌜σπηροντος Θ

14:27 ⌜φοβεισθε rell |⌜φοβισθε ℵ |⌜φοβεισθαι C D P 2 28 157 579 |⌜φοβησθε E* 565 1071 |⌜φοβισθαι W |⌜φωβεισθε Θ

16:1 (επηδειξαι K |δειξαι 2); 24:1 ⌜επιδειξαι rell |⌜επιδιξε ℵ |⌜επιδειξε L |⌜επιδιξαι Θ

18:34 ⌜οργισθεις rell |⌜οργισθις ℵ |⌜οργισθης E* |⌜οργησθεις G 2 |⌜οργεισθεις W |⌜οργησθης Θ* |⌜οργησθις Θ^c |⌜οργισθης 579

20:10 ⌜πλειον B C* L N Z $f^{1.13}$ 124 579 788 1346 NA²⁸ |⌜πλιονα ℵ |⌜πλειονα rell |⌜πλειω D |⌜πλιον W Θ |⌜πλειωνα 1071 |⌜πλεων Or^semel
Matt.XV.30

21:3 ⌜αποστελει B D M 69 157 700 1582* NA²⁸ |⌜αποστελι ℵ |⌜αποστελλει rell |⌜αποστελλι Θ |⌜απεστειλε 349 1293 (1424) 1675

21:41 ⌜εκδωσεται rell |⌜εκδωσετε ℵ |⌜εκδωσει C |⌜εκδοσεται f^{13} 2 118 157 565 788 1346 1424 |⌜εκδοσετε 1346

22:18 ⌜πειραζετε rell |⌜πιραζετε ℵ |⌜πειραζεται D L W Δ 13 33 579 1071 |⌜πιραζεται Θ |⌜πηραζεται 2*

23:13 ⌜κλειετε rell |⌜κλιετε ℵ |⌜κλειεται D L 2 13 |⌜κλιεται W |⌜κλιεσται Θ

26:38 ⌜γρηγορειτε rell |⌜γρηγοριτε ℵ |⌜γρηγορειται D 700 |⌜γριγοριτε Θ |⌜γρηγροητε 2

27:12 ⌜κατηγορεισθαι rell |⌜κατηγορισθε ℵ |⌜κατηγορισθαι W |⌜κατεγορεισθε Θ |⌜κατηγορεισθε 1346

APPENDIX 13
ITACISMS IN VATICANUS IN MATTHEW

1. ι > ει

1:6   του ⌈Ουριου *rell* |⌈Ουρειου □¹ B |⌈ριου L |⌈Οριου 124

1:25   ⌈εγινωσκεν *rell* |⌈εγνω D |⌈εγεινωσκεν B

2:22; 3:13; 4:18; 15:29; 21:11 (Γαλιλεας ℵ); 27:55 (Αγιλειλαιας A Y W Δ Π |Γαληλαιας K L) ⌈Γαλιλαιας *rell* |⌈Γαλειλαιας B

3:7; 5:20 (Φαρισσεων Θ |Φαρησαιων 2*); 16:6; 22:41 (Φαρισεων ℵ) ⌈Φαρισαιων *rell* |⌈Φαρεισαιων B

3:10   ⌈αξινη *rell* |⌈αξεινη B |⌈αξηνη 28

3:12   ⌈σιτον *rell* |⌈σειτον B |⌈συτον 788ᶜ

4:12   ⌈Γαλιλαιαν *rell* |⌈Γαλειλαιαν B

4:15   ⌈Γαλιλαια *rell* |⌈Γαλειλαια B |⌈Γαλιλαιας D* L |⌈Γαλιλαιαν f¹³

4:23   ⌈Γαλιλαια ℵ* C NA²⁸ |⌈Γαλειλαια B |⌈Γαλιλαιαν *rell*

7:2   ⌈κρινετε *rell* |⌈κρεινετε B

8:15   ⌈διηκονει *rell* |⌈διεκονει B*

8:26   ⌈επετιμησεν *rell* |⌈επετειμησεν B |⌈επετιμησε K U 13 118 157 700ᶜ 788 |⌈επετημησεν L |⌈επετημησε 1071

8:28 ⌜λιαν rell |⌜λειαν B

9:11, 14; 12:2, 24; 15:1, 2; 16:1; 19:3 (Φαρισεοι ℵ); 21:45; 22:15 (Φαρισεοι ℵ), 41; 23:2 (Φαρισεοι ℵ), 13, 15, 23, 25 (Φαρισεοι ℵ), 27 (Φαρισεοι ℵ), 29 (Φαρισεοι ℵ*); 27:62 ⌜Φαρισαιοι rell |⌜Φαρεισαιοι B

9:30 ⌜ενεβριμησατο rell |⌜ενεβριμηθη ℵ f^1 NA²⁸ |⌜ενεβρειμηθη B*

10:28 ⌜αποκτεννοντων ℵ C D W Θ 33 700* NA²⁸ |⌜αποκτενοντων rell |⌜αποκτεινοντων B

10:42 ⌜μικρων rell |⌜ελαχιστων D |⌜μεικρων B

11:4 ⌜Ιωαννη rell |⌜Ιωανει B* |⌜Ιωανη B^{c2} |⌜Ιωαννει D W Δ |⌜Ιωαννην E

11:19 ⌜εσθιων rell |⌜εσθειων B

12:20a ⌜συντετριμμενον rell D^{mg} |⌜συντετρειμμενον B |⌜om. D*

12:20b ⌜νικος rell |⌜νεικος B

13:21 ⌜θλιψεως rell |⌜θλειψεως B |⌜θλειψαιως D

13:25, 26, 27, 29, 30, 36, 38, 40 ⌜ζιζανια rell |⌜ζειζανια B

15:27a ⌜εσθιει rell |⌜εσθιουσιν D |⌜εσθειει B

15:27b ⌜ψιχιων rell |⌜ψειχιων B |⌜ψυχιων 565 1071 |⌜ψειχων D

17:15 ⌜πιπτει rell |⌜πειπτει B

19:13 οι δε μαθηται ⌜επετιμησαν ℵ L M W □ $f^{1.13}$ 33 pc NA²⁸ |⌜επετειμησαν B |⌜επετιμων C 66 it vg

23:26 ⌐Φαρισαιε rell |⌐Φαρεισαιοιε C* |⌐Φαρεισαιε B

23:34 ⌐μαστιγωσετε rell |⌐μαστειγωσετε B

24:29 την ⌐θλιψιν rell |⌐θλειψειν D |⌐θλειψιν B

25:44 ⌐διηκονησαμεν σοι rell |⌐διακονησαμεν A*vid |⌐ηδιηκονησαμεν ℵ |⌐διεκονησαμεν B* Δ |⌐διηκονισαμεν 565

26:7 ⌐βαρυτιμου rell |⌐πολυτιμου ℵ A L M Θ Π 33 157 565 1424 pc |⌐βαρυτειμου B |⌐πολυτειμου D |⌐βαρυτυμου K

26:62 ουδεν ⌐αποκρινη rell (-ℵ* 243 983 1689 l183) |⌐αποκρεινη B |⌐αποκρινει H 28 517

27:9a του ⌐τετιμημενου rell |⌐τεμειμενου Δ |⌐τετειμημενου B

27:9b ον ⌐ετιμησαντο rell |⌐ετειμησαντο B

27:46¹, 46² ⌐ηλι rell (157) |⌐ελωι ℵ 33 |⌐ελωει B |⌐ηλει D E Δ Θ Σ Φ 090 1 1582 1604 |⌐heloi vg^mu cop aeth |⌐heli it vg^pler arm geo Clem Cyp Aug |om. sy^s.pesh.hier

28:7, 10; 28:16 την ⌐Γαλιλαιαν rell |⌐Γαλειλαιαν B

2. Singular Readings with Non-Singular Orthographic Exchanges

24:32 ⌐γινωσκετε rell |⌐γεινωσκετε B* |⌐γινωσκεται L Θ 2* 579 |⌐γιγνωσκεται W |⌐γεινωσκεται B² D Γ 348 1187 al.

24:44 ⌐γινεσθε rell |⌐γεινεσθε B |⌐γεινεσθαι D |⌐γινεσθαι W Θ 2* 28 579

APPENDIX 14
ITACISMS IN EPHRAEMI IN MATTHEW

1. αι > ε

10:16 ⌜περιστεραι rell |⌜περισταιρε C

2. ε > αι

7:7 ⌜αιτειτε rell |⌜αιτειται C |⌜αιτιτε N W Θ 579

10:16 ⌜περιστεραι rell |⌜περισταιρε C

3. ει > ι

4:9 ⌜προσκυνησης rell |⌜προσκυνησις C |⌜προσκυνησεις E L Δ Σ 2 253 346 692 788* 1241 1346 1424 *l*47 *l*183 al. mu.

4:10 ⌜προσκυνησεις rell |⌜προσκυνησης ℵ L P 28 |⌜προσκυνησις C

17:20 ⌜ερειτε rell |⌜εριτε C |⌜ερειται W 2*

4. ι > ει

3:11 ⌜ειμι rell |⌜ειμει C |⌜ειμη L 1346

4:8 ⌜δεικνυσιν rell |⌜δικνυει ℵ |⌜δικνυσειν C |⌜εδειξεν D 372 |⌜δικνυσιν P W Δ Θ

13:15 και τη καρδια ⌜συνωσιν rell |⌜συνιωσιν 2 33 1071 |⌜συνειωσιν C

13:23 ⌜συνιεις ℵ B D Θ NA²⁸ |⌜συνειων C |⌜συνιων rell

14:8 ⌜προβιβασθεισα rell |⌜προβιβασθισα ℵ 788 |⌜προβειβασθεισα C |⌜προβιβασθησα E* Θ 13 2ᶜ 579 |⌜προβηβασθισα K |⌜προβηβασθησα L 2* 1346

15:10 ⌜σινιετε rell |⌜συνειετε C |⌜συνιεται W 2* 579 |⌜συνετε 1424

22:19 ⌜επιδειξατε rell |⌜επιδιξατε ℵ W Θ |⌜επειδειξατε C |⌜υποδειξατε S 28 71 349 399* 700 1187

23:26 ⌜Φαρισαιε rell |⌜Φαρεισαιοιε C* |⌜Φαρεισαιε B

24:9 εις ⌜θλιψιν και rell |⌜θλειψιν B D |⌜θλιψις 157 |⌜θλιψεις L 047 f¹ 1071 1582 plu syᵖ·ʰ·ᵐᵍ Orⁱⁿᵗ |⌜θλιψειν C

26:31 ⌜νυκτι rell |⌜νυκτει C |⌜νοικτι 2 |⌜νυκτη 1424

26:75 ⌜πριν rell |⌜πρειν C

5. Singular Readings with Non-Singular Orthographic Exchanges

23:31 ⌜μαρτυρειτε rell |⌜μαρτυριτε ℵ Θ |⌜μαρτυρειται C |⌜μαρτυριται W |⌜μαρτυρητε 579

24:9 ⌜θλιψιν rell |⌜θλειψιν B |⌜θλιψειν C |⌜θλειψειν D |⌜θλιψεις L 047 f¹ 4 273 pler |⌜θληψιν 2 |⌜θλιψις 157

APPENDIX 15
ITACISMS IN CODEX D IN MATTHEW

1. αι > ε

1:23   ⌜τεξεται *rell* |⌜τεξετε D

2:23   ⌜Ναζωραιος *rell* |⌜Ναζωρεος D W

5:10 (εστιν *rell* | erit *d*); 16:19², 22; 19:27 (εστιν 251); 22:28 ⌜εσται *rell* |⌜εστε D

9:2   ⌜αφιενται ℵ B NA²⁸ |⌜αφεωνται *rell* |⌜αφιοντε D

21:37 ⌜εντραπησονται *rell* |⌜εντραπησοντε D |⌜εντραπεισονται 2* |⌜εντραπησωνται 579

2. ε > αι

2:8b   ⌜εξετασατε *rell* |⌜εξετασαται D

2:8d   ⌜απαγγειλατε *rell* |⌜αναγγειλατε 124 |⌜επαγγειλαται D* |⌜απαγγειλαται Dᴮ

2:16a εν ⌜βηθλεεμ *rell* |⌜βλεεμ C |⌜βεθλεαιμ D* |⌜βηθλεεμ Dᴮ |⌜βιθλεεμ L Ω 349 1071

6:19   ⌜θησαυριζετε *rell* |⌜θησαυρισεται D

12:1   ⌜εσθιειν *rell* |⌜αισθιειν D |⌜εσθειειν 1071

13:21 ⌜θλιψεως *rell* |⌜θλειψεως B |⌜θλειψαιως D

APPENDIX 15: ITACISMS IN CODEX D IN MATTHEW 297

14:21 ⌜εσθιοντες *rell* |⌜αισθιωντες D* |⌜αισθιοντες D^c |⌜εσθιωντες 579

15:38 ⌜εσθιοντες *rell* |⌜αισθιοντες D

16:21 ⌜αρχιερεων *rell* |⌜αρχειεραιων D

21:2 ⌜αγαγετε *rell* |⌜αγετε B 56 58 |⌜αγεται D |⌜αγαγεται W

21:31 ⌜πρωτος *rell* |⌜υστερος B |⌜αισχατος D |⌜εσχατος Θ f^{13} 700 788 *pc*

21:32 ⌜επιστευσατε *rell* |⌜επιστευσαται D |⌜αιπιστευσαται L |⌜επιστεισαν 1424

24:42 ⌜οιδατε *rell* |⌜οιδεται D

25:28 ⌜αρατε *rell* |⌜αραται D

25:35 ⌜εποτισατε *rell* |⌜εποτεισαται D |⌜εποτησατε L U Δ Θ 2 33 579 1346 1424

25:40¹, 40² ⌜εποιησατε *rell* |⌜εποιησαται D

26:49; 27:29 ⌜χαιρε *rell* |⌜χαιραι D

26:50 ⌜εταιρε *rell* |⌜ετεραι D

27:64 ⌜κελευσον *rell* |⌜καιλευσον D

27:64 ⌜εσχατη *rell* |⌜αισχατη D |⌜σχατη C |⌜εσχατι 2*

28:9 ⌜χαιρετε *rell* |⌜χαιραιται D |⌜χαιρεται W Θ 2*

3. ει > ι

5:33 ⌜επιορκησεις *rell* | ⌜εφιορκησεις ℵ |⌜επειορκησις D |⌜εποιρκισεις 118 |⌜επιορκισης 1346

6:12 ⌜οφειληματα *rell* |⌜οφιλεματα D |⌜οφεληματα K L

9:3 ⌜βλασφημει *rell* |⌜βλασφημι D |⌜βλασφημη L

9:19 ⌜ηκολουθησεν *rell* |⌜ηκολουθει ℵ C 21 33 399 1396 1604 |⌜ηκολουθι D |⌜ηκολουθησαν E M 4 273 471 713 *l*49 *l*184

14:29 ⌜περειπατησεν *rell* |⌜περιπατησεν D Δ *d e* vg

16:21 ⌜αρχιερεων *rell* |⌜αρχειεραιων D

17:12/13 ⌜πασχειν *rell* |⌜πασχιν D

18:33 ⌜εδει *rell* |⌜εδι D

21:34 ⌜λαβειν *rell* |⌜λαβον ℵ |⌜λαβιν D

23:27 ⌜γεμουσιν *rell* |⌜γεμι D (Clem[282] Cyr[iulian335] Ir[int250])

24:48 ⌜χρονιζει *rell* |⌜χρονιζι D |⌜χρονηζει 2*

25:41 ⌜ερει *rell* |⌜ερι D

4. ι > ει

2:13 (om. sy[c.s.pesh]); 11:8; 12:42 ⌜ιδου *rell* |⌜ειδου D

3:3 ⌜τριβους *rell* |⌜τρειβους D

APPENDIX 15: ITACISMS IN CODEX D IN MATTHEW

3:4 ⌜δερματινην *rell* |⌜δερματεινην D

4:6; 5:23; 13:5; 26:39 ⌜επι *rell* |⌜επει D

4:16a ⌐σκοτια   ℵᶜ B |⌐τη W
       ⌜σκοτει   *rell* |⌜σκοτι ℵ* C Δ 2* 565 |⌜σκοτη Θ
       τη σκοτεια   D

4:16f ⌜σκια θανατου *rell* Dᴮ |⌜σκεια D* |⌜σκηα L

4:19 ⌜οπισω *rell* |⌜οπεισω D

5:16 ⌜ιδωσιν *rell* |⌜ειδωσιν D |⌜ιδοσιν 1071 |⌜ιδωσι 1346

5:17 ⌜νομισητε *rell* |⌜νομεισητε D |⌜νομησητε L Θ 124 2 28 788 1346 |⌜νομισηται W Δ 157 |⌜νομησεται 118* |⌜νομησηται 118ᶜ |⌜νομιζητε 346

5:18, 22, 28, 32, 34, 39, 44; 6:1, 5, 14, 16, 19, 20; 9:29; 10:15, 20, 23 (υμην 1071), 27, 42; 11:9, 11, 17, 21, 22¹, 22² (σοι M |om. 1346), 24; 12:6, 31, 36; 13:11, 17; 15:15; 16:28 (υμην 579); 17:12, 20¹, 20²; 18:3, 10, 12, 13, 18, 19, 35; 19:8, 9, 23, 24, 28; 20:4, 26¹, 26², 27, 32; 21:21, 24, 27, 31, 43; 22:31, 42; 23:9, 13, 15, 16, 23, 25a, 27, 29, 36, 39; 24:23, 25, 26, 34, 47; 25:12, 34, 40, 45; 26:13, 15, 21, 29, 64, 66; 27:17, 21 (υμην E*); 28:7 (om. Π*), 20 (ημιν 579) ⌜υμιν *rell* |⌜υμειν D

5:25 ⌜ισθι *rell* |⌜ισθει D |⌜ισθη Θ

5:25 ⌜αντιδικος *rell* |⌜αντιδεικος D |⌜αντηδικος L

5:36; 17:4¹, 4² (μια Θ), 4³; 19:5; 21:19; 28:1 ⌜μιαν *rell* |⌜μειαν D

5:40 ⌜ιματιον *rell* |⌜ειματιον D |⌜ηματιον Θ 2

5:42 ⌐αιτουντι rell |⌐αιτουντει D

5:44 ευλογειτε τους καταρωμενος ⌐υμας L W Δ Θ Π Σ 𝔐 f¹³ pler |om. ℵ B f¹ pler NA²⁸ |⌐υμειν D* |⌐υμιν 118

5:44 ⌐μισουσιν 𝔐 K L M U W pler (om. ℵ B 1071 pler NA²⁸) |⌐μεισουσιν D |⌐μησουσιν L |⌐μησουντας 2* |⌐μισουντας 1582ᶜ

5:46 ⌐μισθον rell |⌐μεισθον D |⌐μισθην Δ

6:3; 27:29 (δεχιαν 𝔐 K M U W Γ Δ Π 064 plu) ⌐δεξια rell |⌐δεξεια D

6:11, 12; 13:36 (ημην L); 15:33; 20:12; 21:25; 22:25 (εμιν Θ); 24:2, 3; 25:8 (υμιν 157), 11 (υμιν 1346); 26:63, 68 ⌐ημιν rell |⌐ημειν D

6:16 ⌐υποκριται rell |⌐υποκρειται D |⌐υποκριτε L

9:6 ⌐αμαρτιας rell |⌐αμαρτειας D

9:8, 11; 27:54 ⌐ιδοντες rell |⌐ειδοντες D

9:16a ⌐ιματιω rell |⌐ειματιω D |⌐ηματιω L 2

9:16b ⌐ιματιου rell |⌐ειματειου D |⌐ηματιου 2

9:16c ⌐σχισμα rell |⌐σχεισμα D |⌐σχιμα K

9:22 (ιδον Θ | om. syˢ); 21:19 ⌐ιδων rell |⌐ειδων D

9:35 ⌐μαλακιαν rell |⌐μαλακειαν D |⌐μαλακηαν 2*

10:6; 15:24 ⌐Ισραηλ rell |⌐Εισραηλ D

10:8   λεπρους ⌜καθαριζετε rell (א P W Δ Θ 2* 579) -1424* |⌜καθαρεισατε D

10:15 ⌜μαστιγωσουσιν rell |⌜μαστειγωσουσιν D |⌜μιστηγωσουσιν E L 2*

10:42 ⌜ποτιση rell |⌜ποτειση D |⌜ποτησει L 1071 1424 |⌜ποτηση Δ 13 124 |⌜ποτισει 2 33* 346 1346 *l*53 *l*184

11:22 ⌜κρισεως rell |⌜κρεισεως D |⌜κρησεως 2*

11:25 (αποκριθις א | αποκριθης 579); 13:37; 14:28 (αποκριθις א |αποκριθει Θ | om. Sy^c); 15:13 (αποκριθις א | αποκρηθης Θ); 21:24, 29, 30 (αποκριθις א^c | απεκριθη W* | απεκριθεις W^c | αποκφιθης 579 | απηλθε Y 118 157); 22:29 (αποκριθις א); 24:2 (om. C 𝔐 W *pler*); 25:40 ⌜αποκριθεις rell |⌜αποκρειθεις D

11:27 ⌜επιγινωσκει rell |⌜επιγινωσκι א |⌜γινωσκι C |⌜επιγεινωσκει D |⌜επιγιγνωσκει W

12:5   ⌜ιερεις rell |⌜ιερις א |⌜ειερεις D |⌜ερεις Θ*

12:41 ⌜Νινευιται B C L W Δ Θ NA²⁸ |⌜Νινευειτε א |⌜Νεινευεται D* |⌜Νεινευειται D^c |⌜Νηνευιται Γ |⌜Νινευιται rell

12:42 ⌜κατακρινει rell |⌜κατακρινι א |⌜κατακρεινι D |⌜κατακρινη L |⌜κατακρινουσιν U 346 1346

12:43 ⌜ευρισκει rell |⌜ευρεισκει D |⌜ευρισκον 700

13:47 ⌜παλιν rell |⌜παλειν D

13:54 ⌜σοφια rell |⌜σοφεια D |⌜σοφι F* |⌜σωφια L

14:4 ⌜γενεσιοις ℵ B L NA²⁸ |⌜γενεσιων rell |⌜γενεσειοις D |⌜γενεσιον 13 124 788 1346

14:13 ⌜ιδιαν rell |⌜ειδιαν D |⌜ηδιαν L 579

14:15 ⌜οψιας rell |⌜οψειας D

15:5 ⌜τιμησει B C N W Δ Θ Π² Σ Ω 047 f¹³ 1 33 124 543 565 788 1071 1295 1346 1582* NA²⁸ |⌜τιμηση rell |⌜τειμησει D |⌜τημηση E* K |⌜τημησει Eᶜ 2* |⌜τιμισει Θ |⌜τημισει 579

15:8 ⌜τιμα rell |⌜τειμα D |⌜τημα L 2 |⌜om. Ω

15:17 ⌜κοιλιαν rell |⌜κοιλειαν D

15:20 ⌜ανιπτοις rell |⌜ανειπτοις D

16:2 ⌜οψιας rell |⌜οψειας D

16:3 ⌜πρωι rell |⌜πρωει D |⌜πρωιας E M^{mg} 33 71 213 235 473 477 485 655 1071 1207 1223 1365 1396 1574 |⌜προι Θ* 1424

16:3 ⌜διακρινειν rell |⌜διακρεινειν D |⌜διακρινην Θ

16:22 ⌜πιτιμαν pler NA²⁸ |⌜ επειτειμαν D (it)

16:24 ⌜τις rell |⌜τεις D |⌜της L |⌜οστις 1071

16:28 ⌜ιδωσιν rell |⌜ειδωσιν D |⌜ιδωσι Y K L M S U Ω f¹ 28 118 157 700 1071

17:2a (ηματια 2*); 21:7 (ιματι K*), 8 (ηματια 2*); 27:35 (ειματια A) ⌜ιματια rell |⌜ειματεια D

APPENDIX 15: ITACISMS IN CODEX D IN MATTHEW

17:2a (ηματια 2*); 21:7 (ιματι K*), 8 (ηματια 2*); 27:35 (ειματια A) ⌜ιματια rell ⌜ειματεια D

17:2b το φος   rell
       χιων   it vg Syr^{cu} aeth arm^{cdd} bo^{mss} Hil pc ⌜χειων D

17:24² τα ⌜διδραχμα   rell ℵ^{ca} ⌜διδραγμα 𝔐 L (W) 118 f^{13} 28 157 565 700 1071 ⌜διδραχματα 579 ⌜διδραχμον 1093 ⌜tributum a d e f ff^{1} n vg$^{(pler)}$ aeth ⌜didgrama uel censum b ⌜didgramam g^{1}
    ⌜δειδραγμα   D ⌜διδραχα ℵ* mae bo
    το διδραχμον   Cyr^{4,791}

17:27 ⌜σκανδαλισωμεν rell ⌜σκανδαλιζωμεν ℵ L Z ⌜σκανδαλεισωμεν D ⌜σκανδαλισομεν 28 ⌜σκανδαλησωμεν 2 579 1424

18:6 ⌜σκανδαλιση rell ⌜σκανδαλειση D ⌜σκανδαληση E 1346 ⌜σκανδαλησει L 579 ⌜σκανδαλισει H Θ 2* 1071

18:16; 26:61 ⌜τριων rell ⌜τρειων D

18:17 ⌜εκκλησια rell ⌜εκκλησεια D ⌜εκληδσια H K

18:17 ⌜εκκλησιας rell ⌜εκκλησειας D ⌜εκκλησια 472 478 565 1675 *l*184

19:6; 24:41¹, 41² ⌜μια rell ⌜μεια D

19:7 ⌜αποστασιου rell ⌜αποστασειου D

19:10 ⌜αιτια rell ⌜ετιος 𝔓^{25} ⌜αιτεια D ⌜αιτηα L

19:19 ⌜πλησιον rell ⌜πλησειον D ⌜πλησιων 579

19:28 ⌜παλιγγενεσια rell |⌜παλινγενεσια ℵ B* C E 𝔐 L W Z Δ Θ f¹³ 2 33 579 1071 |⌜παλινγενεσεια D |⌜παληνγενεσια Θ |⌜παλινενγενεσια Σ

20:1 ⌜μισθωσασθαι rell |⌜μισθωσασθε ℵ |⌜μεισθωσασθαι D |⌜μησθωσασθαι 2*

20:7 ⌜εμισθωσατο rell |⌜εμεισθωσατο D* |⌜εμισθωσατω Θ

20:13 ⌜αποκριθις rell |⌜αποκρειθις D

20:18 ⌜κατακρινουσιν rell |⌜κατακρεινουσιν D

20:19 ⌜μαστιγωσαι rell |⌜μαστειγωσαι D |⌜μαστηγωσαι M 2* 1071

20:22a ⌜πιειν rell |⌜πειειν D |⌜πιν W |⌜ποιειν f¹³

20:22b ⌜πινειν rell |⌜πινιν ℵ |⌜πιειν B G 085 245 477 482 485 579 1365 1689 2145 |⌜πεινειν D |⌜πινει 13 |⌜πινην 2* |⌜πινω 118 1424

20:31a ⌜επετιμησεν rell |⌜επετειμησεν D |⌜επετημησεν K Θ 565 1071 |⌜επιτιμησεν M |⌜επετιμησαν N

20:31b ⌜σιωπησωσιν rell |⌜σειωπησωσιν D |⌜σιωπισωσιν E K Ω |⌜σιωπησουσιν L N O Δ Σ 579 |⌜σιωπησωσι 1071

21:16 ⌜νηπιων rell |⌜νηπειων D |⌜νιπιων E K

21:23a ⌜διδασκοντι rell |⌜διδασκοντει D |⌜διδασκοντες 118 |⌜διδασκωντι 579

21:23b, 27 ⌜εξουσια rell |⌜εξουσεια D

21:23c ⌜εξουσιαν rell |⌜εξουσειαν D

21:27 ⌜αποκριθεντες rell |⌜αποκρειθεντες D

21:35 ⌜ελιθοβολησαν rell |⌜ελειθοβολησαν D |⌜ελιθοβολισαν 69 1071

21:42a ⌜απεδοκιμασαν rell |⌜απεδοκειμασαν D |⌜απεδοκημασαν 2 28 1424 |⌜απεδωκιμασαν 579 1346 |⌜απεδωκημασαν 1071

21:42b ⌜γωνιας rell |⌜γωνειας D |⌜γονιας E L U 2* 565 579 1424

22:5 ⌜ιδιον rell |⌜ειδιον D

22:6 ⌜υβπισαν rell |⌜υβρεισαν D |⌜υβρησαν 28

22:18 ⌜υποκριται rell |⌜υποκρειται D |⌜υποκριτε 2*

22:30 ⌜γαμιζονται ℵ B D L 047 f^1 22 pler NA^{28} |⌜εκγαμιζονται 𝔐 Γ Δ Π Σ Φ 2 pler |⌜γαμειζονται D |⌜γαμισκονται W 33 124 157 700 713 788 1295 |⌜γαμησκονται Θ |⌜εκγαμηζονται 2* |⌜ενγαμιζονται 13 |⌜εγγαμισκονται 69 1346 Clem^{semel} pc |⌜εγγαμιζονται 1093 1241 1515 Or^{semel} |⌜εκξαμιζουσιν 1194

22:37 ⌜καρδια rell |⌜καρδεια D

22:46 ⌜αποκριθηναι rell |⌜αποκριθηνε ℵ* |⌜αποκρειθηναι D

23:6 ⌜πρωτοκλισιαν rell |⌜πρωτοκλισιας ℵ^{ca} 157 713 892 a c f ff^1 g^1 h l m r$^{1.2}$ aur vg sy$^{c.s.pesh(pler).hl.hier}$ sa bo aeth Hil |⌜πρωτοκλεισιαν D |⌜πρωτοκλησιαν F G Γ Δ 2* 28 69 565 579 1071 |⌜πρωτοκλησιας L f^1 33 |⌜προτοκλισιαν Θ

23:13 (αφιεται W Θ 579 |αφηεται 2); 24:40 (αφιετε ℵ 28), 41 (αφιετε ℵ 28) ⌜αφιετε rell |⌜αφειεται D

23:25c αρπαγης και ⌜ακρασιας rell |⌜ακρασειας D |⌜αδικιας C E F G H K S U V Γ Ω 28 157 579 700 pm sy^{p}et$^{p.cod}$ Bas$^{eth\ 236\ cod}$ Chr$^{mo\ 5}$ Op pc |⌜ακαθαρσιας Ο Σ 66 71 1295 1515 *1844* Cl |⌜πλεονεξιας M 1093 Chr^{montf} Dam^{par517} |⌜ακρασιας αδικειας W |⌜πονηριας 999 |⌜intemperantia lat |⌜intemperantiae d |⌜iniquitate r^2 sy^{pesh} |⌜incontinentia e r^1 |⌜iniustitia f |⌜immunditia ff^1 g$^{1.2}$ l m aur vg sah sy^s sa bo geo |⌜iniquitate auaritia aeth |⌜intemperantia et iniquitate sy^{hl}

23:27 ⌜ακαθαρσιας rell |⌜ακαθαρσειας D

23:28 ⌜ανομιας rell |⌜ανομειας D

23:37 ⌜νοσσια rell |⌜νοσσεια D |⌜νοσια Ε* Η Θ Π 565* 579 1424

24:15 ⌜ιδητε rell |⌜ειδητε D |⌜ιδηται W |⌜ιδιτε 579

24:15 ⌜αναγινωσκων rell |⌜αναγεινωσκων D |⌜αναγιγνωσκων W |⌜αναγινοσκων Θ |⌜αναγινωσκον 118 565

24:18 ⌜ιματιον rell |⌜ειματειον D

24:27, 37, 39 ⌜παρουσια rell |⌜παρουσεια D

24:29 την ⌜θλιψιν rell |⌜θλειψειν D |⌜θλειψιν Β

24:38a ⌜αχρι rell |⌜αχρει D |⌜αχρις f^{13} 69 124 543 788 1346 |⌜αχι Θ*

24:38b γαμουντες και ⌜γαμιζοντες ℵ 33 1346 1355 1396 NA^{28} |⌜γαμισκοντες Β 1675 |⌜εκγαμιζοντες rell |⌜γαμειζοντες D |⌜εκγαμισκοντες W 517 1424 |⌜εκγαμειζοντες Δ |⌜εκγαμηζοντες Θ |⌜εγγαμιζοντες Σ 047 13 124 543 174 230 348 788 826 828 892 983 1093 1241 1346 1473 1515 1689
24:42a ⌜κλινης rell |⌜κλεινης D |⌜κληνης 1346

24:42b ⌜μιας rell |⌜μειας D

24:43 ⌜οικιαν rell |⌜οικειαν D |⌜οικον L W

25:25 ⌜ιδε rell |⌜ειδου D

25:33 ⌜εριφια rell |⌜εριφεια D

25:35 ⌜εποτισατε rell |⌜εποτεισαται D |⌜εποτησατε L U Δ Θ 2 33 579 1346 1424

25:37 ⌜διψωντα rell |⌜δειψωντα D

25:42 ⌜εποτισατε rell |⌜εποτεισατε D |⌜εποτησατε E L Θ 2* 33 579 1071 1424 |⌜εποτισαται W

25:44 ⌜διψωντα rell |⌜δειψωντα D |⌜δηψωντα 579 |⌜διψοντα E* K

26:3 ⌜αρχιερεις rell |⌜αρχειερεις D

26:7 ⌜βαρυτιμου rell |⌜πολυτιμου ℵ A L M Θ Π 33 157 565 1424 pc |⌜βαρυτειμου B |⌜πολυτειμου D |⌜βαρυτυμου K

26:27 ⌜πιετε rell |⌜πειεται D |⌜πιεται W 579

26:29a ⌜αρτι rell |⌜αρτει D

26:29b ⌜βασιλεια rell |⌜βασειλεια D

26:40 ⌜ισχυσατε rell |⌜ισχυσας A 1396 |⌜εισχυσαται D |⌜ισχυσαται L

26:51 ⌜ωτιον rell |⌜ωτειον D |⌜οτιον Δ

26:58 ⌜ιδειν rell |⌜ειδειν D

26:59 εζητουν ⌜ψευδομαρτυριαν rell |⌜ψευδομαρτυραν B* |⌜ψευδομαρτυρειαν D

26:65 ⌐ιματια rell |⌐ειματια D |⌐ηματια 2*

26:67 ⌐εραπισαν rell |⌐εριπισαν W |⌐εραπιζον 157 |⌐ερραπισαν 𝔐 G $f^{1.13}$ 22 33 543 565 579 700 892 al. pler. |⌐ερραπησαν 118 |⌐εραππισαν Φ |⌐εραπεισαν D

27:28 αυτον   rell
       αυτον τα ιματια αυτου   33 pc sy^{hmg} sa^{ms} mae bo^{ms}
       αυτον ιματιον πορφυρουν^T 157|⌐και 157 a b c d f ff^2
h (q) gat mm (Or^{int} sy^s)
       αυτον ειματιον πορφυρουν και   D

27:48 ⌐εποτισεν rell |⌐εποτειζεν D |⌐εποτηζεν Ω 579

27:49 Ηλιας ⌐σωσων   pler NA^{28} |⌐και σωσει 1 1582*
       Ηλειας και σωσει   D

27:63 ⌐τριτης rell |⌐τρειτης D

5. Singular Readings with Non-Singular Orthographic Exchanges

16:22 ⌐ιλεως rell |⌐ειλεως ℵ B W Θ |⌐ειλεος D* |⌐ιλεος F S 13 124 788

17:27 ⌐αγκιστρον rell |⌐ανκιστρον D |⌐αγκηστρον L |⌐αγγιστρον Θ Σ Ω 2* |⌐ανκυστρου 2²

18:28 ⌐επνιγεν rell |⌐επνειγε B |⌐επνειγεν D |⌐επνιγε H Y U 13 118 157 700 788 1346 |⌐επνηγεν Κ Ω 2* |⌐επνηγε 28 1071
23:27 ⌐φαινονται rell |⌐φενοντε ℵ |⌐φαινετε D

23:28 ⌐φαινεσθε rell |⌐φενεσθε ℵ 2* |⌐φαινεσθαι C E W Θ 13 33 579 |⌐φενεσθαι D

24:9 ⌜θλιψιν rell |⌜θλειψιν B |⌜θλιψειν C |⌜θλειψειν D |⌜θλιψεις L 047 f^1 4 273 pler |⌜θληψιν 2 |⌜θλιψις 157

24:44 ⌜γινεσθε rell |⌜γεινεσθε B |⌜γεινεσθαι D |⌜γινεσθαι W Θ 2* 28 579

27:64 ⌜χειρων rell |⌜χειρον ℵ Σ Φ 28 33 69 245 565 579 1424 |⌜χειρω D |⌜χερω L |⌜μειζων 247

28:5 ⌜ζητειτε rell |⌜ζητειται D |⌜ζητιται W Θ |⌜ζητιτε 2 |⌜ζητητε 565

APPENDIX 16
Itacisms in Washingtonianus in Matthew

1. αι > ε

6:17   ⌜νιψαι rell |⌜νιψε W

10:2; 26:37   ⌜Ζεβεδαιου rell (|⌜Ζεβεδεου D |⌜Ζεβεδεου ℵ L) |⌜Ζεβαιδεου W

13:2   ⌜αιγιαλον rell |⌜εγειαλον W

13:14   ⌜αναπληρουται rell |⌜πληρωθησεται D 7 517 954 1424 1675 |⌜αναπληρουτε W* |⌜αναπληρουνται Θ 579 |⌜πληρουται 1 485 1582*

13:48   ⌜αιγιαλον rell |⌜αγιαλον B* |⌜εγιαλον W

16:1   ⌜Σαδδουκαιοι rell |⌜Σαδουκαιοι L Y* Θ* |⌜Σαδδουκεοι W

16:6 (-U 157 haplography), 11, 12 (-579 f¹) ⌜Σαδδουκαιων   rell |⌜Σαδδουκεων W

16:13   ⌜Καισαρειας B F G plu NA²⁸ |⌜Καισαριας ℵ C D L plu |⌜Κεσαριας W

17:9   ⌜καταβαινοντων rell |⌜καταβαινοντες D d sy^{c.p} |⌜καταβενοντων W |⌜καταβαντων 655

25:10   ⌜αγορασαι rell |⌜αγορασε W |⌜αγωρασαι 579

26:35   ⌜απαρνησομαι rell |⌜απαρνησωμαι A 𝔐 K U Π 1582 118 157 1071 |⌜αρνησομαι H |⌜απαρνησομε W

26:56 ⌈μαθηται *rell* |⌈μαθητε W

26:75 ⌈φωνησαι *rell* exc. f^1 |⌈φωνησε W

27:20 ⌈αιτησωνται *rell* |⌈αιτησονται Ε Η Ω 2 1071 1346 1424 |⌈ετησωνται W |⌈αιτισονται 13

27:42 ⌈δυναται *rell* |⌈δυνατε W

27:42 ⌈σωσαι *rell* |⌈σωσε W

2. ϵ > αι

5:44 ⌈ποιειτε *rell* |⌈ποιειται W |⌈ποιητε Κ L 2*

6:16 ⌈νηστευητε *rell* |⌈νηστευηται W |⌈νηστευετε Σ 348 *l*47 |⌈νηστευιετε 2*

6:15 ⌈αφητε *rell* |⌈αφηται W

6:33 ⌈ζητειτε *rell* |⌈ζητιτε Ν |⌈ζητειται W |⌈ζητητε Θ

6:34 ⌈μεριμνησητε *rell* |⌈μεριμνησειτε Ε Ω 2 |⌈μερημνσιτε L |⌈μεριμνησηται W |⌈μερημνησειτε 1071

7:23 ⌈αποχωρειτε *rell* |⌈αποχορητε L 2* |⌈αποχωριται W |⌈αποχωριτε Δ |⌈αναχωριτε Θ |⌈αναχωρειτε f^{13} 788

10:8 ⌈δοτε *rell* |⌈δωτε G L 2 13 1346 |⌈δοται W

10:11 ⌈μεινατε *rell* |⌈μινατε ℵ Ν |⌈μειναται W |⌈μηνατε Θ 118 |⌈μενετε 28

10:19 ⸀μεριμνησητε rell |⸀μεριμησητε B* |⸀μεριμνησηται W |⸀μεριμνησετε Γ Θ 253 *l*54 |⸀μεριμνησειτε |⸀μεριμνησιτε 1424

14:27 ⸀φοβεισθε rell |⸀φοβισθε ℵ |⸀φοβεισθαι C D P 2 28 157 579 |⸀φοβησθε E* 565 1071 |⸀φοβισθαι W |⸀φωβεισθε Θ

17:7 ⸀εγερθητε rell |⸀εγειρεσθαι D *l*33 |⸀εγερθηται W

17:9 ⸀ειπητε rell |⸀ειπηται W |⸀ειπειτε 1071

18:10 ⸀ορατε rell |⸀οραται W

18:35 ⸀αφητε rell |⸀αφηται W |⸀αφειτε 579

21:2 ⸀πορευεσθε ℵ B L Θ f^1 33 157 788 1346 1424 NA²⁸ |⸀πορευθητε rell |⸀πορευθηται W |⸀πορευεσθαι 13

21:2 ⸀αγαγετε rell |⸀αγετε B 56 58 |⸀αγεται D |⸀αγαγεται W

21:21 ⸀εχητε rell |⸀εχειτε E 2 579 1071 |⸀εχηται W

21:21 ⸀ειπητε rell |⸀ειπηται W

21:24 ⸀ειπητε rell |⸀ειπιτε L |⸀ειπηται W |⸀ειπειτε 1071

21:25 ⸀επιστευσατε rell |⸀αιπιστευσατε L |⸀επιστευσαται W

23:3 ειπωσιν υμιν ⸀ποιειτε rell (D) |⸀ποιησατε ℵ B L Θ 124 NA²⁸ |⸀ποιετε F K Y (Γ) 2 |⸀ποιειται W |⸀ποιειν (Γ) f^1 118 700 |⸀ποιητε 565 |⸀ποιηται 579

23:14 om. verse ℵ B D L Θ pler NA²⁸ |⸀κατεσθιετε rell |⸀καταισθειεται W |⸀κατεσθιεται 13 579

23:39 ⸀ειπητε rell |⸀ειπηται W |⸀ιπειτε 13

24:2 ⸀βλεπετε rell |⸀βλεπεται W

24:15 ⌜ιδητε rell |⌜ειδητε D |⌜ιδηται W |⌜ιδιτε 579

25:42 ⌜εποτισατε rell |⌜εποτεισατε D |⌜εποτησατε E L Θ 2* 33 579 1071 1424 |⌜εποτισαται W

3. ει > ι

1:21 ⌜καλεσεις rell |⌜καλεσει L* |⌜καλεσις W

2:4 (γραμματης S*); 15:1 (γραματεις Θ); 17:10; 23:2 ⌜γραμματεις rell |⌜γραμματις W

5:43 ⌜αγαπησεις rell |⌜αγαπησις W |⌜αγαπησης 2* 788

9:26 ⌜εκεινην rell |⌜εκινην W

11:11[1] ⌜μειζων rell |⌜μιζων ℵ N Θ |⌜μιζον W |⌜μειζον 565 892

11:22 ⌜Σειδωνι rell |⌜Σοσομνι N |⌜Σιδονει W

12:40[4] ⌜τρεις rell |⌜τρις W

13:34 ⌜ελαλει rell |⌜ελαλησεν ℵ* Δ 1675 sah |⌜ελαλη E M Γ 2 565 579 |⌜ελαλι W |⌜ηλαλη Θ

16:23 ⌜φρονεις rell |⌜φρονις W |⌜εφρωνεσας Θ

17:4 ⌜Μωυσει rell |⌜Μωση uel Μωσει C E F pc 700 2 33 𝔐 L M U Θ Π^c f^13 157 1071 579 |⌜Μωυση L Θ Π2 Φ 892 |⌜Μωυσι W

19:19 ⌜αγαπησεις rell |⌜αγαπησις W |⌜αγαπησες Θ* |⌜αγαπησης 579

20:22 δυνασθε ⌜πιειν rell |⌜πειειν D |⌜πιν W |⌜ποιειν f^13

25:26 ⌐ηδεις rell |⌐ηδις W |⌐ιδης 69 |⌐ηδης 1424

25:27 ⌐βαλειν rell |⌐βαλιν W |⌐καταβαλειν 517 1424 |⌐λαβειν 697

26:41 ⌐γρηγορειτε rell |⌐εγρηγορειτε 𝔓³⁷ |⌐γρηγορειται D L 579 |⌐γρηγοριτε W |⌐γρηγορητε Θ 69

27:4b ειπαν L f¹³ 33 788 1346 NA²⁸ |⌐ειπον rell |⌐ι(πον) W*

4. ι >ει

1:5   ⌐Ιεσσαι plu NA²⁸ | ⌐Ειεσσαι W

2:6   ⌐ελαχιστη rell |⌐ελαχειστη W

2:13 ⌐ισθι rell |⌐εισθει W |⌐ισθει 2*

3:4   ⌐μελι rell |⌐μελει W

5:1   ⌐καθισαντος rell |⌐καθεισαντος W

5:15 ⌐οικια rell |⌐οκεια W

6:26 ⌐ουχ   rell |⌐ουχει W |⌐ουχι Θ
      ου πολλω   28

6:27 ⌐ηλικιαν rell |⌐ηλικειαν W

6:34 ⌐κακια rell |⌐κακεια W

7:14 ⌐ολιγοι rell |⌐ολειγοι W

7:25 ⌐οικια rell |⌐οικεια W

Appendix 16: Itacisms in Washintonianus in Matthew

8:9; 22:32; 24:5; 26:22, 25 (ειμη 579); 27:24; 28:20 (ημι E* F 28 |om. 579) ⌐ειμι *rell* |⌐ειμει W

8:11   ⌐ανακλιθησονται *rell* |⌐ανακληθησονται V 13 251 252 471 485 517 543 al. |⌐ανακλειθησονται W

8:16   ⌐οψιας *rell* |⌐οψειας W

9:37   ⌐ολιγοι *rell* |⌐ολειγοι W

10:34 ⌐νομισητε *rell* |⌐νομισηται ℵ D Δ |⌐νομησειτε L |⌐νομεισηται W |⌐νομησητε Θ 2 28 788 1346

11:22 ⌐Σειδωνι *rell* |⌐Σοσομνι N |⌐Σιδονει W

13:2   ⌐αιγιαλον *rell* |⌐εγειαλον W

13:48 ⌐καθισαντες *rell* |⌐καθησαντες L Θ Ω 2* 28 1071 1346 |⌐καθεισαντες W

14:11 ⌐πινακι *rell* |⌐πινακει W |⌐πινακη 2*

14:23 ⌐ιδιαν *rell* |⌐ειδιαν W |⌐ηδιαν 2*

18:34 ⌐οργισθεις *rell* |⌐οργισθις ℵ |⌐οργησθης E* |⌐οργησθεις G 2 |⌐οργεισθεις W |⌐οργησθης Θ* |⌐οργισθις Θ^c |⌐οργισθης 579

20:1   ⌐πρωι *rell* |⌐πρωει W

21:7 ⌐επεκαθισεν B C F M S U V X Z^{vid} Γ Δ *f*¹³ *pler* it^{pler} sy^{utr.cu} sa *pc* Or *pc* NA²⁸ |⌐εκαθισαν ℵ* |⌐επεκαθισαν ℵ^{ca} 4 16 245 291 892 |⌐εκαθητο D 700 |⌐επεκαθησεν H 118 1071 |⌐εκαθησεν K Θ |⌐επεκαθησαν L 579 |⌐εκαθισεν N Y Π Σ 1241 |⌐εκαθεισεν W |⌐επεκαθισε 69

21:34 ⌜ηγγισεν rell |⌜ηγγεισαν W |⌜ηγγησεν Θ

22:14 ⌜ολιγοι rell |⌜ολειγοι W

23:14 om. verse ℵ B D L Θ pler NA²⁸ |⌜κατεσθιετε rell |⌜καταισθειεται W |⌜κατεσθιεται 13 579

23:15 ⌜υποκριται rell |⌜υποκρειται W |⌜οιποκριται 579

24:33 ⌜ιδητε rell |⌜ειδηται W |⌜ιδηται Θ |⌜ηδητε 1424

25:22 (ιδου D 2145 it^pler vg^pler VSS rell), 25 (ειδου D VSS pler |ο δε 1515); 26:65 (ιδου Θ 157)   ⌜ιδε rell |⌜ειδε W

25:23 ⌜ολιγα rell |⌜οληγα L |⌜ολειγα W

25:26 οτι ᵀ θεριζω rell |ᵀεγω ανθρωπος αυστηρος ειμει W (sy^p (1 MS) sah^(1 MS))

26:67 ⌜εραπισαν^T rell |⌜εραπεισαν αυτον D |⌜εριπισαν W |⌜εραππισαν αυτον Φ|⌜ερραπισαν 𝔐 f^1.13 1582 22 543 33 565 700 892 al. |⌜εραπιζον 157 |ᵀαυτον G f¹ 579 700 1071 1241 1295 1582 1604 2145 f ff¹ g^1(2) i q aur vg (pler)

27:1 ⌜πρωιας rell |⌜πρωειας W |⌜προιας 2

27:2 ⌜ηγεμονι rell |⌜ηγεμονει W |⌜ηγεμωνη 124 788 |⌜ηγεμωνι 1424

5. οι > υ

7:7 ⌜ανοιγησεται rell |⌜ανυγησεται W |⌜ααγισεται 2

6. Singular Readings with Non-singular Orthographic Exchanges

5:44 εχθρους υμων ᵀ ℵ B 1 1582* NA²⁸ |ᵀευλογειτε (rell) |ᵀευλογητε L Θ 2* |ᵀευλογειται W |ᵀευλογιτε 2ᶜ |ευλογιται 1071

6:31 ⌈μεριμνησητε rell |⌈μεριμνησειτε Lᶜ |⌈μεριμνησηται W |⌈μερημνησητε Δ |⌈μεριμνισηται Θ |⌈μεριμνησετε 118 209

7:6 ⌈βαλητε rell |⌈βαλειτε E |⌈βαλλετε L |⌈βαληται W |⌈βαλεται 2* |⌈om. 13 |⌈βαλλητε 473 |⌈βαλετε 1424

9:4 ⌈ενθυμεισθε rell |⌈ενθυμεισθαι D 13 33 157 1071 |⌈ενθυμισθε ℵ |⌈ενθυμισθαι W

10:14 ⌈εκτιναξατε rell |⌈εκτειναξατε D G L Δ 13 28 33 565 788 |⌈εκτιναξαται W |⌈εκτιναξα Y* |⌈εκτηναξατε Θ 2 |⌈εκτειναξατε 124 1071 1346 |⌈εκτειναξαται 1424

10:19² ⌈λαλησητε rell |⌈λαλησετε E S U Π Ω 157ᶜ 700 1071 1582ᶜ |⌈λαλησεται M 579 |⌈λαλησηται W |⌈λαλησιτε Δ

10:27 ⌈κηρυξατε rell |⌈κηρυσσεται D Θ |⌈καιρυξητε E* |⌈κηρυθησετε L |⌈κηρυξαται W

18:3 ⌈γενησθε rell |⌈γενεσθε L |⌈γενεσθαι W |⌈γηνεσθαι 13 2* |⌈γενησεσθαι 579

20:19 ⌈εμπαιξαι rell |⌈εμπεξε ℵ |⌈εμπεξαι C Δ 2* 28 33 565 1071 |⌈ενπαιξαι D E |⌈ενπεξαι W

23:13 ⌈κλειετε rell |⌈κλιετε ℵ |⌈κλιεται D L 2 13 |⌈κλιεται W |⌈κλιεσται Θ

23:31 ⌈μαρτυρειτε rell |⌈μαρτυριτε ℵ Θ |⌈μαρτυρειται C |⌈μαρτυριται W |⌈μαρτυρητε 579

23:39 ⌜ιδητε rell ⌜ειδητε C M Δ ⌜ιδετε E 2ᶜ ⌜ιδηται W ⌜ιδεται 2* ⌜ιδειτε 13

24:42 ⌜γρηγορειτε rell ⌜γρηγορηται L* ⌜γρηγορειται Lᶜ Δ 579 1071 ⌜γρηγοριται W ⌜γρηγοριτε Θ

26:36 ⌜Γεθσημανι ℵ L U Π Ω 33 124 NA²⁸ ⌜Γεσσημανει 𝔓⁴⁵ 𝔐 Δ ⌜Γεθσημανει A B C pc ⌜Γεθσαμανει D ⌜Γεδσημανι W ⌜Γεθσσημανει K ⌜Γεθσημανη M* 1582ᶜ 118 2 157 1071 ⌜Γηθσημανη Mᶜ² ⌜Γηθσημανι Θ ⌜Γεθσεμανι Σ ⌜Γεσσημανι E G* H V Ω 124 461 pc ⌜Γεσσιμανι 124 ⌜Γετσημανει 565 ⌜Γευδσημανι 579 ⌜Γεθσιμανη 700 1424

27:12 ⌜κατηγορεισθαι rell ⌜κατηγορισθε ℵ ⌜κατηγορισθαι W ⌜κατεγορεισθε Θ ⌜κατηγορεισθε 1346

APPENDIX 17
SINGULAR OMISSIONS (-) AND ADDITIONS (+) OF WORDS

Table A17.1 Codex Sinaiticus[1]

-13	24:35
-9	9:15
-8	10:39
-6	5:45; 13:39
-5	28:2–3
-4	7:27b; 19:18; 21:30
-3	12:46; 13:44; 14:23; 18:12; 24:10b
-2	10:9; 19:26; **24:37**; 27:48; 28:5a
-1	1:21; 1:23; 2:2; 4:23a; 6:9; 8:3; 8:15b; 9:9; 9:28a; 9:30; 9:35a; 9:35b; 12:11; 12:37; 12:44; 18:20; 19:10; 20:7; 20:19; 21:19; 22:1; 22:15; 22:32a; 22:32b; 22:42; 23:11; **25:22**; 26:33; 27:11; 27:33; 27:53a; 27:53b; 28:10
+/-0	1:14^1; 1:14^2; 1:18; 2:9; 3:15; 4:8; 4:12; 4:18; 4:24a; 4:24b; 5:33; 5:39; 5:41; 6:6; 6:14; 7:21; 7:25; 7:27a; 7:28; 8:15a; 8:26; 8:28; 9:6; 9:12; 9:20; 9:27; 9:28b; 10:21; 10:40; 11:23; 12:22; 12:33; 12:34; 12:49; 13:25; 13:28; 13:54; 14:1; 14:7; 14:17; 15:12; **16:13**; **16:17**; **16:19**^{1}; **17:8**; **17:10**; **17:17**; **18:3**; **18:8**; 18:18; 18:19; 18:30a; 18:30b; 19:15; 19:21; 20:13; 20:14a; 20:14b; 20:31b; 20:34; 21:7a; 21:25; 21:39; 21:42; 21:43; 22:9; 22:16; 22:21; 22:30; 23:34; 23:37; 24:10a; 24:15; 24:17; 24:22; 24:24; 24:28; **24:49**; **25:16**; **25:36**; **25:44a**; **25:44b**; 26:15a; 26:15b; 26:21; 26:44; 26:46; 26:65; 27:15; 27:23; 27:54a; 27:56ab; 27:64; 28:5b; 28:7; 28:12; 28:13
+1	4:23b; 6:16a; 6:16b; 6:28; 7:22; 7:26; 10:4; 11:19; 14:29; 15:11; 18:31; 20:18; 20:31a; 21:7b; 21:34–35; 23:4; 23:16; **24:39**; 27:3; 27:16; 27:24; 27:54b
+2	8:7; 15:5; 19:1

---

[1] Codex Sinaiticus: In this table, the citations in bold signify omissions/additions in the work of scribe D of Sinaiticus, otherwise, all citations refer to the work of scribe A of Sinaiticus.

Table A17.2 Codex Vaticanus

-2	10:14; 13:17; 26:3
-1	5:16; 12:48; 14:13; 16:17; 19:17; 20:32; 22:39
+/-0	1:12a; 1:12b; 1:13; 3:4; 3:12; 4:21; 5:10; 5:11; 5:28; 6:19; 6:32; 6:33; 7:16; 7:25; 8:32; 9:3; 9:28; 10:16; 10:19; 10:22; 10:25a; 10:25b; 11:2; 11:4; 11:7; 11:11; 11:12; 11:13; 11:18; 12:1a; 12:1b; 12:33; 13:14; 13:15; 13:24; 13:30^2; 13:39; 13:48; 14:3; 14:4; 14:8; 14:10; 15:11; 15:15; 15:32; 16:4; 17:16; 17:23; 18:9; 18:31; 19:12; 20:13; 20:17; 20:27; 21:17; 21:26; 21:32; 21:33; 21:38a; 21:38b; 21:41; 21:46; 22:43; 23:23; 23:25; 25:6; 25:10; 25:32; 26:14; 26:51; 26:53a, 26:53b; 26:59; 26:63; 27:1; 27:13; 27:45; 28:2–3; 28:11
+1	12:32a; 12:32b; 17:15
+4	2:13
+5	21:4
+6	26:57

Table A17.3 Codex Ephraemi

-4	13:3–4
-2	12:22; 15:30
-1	12:48; 13:15; 13:57; 15:36; 21:17b
+/-0	1:8^1; 1:8^2; 2:16; 3:10; 4:2; 4:14; 4:21a; 4:21b; 7:9; 7:16; 7:22; 8:5; 8:13; 8:17; 8:21; 8:31; 8:32; 9:2; 9:15; 9:30; 10:20; 11:21; 12:4; 12:6; 12:7; 13:44; 14:4; 15:2; 15:11; 15:32; 16:3; 16:12; 16:22; 17:4; 17:15; 19:1; 20:19; 20:32; 21:17a; 21:23; 21:28a; 21:28b; 22:10a; 22:10b; 23:24; 23:26; 24:3b; 24:4; 24:45; 25:6; 26:50; 26:51; 26:57; 26:67; 27:49; 27:58; 27:64
+1	2:20; 5:10; 12:47; 21:1; 22:20; 26:39; 26:65; 27:56
+2	20:11
+3	24:3a

Table A17.4 Codex Bezae

-15	15:37–38
-5	15:32b
-3	14:8; 22:24
-2	12:20a
-1	2:3; 4:16b; 5:3; 5:25a; 5:48; 6:18a; 6:18c; 9:33; 10:13^2; 10:35; 12:1a; 13:16; 13:25; 14:31; 16:23; 19:28b; 21:13; 21:22; 23:16; 24:21; 26:1–2; 27:46; 27:56; 27:61a; 28:1; 28:16
+/-0	2:1; 2:6; 2:8a; 2:8b; 2:8c; 2:9; 2:11; 2:16a; 2:16b; 2:22; 3:2; 3:4; 4:6a; 4:6b; 4:7; 4:13; 4:15; 4:16a; 4:17; 4:18; 4:24; 5:10; 5:12; 5:18; 5:22; 5:24; 5:25b; 5:25c; 5:29; 5:36; 5:40; 5:41; 6:7; 6:12; 6:18b; 6:20; 9:2; 9:10; 9:20; 9:36; 10:8; 10:10; 10:16; 10:25; 10:28; 10:34^2; 10:36; 11:3; 11:8; 11:10; 11:12; 11:20; 11:21; 11:22; 11:24a; 11:24b; 11:25; 11:26; 12:1b; 12:1c; 12:4a; 12:4b; 12:13; 12:18b; 12:19; 12:20b; 12:20c; 12:26; 12:28; 12:34; 12:36; 12:39; 12:40; 12:41a; 12:41b; 12:41c; 12:43; 13:1a; 13:1b; 13:22; 13:30; 13:34; 13:38^1; 13:41; 13:44a; 13:46; 13:48a; 13:49a; 13:49b; 13:52; 14:6; 14:14; 14:24; 14:25; 14:27; 15:1; 15:3; 15:14b; 15:16; 15:22a; 15:27a; 15:27b; 15:29; 15:32a; 15:35; 15:37–38; 15:37; 15:39a; 16:3; 16:4; 16:16; 16:22; 17:2; 17:5; 17:8; 17:18; 17:20; 17:24^1; 18:6; 18:14; 18:15a; 18:15b; 18:19a; 18:22; 18:25; 18:27; 18:28; 19:4; 19:6; 19:10; 19:12; 19:20; 19:26; 19:28a; 19:29; 20:3; 20:10; 20:15; 21:9^1; 21:9^2; 21:15; 21:21; 21:28; 21:29; 21:31; 21:36; 21:39; 21:46; 22:12; 22:44; 23:13; 23:17; 23:33; 23:39; 24:9; 24:12; 24:15; 24:19; 24:30b; 24:33; 24:38; 25:22; 25:28; 25:29; 25:32a; 25:32b; 25:38; 26:1; 26:6; 26:12; 26:13; 26:15; 26:16; 26:18; 26:23a; 26:23b; 26:26; 26:45; 26:53; 26:55; 26:70; 27:1; 27:13; 27:27; 27:29; 27:30; 27:34^1; 27:34^2; 27:41; 27:44; 27:48; 27:53; 27:54; 27:59; 27:60; 27:61b; 27:64; 28:2
+1	10:15; 11:11a; 11:11b; 11:16; 12:12; 12:18a; 12:23; 12:42; 12:45; 13:1c; 13:6; 13:48b; 15:14a; 15:39b; 18:19b; 21:3; 23:6; 24:30a; 27:15; 27:16
+2	13:38a; 15:22b; 23:3

Table A17.5 Codex Washingtonianus

-8	16:2b–3
-3	8:28; 21:8
-2	2:17; 18:4
-1	6:7; 7:17; 17:8; 17:24; 19:9b; 21:32a
+/-0	1:9; 2:6; 2:16; 3:5^2; 3:6; 3:12; 5:22^2; 5:44; 7:8; 8:16; 9:6; 9:15; 9:20; 10:5; 10:40; 11:17a; 11:17b; 11:27^1; 11:27^2; 12:4; 12:12; 12:27; 12:33^1; 12:50; 13:2; 13:38; 13:46; 14:3; 14:25; 14:32; 14:35; 14:36; 16:3a; 16:3b; 16:9; 16:24; 16:27; 18:15; 18:27; 18:34; 19:1; 19:8; 19:9a; 20:1; 20:12; 20:15; 20:29; 20:33; 21:18; 21:23; 21:26; 21:30; 21:32b; 21:32c; 21:41a; 21:41b; 22:7; 23:8; 23:14; 23:37; 24:9; 24:11; 24:15; 24:18; 24:32a; 24:32b; 24:39; 24:49; 25:19; 25:34; 25:46; 26:1; 26:3; 26:14; 26:15; 26:18; 26:19; 26:41; 26:65; 26:67; 26:72; 27:4; 27:39; 27:41; 27:44; 27:46; 27:47; 27:51; 27:55; 27:58; 27:61; 28:11
+1	12:20; 13:20; 13:41; 23:25
+2	6:30; 8:29; 14:30; 17:25
+3	12:15–16

Bibliography

Aland, Kurt, Barbara Aland, Klaus Wachtel, and Klaus Witte, eds. *Text und Textwerk der Griechischen Handschriften des Neuen Testaments IV: Die Synoptischen Evangelien, 2: Das Matthäusevangelium, Bd. 2.2: Resultate der Kollation und Hauptliste sowie Ergänzungen.* Berlin: de Gruyter, 1999.

Anderson, Amy S. *The Textual Tradition of the Gospels: Family 1 in Matthew.* NTTS 32. Leiden: Brill, 2004.

(BHS) *Biblia Hebraica Stuttgartensia.* Edited by K. Elliger and W. Rudolph. Stuttgart: Deutsche Bibelgesellschaft, 1997.

Black, Matthew. *An Aramaic approach to the Gospels and Acts.* 2nd ed. Oxford: Clarendon, 1954.

(BDF) Blass, Friedrich, Albert Debrunner, and Robert W. Funk. *A Greek Grammar of the New Testament and Other Early Christian Literature.* Chicago: The University of Chicago Press, 1961.

British Library, Leipzig University Library, St Catherine's Monastery at Sinai, and the National Library of Russia. "Electronic Version of Codex Sinaiticus." http://www.codexsinaiticus.org/en/ manuscript.aspx.

Callan, Terrance. "Reading the Earliest Copies of 2 Peter." *Bib* 93.3 (2012): 427–50.

Clark, Albert C. *The Acts of the Apostles: A Critical Edition with Introduction and Notes on Selected Passages.* Oxford: Clarendon, 1970.

Colwell, Ernest C. "Method in Evaluating Scribal Habits: A Study of P^{45}, P^{66}, P^{75}." Pages 106–24 in *Studies in Methodology in Textual Criticism of the New Testament.* By Ernest C. Colwell. NTTS IX. Leiden: Brill, 1969.

———. "Scribal Habits in Early Papyri: A Study in the Corruption of the Text." Pages 370–89 in *The Bible in Modern Scholarship.* Edited by J. Philip Hyatt. Nashville: Abingdon, 1965.

Cranfield, C. E. B. *The Gospel According to Mark.* CGTC. Cambridge: Cambridge University Press, 2005.

(BDAG) Danker, Frederick William, Walter Bauer, William F. Arndt, and F. Wilbur Gingrich. *Greek-English Lexicon of the New Testament and Other Early Christian Literature.* 3rd ed. Chicago: The University of Chicago Press, 2000.

Davies, W. D. and Dale C. Allison. *A Critical and Exegetical Commentary on the Gospel According to Saint Matthew.* ICC. Edinburgh: T&T Clark, 1988–1997.

Epp, Eldon Jay. *The Theological Tendency of Codex Bezae Cantabrigiensis in Acts.* SNTSMS 3. Cambridge: Cambridge University Press, 1966.

Finegan, Jack. *Encountering New Testament Manuscripts: A Working Introduction to Textual Criticism.* London: SPCK, 1975.

France, R. T. *The Gospel of Matthew.* NICNT. Grand Rapids: Eerdmans, 2007.

Foster, Paul. *Community, Law and Mission in Matthew's Gospel.* WUNT 2, 177. Tübingen: Mohr Siebeck, 2004.

Funk, Robert W. *A Beginning-Intermediate Grammar of Hellenistic Greek.* SBLSBS 2. Missoula, MT: Scholars Press, 1973.

Gamble, Harry Y. "Codex Sinaiticus in Its Fourth Century Setting." Pages 3–18 in *Codex Sinaiticus: New Perspectives on the Ancient Biblical Manuscript.* Edited by Scot McKendrick, David Parker, Amy Myshrall, and Cillian O'Hogan. London: The British Library, 2015.

Geerlings, Jacob. *Family 13—The Ferrar Group: The Text According to Matthew.* SD 19. Salt Lake City: University of Utah Press, 1961.

Gignac, Francis Thomas. *Grammar of the Greek Papyri of the Roman and Byzantine Periods*, vol. 1 Phonology. Testi e Documenti per lo Studio Dell'antichità 55. Milan: Instituto Editoriale Cisalpino-La Goliardica, 1976.

Goodwin, William W. *A Greek Grammar.* Surrey, UK: Thomas Nelson, 1992.

Gundry, Robert H. *Matthew: A Commentary on His Literary and Theological Art.* Grand Rapids: Eerdmans, 1982.

Hagner, Donald A. *Matthew.* 2 vols. WBC 33a–33b. Dallas: Word, 1995.

Haugh, Dennis. "Was Codex Washingtonianus a Copy or a New Text?" Pages 167–84 in *The Freer Biblical Manuscripts: Fresh Studies of an American Treasure Trove*. Edited by Larry Hurtado. TCSt 6. Atlanta: SBL Press, 2006.
Harris, J. Rendel. *Stichometry*. London: Clay, 1893.
Head, Peter M. "The Gospel of Mark in Codex Sinaiticus: Textual and Reception-Historical Considerations." *TC* 13 (2008). http://rosetta.reltech.org/TC/v13/Head2008.pdf.
_____. "The Habits of New Testament Copyists: Singular Readings in the Early Fragmentary Papyri of John." *Bib* 85.3 (2004): 399–408.
_____. "Observations on Early Papyri of the Synoptic Gospels, especially on the 'Scribal Habits.'" *Bib* 71. 2 (1990): 240–47.
Hernández, Juan, Jr. *Scribal Habits and Theological Influences in the Apocalypse: The Singular readings of Sinaiticus, Alexandrinus, and Ephraemi*. WUNT 2, 218. Tübingen: Mohr Siebeck, 2006.
_____. "A Scribal Solution to a Problematic Measurement in the Apocalypse." *JSNT* 56.2 (2010): 273–78.
Holmes, Michael W. "Early Editorial Activity and the Text of Codex Bezae in Matthew." Ph.D. diss., Princeton Theological Seminary, 1984.
Hort, Fenton John Anthony. *The New Testament in the Original Greek: Introduction and Appendix*. Cambridge: Macmillan, 1881.
Hoskier, H. C. *Codex B and its Allies: Part I, A Study and an Indictment*. London: Bernard Quaritch, 1914.
Hurtado, Larry W. *Text-Critical Methodology and the Pre-Caesarean Text: Codex W in the Gospel of Mark*. SD 43. Grand Rapids: Eerdmans, 1981.
Institut für Neutestamentliche Textforschung. "New Testament Transcripts Prototype." http://nttranscripts.uni-muenster.de/.
_____. "Virtual Manuscript Room." http://ntvmr.uni-muenster.de/home.
Jongkind, Dirk. *Scribal Habits of Codex Sinaiticus*. TS 3rd series, ed. D. C. Parker and D. G. K. Taylor, vol. 5. Piscataway, NJ: Gorgias, 2007.
Jülicher, Adolf, ed. *Itala das Neue Testament in Altlateinischer Überlieferung: 1, Matthäus-Evangelium*. Berlin: de Gruyter, 1938.

(*Liste*) *Kurzgefasste Liste des Griechischen Handschriften des Neuen Testaments*. Rev. and enl. ed. Edited by Kurt Aland. ANTF 1. Berlin: Walter de Gruyter, 1994.

Lake, Kirsopp. *Codex 1 of the Gospel and its Allies*. TS: Contributions to Biblical and Patristic Literature, ed. J. Armitage Robinson, vol. 7 no. 3. Cambridge: Cambridge University Press, 1902.

Legg, S.C.E., ed. *Nouum Testamentum Graece: Secundum Textum Westcotto-Hortianum, Euangelium Secundum Matthaeum*. Oxford: Clarendon, 1940.

(Liddell-Scott) Liddell, Henry George and Robert Scott. *A Greek-English Lexicon*. New ed. Henry Stuart Jones and Roderick McKenzie. Oxford: Clarendon, 1966.

Luz, Ulrich. *Matthew*. 3 vols. Vol. 1 translated by Wilhelm C. Linss. CC. Minneapolis: Fortress, 1992. Vols. 2–3 translated by James E. Crouch. Edited by Helmut Koester. Hermeneia. Minneapolis: Fortress, 2001–2005.

Lyon, Robert W. "A Re-Examination of Codex Ephraemi Rescriptus." Ph.D. diss., The University of St. Andrews, 1958.

Martini, Carlo M. *Novum Testamentum e Codice Vaticano Graeco 1209 (Codex B)*. Vatican City: Bibliotheca Apostolica Vaticana, 1968.

McNeile, Alan Hugh. *The Gospel According to St. Matthew: The Greek Text with Introduction, Notes, and Indices*. Grand Rapids: Baker, 1980.

Metzger, Bruce M. *Manuscripts of the Greek Bible: An Introduction to Greek Palaeography*. New York: Oxford University Press, 1981.

————. *A Textual Commentary on the Greek New Testament*, 2nd ed. Stuttgart: Deutsche Bibelgesellschaft, 2002.

Metzger, Bruce M. and Bart D. Ehrman. *The Text of the New Testament: Its Transmission, Corruption, and Restoration*, 4th ed. New York: Oxford University Press, 2005.

Milne, H. J. M. and T. C. Skeat. *Scribes and Correctors of the Codex Sinaiticus*. Oxford: Oxford University Press, 1938.

Min, Kyoung Shik. *Die Früheste Überlieferung des Matthäus-evangeliums (bis zum 3./4. Jh.)*. ANTF 34. Berlin: de Gruyter, 2005.

Montefiore, C. G. *The Synoptic Gospels, edited with an Introduction and a Commentary*. London: Macmillan, 1909.
(Moulton-Milligan) Moulton, James Hope and George Milligan. *The Vocabulary of the Greek Testament: Illustrated from the Papyri and Other Non-Literary Sources*. Grand Rapids: Eerdmans, 1930.
Mounce, William D. *The Morphology of Biblical Greek*. Grand Rapids: Zondervan, 1994.
Myshrall, Amy. "The Presence of a Fourth Scribe?" Pages 139–48 in *Codex Sinaiticus: New Perspectives on the Ancient Biblical Manuscript*. Edited by Scot McKendrick, David Parker, Amy Myshrall, and Cillian O'Hogan. London: The British Library, 2015.
Nolland, John. *The Gospel of Matthew*. NIGTC. Grand Rapids: Eerdmans, 2005.
(NA^{27}) *Novum Testamentum Graece*. 27th ed. Edited by Barbara and Kurt Aland, Johannes Karavidopoulos, Carlo M. Martini, Bruce M. Metzger. Stuttgart: Deutsche Bibelgesellschaft, 2001.
(NA^{28}) *Nestle-Aland Novum Testamentum Graece*. 28th ed. Edited by Barbara and Kurt Aland, Johannes Karavidopoulos, Carlo M. Martini, Bruce M. Metzger, revised by Luc Herren, Marie-Luise Lakmann, Beate von Tschischwitz, and Klaus Wachtel, under the direction of Holger Strutwolf. Stuttgart: Deutsche Bibelgesellschaft, 2012.
Novum Testamentum Graecum Editio Critica Maior: Parallel Pericopes. Edited by Holger Strutwolf and Klaus Wachtel. Stuttgart: Deutsche Bibelgesellschaft, 2011.
Novum Testamentum Graecum Editio Critica Maior. Edited by the Institute for New Testament Textual Research, IV Catholic Letters, ed. Barbara Aland, Kurt Aland, Gerd Mink, and Klaus Wachtel (and Holger Strutwolf for Installment 4), Installment 1: James, Installment 2: The Letters of Peter, Installment 3: The First Letter of John, Installment 4: The Second and Third Letter of John and the Letter of Jude. Stuttgart: Deutsche Bibelgesellschaft, 1997, 2000, 2003, 2005.
Parker, David C. *Codex Bezae: An Early Christian Manuscript and its*

Text. Cambridge: Cambridge University Press, 1992.

(PG) *Patrologia Graeca*. Edited by J.-P. Migne. 162 vols. Paris, 1857-1886.

Pisano, Stephen. "The Text of the New Testament." Pages 27–41 in *Prolegomena: Exemplum Quam Simillime Phototypice Expressum Codicis Vaticani B (Vat. Gr. 1209) Praestantis Humanitatis Operis Rei Publicae Italicae Officina Typographica et Argentaria Sumptibus Suis Comparauit*. Vatican City: La Biblioteca Apostolica Vaticana e L'Instituto Poligrafico e Zecca Dello Stato, 1999.

Porter, Calvin L. "Papyrus Bodmer XV (P75) and the Text of Codex Vaticanus." *JBL* 81.4 (1962): 363–76.

Rahlfs, Alfred, ed. *Septuaginta: Id est Vetus Testamentum graece iuxta LXX interpretes*. Duo volumina in uno. Stuttgart: Deutsche Bibelgesellschaft, 1979.

Read-Heimerdinger, Jenny. *The Bezan Text of Acts: A Contribution of Discourse Analysis to Textual Criticism*. JSNTSup 236. London: Sheffield Academic, 2002.

Reinmuth, Eckart, ed. *Joseph und Aseneth*. SAPERE XV. Tübingen: Mohr Siebeck, 2009.

Robertson, A.T. *A Grammar of the Greek New Testament in the Light of Historical Research*. Nashville: Broadman, 1934.

Ropes, J.H. *The Text of Acts*. Vol. 3 of *The Beginning of Christianity*. Edited by F.J. Foakes Jackson and Kirsopp Lake, part 1. London: Macmillan, 1926.

Royse, James R. "The Corrections in the Freer Gospels Codex." Pages 185–226 in *The Freer Biblical Manuscripts: Fresh Studies of an American Treasure Trove*. Edited by Larry Hurtado. TCSt 6. Atlanta: SBL Press, 2006.

_____. "Scribal Habits in Early Greek New Testament Papyri." Th.D. diss., Graduate Theological Union, 1981.

_____. *Scribal Habits in Early Greek New Testament Papyri*. NTTSD 36. Leiden: Brill, 2008.

Sanders, Henry A. *Facsimile of the Washington Manuscript of the Four Gospels in the Freer Collection*. Ann Arbor: University of Michigan, 1912.

———. *The New Testament Manuscripts in the Freer Collection, Part I: The Washington Manuscript of the Four Gospels*. University of Michigan Studies, Humanistic Series 9/1. New York: Macmillan, 1912.

Schmid, Ulrich. "Reassessing the Palaeography and Codicology of the Freer Gospel Manuscript." Pages 227–51 in *The Freer Biblical Manuscripts: Fresh Studies of an American Treasure Trove*. Edited by Larry Hurtado. TCSt 6. Atlanta: SBL Press, 2006.

Schnackenburg, Rudolph. *The Gospel of Matthew*. Translated by Robert R. Barr. Grand Rapids: Eerdmans, 2002.

Scrivener, Frederick H. *Bezae Codex Cantabrigiensis: Being an Exact Copy, in Ordinary Type, of the Celebrated Uncial Graeco-Latin Manuscript of the Four Gospels and Acts of the Apostles, Written Early in the Sixth Century, and Presented to the University of Cambridge by Theodore Bezae, A.D. 1581. Edited with a Critical Introduction, Annotations, and Facsimiles*. Cambridge: Deighton, Bell, and Co., 1864.

Strutwolf, Holger. "Scribal Practices and the Transmission of Biblical Texts: New Insights from the Coherence-Based Genealogical Method." Pages 139–60 in *Editing the Bible: Assessing the Task Past and Present*. Edited by John S. Kloppenborg and Judith H. Newman. RBS 69. Atlanta: SBL Press, 2012.

Swanson, Reuben, ed. *Matthew*. Vol. 1 of *New Testament Greek Manuscripts: Variant Readings Arranged in Horizontal Lines Against Codex Vaticanus*. Sheffield: Sheffield Academic, 1995.

(TDNT) *Theological Dictionary of the New Testament*. Edited by Gehard Kittel and Gerhard Friedrich. Translated by Geoffrey W. Bromiley. 10 vols. Grand Rapids: Eerdmans, 1964–1976.

(TLG) *Thesaurus Linguae Graecae*. Edited by Maria C. Pantelia. University of California, Irvine. http://www.tlg.uci.edu.

Tischendorf, Constantine, ed. *Codex Ephraemi Syri Rescriptus sive Fragmenta Novi Testamenti e Codice Graeco Parisiensi Celeberrimo Quinti ut Videtur Post Christum Seculi*. Leipzig: Bernh. Tauchnitz, 1843.

---. *Novum Testamentum Graece*. 8th ed. Lipsiae: Giesecke & Devrient, 1869.

---. *Vetus Testamentum Graece*. Lipsaie: F.A. Brockhaus, 1869.

Turner, Nigel G. *Syntax*. Vol. 3 of A Grammar of New Testament Greek. By James Hope Moulton. Edinburgh: T&T Clark, 1963.

Urbán, Ángel. "Bezae Codex Cantabrigiensis (D): Intercambios Vocálicos en el Texto Griego de Marcos." *CCO* 4 (2007): 245–68.

Van Aarde, Andries G. "ΙΗΣΟΥΣ, the Davidic Messiah, as Political Saviour in Matthew's History." Pages 7–31 in *Salvation in the New Testament: Perspectives on Soteriology*. Edited by Jan G. van der Watt. NovTSup 121. Leiden: Brill, 2005.

Voelz, James W. "The Greek of Codex Vaticanus in the Second Gospel and Marcan Greek." *NovT* 47.3 (2005): 209–49.

Vogels, Heinrich Joseph. "Die Harmonistik im Evangelientext des Codex Cantabrigiensis: Ein Beitrag zur Neutestamentlichen Textkritik." Pages 1–118 in TUGAL 6 no. 3. Edited by Adolf Harnack and Carl Schmidt. Leipzig: J.C. Hinrichs'sche Buchhandlung, 1913.

Von Soden, Hermann Freiherr. *Die Schriften des Neuen Testaments in Ihrer Ältesten Erreichbaren Textgestalt Hergestellt auf Grud Ihrer Textgeschichte. II. Teil: Text mit Apparat. Nebst Ergänzungen zu Teil I*. Göttingen: Vandenhoeck und Ruprecht, 1913.

Wallace, Daniel B. *Greek Grammar Beyond the Basics: An Exegetical Syntax of the New Testament*. Grand Rapids: Zondervan, 1996.

Wiarda, Timothy. *Peter in the Gospels: Pattern, Personality and Relationship*. WUNT 2, 127. Edited by Martin Hengel and Otfried Hofius. Tübingen: Mohr Siebeck, 2000.

Zerwick, Maximilian. *Biblical Greek: Illustrated Examples*. English edition adapted from the fourth Latin edition by Joseph Smith, 2nd reprint. Scripta Pontificii Instituti Biblici 114. Roma: Editrice Pontificio Istituto Biblico, 1985.

---. *A Grammatical Analysis of the Greek New Testament*. 5th ed. Roma: Editrice Pontificio Istituto Biblico, 1996.

Ziegler, Joseph, ed. *Isaias*. Septuaginta Vetus Testamentum Graecum Auctoritate Societatis Litterarum Gottingensis. Vol. 14. Göttingen: Dandenhoed & Ruprecht, 1939.

Index of Modern Authors

Aland, Kurt 4–5
Anderson, Amy S. 9 n. 7
BDAG 27 n. 96, 30 n. 114, 31 n. 118, 34 n. 133, 37 nn. 144–5, 47 n. 16, 52 n. 44, 53 n. 50, 55 n. 59, 61 n. 11, 78 n. 27, 82 n. 61, 88 n. 108, 90 n. 120, 91 n. 133, 92 n. 137, 98 n. 162, 112 n. 50, 116 nn. 75–6, 117 n. 78
BDF 23 nn. 66 and 73, 27 nn. 97 and 98–100, 30 nn. 114 and 117, 34 nn. 132–3, 35 nn. 136 and 138, 41 n. 162, 51 n. 38, 53 nn. 47 and 50–1, 54 nn. 54 and 56, 55 n. 61, 75 n. 8, 86 nn. 95 and 97–9, 87 nn. 101–2 and 105, 94 n. 148, 99 n. 172, 100 n. 175, 108 n. 21, 114 nn. 59–62, 114 n. 63, 115 n. 64, 119 n. 91, 120 nn. 92 and 97
Black, Matthew 96 n. 57
Callan, Terrance 14 n. 6
Clark, Albert C. 92–3
Clark, Kenneth W. 4–5
Colwell, Ernest C. 1, 4, 8
Cranfield, C.E.B. 30 n. 114, 69, 94 n. 143

Davies, W.D. and Dale C. Allison 32 n. 121, 33 nn. 124 and 126–27, 35 nn. 139–140, 36 n. 143, 49 n. 28, 55 n. 59, 64 n. 27, 68 n. 56, 82 n. 60, 83 n. 66, 87 nn. 103 and 105, 95 n. 155, 96 n. 158, 96 n. 159, 98 n. 163, 100 n. 176–7, 116 nn. 75–76, 119 n. 86
ECM (*Editio Critica Maior*) 6–9
Epp, Eldon Jay 96 n. 159
Finegan, Jack 110 n. 37
France, R.T. 22 n. 65, 35 n. 139, 38 n. 137, 51 n. 37, 52 n. 44, 55 n. 59, 88 n. 111, 89 m. 118, 92 n. 139, 96 n. 159, 100 n. 176, 116 n. 76
Foster, Paul 22 n. 64
Funk, Robert W. 114 n. 63
Gamble, Harry Y. 31 n. 118
Geerlings, Jacob 9 n. 37
Gignac, Francis Thomas 15 nn. 9 and 12, 39 n. 150, 46 n. 5, 47 nn. 7–9 and 16, 61 n. 7, 75 nn. 6 and 9, 86 n. 96, 107, 108 n. 23, 115 n. 66
Goodwin, William W. 34 n. 133, 119 n. 90

Gundry, Robert H. 22 n. 65, 24 n. 75, 29 n. 112, 38 n. 147, 48 n. 23, 49 n. 24, 67 n. 53, 86 n. 95, 89 n. 118, 90 n. 123, 92 n. 139, 95 n. 155, 96 n. 159, 99 n. 167, 101 n. 179, 119 n. 86

Hagner, Donald 24 n. 75, 33 n. 129, 38 n. 147, 81 n. 59, 82 n. 63, 83 n. 64, 89 n. 114, 93 n. 141, 96 n. 159, 99 n. 173, 99 n. 173, 100 n. 177, 114 n. 62, 116 n. 76

Haugh, Dennis 105 n. 2, 122 n. 102, 122 n. 102

Harris, J. Rendel 30–1

Head, Peter M. 2, 3 n. 8, 8 n. 30, 41 n. 165, 114 n. 62

Hernández, Juan, Jr. 1–2, 5, 13 n. 3, 13 nn. 4 and 5, 15 n. 13, 25 n. 84, 42, 59 n. 4, 60, 62 n. 13, 64 n. 31, 66–7, 69 n. 60, 70, 100 n. 177, 130–2

Holmes, Michael W. 35 n. 140, 68 n. 55, 77 n. 18, 82 n. 62, 90 n. 26, 91 n. 128, 93 n. 142, 94 n. 147, 96 n. 157, 99 n. 166, 100 n. 177, 102

Hort, Fenton John Anthony 56–58

Hoskier, H.C. 5, 52 n. 42

Hurtado, Larry W. 8 n. 30, 105 n. 2, 111, 113, 115, 119 n. 87, 119–20, 122 n. 102, 132

Jongkind, Dirk 8 n. 30, 26, 39

Jülicher, Adolf 9 n. 37

Lake, Kirsopp 9 n. 37

Legg, S.C.E. 4–5, 8–9, 21 nn. 56–7, 110 n. 36

Liddell-Scott 29 n. 111, 30 n. 117, 47 n. 16, 82 n. 62, 86 n. 100, 95 n. 154, 98 nn. 161–2

Luz, Ulrich 22 nn. 64–5, 23 n. 73, 37 n. 145, 48 n. 23, 52 n. 44, 53 n. 49, 83 n. 66, 96 n. 159, 98 n. 165, 99 n. 172, 100 n. 76, 112 n. 45, 114 n. 62, 119 n. 88

Lyon, Robert W. 59 nn. 1 and 3, 62 nn. 12 and 14–17, 65 n. 39, 66 n. 44, 67 n. 50

Martini, Carlo M. 57 n. 69

McNeile, Alan Hugh 17 n. 29, 22 n. 64, 32 n. 120, 33 n. 126, 36 n. 142, 40 n. 156, 48 n. 123, 54 n. 53, 66 n. 47, 78 n. 26, 87 n. 105, 89 nn. 117–8, 96 n. 159, 100 n. 174, 118 n. 84

Metzger, Bruce M. 25 n. 81, 36 n. 142, 37 n. 144, 51 n. 37, 56, 95 n. 151, 109 n. 32, 118 n. 83, 121 n. 99

Metzger, Bruce M. and Bart D. Ehrman 74 n. 3
Milne, H.J.M. and T.C. Skeat 13 n. 1, 30–1, 39, 45 n. 1
Min, Kyoung Shik 2, 9 n. 37
Montefiore, C.G. 116 n. 76, 119 n. 90
Moulton-Milligan 47 n. 16, 53 n. 50, 76 n. 14, 83 n. 65, 86 n. 99–100, 98 n. 162, 114 n. 62, 116 n. 73
Mounce, William D. 97 n. 160
Myshrall, Amy 13 n. 1
NA^{25} 4–5
NA^{26} 4–5
NA^{27} 4–5, 8–10, 74 n. 4, 75 n. 5
NA^{28} 3, 8–9, 21 n. 56, 24 n. 74, 29 n. 112, 35 n. 137, 59 n. 2, 82 n. 62, 90 , 125, 94 n. 143, 109 n. 31, 117 n. 82
Nolland, John 22 n. 64, 24 nn. 75 and 78, 25 n. 83, 29 n. 113, 33 n. 126, 35 n. 140, 36 n. 142, 37 nn. 144–5, 38 n. 137, 48 n. 23, 49 n. 28, 51 n. 41, 52 n. 44, 89 n. 118, 96 n. 156, 96 n. 159
Parker, David C. 73 n. 1, 78 n. 28, 85, 90 n. 122, 96 n. 159, 101 nn. 180–1
PG (*Patrologia Graeca*) 108 n. 21
Pisano, Stephen 46 n. 4, 56 n. 65
Porter, Calvin L. 56 n. 65

Rahlfs, Alfred 10, 78 n. 23
Read-Heimerdinger, Jenny 85
Robertson, A.T. 15 n. 10
Ropes, J.H. 30–1
Royse, James R. 1, 2 n. 7, 4–8, 15 n. 13, 105 n. 2, 106 n. 7, 107 nn. 10–1, 108 n. 23, 109 nn. 28 and 33, 110 n. 34, 111 n. 38, 112 n. 49, 114 n. 61, 118 n. 85, 119 n. 88, 120 nn. 94 and 97
Sanders, Henry A. 9 n. 37, 105 nn. 1–3, 106 n. 8, 107 n. 14, 108 n. 25, 109 n. 33, 110, 111 n. 39, 115–6, 117 n. 82, 121 nn. 99–101
Schmid, Ulrich 105 n. 2
Schnackenburg, Rudolph
Scrivener, Frederick H. 33 n. 124
Strutwolf, Holger 6–7
Swanson, Reuben 5, 8–10, 20 n. 52, 21 n. 56, 47 n. 15, 49 n. 28, 50 n. 30, 53 n. 48, 73 n. 2, 101 n. 180
TDNT (*Theological Dictionary of the New Testament*) 98 n. 162
Text und Textwert 9, 13 n. 3, 45 n. 2, 59 n. 3, 73 n. 2, 105 n. 4

Tischendorf, Constantine 4–5, 8–9, 13 n. 1, 21 n. 56, 59 n. 3, 61 n. 11, 62 n. 14, 63 n. 21, 65 nn. 36 and 39, 66 n. 44, 78 n. 23

TLG (*Thesaurus Linguae Graecae*) 47 n. 16, 108 n. 25

Turner, Nigel G. 40 n. 156, 49 n. 28, 50 n. 31, 53 n. 49, 55 n. 61, 83 n. 68, 94 n. 148, 95 n. 150, 118 n. 84, 120 n. 92

Urbán, Ángel 74 n. 4, 75 n. 5

Van Aarde, Andries G. 37 n. 144

Voelz, James W. 46 n. 4, 53–4, 55 n. 62

Vogels, Heinrich Joseph 101 n. 181

Von Soden, Hermann Freiherr 4–5, 8–9

Wallace, Daniel B. 32 n. 123, 35 n. 140, 49 n. 28, 53 n. 48, 54 n. 53, 79 n. 37, 85 nn. 84 and 91, 112 n. 48

Wiarda, Timothy 118 n. 83

Zerwick, Maximilian 27 n. 92, 29 n. 113, 34 n. 133, 37 n. 146, 38 n. 137, 40 nn. 155–6, 53 n. 52, 54 n. 53, 62 n. 20, 68 n. 56, 79 nn. 37 and 39, 85 n. 84, 86 nn. 95 and 97, 98 n. 165, 114 nn. 60 and 63, 115 n. 64, 120 n. 92

Ziegler, Joseph 22 n. 65, 78 n. 23

Index of Subjects

Alexander of Aphrodisias 82 n. 62
Alexandrinus/02 3–4, 100 n. 177
Anaptyxis 75–76
Aramaic 40 n. 156, 95 n. 150, 96 n. 157
Archigenes 82 n. 62
Aretaeus 82 n. 62
Aristotle 87 n. 100
(A)syndeton/asyndetic 27, 95, 120, 122
Contraction, un-, non- 14 n. 4, 15, 16, 28 n. 104, 48 n. 22, 80 n. 40, 107 n. 14
Elders (in Matthew) 117 n. 79, 120
Elision 39, 107 n. 19
Epistle of Aristeas 78 n. 27
Eustathius 82 n. 62
Felix 29 n. 110
Hapax Legomenon 82 n. 60, 86 n. 100, 88 n. 108, 98 n. 162, 100 n. 174, 119 n. 86
Herod 21 n. 61, 29 n. 110, 31 n. 118, 86 n. 106, 94 n. 143, 100 n. 176
Herodotus 34 n. 133
Hesychius 82 n. 62
Homer 29 n. 111, 34 n. 133
INTF 3 n. 11
Israel 16, 84
Jacob 16 n. 17
John (disciple of Jesus) 46–47
John the Baptist 35 n. 138, 46–47, 100, 117 n. 79
Josephus 78 n. 27
Lectio Brevior Potior 7–8
Mary 21 n. 57, 32, 116 n. 72
Metathesis 31 n. 119, 76, 108
Metaplasm 34
NTTranscripts 9–10, 49 n. 28
Nomina Sacra/Nomen Sacrum 16 n. 17, 18 n. 32, 62 n. 17, 80 n. 40, 83 n. 67, 118 n. 85
Numeral 18 n. 34, 106 n. 5
Paul, Apostle 29 n. 110,
Pharisees 29 n. 110, 83 n. 64, 94 n. 147, 99 n. 166, 120, 122
P.Lond 951 86 n. 100
Plutarch 82 n. 62
P.Mich 123 47 n. 9
Pre-Harmonization 91 n. 127, 113 n. 53
Provenance 31 n. 118, 126
Q Source 87 n. 103
Scribes (in Matthew) 94 n. 147, 120 n. 98
VMR 9–10
Western Order of Gospels 126
Western Text 74, 101, 102, 103

Scripture Index

Septuagint/Old Testament

Genesis
1:27 94 n. 144
35:10 16 n. 17
46:28–1 Kings 19:11 45 n. 1

Exodus
3:6 28 n. 106
12:39 54 n. 57

Leviticus
19:18 22 n. 65
26:35 54 n. 56

Numbers
28:10 54 n. 56

Deuteronomy
6:16 98 n. 165
25:5 93 n. 142
32:35 22 n. 65

Joshua
15:63 54 n. 57
17:12 54 n. 57

Judges
1:19 54 n. 57
2:14 54 n. 57
14:14 54 n. 57

1 Kings
19:11–2 Esdras and Hosea–Daniel 45 n. 1

2 Kings
3:26 54 n. 57

1 Chronicles
23:31 54 n. 56

2 Chronicles
8:13 54 n. 56
30:3 54 n. 57

Ezra
2:59 54 n. 57

Nehemiah
7:61 54 n. 57

Job
32:3 54 n. 57

Psalms
Psalms–Tobit 45 n. 1
90:12 96 n. 160
117:22–23 37 n. 146
117:23 28 n. 106, 37 n. 146
118:26 83 n. 67
129:2 54 n. 57

Proverbs
20:22 22 n. 65
24:29 22 n. 65
25:21–22 22 n. 65

Isaiah
7:1 54 n. 57
7:12 98 n. 165
9:1 78 n. 23
9:2 78 n. 23
42:1–4 98 n. 163, 99 n. 169, 101 n. 178, 114 n. 60
50:8 22 n. 65

Ezekiel
45:17 54 n. 56
46:3 54 n. 56

Daniel
5:15 54 n. 57

Obadiah
7 54 n. 57

Zechariah
8:13 54 n. 56
11:4 82 n. 61
11:7 82 n. 61

Apocrypha and Pseudepigrapha of the Old Testament

Tobit
2:12 52 n. 44
2:13 52 n. 44

Susanna
1:60 46 n. 5

Sirach
28:1–7 22 n. 65

Joseph and Aseneth
4:7 15 n. 11

Scripture Index

New Testament

Matthew
1:1–2 59
1:1–16 55 n. 58
1:1–20 73
$1:8^1$ 61, 70 n. 62
$1:8^2$ 61, 70 n. 62
1:9 108
1:12–16 55 n. 58
1:12a 54–5, 57
1:12b 54–5, 57
1:13 54–5, 57
$1:14^1$ 15
$1:14^2$ 15
1:18 19
1:21 32, 32 n. 123
1:23 32, 88 n. 109
1:25 32 n. 123
2:1 87
2:2 34
2:3 100
2:6 75, 114
2:7 25 n. 85
2:8a 75
2:8b 81–2
2:8c 75
2:9 24 n. 74, 25, 79
2:10 34 n. 132
2:11 87–8
2:12 51 n. 39
2:13 51
2:16 62, 108
2:16a 75
2:16b 75
2:17 109–10
2:20 29 n. 110, 64, 64 n. 31, 65–6
2:21 73 n. 2
2:22 77
3:2 76
3:4 40 n. 156, 46–7, 87–8

3:5 100 n. 176
$3:5^2$ 106–7
3:6 106–7
3:7 23 n. 71, 76 n. 15
3:7–16 73
3:10 48 n. 23, 61
3:12 47, 107
3:15 35
3:17 91 n. 128
4:2 61–2, 64 n. 31, 70 n. 63
4:6a 80
4:6b 97–8
4:7 97–8
4:8 34–5
4:12 21–2
4:13 75
4:14 62, 70 n. 61
4:15 76
4:16a 77
4:16b 78
4:17 76
4:18 15, 77
4:21 22 n. 64, 46–7, 49 n. 28
4:21a 61
4:21b 61–2, 64 n. 31, 70 n. 63
4:22 22 n. 64
4:23 9 n. 35, 13 n. 3, 22 n. 64, 45 n. 1
4:23a 13 n. 3, 33
4:23b 22–3
4:24 81
4:24a 25
4:24b 20
5:3 84–5, 88 n. 109
5:3–12 66 n. 47
5:4 88 n. 109
5:5 88 n. 109
5:6 66 n. 47, 88 n. 109
5:7 88 n. 109

5:8 88 n. 109
5:9 88 n. 109
5:10 51 n. 37, 53–54, 66, 88–90
5:11 53–4, 73 n. 2
5:12 88–90
5:14 24 n. 74
5:15–7:5 59
5:16 48
5:18 81
5:20 51 n. 37
5:22 97–8
$5:22^2$ 107
5:23–24 88 n. 111
5:24 88–90
5:25–26 88 n. 111
5:25a 78
5:25b 86–7
5:25c 86–7
5:28 55
5:29 81
5:33 15
5:36 88–90
5:38 22 n. 65
5:39 22–3
5:40 86–7
5:41 14, 77, 107, 126 n. 1
5:44 107
5:45 17
5:48 84–5
6:6 15–6, 38
6:7 97–8, 120
6:8 55 n. 59
6:9 28
6:12 75
6:14 18, 25 n. 82
6:16a 27–8
6:16b 22–3
6:18a 84 n. 77, 84–5
6:18b 77
6:18c 84–5
6:19 46

6:20 80
6:20–9:2 73
6:28 25
6:30 113, 117, 127
6:32 55
6:33 9 n. 35, 45 n. 1, 50–1, 56, 128
7:8 112
7:9 61–2, 64 n. 31, 70 n. 63
7:16 47, 62, 70
7:17 48 n. 23, 109–10
7:18 48 n. 23
7:19 48 n. 23
7:21 34, 38
7:22 23–25, 64–5
7:25 23–25, 26, 55
7:25–9:28 57
7:26 19
7:27a 34–5
7:27b 16–7
7:28 21–2, 79 n. 37
7:29 22 n. 64
8:3 17, 35 n. 139
8:5 61, 70 n. 62
8:7 23–5
8:10 24 n. 78
8:13 64–5, 70 n. 61
8:15 35 n. 139
8:15a 34, 38
8:15b 27
8:16 106–7
8:17 64–5, 70 n. 61
8:21 62
8:26 19
8:28 15, 109–10
8:29 121, 121 n. 99, 128
8:31 61
8:32 55, 61
9:2 68, 70, 77, 88 n. 109, 107, 126 n. 1
9:2–8 29 n. 110

9:3 55
9:6 29, 29 n. 112, 110–1, 127
9:9 27, 49 n. 28
9:10 92
9:12 22–3
9:15 16–7, 61, 79–80, 116
9:18 35 n. 139
9:20 14, 77, 107
9:27 29–30, 29 n. 112, 49 n. 28
9:28 55
9:28a 28
9:28b 20
9:29 19 n. 41, 35 n. 139, 64 n. 27
9:30 19, 62
9:32 68 n. 55
9:33 68 n. 55, 84
9:34 68 n. 55
9:35 22 n. 64
9:35a 27
9:35b 33
9:36 75
10:3 59 n. 3, 73 n. 2
10:4 28, 56 n. 66
10:4a 73 n. 2
10:5 112
10:8 75
10:9 17
10:10 76
10:13^2 84–5
10:14 48
10:15 80
10:16 53–4, 83
10:17 22 n. 64
10:19 47
10:20 64–5
10:21 22–3, 26
10:22 46
10:23 73 n. 2
10:25 99

10:25a 53–4
10:25b 53–4
10:28 82
10:29 33 n. 128
10:32^1 76 n. 16
10:32^2 76 n. 16
10:33^1 76 n. 16
10:33^2 76 n. 16
10:34^2 79
10:35 84–5
10:36 76
10:39 17, 76
10:40 27, 115
10:41 49 n. 24
11:1 22 n. 64, 49 n. 28, 79 n. 37
11:2 46–7
11:3 88–90
11:4 46–7
11:7 46–7
11:8 75
11:10 76
11:11 46–7
11:11a 84–5
11:11b 84–5
11:12 46–7, 87
11:13 46–7
11:16 84–5
11:17a 115
11:17b 119
11:18 46–7
11:19 19
11:20 99
11:20–24 99 n. 172
11:21 61, 70 n. 62, 99
11:22 91–2, 91 n. 131
11:23 22–3
11:24a 80
11:24b 91–2
11:25 75
11:26 76
11:27^1 115

SCRIPTURE INDEX 339

11:27² 115
11:30 25 n. 81
12:1a 54, 84–5
12:1b 46, 81
12:1c 79
12:4 62, 70 n. 61, 114
12:4a 77
12:4b 81
12:6 35 n. 140, 62, 70
12:7 62, 70 n. 61
12:9 22 n. 64, 49 n. 28
12:11 27
12:12 54 n. 56, 84–5, 107
12:13 76
12:14 30 n. 114
12:15 49 n. 28
12:15–16 121, 121 n. 99, 128
12:18a 91
12:18b 97–8
12:19 77, 107, 126 n. 1
12:20 114
12:20a 100–1
12:20b 75, 98–9
12:20c 76
12:22 22–3, 26, 67–8
12:23 68 n. 55, 95
12:24 68 n. 55
12:25 89 n. 114
12:25–26 68 n. 55
12:26 88–90, 101 n. 181
12:27 101 n. 181, 111
12:28 88–90
12:32a 51, 56, 128
12:32b 53–54
12:33 15, 23 n. 71, 47, 48 n. 23
12:33–35 119 n. 90
12:33¹ 119
12:34 22–23, 76 n. 15, 88–90

12:36 9 n. 35, 33 n. 126, 73 n. 2, 97–8
12:37 33
12:38 94 n. 147
12:39 94–5
12:40 77
12:40⁴ 106 n. 5
12:41a 75
12:41b 75
12:41c 79
12:42 84
12:43 75
12:44 17
12:45 17 n. 29, 95
12:46 36, 67 n. 50, 78 n. 26, 128
12:47 36 n. 142, 65–6, 67 n. 50
12:48 36 n. 142, 52–3, 67
12:49 15
12:50 34 n. 131, 106–7
13:1 9 n. 35, 73 n. 2
13:1a 75
13:1b 75
13:1c 73 n. 2, 78
13:2 112–3
13:3–4 65–6
13:6 85
13:14 46
13:15 47, 65–6
13:16 84–5
13:17 48, 56 n. 66
13:20 112–3
13:22 80
13:24 55
13:25 15, 78, 101 n. 179
13:28 19
13:30 79
13:30² 48
13:31 101 n. 179
13:34 77
13:38 89 n. 118, 114

13:38a 80
13:38¹ 77, 80 n. 41
13:39 16–7, 50, 89 n. 118
13:40 89 n. 118
13:41 76, 119–20
13:44 18, 61, 70 n. 62
13:44a 87–8
13:44b 101
13:46 86, 108
13:47–48 89 n. 118
13:48 46
13:48a 88–90
13:48b 90
13:49a 88–90
13:49b 76, 90
13:52 76
13:53 49 n. 28, 79 n. 37
13:54 22 n. 64, 30–1
13:57 67–8
14:1 21–2
14:3 46–7, 108
14:4 46–7, 61
14:6 93–4
14:7 15
14:8 46–7, 100
14:10 46–7
14:11 100 n. 177
14:13 49
14:14 94
14:17 20
14:23 18
14:24 91–2
14:25 86, 116–7
14:27 75
14:29 36–37, 128
14:30 117–8
14:31 84
14:32 108
14:33 38 n. 147
14:35 115
14:36 116
15:1 75

15:2 62, 70 n. 61, 100 n. 174
15:3 37 n. 145, 99–100
15:5 36–37, 128
15:6 37 n. 145
15:11 23–5, 52, 61
15:12 34–5, 83 n. 64
15:13 83 n. 64
15:14a 82–3
15:14b 76
15:15 50–1
15:16 76
15:21 49 n. 28
15:22a 77
15:22b 90–1
15:26 91 n. 133
15:27a 82
15:27b 91–2
15:28 64 n. 27
15:29 49 n. 28, 79
15:30 65–6
15:32 47, 67, 127
15:32a 76
15:32b 93
15:35 76
15:36 65–6
15:37 76
15:37–38 101
15:39a 99
15:39b 84
16:1 98 n. 165
16:1–4 82 n. 63
16:2b–3 109–10
16:3 3 n. 9, 4 n. 14, 62, 82
16:3a 115
16:3b 119
16:4 55, 75
16:9 13, 116
16:12 61
16:13 39–40
16:16 96
16:17 9 n. 35, 39, 52–3
16:19[1] 40
16:19[2] 88 n. 109
16:21 34 n. 133, 81 n. 59
16:22 61–2, 70 n. 63, 81, 88 n. 109
16:23 95
16:24 119
16:27 106–7
17:1 47 n. 14
17:2 76
17:4 64–5
17:5 91 n. 128, 97–8
17:7 35 n. 139
17:8 39–40, 75, 119
17:10 39
17:15 51, 56 n. 66, 61
17:16 54
17:17 41
17:18 75
17:19 47 n. 14
17:20 66 n. 46, 77
17:21 3 n. 9, 4 n. 14
17:23 47
17:24 108
17:24[1] 76
17:25 118
17:26–18:28 59
18:3 39
18:4 35 n. 140, 109–10
18:6 76
18:8 39
18:9 47, 39 n. 153
18:11 3 n. 9, 4 n. 14
18:12 13, 31–2, 33 n. 128
18:14 34 n. 131, 76
18:15 112
18:15a 76
18:15b 75
18:18 15
18:19 20
18:19a 76
18:19b 84–5
18:20 18
18:21–22 89 n. 119
18:22 88–90
18:25 79
18:27 76, 108
18:28 40 n. 158, 81
18:29 40 n. 158
18:30a 27
18:30b 34–5
18:31 27, 40 n. 158, 50–1
18:33 40 n. 158
18:34 108
19:1 19, 64, 79 n. 37, 109–10
19:4 94
19:5 53 n. 50
19:6 88–90
19:8 110–1, 127
19:9a 112
19:9b 119–20
19:10 18, 76
19:12 46, 75
19:13 35 n. 139
19:15 35, 49 n. 28
19:17 45 n. 1, 48–9, 73 n. 2
19:18 17
19:20 95
19:21 22–3, 26
19:24 9 n. 37
19:26 18, 96, 128
19:27 88 n. 109
19:28 92 n. 138
19:28a 86, 114 n. 62
19:28b 84–5
19:29 53 n. 50, 77
20:1 19 n. 42, 99 n. 167, 108
20:3 97–8
20:5 99 n. 167
20:6 99 n. 167
20:7 19

20:10 83, 94 n. 146
20:11 65–6
20:12 112
20:13 15, 50–1
20:14a 18
20:14b 16, 38
20:15 91–2, 112
20:17 47
20:18 22–3
20:19 18, 61, 70 n. 62
20:26 32 n. 120
20:27 50–1
20:29 106–7
20:30 16 n. 16
20:31a 35, 127
20:31b 35
20:32 52, 57, 63
20:33 108
20:34 16, 38
21:1 68, 70
21:3 80
21:4 50, 56 n. 66
21:7 24 n. 74
21:7a 29–30, 29 n. 112
21:7b 22–3, 26
21:8 118–9
21:9 83 n. 64
21:9^1 87–8
21:9^2 87–8
21:10 100 n. 176
21:13 84–5
21:15 87–8
21:17 47
21:17a 63
21:17b 67–8
21:18 116
21:19 17
21:21 77–8
21:22 79
21:23 52 n. 45, 63, 112
21:25 15
21:26 46–7, 117

21:27 63 n. 25
21:28 33 n. 127, 63 n. 25, 75
21:28a 63
21:28b 64–5, 70 n. 61
21:29 33 n. 127, 80
21:30 33, 108
21:31 34 n. 131, 75
21:32 46–7
21:32a 119–20
21:32b 108
21:32c 119
21:33 48
21:34–35 20
21:35 108 n. 24
21:36 95
21:37 88 n. 109
21:38a 46
21:38b 49
21:39 23–5, 88–90
21:40 48 n. 21
21:41 47
21:41a 77 n. 18, 107, 126 n. 1
21:41b 106–7
21:42 28 n. 106, 37–8, 128
21:43 19
21:44 3 n. 9, 4 n. 14
21:46 47, 79
22:1 18–9
22:4 21 n. 58, 95 n. 154
22:7 117
22:9 29, 29 n. 112
22:10a 61–2, 70 n. 63
22:10b 62, 70 n. 61
22:12 94–5
22:15 18–9, 30 n. 114
22:16 15
22:19 66 n. 46
22:20 66
22:21 15

22:21–23:17 59
22:24 93
22:28 88 n. 109
22:30 15
22:32a 28
22:32b 28
22:35 33 n. 128
22:38 11 n. 40
22:39 53, 57, 128
22:42 28
22:43 50
22:44 76
23:3 13 n. 3, 80
23:4 23–5
23:5 25 n. 81
23:6 80
23:8 110–1
23:11 31–2, 35 n. 140
23:13 76
23:14 3 n. 9, 4 n. 14, 77 n. 18, 107, 126 n. 1
23:16 28, 37 n. 145, 85
23:17 35 n. 140, 94
23:18 24 n. 74
23:19 35 n. 140
23:20 24 n. 74
23:22 24 n. 74, 92 n. 138
23:23 55
23:24 63
23:25 47, 121, 128
23:26 62, 70
23:33 23 n. 71, 76
23:34 21–2, 22 n. 64
23:37 23–5, 108
23:39 83
24:2 68 n. 58
24:3 21 n. 58, 47 n. 14
24:3–5 112 n. 52
24:3a 68–9, 70
24:3b 62–3
24:4 61, 112 n. 52
24:5 68 n. 58, 112 n. 52

24:6 68 n. 58
24:6–8 112 n. 52
24:9 75, 106–7, 112 n. 52
24:9–13 112 n. 52
24:10 112 n. 52
24:10–11 24 n. 75
24:10–45 59
24:10a 22–3
24:10b 22–3
24:11 112
24:12 97–8, 112 n. 52
24:15 16, 78, 115
24:17 23–5
24:17–18 25 n. 83
24:18 106–7
24:19 86
24:20 111 n. 44
24:21 84–5
24:22 20
24:24 19–20
24:27 30 n. 117
24:28 29–30, 29 n. 112
24:29 90 n. 122
24:29–30 90 n. 122
24:30a 90
24:30b 88–90
24:32a 115
24:32b 112–3, 113 n. 55, 116, 128
24:33 76
24:35 31–2
24:36 13, 32 n. 121
24:37 39
24:38 92
24:39 40, 117–8, 128
24:40 39 n. 149
24:45 67–8
24:48 40 n. 158
24:49 40, 112–3
24:51 113 n. 54
25:1 66 n. 48
25:2 33 n. 128

25:6 53–4, 66
25:7–end 3–4
25:10 46
25:16 39, 96 n. 156
25:19 112–3, 113 n. 55, 116
25:20 96 n. 156
25:22 41, 75
25:28 95–6
25:29 99
25:30–26:22 59
25:32 9 n. 37, 52
25:32a 75–6
25:32b 76
25:33 52 n. 44
25:34 106–7
25:35–36 40 n. 159, 95 n. 155
25:36 40
25:37–39 95 n. 155
25:38 95
25:40 33 n. 129
25:44a 40
25:44b 40–1
25:46 107
26:1 79, 109–10
26:1–2 96, 128
26:2 108 n. 25
26:3 52, 57, 120
26:6 13, 87–8
26:7 32 n. 121
26:10 48 n. 23
26:12 80
26:13 33 n. 124, 75
26:14 46, 114
26:15 91–92, 114–5
26:15a 15
26:15b 14
26:16 79
26:17 108 n. 25
26:18 76, 108
26:19 108 n. 25, 116–7

26:21 23–5
26:23a 77–8
26:23b 75–6
26:26 81, 88 n. 108
26:33 27
26:39 65–6
26:40 107 n. 11
26:41 107
26:44 21–2
26:45 77
26:46 34–5
26:47 52 n. 45, 120 n. 98
26:50 52 n. 42, 61–2, 70 n. 63
26:51 51–5, 61, 70 n. 62
26:53 91
26:53a 46
26:53b 46
26:55 92
26:56 50 n. 30
26:57 50, 64–5, 70 n. 61
26:59 46
26:63 47
26:65 15, 65–6, 66 n. 45, 107
26:67 62, 70 n. 61, 106–7
26:70 76
26:72 108
27:1 30 n. 114, 47, 52 n. 45, 86
27:2–12 73
27:3 27
27:4 107
27:11 28
27:11–46 59
27:13 55, 76
27:15 29, 84–5, 127
27:16 25, 85
27:17 29 n. 112
27:21 29 n. 112
27:23 15
27:24 27

SCRIPTURE INDEX

27:24a 90 n. 124
27:27 100
27:29 76
27:30 76
27:33 18–9
27:34¹ 76
27:34² 76
27:37 24 n. 74
27:39 111
27:40 38 n. 147
27:41 76, 107
27:43 38 n. 147
27:44 94–5, 106–7
27:45 49
27:46 84, 109–10
27:47 101 n. 181, 107
27:48 33, 76
27:49 64–5, 70 n. 61
27:51 117
27:53 92, 128
27:53a 17
27:53b 27
27:54 77
27:54a 37–8, 128
27:54b 37–8, 128
27:55 106–7
27:56 65–6, 84
27:56ab 20
27:58 61–2, 70 n. 63, 90 n. 123, 107
27:59 88–90
27:60 80
27:61 116
27:61a 84, 127
27:61b 88–90
27:64 14, 61, 70 n. 62, 86–7
27:65 47 n. 16
27:66 47 n. 16
28:1 84
28:2 24 n. 74, 86
28:2–3 16–7, 46

28:4 36 n. 143
28:5a 36, 128
28:5b 29, 29 n. 112
28:7 15
28:8 36 n. 143
28:10 33
28:11 47, 115
28:12 18 n. 39, 29, 29 n. 112
28:13 21–2
28:15–end 59
28:16 84
28:19 33 n. 124

Mark
1:9 119–20
1:39 33 n. 124
2:3 68 n. 56
2:10 111 n. 39
2:21 40 n. 156
2:26 114 n. 63
3:6 30 n. 114
3:22 68 n. 55
3:25–26 68 n. 55
3:33 53 n. 47
4:1 96 n. 159
5:1 109 n. 32
6:5 35 n. 139
6:10 119 n. 87
6:17 40 n. 156
6:18 40 n. 156
6:22 40 n. 156
6:22 94 n. 143
6:38 66 n. 46
7:9 100 n. 174
7:28 82 n. 62
7:32 35 n. 139
8:1 67 n. 51
8:1–3 93 n. 141
8:23 35 n. 139
8:25 35 n. 139
8:34 119 n. 88

9:19 41 n. 163
9:35 32 n. 120
10:4–5 111 n. 38
10:16 35 n. 139
10:19 17 n. 25
10:20 95 n. 151
10:32–34 23 n. 73
10:44 50 n. 32
10:48 35 n. 140, 36 n. 141
11:1 68 n. 57
11:7 30 n. 116
11:8 119 n. 86
12:4 95 n. 154
12:19 93 n. 142
12:31 53 n. 49
12:35 28 n. 107
12:36 40 n. 156
12:37 40 n. 156
13:2 68 n. 58
13:3 68–9
13:6 68 n. 58
13:7 68 n. 58
13:9 53 n. 50
13:17 86 n. 100
14:1 120 n. 98
14:3 88 n. 108
14:5 24 n. 74
14:10 115 n. 64
14:54–end 13 n. 2
15:1 30 n. 114
15:6 29 n. 112
15:9 29 n. 112
15:13–15:38 105 n. 3
15:23 94 n. 148
15:40 21 n. 57
15:47 84 n. 71
16:6 66 n. 46
16:9 92 n. 139
16:12 92 n. 139

Luke
1:1–56 13 n. 2
3:7 76 n. 15
4:34 121 n. 100
4:39 24 n. 74
4:40 35 n. 139
5:18 68 n. 56
5:24 29 n. 110
6:4 114 n. 63
6:22 53 n. 50
7:9 21 n. 58
7:50 29 n. 110
8:26 109 n. 32
8:48 29 n. 110
9:36 119 n. 87
9:40 54 n. 57
10:19 24 n. 74
10:37 29 n. 110
11:14 68 n. 55
11:15 68 n. 55
11:17–18 68 n. 55
11:22 82 n. 60
11:34 82 n. 60
11:44 24 n. 74
12:18 117 n. 82
12:20 51 n. 41
12:28 117 n. 82
12:50 78 n. 24
12:58 87 nn. 102 and 103
13:8 78 n. 24
13:13 35 n. 139
13:27 21 n. 58
13:31 29 n. 110
13:35 83 n. 64
15:17 99 n. 173
15:29 52 n. 44
16:21 82 n. 62
17:19 29 n. 110
18:21 95 n. 151
18:39 35 n. 140, 36 n. 141
19:17 24 n. 74
19:19 24 n. 74

19:29 68 n. 57
19:36 119 n. 86
19:38 83 n. 64
19:40 21 n. 58
20:2 21 n. 58
20:11 95 n. 154
20:28 93 n. 142
20:41 28 n. 107
21:12 53 n. 50
21:23 86 n. 100
22:1 96 n. 159
22:2 120 n. 98
22:4 115 n. 64
22:16 78 n. 24
22:30 92 n. 138
22:34 21 n. 58

John
1:1–5:12 105 n. 2
2:18 34 n. 133
3:31 24 n. 74
4:50 29 n. 110
5:20 34 n. 133
6:19 117 n. 77
6:20 66 n. 46
8:11 29 n. 110
9:13 40 n. 156
9:18 78 n. 24
10:32 48 n. 23
11:47 120 n. 98
12:13 83 n. 64, 119 n. 86
14:25–16:7 105 n. 3
18:39 29 n. 112
20:17 29 n. 110
21:19 21 n. 58

Acts
3:17 96 n. 159
6:6 35 n. 139
8:5 31 n. 118
8:17 35 n. 139
8:18 35 n. 139

8:19 35 n. 139
8:26 29 n. 110
9:12 35 n. 139
9:15 29 n. 110
9:17 35 n. 139
10:20 29 n. 110
13:3 35 n. 139
19:6 35 n. 139
19:32 53 n. 50
22:10 29 n. 110
22:21 29 n. 110
24:25 29 n. 110
25:12 30 n. 114
26:21 53 n. 50
28:3 76 n. 15
28:8 35 n. 139

Romans
8:36 53 n. 50

1 Corinthians
15:6 24 n. 74

2 Corinthians
2:13 120 n. 92

Galatians
4:11 87 n. 102

Philippians
4:5 116 n. 75

1 Thessalonians
2:14–end 13 n. 2

Hebrews
3:12 87 n. 102
3:19 54 n. 57
4:16–8:1 13 n. 2

Revelation
1:1–5   13 n. 2
1:3   116 n. 75
2:28   34 n. 132
3:4   67 n. 54
3:7   64 n. 31
4:2   92 n. 138
4:3   92 n. 138
4:4   92 n. 138
4:9   92 n. 138
4:10   92 n. 138
5:1   92 n. 138
5:6   82 n. 61
5:7   92 n. 138
5:12   82 n. 61
5:13   92 n. 138
6:2   62 n. 13
6:8   24 n. 74
6:9   82 n. 61
6:16   92 n. 138
7:10   92 n. 138
7:15   92 n. 138
9:1   34 n. 132
13:8   82 n. 61
16:8   25 n. 84
16:31a   25 n. 84
18:19a   67 n. 54
19:4   92 n. 138
20:3   24 n. 74
20:4   100 n. 177
20:11   92 n. 138
21:5   92 n. 138
22:8   34 n. 133
22:10   116 n. 75

www.ingramcontent.com/pod-product-compliance
Lightning Source LLC
Chambersburg PA
CBHW050850160426
43194CB00011B/2101